AMERICAN DATELINES

AMERICAN DATELINES

Major News Stories from
Colonial Times to the Present

EDITED BY

Ed Cray

Jonathan Kotler

Miles Beller

UNIVERSITY OF ILLINOIS PRESS

URBANA AND CHICAGO

First Illinois paperback, 2003
©1990, 2003 by Ed Cray, Jonathan Kotler, and Miles Beller
Reprinted by arrangement with the editors
All rights reserved
Manufactured in the United States of America
P 5 4 3 2 1

Pages 395–97 constitute an extension of the copyright page.

This book is an updated edition of *American Datelines: One Hundred and Forty Major News Stories from Colonial Times to the Present* (New York: Facts on File, 1990).

This book is printed on acid-free paper.

Library of Congress Cataloging-in-Publication Data
American datelines : major news stories from colonial times to the present /
edited by Ed Cray, Jonathan Kotler, and Miles Beller.
p. cm.
Rev. ed. of: American datelines /
by Ed Cray, Jonathan Kotler, Miles Beller, 1990.
Includes index.
ISBN 0-252-07116-6 (pbk. : alk. paper)
1. Journalism—United States.
2. Reportage literature, American.
3. Reportage literature, American—History and criticism.
I. Cray, Ed.
II. Kotler, Jonathan.
III. Beller, Miles.
IV. Cray, Ed. American datelines.
PN4726.A48   2003
071'.3—dc21   2002027190

For
Jennifer Cray and Marc Igler
Brendan W. Kotler and John R. Hubbard
Laurette Hayden and Eli Beller

TABLE OF CONTENTS

2000

It was a political cliff-hanger that seemingly would not end, the post–Election Day battle between the Democratic candidate, Vice President Al Gore, and the Republican standard-bearer, Texas governor George W. Bush. The battleground was Florida, its 25 electoral votes defiantly claimed by both candidates. In the weeks after the polls closed, Americans would become familiar with such formerly arcane terms as "butterfly ballot" and "pregnant chad." Finally, after more than a month without a president-elect, a U.S. Supreme Court ruling effectively handed the victory to Bush.

INTRODUCTION

This, dear reader, is a family photograph album, a collection of historical snapshots, word pictures of a handful of memorable moments in American history. It is also, as it were, a book of history, the stuff of memory, of culture, something of a national biography.

It is unique in one way. It is, we believe, the first attempt to sketch the American adventure using contemporary newspaper accounts of the significant events that have shaped us as a nation and a people. Here are the first news reports of the pillage that was the Boston "tea party," the promulgation of a national constitution, of Nat Turner's rebellion, and the discovery of gold in Coloma. Not all are accounts of what a friend calls "state journalism," those to-ings and fro-ings of presidents, or acts of Congress, or court decisions, the familiar ingredients of conventional history texts. Indeed, there are battles—Lexington-Concord, New Orleans, first Manassas, Vicksburg, Little Big Horn, Manila Bay, the Marne, D-Day, Tet—but there is more too.

We have sought to include some of those other events that gave that new nation a soul or a heart: the coming of the railroad, the murder of Jesse James, the publication of *Huckleberry Finn,* Cy Young's perfect game and Babe Ruth's sixtieth, Peary's claim of the North Pole, and Ford's startling $5-a-day, and Benny Goodman's Carnegie Hall concert.

Some stories and illustrations are well known, and earlier, deservedly reprinted: the Norfolk, Virginia, *News-Pilot*'s account of the first flight at Kitty Hawk; Grantland Rice's report of the 1924 Army-Notre Dame game; or Ernie Pyle's moving description of grief in the mountains of Italy in 1944. Some are by famous writers, or writers who would later become famous, for a significant number of the United States' finest novelists and poets, from Poe to Runyon to Hemingway, spent their formative years in newsrooms, practicing the journalist's craft. Many are by anonymous writers, truly correspondents, like the soldier at Fort Kennedy, Nebraska, who wrote to describe those a later generation would hail as "the Forty-niners."

In compiling this anthology, we have attempted to identify those events in American history we deemed pivotal or, at the very least, to be important, and then to locate the newspaper story that offered the most immediate eyewitness account. Papers covering these events as *local* news were to be preferred wherever possible. These are not necessarily the finest examples of the newswriter's craft—as if there could ever be agreement on the 100 or 200 best stories—but they are representative of their times. Many of these accounts, generally from weeklies prior to the Civil War, and from dailies after that, were written hastily. Time and again, the sense of urgency in the copy, of momentous events retold, is genuine. The immediacy, the fact that these news stories are chronicling American history literally in the making, gives them a special validity and a vitality.

Because journalism is, to use Philip Graham's pithy phrase, the first rough draft of history, here and there the hastily gathered information as originally reported is wrong, or the story not as complete as later historians would make it. Despite that, the editors have not attempted to hide the sins of our fathers. Indeed, we have deliberately preserved the writing styles of the authors, for as wordy as some accounts may seem to us, the accepted, applauded, imitated journalistic style has changed markedly over the years. *American Datelines* then offers an array of newspaper and/or literary styles as these have evolved over the years.

We have edited these stories only for length, attempting to preserve the sensibility or style of the original. Where we have cut, we have used the conventional ellipse. The italics, the sometimes idiosyncratic spellings of the 18th Century, we have preserved. Typographic errors we have left standing.

We are grateful to a number of people who helped to compile the 141 stories in this anthology. Elizabeth Kaufman, Stephanie Johns and Valerie Johnson served as researchers. At the Library of Congress's Serial and Government Publications Division, headed by Donald F. Wisdom, John Connell, Jim Hicks, Susan Manakul, Joe Puccio, and Travis Westly guided us in the paths of righteousness. Ronald Grantz, curator of the National Automotive History Collection of the Detroit Public Library forwarded material at our request. The staffs of the Library of the American Antiquarian Society in Worcester, Massachusetts, and at the Huntington Library in San Marino, California, were ever helpful.

Update

The start of a decade, the turn of a century, the dawn of a new millennium—all have historically served as moments for looking forward by gazing backward. They are dates that prompt us to consider the future by weighing the past.

The years 1900-1999 were brashly (and prematurely) identified as "The American Century" by Henry Robinson Luce, cofounder of the Time-Life publishing empire. Luce, with chauvinistic assurance, assumed the supremacy of the United States in political, scientific, and cultural affairs. Though the nation endures as the last superpower, its once-strong sense of purpose, of a Divinely ordained destiny, is less sure.

In the years since the first edition of *American Datelines* appeared in 1990, a number of truly significant events have occurred. From them we have chosen nine, including the O. J. Simpson trial, a televised courtroom drama of tense racial themes that surpassed the most lurid of crime fiction, and the September 11, 2001, attack on the World Trade Center by international terrorists, who made murderously clear the grim realities of a new world order.

We also look at some uplifting moments, such as the fall of the Berlin Wall, and with it the symbolic end of both Soviet totalitarianism and the cold war; Tiger Woods's triumphant ascent to country club acceptance and golfing greatness; and the home run contest between Mark McGwire and Sammy Sosa, an intense but gentlemanly competition that played to the highest ideals of good sportsmanship.

All these events and more have been incisively reported as the nation enters a new, yet undefined, age. In daily installments, the great American adventure continues.

Ed Cray
Jonathan Kotler
Miles Beller

AMERICAN DATELINES

1704

The first English-language newspaper printed in colonial America was Benjamin Harris's *Publick Occurrences, Both Forreign and Domestick,* which appeared in Boston on September 25, 1690. However, it was promptly shut down by the Massachusetts government after only one issue. Harris's paper lacked a government license, and an unlicensed press was strictly forbidden in North America. The thinking in London during these first years of colonization was that an unlicensed press had a tremendous potential to cause mischief.

The distinction of being the first regularly appearing newspaper in the British American colonies goes to the *Boston News-Letter,* which was published weekly by Boston postmaster John Campbell beginning on April 24, 1704. As it proudly proclaimed on its first page, the *News-Letter* was "Published by Authority," meaning, that it was licensed, and censored, by the government. This resulted, more often than not, in bland, passionless journalism. Most of the *News-Letter's* contents was nothing more than information lifted by Campbell from months' old London newspapers that had reached the Massachusetts Bay Colony after a lengthy ocean crossing from Britain.

But at least America had a newspaper, albeit one without competition. In its first issue, the *News-Letter* told the tale of pirates operating off the coast of Rhode Island.

Capt. *Toungrello* has taken Five Prizes off of *Currosoa,* one of which is come in to *Rhode Island* mostly Loaden with *Cocco, Tobacco, Liquors, Etc.* She is a *Currasoe* Trader, as all the rest were. One of the five was one *Larew* a *French-man,* a Sloop of 8 Guns & 8 Patteraro's, 76 Men, Fought him Board and Board, and three Glasses; Captain *Larew* was kill'd, and 20 of his Men kill'd and wounded; Capt. *Toungrello* wounded thro' the Body, and five of his men, but none kill'd, he had but 40 Fighting Men, when he took *Larew.*

The 18 Currant, came in a Sloop to this Port from *Virginia,* the Master informed Governour *Cranston* Esq. he was chased by a Topsail Shallop off of *Block-Island,* which he judged to be a *French* Privateer, and that there was two other Vessels in her Company, which he judged to be her Prizes. Whereupon his Honour being concerned for the Publick Weal and Safety of Her Majesties good Subjects immediately caused the Drum to beat for Volunteers, under the Command of Capt. *Wanton,* and in 3 or four hours time Fitted and Man'd a Brigantine, with 70 brisk young men-well Arm'd, who Sail'd the following Night, returned last Evening, and gave his Honour an Account that they found the aforesaid Shallop with one other, and a Ketch at *Tarpolian Cove,* who were all Fishing Vessels belonging to *Marblehead* or *Salem,* who were fishing off of *Block-Island,* one of them was *French* built Shallop with a Topsail, which gave the great suspicion that they were Enemies.

Under a bold-faced **Advertisement** was the following notation:

This News Letter is to be continued Weekly; and all Persons who have any Houses, Lands, Tenements, Farmes, Ships Vessels, Goods, Wares or Merchandizes, Etc., to be Sold or Lett; or Servants Runaway; or Goods Stoll or Lost, may have the same Inserted at a Reasonable Rate; from Twelve Pence to Five Shillings and not to exceed: Who may agree with *Nicholas Boone* for the same at his Shop, next door to Major *Davis's* Apothecary in *Boston*, near the Old Meeting House.

All Persons in Town and Country may have said News-Letter Weekly upon reasonable terms, agreeing with *John Campbell* post-Master for the same.

1734

The case of John Peter Zenger is one of the enduring myths of American history. Generations of budding reporters have been taught that the immigrant German printer's exoneration on a charge of printing seditious libel about the royal governor of New York established truth as a defense to defamation charges. In fact, while the Zenger trial took place in 1735, truth did not become a defense to a charge of defamation under New York law until 1805, 70 years later.

Under the British law of seditious libel, criticism of government was criticism of the government's authority. The rule was "the greater the truth, the greater the libel." After all, truth might cause greater harm than a falsehood, since a lie could not be verified. Under such a rule, once the defendant admitted printing the material, the case was over, and the accused had to be found guilty.

But, under the tutelage of Philadelphia attorney Andrew Hamilton, Zenger's jury ignored the law and decided to make its own rule, that truth should be a defense to a charge of seditious libel. The jury found Zenger not guilty. Still, the real, although unsung, hero of this story was the crown-appointed judge, James Delancy. After the jury disregarded his instructions to find Zenger guilty—since

Zenger previously had admitted printing the offending material about Governor William Cosby, including a letter that accused the Royal Governor of manipulating the colony's legal system to his personal benefit and that of his political allies—Delancy could have declared a mistrial. Or he could have reversed the jury's decision, since it did not properly follow the law. Instead, he bowed to the people's will and let the verdict stand.

The Zenger case did not change the law, but it had many important consequences because it established the precedent of the press being able to criticize public figures, and to get away with it. It also helped develop the concept of "freedom of the press" as we know it today—the right of the press to express a particular partisan point of view. Prior to this time, "freedom of the press" meant little more than the right of all people to have access to the pages of their local newspapers, without regard to the political persuasions of the paper's publisher. The trial's result also demonstrated to Great Britain the power of popular opinion. After the Zenger trial, there were no further reported cases of crown prosecutions against newspaper publishers in colonial America.

The following is the story of the Zenger arrest and trial in John Peter Zenger's own words, as they appeared in his *New York Weekly Journal,* on November 24, 1734, following his arrest, and on August 18, 1735, following his acquittal.

To all my Subscribers and Benefactors who take my weekly Journal Gentlemen, Ladies and Others;

As you last week were Disappointed of my Journall, I think it Incumbent upon me, to publish my Apology which is this. On the Lord's Day, the Seventeenth of this Instant, I was Arrested, taken and Imprisoned in the common Goal [sic] of this City, by Virtue of a Warrant from the *Gouvernour,* and the Honorable *Francis Harrison,* Esq; and others in Council of which (God willing) yo'l have a Coppy whereupon I was put under such Restraint that I had not the Liberty of Pen, Ink or Paper, or to see, or speak with People, till upon my complaint to the Honourable the Chief Justice, at my appearing before him upon my *Habeas Corpus* on the *Wednesday* following. Who discountenanced that Proceeding, and therefore I have had since that Time, the Liberty of Speaking through the Hole of the Door, to my Wife, and Servants by which I doubt not yo'l think me sufficiently Excused for not sending my last weeks *Journall,* and I hope for the future by the Liberty of Speaking to my Servants thro' the Hole of the Door of the Prison, to entertain you with my weekly *Journal* as formerly.

And am your obliged Humble Servant
J. Peter Zenger

1735

To my Subscribers and Benefactors.
Gentlemen;
I Think my self in Duty bound to to [sic] make publick Acknowledgment for the many Favours received at your Hands, which I do in this Manner return you my hearty Thanks for. I very soon intend to print my Tryal at Length, that the World may see how unjust my Sufferings have been, so will only at this Time give the short Account of it.

On *Monday* the *4th* Instant my Tryal for Printing Parts of my Journal No. 13. and 23. came on, in the Supreme Court of this Province, before the most numerous Auditory of people, I may with Justice say, that ever were seen in the Place at once; my Jury sworn were,

1.	*Harmanus Rutgers,*	5.	*Samuel Weaver,*
2.	*Stanley Holms,*	6.	*Andrew Marschalk,*
3.	*Edward Man,*	7.	*Egbert Van Borsen,*
4.	*John Bell,*	8.	*Thomas Hunt,*

9. *Benjamin Hildrith,*   11. *John Goelet,*
10. *Abraham Kiteltass,*   12. *Hercules Wendover*

John Chambers, Esq; had been appointed the Term before by the Court as my Council, in the place of *James Alexander* and *William Smith,* who were then silenced on my Account, and to Mr. *Chambers's* Assistance came *Andrew Hamilton,* Esq; of Philadelphia Barrister at Law; when Mr. Attorney offered the Information and the Proofs, Mr. *Hamilton* told him, he would acknowledge my Printing and Publishing the Papers in the Information, and save him the Trouble of that Proof; and offered to prove the Facts of those Papers true, and had Witnesses ready to prove every Fact; he long insisted on the Liberty of Making Proof thereof, but was over-ruled therein. Mr. Attorney offered no Proofs of my Papers being *false, malicious and seditious,* as they were charged to be, but insisted that they were Lybels tho' true. There were many Arguments and Authorities on this point, and the Court were of Opinion with Mr. Attorney on that Head: But the Jury having taken the Information out with them, they were returned in about Ten Minutes, and found me *Not Guilty;* upon which there were immediately three Hurra's of many Hundreds of People in the presence of the Court, before the Verdict was returned. The next Morning my Discharge was moved for and granted, and sufficient was subscribed by my fellow Citizens for payment of sundry Debts, for which I was also charged in Custody, and about Noon I had my Liberty from my long Imprisonment above eight Months. Above Forty of the Citizens entertained Mr. *Hamilton* at the black *Horse* that Day at Dinner, to express their Acknowledgment of his Generosity on this Occasion, and at his Departure next Day he was saluted with the great Guns of several Ships in the Harbour, as a public Testimony of the glorious Defence he made in the Cause of Liberty in this Province.

1755

On July 9, 1755, a large body of regular British soldiers and colonial militia was ambushed by a combined force of French and Indians at Fort Duquesne, the site of what today is Pittsburgh, Pennsylvania. The loss of several hundred troops, including Edward Braddock, the commanding general of all British forces in North America, led to the demand by Parliament in London for increased taxation of American colonials in order to pay for the cost of maintaining the British military presence in the New World. In time, Westminster would pass both the Stamp Act and the tax on tea as a way of supporting the North American colonies. To the British, this made economic sense. To the Americans, this was taxation without representation. Accordingly, Braddock's defeat in the French and Indian War can be seen as the opening shot of the American Revolution.

Nearly a month after the battle, on August 9, 1755, the *New York Mercury* published an account of this fateful incident, written by one of Braddock's officers, whose name, unfortunately, has been lost to the ages. Of special note is his reference to the heroics of one of Braddock's aides, George Washington, for the twenty-three-year-old Washington's service in the French and Indian War led to his appointment as commander of the Continental Army during the Revolution, still more than two decades in the future.

Extracts of a Letter from an Officer; dated at Fort Cumberland, July 18, 1755

The 9th Inst. we passed and repassed the Monongahela, by advancing first a Party of 300 Men, which was immediately followed by another 200. The General, with the Column of Artillery, Baggage, and the main Body of the Army, passed the River the last Time about One a'Clock. As soon as the whole had got on the Fort Side of the Monongahela, we heard a very heavy and quick Fire in our Front; we immediately advanced in order to sustain them; but the Detachment of the 200 and 300 Men gave Way, and fell back upon us, which caused such Confusion, and struck so great a Panick among our Men, that afterwards no military Expedient could be made use of that had any Effect upon them: The Men were so extremely deaf to the Exhortations of the General, and the Officers, that they fired away, in the most irregular Manner, all their Ammunition, and then run off, leaving to the Enemy, the Artillery, Ammunition, Provision and Baggage; nor could they be persuaded to stop till they got as far as Geist's Plantation, nor there only in Part, many of them proceeding as far as Col. Dunbar's Party, who lay six Miles on this Side.

The Officers were absolutely sacrificed, by their unparalleled good Behaviour, advancing sometimes in Bodies, and sometimes separately, hoping by such Example to engage the Soldiers to follow them, but to no Purpose.

The General had five Horses killed under him, and at last received a Wound thro' his Right Arm into his Lungs, of which he died the 13th Instant. Secretary Shirley was shot thro' the Head; Capt. Morris wounded; Mr. [George] Washington had two Horses shot under him, and his Clothes shot thro' in several Places, behaving the whole Time with the greatest Courage and Resolution. Sir Peter Halket was killed upon the Spot. Col. Burton, and Sir John St. Clair wounded; and enclosed I have sent a List of Killed and Wounded, according to as exact Account as we are yet able to get. . . .

As our Number of Horses was so much reduced, and those extremely weak, and many Carriages being wanted for the wounded Men, occasioned our destroying the Ammunition and superfluous Part of the Provision left in Col. Dunbar's Convoy, to prevent it falling into the Hands of the Enemy.

As the whole of the Artillery is lost, and the Troops are so extremely weakened by Deaths, Wounds and Sickness, it was judged impossible to make any further Attempt; therefore Col. Dunbar is returning to Fort Cumberland, with every Thing he is able to bring with him.

By the particular Disposition of the French and Indians, it was impossible to judge of the Numbers they had that Day in the Field.

1771

Writing under several different pen names, including "Candidus," Samuel Adams of Massachusetts was the unofficial propagandist to the American revolution. Adams railed against the evils of "taxation without representation," that is, the inability of Americans to control their own political destiny owing to the absence of their representatives at the Imperial Parliament in London. Ultimately, Adams's diatribes found a sympathetic audience throughout the American colonies, and his invectives were printed and reprinted in newspapers up and down the Atlantic seaboard. The following tract appeared originally in the *Boston Gazette and Country Journal* on October 7, 1771.

. . . Is it impossible to form an idea of *slavery* more complete, more miserable, more *disgraceful,* than that of a people where justice is administer'd, government exercis'd, and a standing army maintain'd at the expense of the people, and yet without the least dependence upon them? If we can find no relief from this infamous situation,—I repeat it, *"if we can find no relief from this infamous situation,*—let the ministry, who have stripped us of our property and liberty, deprive us of our understanding too; that, unconscious of what we have been or are, and ungoaded by tormenting reflections, we may tamely bow down our necks with all the stupid serenity of servitude to any drudgery which our lords and masters may please to command.''—I appeal to the common sense of mankind to what a state of infamy and misery must a people be reduced! To have a Governor by the sole appointment of the crown; under the absolute control of a weak and arbitrary minister, to whose dictates he is to yield unlimited obedience or forfeit his political existence; while he is to be supported at the expense of the people by virtue of an authority claimed by *strangers* to oblige them to contribute for him such an annual stipend, however unbounded, as the Crown shall be advised to order? If this is not a state of despotism, what is? Could *such* a governor, by all the *arts of persuasion,* prevail upon a people to be quiet and contented under *such* a mode of government, his noble patron might spare himself the trouble of getting a Charter vacated by a formal decision of parliament or in the tedious process of law.—Whenever the relentless enemies of America shall have completed their system, which they are still, though more silently pursuing, by subtle arts, deep dissimulation, and manners calculated to deceive, our condition will then be more humiliating and miserable, and perhaps more *inextricable too,* than that of the people of England in the infamous reigns of the Stuarts, which blacken the pages of history, when,

"Oppression stalk'd at large and pour'd abroad
Her *unrelenting* Train; *Informers—Spies—*
Hateful Projectors of *aggrieving* Schemes,
To sell the starving many to the few,
And drain a thousand Ways th' exhausted Land.

_____And on the *venal* Bench,
Instead of Justice, *Party* held the *Scale*
And *Violence* the *Sword.*"

Your's,
CANDIDUS

1773

To show their displeasure with the tax on tea passed by Parliament to help finance the British administration of North America, Massachusetts residents staged what has since become known as "The Boston Tea Party." Faintly disguised as so many stage Indians, a band of enthusiastic American patriots boarded tea-carrying ships in Boston harbor on December 16, 1773. They then proceeded to dump the chests of tea on board into the waters of Massachusetts Bay.

Immediately prior to this event, a group of Bostonians assembled at Boston's Old South Meeting-House to discuss the tea tax. *The Massachusetts Gazette and Boston News-Letter* was there, and what follows is the report of that meeting and subsequent "tea party," which was carried in that paper's edition of December 23, 1773.

. . . Just before the Dissolution of the Meeting, a number of brave and resolute Men, dressed in the Indian Manner, approached near the Door of the Assembly, and gave the War Whoop, which rang through the House and was answered by some in the Galleries, but Silence being commanded, and a peaceable Deportment was again enjoined till the Dissolution: The Indians, as they were then called, repaired to the Wharf, where the Ships lay that had the Tea on board, and were followed by Hundreds of People, to see the Event of the Transactions of those who made so grotesque an appearance:— They, the Indians, immediately repaired on board Capt. Hall's Ship, where they hoisted the Chests of Tea and when upon the Deck stove the Chests and emptied the Tea overboard; having cleared this Ship, they proceeded to Capt. Bruce's and then to Capt. Coffin's Brig.—They applied themselves so dexterously to the Destruction of this Commodity that in the Space of three Hours they broke up 342 Chests, which was the whole Number in those Vessels, and discharged their Contents into the Dock; when the Tide rose it floated the broken chests and the Tea insomuch that the Surface of the Water was filled therewith a considerable Way from the South Part of the town to Dorchester-Neck, and lodged on the shores.—There was the greatest Care taken to prevent the Tea from being purloined by the Populace: One or two being detected in endeavoring to pocket a small quantity were stripped of their Acquisitions and very roughly handled.—It is worthy of Remark that although a considerable Quantity of Goods were still remaining on board the Vessels, no Injury was sustained: Such Attention to private Property was observed that a small padlock belonging to the Captain of one of the Ships being broke, another was procured and sent to him.—The Town was very quiet during the whole Evening and the Night following: Those Persons who were from the Country returned with a merry Heart; and the next Day Joy appeared in almost every Countenance, some on Occasion of the Destruction of the Tea, others on Account of the Quietness with which it was effect.— One of the Monday's Papers says that the Masters and Owners are well pleased that their Ships are thus cleared. . . .

1775

Ultimately, at Lexington, Massachusetts, the hastily assembled Minutemen fired the "shot heard round the world," beginning the American Revolution. The opening days of the battle for independence were chronicled by a dedicated Son of Liberty, Isaiah Thomas, in the May 3, 1775, edition of his newspaper, *The Massachusetts Spy*. Thomas, who carried a musket at Lexington to be used, if necessary, against the British, hardly was an objective correspondent—but, then, few war correspondents are.

Following the first altercations, Thomas moved his press and printing business to the inland Massachusetts town of Worcester, where he built a printing empire and eventually became a very wealthy man. His concern for collecting the sources of American history resulted in the founding of the American Antiquarian Society in Worcester in 1812. Thomas's printing press and many early editions of the *Massachusetts Spy*, as well as the largest collection of early American newspapers anyplace in the world, may be found there today.

AMERICANS! LIBERTY OR DEATH! JOIN OR DIE!

AMERICANS! forever bear in mind the BATTLE OF LEXINGTON!—where British troops, unmolested and unprovoked, wantonly and in a most inhuman manner, fired upon and killed a number of our countrymen, then robbed, ransacked, and burnt their house! nor could the tears of defenseless women, some of whom were in the pains of childbirth, the cries of helpless babes, nor the prayers of old age, confined to beds of sickness, appease their thirst for blood!—or divert them from their DESIGN of MURDER and ROBBERY!

The particulars of this alarming event will, we are credibly informed, be soon published by authority, as a Committee of the Provincial Congress have been appointed to make special inquiry and to take the depositions on oath, of such as are knowing in the matter. In the meantime, to satisfy the expectations of our readers, we have collected from those whose veracity is unquestioned the following account, viz. A few days before the battle, the Grenadier and Light-Infantry companies were all drafted from the several regiments in Boston; and put under the command of an officer, and it was observed that most of the transports and other boats were put together, and fitted for immediate service. This maneuver gave rise to a suspicion that a more formidable expedition was intended by the soldiery, but what or where the inhabitants could not determine. However, town watches in Boston, Charlestown, Cambridge, etc., were ordered to look well to the landing place. About ten o'clock on the night of the eighteenth of April, the troops in Boston were disclosed to be on the move in a very secret manner, and it was found they were embarking on boats (which they privately brought to the place in the evening) at the bottom of the Common; expresses set off immediately to alarm the country, that they might be on their guard. . . . The body of troops, in the meantime, under the command of Lieutenant Colonel Smith, had crossed the river and landed at Phipp's Farm. They immediately, to the number of 1000, proceeded to Lexington, about six miles below Concord, with great silence. A company of militia, of about eighty men, mustered near the meetinghouse; the troops came in sight of them just before sunrise. The militia, upon seeing the troops, began to disperse. The troops then set out upon the run, hallooing and huzzaing, and coming within a few rods of them, the commanding officer accosted the militia, in words to this effect, *"Disperse, you damn'd rebels!—Damn you, disperse!"* Upon which the troops again huzzaed and immediately one or two officers discharged their pistols, which were instantaneously followed by the firing of four or five of the soldiers; and then there seemed to be a general discharge from the whole body. It is to be noticed that they fired on our people as they were dispersing, agreeable to their command, and that we did not even return the fire. Eight of our men were killed and nine wounded. The troops then laughed, and damned the Yankees, and said they could not bear the smell of gunpowder. A little after this the troops renewed their march to Concord, where, when they arrived, they divided into parties, and went directly to several places where the province stores were deposited. Each party was supposed to have a Tory pilot. One party went into the jailyard and spiked up the otherwise damaged cannon, belonging to the province, and broke and set fire to the carriages. Then they entered a store and rolled out about a hundred barrels of flour, which they unheaded and emptied about forty into the river. At the same time others were entering the houses and shops, and unheading barrels, chests, etc., the property of private persons. Some took possession of the town house, to which they set fire, but was extinguished by our people without much hurt. Another party of the troops went and took possession of the North Bridge. About 150 provincials who mustered upon the alarm, coming toward the bridge, the troops fired upon them without ceremony and killed two on the spot! (Thus had the troops of Britain's king fired FIRST at two separate times upon his loyal American subjects, and put a period to two lives before one gun was fired upon them.) Our people THEN fired and obliged the troops to retreat, who were soon joined by their other parties, but finding they were still pursued the whole body retreated to Lexington, both provincials and troops firing as they went. During this time an express from the troops was sent to General Gage, who thereupon sent out a reinforcement of about 1400 men, under the command of Earl Piercy, with two fieldpieces. Upon the arrival of this reinforcement at Lexington, just as the retreating party had got there, they made a stand, picked up their dead, and took all the carriages they could find and put their wounded thereon. Others of them, to their eternal disgrace be it spoken, were robbing and setting houses on fire, and discharging their cannon at meeting-house. Whilst this was transacting, a few of our men at Menotomy, a few miles distant, attacked a party of twelve of the enemy (carrying stores and provisions to the troops), killed one of them, and took possession of their arms, stores, provisions, etc. without any loss on our side. The enemy, having halted about an hour at Lexington, found it necessary to make a second retreat, carrying with them many of their dead and wounded. They continued their retreat from Lexington to Charlestown with great precipitation. Our people continued their pursuit, firing till they got to Charlestown Neck (which they reached a little after sunset), over which the enemy passed, proceeded up Bunker's Hill, and the next day went into Boston, under the protection of the *Somerset,* man-of-war of 64 guns. . . .

Immediately upon the return of the troops to Boston, all communications to and from the town was stopped by General Gage. The provincials, who flew to the assistance of their distressed countrymen, are posted in Cambridge, Charlestown, Roxbury, Watertown, etc., and have placed a guard on Roxbury Neck, within gunshot of the enemy. Guards are also placed everywhere in view of the town, to observe the motions of the King's troops: The Council of War and the different Committees of Safety and Supplies sit at Cambridge, and the Provincial Congress at Watertown. The troops in Boston are fortifying the place on all sides, and a frigate of war is stationed up Cambridge river, and a sixty-four-gun ship between Boston and Charlestown.

Deacon Joseph Loring's house and barn, Mrs. Mulliken's house and shop, and Mr. Joshua Bond's house and shop, in Lexington, were all consumed. They also set fire to several other houses, but our people extinguished the flames. They pillaged almost every house they passed by, breaking and destroying doors, windows, glass, etc., and carrying off clothing and other valuable effects. It appeared to be their design to burn and destroy all before them, and nothing but our vigorous pursuit prevented their infernal purposes from being put into execution. But the savage barbarity exercised upon the bodies of our unfortunate brethren who fell is almost incredible. Not content with shooting down the unarmed, aged, and infirm, they disregarded the cries of the wounded, killing them without mercy, and mangling their bodies in the most shocking manner.

We have the pleasure to say that notwithstanding the highest provocations given by the enemy, not one instance of cruelty that we have heard of was committed by our militia; but, listening to the merciful dictates of the Christian religion, they "breathed higher sentiments of humanity.". . .

1776

Thomas Paine, a former London corset-maker, also took up the propagandist's pen. The author of *Common Sense,* a pro-independence pamphlet that sold 120,000 copies after its 1776 printing, Paine also wrote a series of articles called "The American Crisis." In these "Crisis Papers," Paine attempted to convey the sense of urgency facing the fledgling nation and its beleaguered military forces. Ultimately, Paine proved to be too revolutionary even for the United States. Arguing for social, as well as for economic and political, revolt, Paine scared the largely bourgeois, new-made American establishment who saw him as a threat. Others, possessed by the business of nation-building, merely ignored him until he died, penniless, in 1809.

What follows is the first of Paine's influential and widely published "Crisis Papers," as it appeared in the Philadelphia weekly, *Dunlap's Pennsylvania Packet or the General Advertiser,* on December 27, 1776, following the Continental Army's retreat across the frozen ground of New Jersey.

THE AMERICAN CRISIS, NO. 1

These are the times that try men's souls. The summer soldier and the sunshine patriot will, in this crisis, shrink from the service of his country; but he that stands it NOW deserves the love and thanks of man and woman. Tyranny, like hell, is not easily conquered; yet we have this consolation with us, that the harder the conflict, the more glorious the triumph. What we obtain too cheap, we esteem too lightly:—'Tis dearness only that gives every thing its value. Heaven knows how to put a proper price upon its goods; and it would be strange indeed, if so celestial an article as FREE-DOM should not be highly rated. Britain, with an army to enforce her tyranny, has declared that she has a right (*not only to* TAX but) "*to* BIND *us in* ALL CASES WHATSOEVER," and if being *bound in that manner,* is not slavery, then is there not such a thing as slavery upon earth. Even the expression is impious, for so unlimited a power can belong only to God. . . .

I have as little superstition in me as any man living, but my secret opinion has ever been, and still is, that God Almighty will not give up a people to military destruction, or leave them unsupportedly to perish, who have so earnestly and so repeatedly sought to avoid the calamities of war, by every decent method which wisdom could invent. Neither have I so much of the infidel in me, as to suppose that He has relinquished the government of the world, and given us up to the care of the devils; and as I do not, I cannot see on what grounds the king of Britain can look up to heaven for help against us: a common murderer, a highwayman, or a house-breaker, has as good a pretence as he. . . .

As I was with the troops at fort Lee, and marched with them to the edge of Pennsylvania, I am well acquainted with many circumstances, which those who live at a distance know but little or nothing of. Our situation there was exceedingly cramped, the place being a narrow neck of land between the North River and the Hackensack. Our force was inconsiderable, being not one fourth so great as [General William] Howe could bring against us. We had no army at hand to have relieved the garrison, had we shut ourselves up and stood on our defence. Our ammunition, light artillery, and the best part of our stores, had been removed, on the apprehension that Howe would endeavor to penetrate the Jerseys, in which case fort Lee could be of no use to us; for it must occur to every thinking man, whether in the army or not, that these kind of field forts are only for temporary purposes, and last in use no longer than the enemy directs his force against the particular object, which such forts are raised to defend. Such was our situation and condition at fort Lee on the morning of the 20th of November, when an officer arrived with information that the enemy with 200 boats had landed about seven miles above: Major General [Nathanael] Greene, who commanded the garrison, immediately ordered them under arms, and sent express to General [George] Washington at the town of Hackensack, distant by way of the ferry six miles. Our first object was to secure the bridge over the the the Hackensack, which laid up the river between the enemy and us, about six miles from us, and three from them. General Washington arrived in about three quarters of an hour, and marched at the head of the troops towards the bridge, which place I expected we should have a brush for; however they did not choose to dispute it with us, the greatest part of our troops went over the bridge, the rest over the ferry, except some which passed at a mill on a small creek, between the bridge and the ferry, and made their way through some marshy grounds up to the town of Hackensack, and there passed the river. We brought off as much baggage as the wagons could contain, the rest was lost. The simple object was to bring off the garrison, and march them on till they could be strengthened by the Jersey or Pennsylvania militia, so as to be enabled to make a stand. We staid four days at Newark, collected our outposts with some of the Jersey militia, and marched out twice to meet the enemy, on being informed that they were advancing, though our numbers were greatly inferior to theirs. Howe, in my little opinion, committed a great error in generalship in not throwing a body of forces off from Staten Island through Amboy, by which means he might have seized all our stores at Brunswick, and intercepted our march into Pennsylvania: but if we believe the power of hell to be limited, we must likewise believe that their agents are under some providential control.

I shall not now attempt to give all the particulars of our retreat to the Delaware; suffice it for the present to say, that both officers and men, though greatly harrassed and fatigued, frequently without rest, covering, or provision, the inevitable consequences of a long retreat, bore it with a manly and martial spirit. All their wishes centred in one, which was, that the country would turn out and help them to drive the enemy back. Voltaire has remarked that king William never appeared to full advantage but in difficulties and in action; the same remark may be made on General Washington, for the character fits him. There is a natural firmness in some minds which cannot be unlocked by trifles, but which, when unlocked, discovers a cabinet of fortitude; and I reckon it among those kind of public blessings, which we do not immediately see, that God hath blest him with uninterrupted health, and given him a mind that can even flourish upon care.

I shall conclude this paper with some miscellaneous remarks on the state of our affairs; and shall begin with asking the following question, Why is it that the enemy have left the New-England provinces, and made these middle ones the seat of war? The answer is easy: New-England is not infested with tories, and we are. I have been tender in raising the cry against these men and used numberless arguments to show them their danger, but it will not do to sacrifice a world either to their folly or their baseness. The period is now arrived, in which either they or we must change our sentiments, or one or both must fall. And what is a tory? Good God! what is he? I should not be afraid to go with an hundred whigs against a thousand tories, were they to attempt to get into arms. Every tory is a coward; for servile, slavish, self-interested fear is the foundation of toryism; and a man under such influence, though he may be cruel, never can be brave.

But, before the line of irrecoverable separation be drawn between us, let us reason the matter together: your conduct is an invitation to the enemy, yet not one in a thousand of you has heart enough to join him. Howe is as much deceived by you as the American cause is injured by you. He expects you will all take up arms, and flock to his standard with muskets on your shoulders. Your opinions are of no use to him, unless you support him personally, for 'tis soldiers, and not tories, that he wants.

I once felt all that kind of anger, which a man ought to feel, against the mean principles that are held by the tories: a noted one, who kept a tavern at Amboy, was standing at his door, with as pretty a child in his hand, about eight or nine years old, as I ever saw, and after speaking his mind as freely as he thought was prudent, finished with this fatherly expression, *"Well! give me peace in my day."* Not a man lives on the continent but fully believes that a separation must some time or other finally take place, and a generous parent should have said, *"If there must be trouble, let it be in my day, that my child may have peace;"* and this single reflection, well applied, is sufficient to awaken every man to duty. Not a place upon earth might be so happy as America. Her situation is remote from all the wrangling world, and she has nothing to do but to trade with them. A man can distinguish in himself between temper and principle, and I am as confident, as I am that God governs the world, that America will never be happy till she gets clear of foreign dominion. Wars, without ceasing, will break out till that period arrives, and the Continent must in the end be conqueror; for though the flame of liberty may sometimes cease to shine, the coal can never expire.

1787

Many American newspapers published a verbatim account of the language contained in the draft Constitution adopted on September 17, 1787, by the delegates to the Constitutional Convention in Philadelphia. Some even included George Washington's letter to the Convention urging that the draft be adopted. Still, for most newspapers printing at this time, the Convention in far-off Philadelphia seemed to be of marginal, or uncertain, import at best. Instead of devoting a great deal of space to the story, they concentrated on that to which they always had devoted the lion's share of their pages—local news.

But, occurring as it did in Philadelphia, to the newspapers of that city, the Constitutional Convention *was* local news. What follows is the coverage of September 21, 1787, by Philadelphia's *Pennsylvania Mercury,* which managed to give the story a nice local twist by focusing on the exploits of one of Philadelphia's favorite sons, Benjamin Franklin.

On Monday last the Federal Convention closed their session by signing the Federal Government. The States, we are told, were *unanimous* in this business. The address of his Excellency Dr. FRANKLIN to the Members of the Convention, previous to this solemn transaction (a correspondent assures us) was truly pathetic and extremely sensible. The concurrence of this venerable patriot in this Government, and his strong recommendation of it, cannot fail of recommending it to all his friends in Pennsylvania.

Tuesday last the frame of government was reported by the Delegates of Pennsylvania, agreeably to their instructions, to the General Assembly of this state, and read publicly in the presence of a large crowd of citizens, who stood in the gallery of the Assembly room, and who testified the highest pleasure in seeing that great work at last perfected, which promises, when adopted, to give security, stability, and dignity to the government of the United States.

The division of the power of the United States into three branches gives the sincerest satisfaction to a great majority of our citizens, who have long suffered many inconveniences from being governed by a *single* legislature. All *single* governments are tyrannies—whether they be lodged in *one* man— a *few* men or a *large* body of the people.

The same day Dr. Franklin delivered a letter from the Delegates to the House, which being read consisted of a recommendation to the legislature "that a law should be immediately passed, vesting in the new Congress a tract of land of ten miles square, by which that body might be induced to fix the seat of federal government in this state—an event that must be highly advantageous to the commonwealth of Pennsylvania."

1787

Now the states, one by one, took up the question of whether or not the new Constitution should be adopted. Many argued for the continued loose confederation of states and weak central government by which the former colonies had been governed since the revolution. Others, who called themselves "federalists," felt strongly that the nation could prosper and grow only under a strong central government, which would exercise many of the powers previously exercised by the states. Among this latter group were attorneys such as John Jay and Alexander Hamilton of New York and Virginia's James Madison. Along with others who shared their views, they wrote a series of essays specifically to stir up support for the adoption of the Constitution. Collectively, these essays, known as *The Federalist Papers,* appeared not only in newspapers in each of the thirteen states, but in a widely distributed pamphlet collection, as well.

Under the pseudonym "Publius," Hamilton wrote the first of *The Federalist* essays. It is reprinted below, exactly as it appeared in New York City's *Independent Journal* on October 27, 1787.

For the Independent Journal

THE FEDERALIST. NO. I

To the People of the State of New York

AFTER an unequivocal experience of the inefficacy of the subsisting Federal Government, you are called upon to deliberate on a new Constitution for the United States of America. The subject speaks its own importance; comprehending in its consequences nothing less than the existence of the UNION, the safety and welfare of the parts of which it is composed, the fate of an empire, in many respects the most interesting in the world. It has been frequently remarked that it seems to have been reserved to the people of this country, by their conduct and example, to decide the important question, whether societies of men are really capable or not, of establishing good government from reflection and choice, or whether they are forever destined to depend, for their political constitutions, on accident and force. If there be any truth in the remark, the crisis at which we are arrived, may with propriety be regarded as the era in which that decision is to be made; and a wrong election of the part we shall act, may, in this view, deserve to be considered as the general misfortune of mankind. . . .

Among the most formidable of the obstacles which the new Constitution will have to encounter, may readily be distinguished the obvious interest of a certain class of men in every State to resist all changes which may hazard a diminution of the power, emolument and consequence of the offices they hold under the State-establishments—and the perverted ambition of another class of men, who will either hope to aggrandise themselves by the confusions of their country, or will flatter themselves with fairer prospects of elevation from the subdivision of the empire into several partial confederacies, than from its union under one government.

It is not, however, my design to dwell upon observations of this nature. I am well aware that it would be disingenuous to resolve indiscriminately the opposition of any set of men (merely because their situations might subject them to suspicion) into interested or ambitious views. Candour will oblige us to admit, that even such men may be actuated by upright intentions; and it cannot be doubted, that much of the opposition which has made its appearance, or may hereafter make its appearance, will spring from sources, blameless at least, if not respectable, the honest errors of minds led astray by preconceived jealousies and fears. So numerous indeed and so powerful are the causes, which serve to give a false bias to the judgment, that we upon many occasions, see wise and good men on the wrong as well as on the right side of questions, of the first magnitude to society. This circumstance, if duly attended to, would furnish a lesson of moderation to those, who are ever so much persuaded of their being in the right in any controversy. And a further reason for caution, in this respect, might be drawn from the reflection, that we are not always sure, that those who advocate the truth are influenced by purer principles than their antagonists. Ambition, avarice, personal animosity, party opposition, and many other motives, not more laudable than these, are apt to operate as well upon those who support as upon those who oppose the right side of a question. Were there not even these inducements to moderation, nothing could be more ill-judged than that intolerant spirit, which has, at all times, characterised political parties. For, in politics as in religion, it is equally absurd to aim at making proselytes by fire and sword. Heresies in either can rarely be cured by persecution.

And yet however just these sentiments will be allowed to be, we have already sufficient indications that it will happen in this as in all former cases of great national discussion. A torrent of angry and malignant passions will be let loose. To judge from the conduct of the opposite parties, we shall be led to conclude, that they will mutually hope to evince the justness of their opinions, and to increase the number of their converts by the loudness of their declamations, and by the bitterness of the invectives. An enlightened zeal for the energy and efficiency of government will be stigmatised, as the off-spring of a temper fond of despotic power and hostile to the principles of liberty. An overscupulous jealousy of danger to the rights of the people, which is more commonly the fault of the head than of the heart, will be represented as mere pretence and artifice; the [stale] bait for popularity at the expense of the public good. It will be forgotten, on the one hand, that jealousy is the usual concomitant of violent love, and that the noble enthusiasm of liberty is too apt to be infected with a spirit of narrow and illiberal distrust. On the other hand, it will be equally forgotten, that the vigour of government is essential to the security of liberty; that, in the contemplation of a sound and well informed judgment, their interest can never be separated; and that a dangerous ambition more often lurks behind the specious mask of zeal for the rights of the people, than under the forbidding appearance of zeal for the firmness and efficiency of government. History will teach us, that the former has been found a much more certain road to the introduction of despotism, than the latter, and that of those men who have overturned the liberties of republics the greatest number have begun their carrier [sic], by paying an obsequious court to the people, commencing Demagogues and ending Tyrants.

In the course of the proceeding observations I have had an eye, my Fellow Citizens, to putting you upon your guard against all attempts, from whatever quarter, to influence your decision in a matter of the utmost moment to your welfare by any impression other than those which may result from the evidence of truth. You will, no doubt, at the same time, have collected from the general scope of them that they proceed from a source not unfriendly to the new Constitution. Yes, my Countrymen, I own to you, that, after having given it an attentive consideration, I am clearly of opinion, it is your interest to adopt it. I am convinced, that this is the safest course for your liberty, your dignity, and your happiness. I affect not reserves, which I do not feel. I will not amuse you with an appearance of deliberation, when I have decided. I frankly acknowledge to you my convictions, and I will freely lay before you the reasons on which they are founded. The consciousness of good intentions disdains ambiguity. I shall not however multiply professions on this head. My motives must remain in the depositary of my own breast: My arguments will be open to all, and may be judged of by all. They shall at least be offered in a spirit, which will not disgrace the cause of truth.

I propose in a series of papers, to discuss the following interesting particulars—*The utility of the UNION to your political prosperity—The insufficiency of the present Confederation to preserve that Union—The necessity of a government at least equally energetic with the one proposed to the attainment of this object—The conformity of the proposed constitution to the principles of republican government—Its analogy to your own state constitution—*and lastly, *The additional security, which its adoption will afford to the preservation of that species of government, to liberty and to property. . . .*

PUBLIUS

1798

Having convinced the country of the need for adopting the Constitution, the Federalists, once in power, seemed to forget that one of the reasons for which the war for independence had been fought was to preserve the right of free speech. Fearful of a revolution of the masses as happened in France, in July, 1798, the Federalist majority in Congress passed, and President John Adams signed, the Sedition Act.

At bottom, the Sedition Act was nothing more than a heavy-handed attempt by the government to stifle dissent. It made it a crime to ''write, print, utter or publish . . . any false, scandalous and malicious writing . . . against the government of the United States, or either house of Congress . . . or the said President . . . or to excite against them the hatred of the good people of the United States . . . or to resist or oppose, or defeat any law. . . ." Not surprisingly, many of the targets of this law, which included penalties upon conviction of up to two years' imprisonment and a fine of up to $2,000, were newspaper editors.

Two such were John D. Burk and James Smith, co-editors of *The New York Time Piece,* who wrote a scathing commentary on July 20, 1798, immediately after the passage of the Sedition Act.

MELANCHOLY, VERY MELANCHOLY INDEED

Congress shall make no law abridging the freedom of speech or of the press. It is pretended that an unconstitutional law has become necessary to keep *the people* in due subordination. If the administration emanated from itself there would be some reason for abridging the rights of the people for its own security; but as the government is the will of the people, for their own happiness and comfort, it is treason against their will to impose restrictions upon them which they did not authorise. If the Government considers itself as a distinct essence and contemplates and provides only for its own benefit, the constitution is a nullity; for this is predicated upon the will of the people, and the government arises out of the constitution. If the people disobey constitutional laws they expose themselves to a punishment which they have assented; but a disobedience of an unconstitutional law ought to subject the authors of it and not the people to punishment. If it is criminal in the people to disobey laws constitutionally made, is it not equally criminal in their representatives to disobey the first and greatest law, the constitution? There is not only a political turpitude in a disobedience, there is also a moral iniquity, for those who administer the constitution are *sworn* to support it.

It is a duty which the people owe themselves to examine the laws that are made, and compare them with the constitution. The sedition bill ought particularly to engage their attention. Let this be compared with the great charter which they have laid down for the regulation of their government. If on enquiry they find that their constitution is violated, they ought to reflect upon the consequences of such a violation thus early. If a casual circumstance shall justify an infraction of it, where is their security? The Constitution was to be inviolable—nothing short of the power who made it was to change it; if it can be made to suit the interest or the designs of any portion of the community, contrary to its true intent and meaning, it is completely annihilated, and all security under it is at an end—we should be as well without such as instrument as with it.

Burk and Smith paid for the exercise of their First Amendment Rights. On July 25, the *Time Piece* ran the following story, under the heading: "COMMENTARY":

Benjamin Franklin Bache, editor of the Aurora, and John D. Burk and James Smith, editors of the Time Piece, have been arrested for publishing libels against government, and given bail for their appearance for trial.

1803

Yankee writer Washington Irving is best remembered for such fanciful tales as "The Legend of Sleepy Hollow" and "Rip Van Winkle," European folktales recast by the author and set in the lush, new world of upstate New York. America's first internationally known author, Irving was a well-known and influential newspaper columnist who wrote for the New York *Morning Chronicle* and *The Corrector,* papers edited by his brother Peter. In the following "letter" to the fictitious Andrew Quoz, Irving (under the pen name of Dick Buckram) satirizes a troupe of actors from the Old American Company in Albany, New York. It ran in the *Morning Chronicle* of December 24, 1803.

FOR THE MORNING CHRONICLE
To Mr. Andrew Quoz

Dear Sir,

The lively interest you appeared to take in Dramatic concerns, last winter, and your friendly vindication of the "Rights of Actors" encourages me to presume, that a brief account of the manner in which your theatric friends passed the summer, would not be unacceptable.

Feeling, in common with my professional brethren, a high sense of the obligations we are under, to you, I have thought it "writ down in my duty," to furnish you, from the pages of my Journal, with a slight sketch of our unfortunate manoeuvres.

Having been disconcerted in our plans, and driven out of our nest, at Mount Vernon Garden, by the Epidemic; we called together a meeting of several of the company, to determine which way we should direct our movements.

Emboldened by the approbation bestowed upon us, in the provincal town of New-York; we determined to repair to the METROPOLIS of the State, though not without great apprehensions of ill-success, in a place that was no doubt the standard of taste and refinement.

Having among our acquaintance, several *Gentlemen of the Law,* whom we were apprehensive might *arrest* us in our departure, and detain us in town with their *friendly importunities,* we determined to retreat without ceremony in the cool of the Evening, and happily succeeded in the attempt.

We now looked forward with impatience, anticipating the attention and curiosity we should attract on our arrival in Albany—Albany! the very name had music in our ears, that seat of opulence and splendor, of elegance and hospitality, there the Muses have fixed their abode! There the Arts and Sciences are encouraged, and there the man of genius receives the reward of his labours.

Such, Mr. Quoz, were the fond ideas that floated in our imaginations! We looked forward to a golden harvest, when our temples should be bound with bays, and our pockets lined with the gifts of Albanian munificence. How can I describe our emotions when the majestic domes and tin steeples of the metropolis slowly rose to view from the bosom of the Hudson. Each breast swelled with joyous expectation, the tear of extacy [sic] trembled in every eye.

We found the city spacious and elegant, the people smiling, courteous and hospitable. An old assembly room was chosen for our exhibitions, and we immediately went to work to prepare the stage and scenery. From the limited state of our funds, we were obliged to make shift with few scenes. One therefore, sufficed for parlor, kitchen and hall; another for grove or garden, forest or street, a white sheet represented the sea, and a dark blue baize curtain hung with red cloaks, the infernal regions. These I must confess were rather meagre contrivances, but to make up for the deficiency, we carried with us a ball of a twelve pounder, and as rosin was cheap we could afford to give them plenty of thunder and lightening!

Thus, Mr. Quoz, did we make shift to get every thing arranged; our prospect of success was trulyflattering [sic]—during our preparations the Citizens were continually running in and out, and appeared to be very curious about our proceedings; generous patrons, thought we, how impatient must you be for the time when you may flock to the theatre and reward our talents and ingenuity!

The important night big with our fate arrived, we made a striking display of the riches of our wardrobe; as I had to act the part of a Lover, I was arrayed in superior style, having on a sky colored silk coat, red jacket, green small clothes, and shoes decorated with large plated buckles; understanding that the Albanians were of Dutch extraction, I made my *debut* in a deliberate manner smoaking [sic] a tobacco piper.

I own, I felt a little aukward [sic] in my dress, having never acted the fine gentleman before, but I am since told that I acquitted myself extremely well, except that I turned in my toes, and was rather stiff in the joints.

My fellow performers were tricked out in equal splendor with myself, and the lady to whom I was to urge my tender suit appeared in all the loveliness of red ribbons and brocade. The candles were close snuffed, the fiddle strings rosined, the thunder bolts ready to roll, and the lightening to flash at a moment's warning, in short every thing was prepared to astonish the good people of Albany into approbation; think then Mr. Quoz what must have been our chagrin, when amongst a numerous audience we could scarcely recognize the bright countenance of a single substantial Albanian. Some of our old patrons who had fled from New-York; a few strangers from different parts of the country and an inconsiderable number of the younger people of the metropolis composed the whole of our auditors.

Our mortification at this neglect from a people so celebrated for patronizing elegant amusements cannot be conceived. The next morning however disclosed the cause. Unfortunately for us, the day before had presented a remarkably fine fish market and the good people were so busily engaged in feasting on sturgeon, that they had no time to attend to any other diversion. With this reason we were perfectly satisfied; had the cause been an assembly, a concert or an oratoria, our chagrin would have been almost insurmountable; but certainly we could not have the egregious vanity to think of rivalling a *sturgeon feast*.

A call to rehearsal interrupts my narration for the present, but I will resume it the first leisure moment.

Your humble servant,
DICK BUCKRAM.

1804

On Wednesday morning, July 11, 1804, two longtime political rivals who had played important roles in the founding of the United States, fought a duel beneath the bluffs of Weehawken, New Jersey, just across the Hudson River from New York City. When it was over, Alexander Hamilton, author of *The Federalist* essays, and secretary of the treasury under John Adams, lay mortally wounded. He had been shot by Aaron Burr, vice president in the Jefferson administration as well as an officer in George Washington's Continental Army.

Hamilton died the next day. News of his death was greeted with an outpouring of grief by his Federalist supporters as well as with a wave of public revulsion against the not uncommon practice of settling disputes between gentlemen upon a field of honor, that is, dueling. *The New York Evening Post,* which was edited by William Coleman and owned by Hamilton, was so overcome with emotion that it was unable to report the details of the event, largely confining its July 13, 1804, story to a republication of a letter written by Anglican Bishop Benjamin Moore, who had attended Hamilton in his last moments.

With emotions that we have not the hand to inscribe, have we to announce the death of ALEXANDER HAMILTON. He was cut off in the 48th year of his age, in the full vigor of his faculties, and in the midst of all his usefulness.

We have not the firmness to depict this melancholy, heart-rending event. Now—when death has extinguished all party animosity, the gloom that overspreads every countenance, the sympathy that pervades every bosom, bear irresistable testimony of the esteem and respect all maintained for him, and assure us that an impression has been made by his loss that no time can efface. It becomes us not to enter into particulars; we have no doubt, that in compliance with the universal anxiety of the inhabitants, a statement will soon be exhibited to them containing all the circumstances necessary to enable them to form a just opinion of this tragic scene. In the mean time we offer the following letter that we have received from the Reverend Bishop Moore. The testimony which this pious and venerable Clergyman bears to the virtues of the deceased, will we are sure, not be lost on a discerning community.

As soon as our feelings will permit, we shall deem it a duty to present a sketch of the character of our ever-to-be-lamented patron and best friend. . . .

THURSDAY EVENING, JULY 12, 1804

Mr. Coleman:

. . . Yesterday morning, immediately after he was brought from Hoboken to the house of Mr. Bayard, at Greenwich, a message was sent informing me of the sad event, accompanied by a request from General Hamilton, that I would come to him for the purpose of administering the holy communion. I went, but being desirous to afford time for serious reflection, and conceiving that under existing circumstances, it would be right and proper to avoid every appearance of precipitancy in performing one of the most solemn offices of our religion, I did not then comply with his desire. At one o'clock I was again called on to visit him. Upon my entering the room and approaching his bed, with the utmost calmness and composure he said, "My dear Sir, you perceive my unfortunate situation and no doubt have been made acquainted with the circumstances which led to it. It is my desire to receive the communion at your hands. I hope you will not conceive there is any impropriety in my request." He added, "It has for some time past been the wish of my heart, and it was my intention to take an early opportunity of uniting myself to the church, by the reception of that holy ordinance." I observed to him, that he must be very sensible of the delicate and trying situation in which I was then placed; that however desirous I might be to afford consolation to a fellow mortal in distress; still, it was my duty, as a minister of the gospel, to hold up the law of God as paramount to all other law; and that, therefore, under the influence of such sentiments, I must unequivocally condemn the practice which has brought him to his present unhappy condition. He acknowledged the propriety of these sentiments, and declared that he viewed the late transaction with sorrow and contrition. I then asked him, "Should it please God to restore you to health, Sir, will you never be again engaged in a similar transaction? and will you employ all your influence in society to discountenance this barbarous custom?" His answer was, "That, Sir, is my deliberate intention."

I proceeded to converse with him on the subject of his receiving the Communion, and told him that with respect to the qualifications of those who wished to become partakers of that holy ordinance, my enquiries could not be made in language more expressive than that which was used by our Church—"Do you sincerely repent of your sins past? Have you a lively faith in God's mercy through Christ, with a thankful remembrance of the death of Christ? And are you disposed to live in love and charity with all men?" He lifted up his hands and said, "With the utmost sincerity of heart I can answer those questions in the affirmative—I have no ill will against Col. Burr. I met him with a fixed resolution to do him no harm. I forgive all that happened." I then observed to him, that the terrors of the divine law

were to be announced to the obdurate and impenitent; but that the consola-
tions of the Gospel were to be offered to the humble and contrite heart, that
I had no reason to doubt his sincerity, and would proceed immediately to
gratify his wishes. The Communion was then administered, which he received with great devotion, and his heart afterwards appeared to be perfectly
at rest. I saw him again this morning, when with his last faltering words he
expressed a strong confidence in the mercy of God through the intercession
of the Redeemer. I remained with him until 2 o'clock this afternoon, when
death closed the awful scene—he expired without a struggle, and almost
without a groan. . . .

> With great respect, I remain,
> Your friend and ser't
> BENJAMIN MOORE

The anti-Federalist *New York Morning Chronicle* stressed in its July 18, 1804, story that the duel had been a fair one, a response to rumors that Hamilton pur-posely had shot wide of his adversary. Oddly, the *Chronicle's* account was printed verbatim in the next day's edition of Hamilton's *Evening Post.*

Colonel Burr arrived first on the ground, as had been previously agreed;
when General Hamilton arrived the parties exchanged salutations, and the
seconds proceeded to make their arrangements. They measured the distance,
ten full paces, and cast lots for the choice of position as also to determine
by whom the word should be given, both of which fell to the second of
General Hamilton. They proceeded to load the pistols in each other's presence, after which the parties took their stations. The gentleman who was to
give the word then explained to the parties the rules which were to govern
them in firing and which were as follows:

"The parties being placed at their stations—the second who gives the
words shall ask them whether they are ready; being answered in the affirmative, he shall say "present," after this the parties shall present and fire
when they please—if one fires before the other, the opposite second shall
say one, two, three, fire—and shall then fire or lose his fire."

He then asked if they were prepared, being answered in the affirmative,
he gave the word *present,* as had been agreed upon, and *both parties took
aim and fired in succession,* the intervening time is not expressed, as the
seconds do not precisely agree on that point. The fire of Colonel Burr took
effect, and General Hamilton almost instantly fell. Colonel Burr then advanced toward General Hamilton with a manner and gesture that appeared
to General Hamilton's friend to be expressive of regret, but without speaking, turned about and withdrew, being urged from the field by his friend as
has been subsequently stated, with a view to prevent his being recognized
by the surgeon and bargeman, who were then approaching. No further communication took place between the principals, and the barge that carried
Colonel Burr immediately returned to the city. We conceive it proper to add

that the conduct of the parties in this interview was perfectly proper, as
suited the occasion. . . .

1812

One of the most famous victories in
the history of the United States Navy was
that of Captain Isaac Hull's "Old Iron-
sides," the 44-gun frigate U.S.S. *Constitution,* over the British frigate *Guerriere* off the coast of Nova Scotia on
August 19, 1812. The battle lasted little
more than an hour before the British
vessel struck her colors. Afterwards, Hull
returned to Boston, British prisoners in
hand, as the first hero of the War of
1812.

Although no reporters witnessed the
battle, as soon as the *Constitution* returned to Boston harbor, on August 30,
1812, the enterprising *Boston Gazette* obtained a copy of the vessel's log from
one of its officers. The next day, New
Englanders read this first-hand account
of the engagement.

BRILLIANT NAVAL VICTORY!

The United States frigate *Constitution,* Captain HULL, anchored yesterday in the outer harbour, from a short cruize, during which she fell in with
the English frigate *Guerriere,* which she captured, after a short, but severe
action.—The damage, sustained by the fire of the Constitution, was so great,
that it was found impossible to tow her into port, and accordingly the crew
were taken out, and the ship sunk. The brilliancy of this action, however
we may regret the occasion that has produced it, will still excite the liveliest
emotions in every American bosom.

Particulars of the late action
between the U.S. frigate
CONSTITUTION, and the British frigate
GUERRIERE

(Communicated to the editors of the Boston Gaz. by an officer
on board the Constitution)

Lat. 41, 42, N. long. 55, 33, W.
Thursday, Aug. 19, fresh breeze from N.W. and cloudy; at 2 P.M. discovered a vessel to the southward, made all sail in chase; at 3, perceived
the chase to be a ship on the starboard tack, close hauled to the wind; hauled
S.S.W. at half past 3, made out the chase to be a frigate; at 4, coming up
with the chase very fast; at quarter before 5, the chase laid her main topsail
to the mast; took in our top gallant sails, stay-sails, and flying gib; took a
second reef in the topsails, hauled the courses up; sent the royal yards down;

and got all clear for action; beat to quarters, on which the crew gave three cheers; at 5 the chase hoisted three English Ensigns, at five minutes past 5, the enemy commenced firing; at 20 minutes past 5, set our colours, one at each mast head, and one at the mizen peak, and began firing at the enemy and continued to fire occasionally, he wearing very often, and we manoeuvering to close with him, and avoid being raked; at 6, set the main top gallant sail, the enemy having bore up; at five minutes past 6, brought the enemy to close action, standing before the wind; at 15 minutes past 6, the enemy's mizen-mast fell over on the starboard side; at 20 minutes past 6, finding we were drawing ahead of the enemy, luffed short round his bows, to rake him; at 25 minutes past 6, the enemy fell on board of us, his bowsprit foul of our mizen rigging. We prepared to board, but immediately after, his fore and main mast went by the board, and it was deemed unnecessary. Our cabin had taken fire from his guns; but soon extinguished, without material injury; at 30 minutes past 6, shot ahead of the enemy, when the firing ceased on both sides; he making the signal of submission, by firing a gun to leeward; set fore sail and main sail, and hauled to the eastward to repair damage; all our braces and much of our standing and running rigging and some of our spars being shot away. At 7, wore ship, and stood under the lee of the prize—sent our boat on board, which returned at 8, with Capt. *Dacres* late of his Majesty's ship *Guerriere,* mounting 49 carriage guns, and manned with 302 men, got our boats out, and kept them employed in removing the prisoners and baggage from the prize to our own ship. Sent a surgeon's mate to assist in attending the wounded, wearing ship occasionally to keep in the best position to receive the boats. At 20 minutes before 2, A.M. discovered a sail off the larboard beam, standing to the south; saw all clear for another action; at 3 the sail stood off again; at daylight was hailed by the lieut. on board the prize, who informed, he had 4 feet of water in the hold, and that she was in a sinking condition; all hands employed in removing the prisoners, and repairing our own damage through the remainder of the day. Friday the 20th commenced with light breezes from the northward, and pleasant; our boats and crew still employed as before; At 3 P.M. made the signal of recall for our boats, (having received all the prisoners) they immediately left her on fire, and a quarter past 3, she blew up; Our loss in the action was 7 killed, and 7 wounded; among the former, Lieut. *Bush* of Marines, and among the latter, Lieut. *Morris* severely*; and Mr. *Aylwin,* the master, slightly. On the part of the enemy, 15 men killed, and 64 wounded. Among the former, Lt. *Ready,* 2d of the ship; among the latter, Capt. *Dacres,* Lieut. *Kent,* 1st; Mr. *Scott,* master, and master's mate. **Now recovering.*

1815

In the days prior to war correspondents, remote bureaus, and swift transportation, newspapers greatly relied upon letters written by eye-witnesses to important events to inform their readers what had happened beyond the community. One such letter, published by the *Daily National Intelligencer* on February 6, 1815, was the report of the Battle of New Orleans sent by General Andrew Jackson to Secretary of War James Monroe.

With a curiously understated headline, the Washington, D.C., paper recounted the battle that had occurred four weeks earlier, ironically, one day after a peace treaty was signed in Paris.

The extent of the victory was made even more clear the following day, when the *Intelligencer* printed the British casualty reports: "killed 700, wounded 1400, prisoners 495."

ALMOST INCREDIBLE VICTORY! FROM NEW ORLEANS

Dates up to the 13th January—the Enemy, attacking our entrenched Army on the 8th, beaten and repulsed by Jackson and his brave associates, with great slaughter

Copy of a letter from Major General Jackson, to the Secretary of War dated

> *Head-quarters, 7th Military District,*
> *Camp, 4 miles below New Orleans,*
> *January 13, 1815*

SIR—At such a crisis, I conceive it my duty to keep you constantly advised of my situation.

On the 10th inst. I forwarded to you an account of the bold attempt made by the enemy on the morning of the 8th to take possession of my works by storm, and of the severe repulse which he met with. That report having been sent by the mail which crosses the Lake, may possibly have miscarried; for which reason, I think it the more necessary briefly to repeat the substance of it.

Early on the morning of the 8th, the enemy, having been actively employed the two preceding days in making preparations for a storm, advanced in two strong columns on my right and left. They were received, however, with a firmness which, it seems, they little expected, and which defeated all their hopes. My men, undisturbed by their approach, which indeed they had long anxiously wished for, opened upon them a fire so deliberate and certain as rendered their scaling ladders and fascines, as well as their more direct implements of warfare, perfectly useless. For upwards of an hour it was continued with a briskness of which there had been but few instances, perhaps, in any country. In just to the enemy it must be said, they withstood it as long as could have been expected from the most determined bravery. At length, however, they fled in confusion from the field—leaving it covered with their dead and wounded. Their loss was immense. It had at first computed it at 1500; but it is since ascertained to have been much greater. Upon information, which is believed to be correct, Col. Haynes, the Inspector General, reports it to be in the total 2600. His report I enclose you. My loss was inconsiderable; being only* seven killed and six wounded. (*This was in the action on the line—afterwards a skirmishing was kept up in which a few more of our men were lost) Such a disproportion in loss, when we consider the number and the kind of troops engaged, must, I know, excite astonishment, and may not, every where, be fully credited; yet I am perfectly satisfied that the account is not exaggerated on the one part, nor underrated on the other.

The enemy having hastily quitted a post which they had gained possession of, on the other side of the river, and we immediately returned to it; both armies at present occupy their former positions. Whether, after their severe losses he has sustained, he is preparing to return to his shipping, or to make still mightier efforts to attain his first object, I do not pretend to determine. It becomes me to act as though the latter were his intention. One thing, however, seems certain, that if he still calculates on effecting what he has hitherto been unable to accomplish, he must expect considerable reinforcements; as the force with which he landed must undoubtedly be diminished by at least 3000. Besides the loss which he sustained on the night of the 23rd ult. which is estimated at 400, he cannot have suffered less between that period and the morning of the 8th instant, than 300—having, within that time, been repulsed in two general attempts to drive us from our position, and there having been continual cannonading and skirmishing, during the whole of it. Yet he is still able to shew a very formidible force.

There is little doubt that the commanding general, Sir Edward Pakenham was killed in the action of the 8th, and that majors general Kean and Gibbs were badly wounded.

Whenever a more leisure moment shall occur, I will take the liberty to make out and forward you a more circumstantial account of the several actions, and particularly that of the 8th, in doing which my chief motive will be to render justice to those brave men I have had the honor to command, and who have so remarkably distinguished themselves.

I have the honor to be, most respectfully, your obedient servant,

ANDREW JACKSON
Major General Com'dg

P.S. A correct list of my killed and wounded will be forwarded by the Adjutant General

1831

In August, 1831, Nat Turner led a bloody revolt of his fellow slaves in Southampton County, Virginia. Although the extent of the violence was greatly exaggerated by a nervous white population, the rebellion caused many a sleepless night thereafter among the slave-owning population of the South. Nat Turner's rebellion also fueled the nascent abolition movement in the North.

On September 2, 1831, *The Washing-* *ton* (D.C.) *Globe,* which published under the motto "The World is Governed Too Much," provided its readers in the southern city that was the national capital a foretaste of the bloodshed to come. The coverage, which was largely ignorant of Turner's leadership role in the uprising, came from news reports first published in Richmond and Norfolk newspapers, the *Norfolk Herald* commenting that slavery was an evil upon the land.

INSURRECTION OF THE BLACKS

From the Norfolk Herald
SOUTHAMPTON

The expedition from this vicinity which was sent off last Wednesday to Southampton have all returned. The mounted volunteers from Norfolk and Portsmouth, got back on Monday afternoon, having been actively employed during their term of service in apprehending the insurgents.

The battalion of U. States artillery from Fortress Monroe, under the command of Lt. Col. WORTH, and the marines and seamen from the Natchez and Warren, embarked at Smithfield yesterday in the steamboat Hampton, and have returned to their respective stations. The exhibition of so formidable an array of arms as these troops presented to the slave population of the counties through which they passed, and the great despatch with which they were marched to the scene of action, cannot fail of producing a lasting and happy effect, it will convince more than volumes of argument, the deluded and infatuated of that unfortunate class of our population, of the utter hopelessness of any attempt by violence to sever the obligations which bind them to us—alas! too fatally bind them—for our evil more than their oppression. . . .

From the Richmond Whig
Extract of a letter from the Senior
Editor of the Whig, dated

JERUSALEM, Southampton Ct. House,
Thursday Evening, August 25

The Richmond Troop arrived here this morning a little after 9 o'clock, after a rapid, hot and most fatiguing march from Richmond. On the road we met a thousand different reports, no two agreeing, and leaving it impossible to make a plausable guess at the truth. On the route from Petersburg, we found the whole country thoroughly alarmed; every man armed, the dwellings deserted by the white inhabitants and the farms most generally left in possession of the blacks. On our arrival at this village, we found Com. Elliott and Col. Worth, with 250 U. States troops, from the neighborhood of Old Point, and a considerable militia force. A Troop of Horse from Norfolk and one from Prince George, have since arrived. Jerusalem was never so crowded from its foundation; for besides the considerable military force assembled here, the ladies from the adjacent country, to the number of 3 or 400, have sought refuge from the appalling dangers by which they were surrounded.

Here, for the first time, we learnt the extent, of the insurrection, and the mischief perpetrated. Rumor had infinitely exaggerated the first, swelling the numbers of the negroes to a thousand or 1200 men, and representing its ramifications as embracing several of the adjacent counties, particularly Isle of Wight and Greensville, but it was hardly the power of rumor itself, to exaggerate the atrocities which have been perpetrated by the insurgents; whole families, fathers, mothers, daughters, sons, suckling babes, and school children, butchered, thrown into heaps, and left to be devoured by hogs and dogs, or to putrify on the spot. At Mr. Levi Waller's, his wife and ten children, were murdered and piled in one bleeding heap on the floor. Waller himself was absent at the moment, but approaching while the dreadful scene was acting, was pursued, and escaped into a swamp, with much difficulty. One small child in the house at the time, escaped by concealing herself in the fire place, witnessing from the place of her concealment, the slaughter of the family, and her elder sisters among them. Another child was cruelly wounded and left for dead, and probably will not survive. All these children were not Mr. Waller's. A school was kept near his house, at which, and between which and his house, the ruthless villains murdered several of the helpless children. Many other horrors have been perpetrated. The killed, as far as ascertained, amount to sixty-two; I send a list believed to be correct, as far as it goes. There are, probably, others not yet known, hereafter to be added. A large portion of these were women and children. It is not believed that any outrages were offered to the females.

How, or with whom, the insurrection originated, is not certainly known. The prevalent belief is that on Sunday week last, at Barnes' church, in the neighborhood of the Cross Keys, the negroes who were observed to be disorderly, took offence at something; (it is not known what) that the plan of insurrection was then and there conceived, and matured in the course of the week following, and carried into execution on Sunday night the 21st August. The atrocities commenced at Mr. Travis'. A negro, who is called captain Moore, and who, it is added, is a preacher, is the reputed leader. On Monday, most of the murders were perpetrated. It is said, that none have been committed since that day. The numbers engaged are not supposed to have exceeded 60—one account says 100—another not so many as 40. Twelve armed and resolute men were certainly competent to have quelled them at any time. But, taken by surprise—with such horrors before their eyes, and trembling for their wives and children, the men, most naturally, only thought in the first place, of providing a refuge for those dependent upon them. Since this has been effected, the citizens have acted with vigor. Various parties have scoured the country, and a number of insurgents (differently reported,) have been killed or taken. There are thirteen prisoners now at this place, one or more of them severely wounded; the principal of them, a man aged 21, called Marmaduke, who might have been a hero, judging from the magnaminity with which he bears his sufferings. He is said to be an atrocious offender, and the murderer of Miss Vaughan, celebrated for her beauty. The Preacher-captain has not yet been taken. At the Cross Keys, summary justice, in the form of decapitation, has been executed on one or more prisoners. The people are naturally enough wound up to a high pitch of rage, and precaution is even necessary to protect the lives of the captives—scouring parties are out, and the insurrection may be considered as already suppressed.

1833

By the early 1830s, the development of new and more efficient presses made it possible to sell newspapers for a penny at a time when most commercial daily papers sold for six cents. The result was a newspaper workers and clerks could afford, papers that deliberately appealed to the working class, papers derisively termed "the penny press" by the often put-out commercial sheets. Relying on street sales as opposed to the subscriptions that sustained their more traditional rivals, the penny papers filled their pages with scandal, crime news, and human interest stories.

While the goal of these papers was large circulations, and therefore, profits for their owners, their appearance made first-time newspaper readers of large segments of the American population. It also caused their "uptown" colleagues to become less formal, out of fear of losing their readers to the livelier upstarts. Concurrently, the penny papers began carrying more serious news amid the sensational, and the gap between the two types of newspapers narrowed. The result was a better informed American public.

The first of the penny papers was Benjamin Day's *New York Sun,* published on September 3, 1833. This initial issue also included stories about murders in Columbus, Ohio, and Charlottesville, Virginia, an earthquake in Charlottesville, a fire in Rochester, New York, a murder trial in Easton, Pennsylvania, an attempted insurrection in the Ohio Penitentiary, consumption deaths in New York, and cholera in Mexico.

MELANCHOLY SUICIDE.—a Mr. Fred. A. Hall, a young gentleman from Boston, who had been a boarder at Webb's Congress Hall, for a week or ten days previous, put an end to his life on Sunday last by taking laudanum. Late in the afternoon Mr. Webb having occasion to go into his room, found the door locked on the inside; but hearing a noise as of a person in distress, after knocking and calling several times without any answer, he burst open the door, and found him apparently dying. Physicians were immediately called and the stomach pump applied, but without success. He was to have sailed yesterday morning for Sumatra, as supercargo of a vessel belonging to a wealthy firm in Boston, one of the members of which was his father. He is supposed to have committed this rash act in a fit of temporary derangement occasioned by an affair of the heart in which his happiness was deeply involved. He was about 24 years of age, of engaging manners, and amiable disposition, and one whose loss even under less affecting circumstances would have been deeply lamented.

The Almshouse Boy.—a youth who was brought up at the Almshouse was lately taken into the family of Mrs.—, in Pearl st. to run of errands. The first day he became an inmate of her house, the following dialogue passed between them:

"Are you not sorry, my dear," said Mrs. M—, "to leave home?"

"No," answered he; "I don't care."

"Is there not somebody at home whom you are sorry to leave?" resumed she.

"No," replied the boy, "I am not sorry to leave any body."

"What, not those who are good to you?" joined she.

"Nobody was ever good to me," said the boy.

Mrs.— was touched with the child's answer, which strongly painted his helpless lot, and the cold indifference of the world. The tear stood in her eye.

"My poor little fellow," said she, after a short pause. "was nobody ever good to you!—have you no friend, my dear?' "

"No, for old dusty Bob, the rag-man, died last week."

"And was he your friend?"

"Yes, that he was," replied the boy, "he once *gave me a piece of gingerbread!*"

And in a column titled "POLICE OFFICE," were, among others, the following pieces:

John Evans, brought up for throwing stones at the house of Eliza Vincent, who refused him admittance. The complainant, a watchman, said he advised the prisoner to desist—the prisoner called the watchman a rascal, and told him to clear out, or at some future time he would get a devil of a flogging; whereupon the watchman seized hold of him and walked him up to the watch-house—held to bail for appearance at court.

John McMan, brought up for whipping Juda McMan, his darling wife—his excuse was, that his head was rather thick, in consequence of taking a wee drap of whiskey. Not being able to find bail he was accommodated with a room in bridewell.

Wm. Scott, from Centre Market, brought up for assaulting Charlotte Gray, a young woman with whom he lived. The magistrate, learning that they never were married, offered the prisoner a discharge on condition that he would marry the injured girl, who was very willing to withdraw the complaint on such terms. Mr. Scott cast a sheep's eye towards the girl, and then looking out of the window, gave the bridewell a melancholy survey; he then gave the girl another look, and was hesitating as to which he should choose— a wife or a prison. The Justice insisted on an immediate answer. At length he concluded that he "might as well marry the critter," and they left the office apparently satisfied.

1836

In 1835, the Mexican province of Texas revolted against General Antonio Lopez de Santa Anna's dictatorial rule. Texans captured the former mission San Antonio de Valero, converted earlier to a barracks and renamed the Alamo. A force of 187 volunteers, including legendary hunter James Bowie and former United States Congressman David Crockett, occupied the walled compound in the heart of San Antonio on February 23, 1836.

Intending to crush the revolt before it could spread, Santa Anna massed an army of 4,000 men to lay siege to the limestone and adobe barracks. The commander of the garrison, Colonel William Barret Travis, answered Santa Anna's surrender demand with a cannon ball and dispatched a futile plea to a rump convention in Austin for aid. On March 6, the thirteenth day of the siege, Santa Anna stormed the Alamo. *The San Felipe de Austin Telegraph and Texas Register* of March 24, 1836, reported the outcome, while managing to misspell the names of both Santa Anna and Crockett.

MORE PARTICULARS RESPECTING THE FALL OF THE ALAMO

That event, so lamentable, and yet so glorious to Texas, is of such deep interest and excites so much our feelings that we shall never cease to celebrate it, and regret that we are not acquainted with the names of all those who fell in that Fort, that we might publish them, and thus consecrate to future ages the memory of our heroes who perished at the Thermopylae of Texas. Such examples are bright ones, and should be held up as mirrors, that by reflection, we may catch the spirit and learn to fashion our own behaviour. The last of names inserted below, was furnished by Mr. Jno. W. Smith, and Mr. Navon, and as we obtain more we will publish them. To Mr. Smith, who has rendered good service to Texas, and to Judge Ponton are we indebted for the particulars, as communicated to them by Mrs. Dickinson, who was in the "Alamo" during the siege and assault.

At daybreak of the 6th inst. the enemy surrounded the fort with their infantry, with the cavalry forming a circle outside to prevent escape on the part of the garrison; the number consisted of at least 4000 against 140! General Santa Ana commanded in person, assisted by four generals and a formidable train of artillery. Our men had been previously as much fatigued and harassed by nightwatching and incessant toils, having experienced for some days past, a heavy bombardment and several real and feigned attacks. But, American valor and American love of liberty displayed themselves to the last: they were never more conspicuous; twice did the enemy apply to the walls their scaling ladders, and twice did they receive a check; for our men were determined to verify the words of the immortal Travis, "to make the victory worse to the enemy than a defeat." A pause ensued after the second attack, which was renewed on the third time, owing to the exertions of Santa Ana and his officers; they then poured in over the walls, "like sheep;" the struggle, however, did not even there cease—unable from the crowd and for want of time to load their guns and rifles, our men made use of the but-ends of the latter and continued to fight and to resist, until life ebbed out through their numberless wounds and the enemy had conquered the fort, but not its brave, its matchless defenders: they perished, but they yielded not: one (Warner) remained to ask for quarter, which was denied by the unrelenting enemy—total extermination succeeded, and the darkness of death occupied the memorable Alamo, but recently so teeming with gallant spirits and filled with deeds of never-failing remembrance. We envy not the feelings of the victors, for they must have been bitter and galling; not proud ones. Who would not be rather one of the Alamo heroes, than of the living of its merciless victors? Spirits of the mighty, though fallen! Honours and rest are with ye: the spark of immortality which animated your forms, shall brighten into a flame, and Texas, the whole world, shall hail ye like demi-gods of old, as founders of new nations, and as patterns for imitation!

From the commencement to its close, the storming lasted less than an hour. Major Evans, master of ordnance, was killed when in the act of setting fire to the powder magazine, agreeably to the previous orders from Travis. The end of David Crocket of Tennessee, the great hunter of the west, was as glorious as his career through life had been useful. He and his companions were found surrounded by piles of assailants, whom they had immolated on the altar of Texas liberties. The countenance of Crocket, was unchanged: he had in death that freshness of hue, which his exercise of pursuing the beasts of the forest and the prairie had imparted to him. Texas places him, exultingly, amongst the martyrs in her cause. Col. Travis stood on the walls cheering his men, exclaiming. "Hurra, my boys!" till he received a second shot, and fell; it is stated that a Mexican general (Mora) then rushed upon him, and lifted his sword to destroy his victim, who, collecting all his last expiring energies, directed a thrust at the former, which changed their relative positions; for the victim became the victor, and the remains of both descended to eternal sleep; but not alike to everlasting fame.

Travis's negro was spared, because, as the enemy said, "his master had behaved like a brave man;" words which of themselves form an epitaph:

they are already engraved on the hearts of Texans, and should be inscribed on his tomb. Col. James Bowie, who had for several days been sick, was murdered in his bed; his remains were mutilated. Humanity shudders at describing these scenes; and the pen, as if a living thing, stops to gain fresh force, that sensibility may give way to duty.

Suspended animation has returned to the instrument of our narration, and we continue. Mrs. Dickinson and her child, and a negro of Bowie's, and as before said, Travis's were spared.

Our dead were denied the right of Christian burial; being stripped and thrown into a pile, and burned. Would that we could gather up their ashes and place them in urns!

It is stated that about fifteen hundred of the enemy were killed and wounded in the last and previous attacks.

On hearing of the total destruction of Col. Travis's men, and reasonably calculating upon a sudden movement of the enemy, Gen. Houston thought it advisable to fall back to the Colorado; and though this was done with a considerable sacrifice to the citizens of Dewit's colony, we do consider that it was the only safe course. It might have been possible that our troops could have checked the enemy at that place, but there being other crossings, the hazard, we think, would have been too great. Gen Houston's force was small and not well provided with ammunition. Whilst his position at the Colorado gives times for more reinforcements to join him, and so renders our efforts more imposing and the issue less doubtful. The laying waste of all the property which could not be removed will convince our enemies that if they overrun our territory they will get no booty.

1838

On April 23, 1838, tangible fruits of the industrial revolution arrived in New York harbor. The first two steamships to successfully make the Atlantic crossing from Great Britain—the *Sirius* and the *Great Western*—steamed up the Narrows, past the Battery, and tied up at piers in Manhattan. The smaller *Sirius* was the first to arrive, stealing the thunder of the much larger, black-hulled *Great Western*, which had been purpose-built by British railway architect Isambard Kingdom Brunel to be an ocean-going link between his London-Bristol Great Western Railroad and America. But although it wasn't the first steamship to make the crossing, Brunel's vessel captured the mythical Atlantic "blue riband," emblematic of the fastest ship between Europe and the United States, by making its journey in a seemingly breathtaking fifteen days, three days fewer than its smaller rival.

In its story of April 24, 1838, James Gordon Bennett's innovative penny sheet, *The New York Morning Herald,* captured the excitement of a day in which the world had grown smaller, and after which the United States would never again be as isolated, or as secure.

Triumph of Steam—The Sirius and the Great Western—The passage of the Atlantic in fifteen days!

The excitement yesterday was tremendous; from an early hour in the morning until dark, myriads of persons crowded the Battery to have a glimpse of the first vessel which had crossed the Atlantic from the British isles, and arrived at this port; indeed, it is said, that every Englishman in the city, at one time or other, during the day, was gazing at the dark looking vessel with American colors at the fore, and the flag of old England at the stern. This excitement was further increased by the arrival of the *Great Western,* from Bristol, which left that port on the 7th instant, making the passage in fifteen days, thus solving the problem of possibility, and showing what can be done by enterprize, expenditure, courage, and skill, in encountering the stormy weather which these two vessels have so successively braved and surmounted. The *Sirius,* however, is the pioneer, and to her glory of the Argonaut is due.

The approach of the "Great Western" to the harbor, and in front of the Battery, was most magnificent. It was about four o'clock yesterday afternoon. The sky was clear—the crowds immense. The battery was filled with the human multitude, one half of whom were females, the faces covered with smiles, and their delicate persons with the gayest attire.—Below, on the broad blue water, appeared this huge thing of life, with four masts, and emitting volumes of smoke. She looked black and blackguard—as all the British steamers generally are—rakish, cool, reckless, fierce, and forbidding in their sombre colors to an extreme. As she neared the Sirius she slackened her movements, and took a sweep round, forming a sort of half circle. At this moment, the whole Battery sent forth a tumultuous shout of delight, at the revelation of her magnificent proportions. After making another turn towards Staten Island, she made another sweep, and shot towards the East River with extraordinary speed. The vast multitudes rent the air with their shouts again, waving handkerchiefs, hats, harraing to a very great degree. After shewing herself thus, she took up her station at the foot of Market street, at a slip assigned to her, and thus let the thousands rest in quiet.

It is a singular coincidence that both vessels should have arrived on St. George's day, the patron saint of the country to which they belong. Old England will exult in the achievement, and great will be the chuckling among its seamen and mercantile people at this prosperous issue of so great an undertaking. These voyages, it must be remembered, are only experimental ones; the *Sirius* was not constructed for the passage of the broad sea, and came off on her expedition almost *impromptu,* and crossed in eighteen days, on eleven of which foul winds prevailed; yet in the eighteen days she ran 3,519 knots! The *Great Western* was built with more preparation, and has, therefore, accomplished her object more speedily;-but the opinion now is that the distance can and will be run in *ten* or *twelve* days, when every thing is arranged and calculated for that purpose.

We have given below the particulars of the construction of the *Great Western,* as we have previously done of the *Sirius* and the *Royal Victoria,* (the name of which has been altered to the *British Queen*). And here we may be permitted to remark that we were in error when we stated that the *Sirius,* now here, was the "pig ship," concerning which an anecdote appeared in the *Herald* on Sunday week;-the *Royal Victoria* also is a different vessel from the *Victoria* on board of which the accident occurred by the bursting of a boiler, as mentioned yesterday morning.

Captain Roberts, of the *Sirius,* was spoken of in the most complimentary of terms by the ladies, his passengers. "They should," they said, "have been dreadfully alarmed by the bad weather, but they felt quite safe when they thought they were under Capt. Roberts' charge, whose celebrity as a steam navigator was proverbial." The cook, who is an authority in such matters, stated that the rolling was very trifling, and not so heavy as in a sailing vessel. In short, nothing could have been more satisfactory for all purposes than this bold expedition, and we trust it will redound to the permanent profit, as it certainly does to the enterprise of all concerned. The results to business, commerce, manners, arts, social life, and the moral approximation of the two hemispheres, we have on divers occasions adverted to, and shall again when we are not so pressed with news. At present, we must conclude with the details relative to the *Great Western,* from the London literary and scientific journals, only promising that the *Sirius* and most probably the *Great Western* will leave this port for London direct, on the 3rd or 5th May. . . .

1840

Edgar Allen Poe, father of the modern horror story, earned his keep as a journalist while developing his compelling literary style. Indeed, around the time he composed his now classic Gothic poem "The Raven" in 1844, Poe was literary critic for the New York *Mirror.* A year later Poe's criticism could be read in the *Broadway Journal,* where he assailed such literary lights as Henry Wadsworth Longfellow, and contributed short fiction such as "The Pit and the Pendulum" and "The Premature Burial."

Apparently his work as a reporter inspired his fiction. "The Trial of James Wood," written by Poe for *Alexander's Weekly Messenger* of April 1, 1840, reports a murder trial that turned on the question of insanity. That subject was to haunt Poe's literature, playing a part in such tales as "The Pit and the Pendulum" and "The Cask of Amontillado."

THE TRIAL OF JAMES WOOD.

The trial of the unfortunate Wood, for the murder of his daughter, Mrs. Sarah Ann Peak, was brought to conclusion on Friday evening last, the jury, after a brief absence, returning a verdict of "Not Guilty, on the ground of insanity.'' This was anticipated by every one, and occasioned no surprise. The witnesses for the defence (of whom the most important was Dr. Meigs, for a long time the family physician of the accused) made out so clear a case of constitutional tendency to mania, if not of existing derangement itself, that but one course was left for the jury. The prosecution was conducted by Mr. Johnson, himself, the Attorney General of the State, who, at the conclusion of the evidence, left the matter, without argument, to the jury. Judge King briefly pointed out the main points for determination, and commented especially upon the question of insanity. Upon this head, it appears to us that a very material argument was strangely omitted by the counsel for the defence—an argument which, with many minds, would have had more weight in bringing about a conviction of the prisoner's insanity than any urged in his behalf. It appears from the testimony that the conduct of Wood, when purchasing his pistols at the shop of the gunsmith, was characterised by an entire self-possession—a remarkable calmness—an evenness of manner altogether foreign to his usual nervous habit. His replies were cool, and without the slightest apparent trepidation. It is just possible that the defence *feared* to broach this striking subject; for, upon a cursory view, the facts do certainly make against the accused, and imply a premeditated and cold-blooded assassination. But the metaphysician, or the skillful medical man, would deduce from them a positive conclusion in favor of Wood. With the deep cause for agitation which he is known to have had, he could not possibly, in the supposition of his sanity, have *assumed* the calmness of demeanor mentioned. A nervous trepidancy would have manifested itself, if not in an ordinary form, at least in an overstrained endeavor to be calm. But, in the supposition of his insanity, all is natural—all is in full accordance with the well known modes of action of the madman. The cunning of the maniac—a cunning which baffles that of the wisest man of sound mind—the amazing self-possession with which at times, he assumes the demeanor, and preserves the appearance, of perfect sanity, have long been matters of comment with those who have made the subject of mania their study.

The acquittal of the accused on the ground of insanity involves his legal confinement as a madman until such time as the Court satisfy themselves of his return to sound mind. We cannot believe, however, that this truly unfortunate man will ever be restored to that degree of reason which would authorise his final discharge. His monomania is essentially periodical; and a perfect sanity for months, or even years, would scarcely be a sufficient guaranty for his subsequent conduct. A time would still come when there would be laid to his charge another—although hardly a more horrible—deed of sudden violence and bloodshed.

1844

Technology was not limited to the oceans. On Friday, May 21, 1844, the first practical use of Samuel Morse's telegraph took place, when the result of a vote in the House of Representatives was transmitted the fifty or so miles from Capitol Hill to waiting representatives of the *Baltimore Patriot and Commercial Gazette,* camped in a railroad freight depot in their home city. For the first time news could travel faster than a man could ride. In Saturday's edition of the paper it was duly reported that the House had rejected a motion to suspend its rules to go into a committee of the whole by a vote of 86 to 79.

Unfortunately for the *Patriot,* this first use of telegraphed information in the service of journalism was only a partial triumph. While the result of the vote in the House had been received in Baltimore within a few minutes of its occurrence, the tally given was incorrect. Indeed, on May 25, the same day in which the *Patriot* reported on this "annihilation of space," another story in the same edition reported that the actual vote count on the question had been "yeas 85, nays 89." Then, as now, new technology was no substitute for accurate reporting.

THE ELECTRO MAGNETIC TELEGRAPH

Morse's Electro Magnetic Telegraph, now connects between the Capitol at Washington and the Railroad Depot in Pratt, between Charles and Light streets in Baltimore. The wires were brought in yesterday from the outer depot and attached to the telegraphic apparatus in a third story room in the depot warehouse building. The batteries were charged this morning and the Telegraph put in full operation, conveying intelligence to and from the Capitol. A large number of gentlemen were present to see the operations of this truly astonishing contrivance. Many admitted to the room had their names sent down, and in less than a second the apparatus in Baltimore was put in operation by the attendant in Washington, and before the lapse of a half minute the same names were returned plainly written. At half-past 11 o'clock, A.M. the question being asked here, "what the news was at Washington?" the answer was almost instantaneously returned—"Van Buren stock is rising"—meaning of course that his chances were strengthening to receive the nomination on Monday next. The time of day was also enquired for, when the response was given from the Capitol—"forty-nine minutes past eleven." At this period it was also asked how many persons were spectators to the Telegraphic experiments in Washington?—the answer was "sixteen." After which a variety of names were sent up from Washington, some with their compliments to friends here, whose names had just been transmitted to them. Several items of private intelligence were also transmitted backwards and forwards, one of them was an order to the agent here not to pay a certain bill. Here, however, the electric fluid proved too slow, for it had been paid a few minutes before.

At half past 12 o'clock, the following was sent to Washington, "Ask a reporter in Congress to send a despatch to the Baltimore Patriot at 2 p.m." In about a minute the answer came back thus. "It will be attended to."

2 o'clock, P.M.—The despatch has arrived, and is as follows:

One o'clock.—There has just been made a motion in the House to go into Committee of the Whole on the Oregon question. Rejected—ayes 79, nays 86.

Half past one.—The House is now engaged on private bills.

Quarter to two.—Mr. Atherton is now speaking in the Senate.

Mr. S. will not be in Baltimore tonight.

So that we are thus enabled to give to our readers information from Washington up to two o'clock. This is indeed the annihilation of space.

1848

Few events have so excited a nation as did the discovery of gold on January 24, 1848, at Captain John Sutter's new lumber mill at Coloma in California. Despite Sutter's attempts to keep secret the discovery by his contractor, James Marshall, the editor of the San Francisco *Californian* broke the story in his issue of March 15, 1848:

GOLD MINE FOUND.—In the newly made raceway of the Saw Mill recently erected by Captain Sutter, on the American Fork, gold has been found in considerable quantities. One person brought thirty dollars worth to New Helvetia, gathered there in a short time. California, no doubt, is rich in mineral wealth; great chances here for scientific capitalists. Gold has been found in almost every part of the country.

Apparently the story excited little interest. Not until an enterprising dry goods merchant from Sutter's Fort, Samuel Brannan, brought a vial of gold dust to San Francisco on May 12 did gold fever set in. Within days, able-bodied men, outfitted in Brannan's store, were making for the gold country in the Sierra Nevada foothills. So many left to seek their fortune that the editor of the *Californian* was forced to print the following notice on May 29, 1848:

TO OUR READERS:

With this slip ceases for the present the publication of the Californian— "Othello's occupation's gone!"

The reasons which have lead to this step are many and cogent. We shall however only state a few of them, merely to satisfy those whose curiosity may be aroused sufficiently to gain for us a perusal, and to show the expediency of the measure.

The majority of our subscribers and many of our advertising patrons have closed their doors and places of business and left town, and we have received one order after another conveying the *pleasant* request that "the printer will please stop my paper. . . ."

The whole country, from San Francisco to Los Angeles and from the sea shore to the base of the Sierra Nevada, resounds with the sordid cry of "*gold!* GOLD! GOLD!!!!" while the field is left half planted, the house half built and everything neglected but the manufacture of shovels and pick-axes. . .

The CALIFORNIAN however may by no means be considered as extinct, though for a time discontinued. Whenever the people of California resume the use of their reading faculties, we shall be ready to serve them with a newspaper, according to the best of our abilities.

The paper suspended publication until July 15, 1848, when a letter from a correspondent who signed himself COSMOPOLITE reported:

I have just returned to Fort Sacramento, from the Gold region, from whence I write this. . . . As near as I can ascertain there are now about 2000 persons engaged and the roads leading to the mines are thronged with people and wagons. . . . The mountains have been explored for about 40 miles, and gold has been found in great abundance in almost every part of them.

1849

"The cowards never started and the weak ones died on the way," Carl Sandburg wrote of them. They were a hardy, and foolhardy breed, those men and women who set off to California in search of gold with the spring thaw of 1849. Brave men and fools, they come alive once more in this long-overlooked account of the first Forty-Niners, written by an unidentified officer at Fort Kennedy, Nebraska. It was published first in the St. Louis *Republican* and reprinted in *The Cincinnati Argus* on June 14, 1849, where it was rediscovered by social historian Henry W. Splitter.

EMIGRANT WAGONS ROLL

Fort Kennedy, Nebraska, May 21, 1849
Gentlemen: The tide of emigration towards the land of promise, via the South Pass, may now be considered as having fairly set in. Daily, hourly, the number of wagons is increasing, and the anxious faces of gold diggers multiply upon us astonishingly. Today 214 wagons passed this post, making

in all 1203. In my last I believe I stated that on an average there were three and a half men to a wagon; it may safely be set down as four, which would give nearly 5,000 for the number already on the road to fortune. The reports of persons recently from the frontiers represent the whole country as filled with white-top wagons, long rifles, bowies, and revolvers. Five thousand wagons, 20,000 to 25,000 men, and 50,000 animals will cross the plains, or attempt to, this season. That there will be great suffering in the mountains, there cannot be the shadow of doubt. Many teams have passed here, that will never reach the mountains, much less pass over them. All talk of going as far as possible with their wagons, then abandoning them and packing over. Already several have been deserted between this point and the frontiers. As for provisions, enough has been thrown away to feed a small village. Every man is desirous of getting to the village a little ahead of his neighbor, and when he finds he is falling behind, out goes a side of bacon, a bag of flour, or a lot of coffee and sugar, until he has reduced his rations to such a nicety that he will just about be starved by the time he is where he can set up his gold washer. The last arrival from the frontiers was an old fellow, who swam the Platte a short distance from here, and was found by some Indian traders on the bank of the river in an exhausted state. They wrapped him up in some buffalo robes, restored him to life, and sent him on his way rejoicing. His clothes he had pushed ahead of him across the river on a log. He considered the Platte "a pretty mighty considerable river," taking it to be about ten miles wide.

1855

Of the many abolitionist newspapers that appeared in the United States during the years before the Civil War, *The Liberator,* first published in Boston, Massachusetts, on January 1, 1831, by William Lloyd Garrison, was the most famous. Never achieving a circulation of more than 3,000 subscribers, Garrison might have been more influential had he been less vitriolic in his attacks not only on the South, but against anyone and anything who had the audacity to disagree with him or his ideas.

And Garrison was not an easy man with whom to agree. Not content merely at calling for the abolition of slavery, the fiery, self-righteous Garrison actually was one of America's first secessionists, urging the North to break away from what he viewed as a Godless South, beyond any hope of moral redemption. His motto was "No Union With Slaveholders." As far as Garrison was concerned, those who would settle for less were as blameworthy as the slaveholders themselves.

While much of *The Liberator* was little more than a reprint of abolitionist tracts published elsewhere, from time to time Garrison would unlimber his own radical views. The following excerpt from the September 28, 1855, issue of his paper is such an example.

THE DISSOLUTION OF THE UNION ESSENTIAL TO THE ABOLITION OF SLAVERY

I do not despair of the triumph of the truth. The slaves in our country are to be set free—that is as certain as that man is man, and God is God. Slavery is doomed, let this country do what it may. But will it go down peaceably? Will the nation relax its grasp willingly? Will it hear the warning voice, and obey the Divine command? Or will it go on, and add iniquity to iniquity, and multiply slaves for the auction-block, and extend the slave system, until its doom is irrevocably sealed? That is the question. I know that our success in the anti-slavery cause has been extraordinary, within the last quarter of a century; I know that, having nothing but the simple truth to begin with, with all that is wealthy, and mighty, and powerful, in Church and State combined against us, our march has been right onward. And yet there is such a thing as a nation sinning away its day of grace, so that it is not possible for it to recover itself. There has never been made a direct and true issue by the North against slavery. Every thing has been and is in the spirit of compromise. In one-half of the country, we have lost our right of speech; the liberty of conscience is cloven down; editors are driven into exile; and their presses destroyed; the Gospel is fettered, and its mouthpiece gagged; and all compacts and agreements are perfidiously overturned. All this is the legitimate fruit of the tree; and unless we lay the axe at the root of the tree, and cut it down, and give it to the consuming fire, we shall do nothing—we are lost. I thank God for any kind of opposition to slavery— and am glad that any issue is raised; and I will respect every honest effort in behalf of freedom. But, until we cease to strike hands religiously, politically and governmentally with the South, and declare the Union to be at an end, I believe we can do nothing even against the encroachments of the Slave Power upon our rights. When will the people of the North see that it is not possible for liberty and slavery to commingle, or for a true Union to be formed between freemen and slaveholders? Between those who oppress and the oppressed, no concord is possible. This Union—it is a lie, an imposture, and our first business is, to seek its utter overthrow. In this Union, there are three millions and a half of slaves, clanking their chains in hopeless bondage. Let the Union be accursed! Look at the awful compromise of the Constitution, by which that instrument is saturated with the blood of the slave! But even if every word of it were unexceptionable, the fact would be none the less palpable, that it is not a question of parchment, but of moral possibilities. "How can two walk together, except they are agreed?" We are against slavery. The slaveholders say to us, "If we catch you south of Mason and Dixon's line, we will lynch you." They declare that no man shall be put into office, who does not go for everlasting and universal slavery. How great the insanity of the North! Like Samson, it has foolishly revealed the secret of its strength, ay, and the source of its weakness; and the Philistines of the South have taken it captive, put out its eyes, and made it grind in the prison-house for them; and if, at last, it shall rise in its returning strength, it will be to feel for the pillars of this heaven-accursed Union, and bring it to the ground. Samson told Delilah that if she should cut off his locks, he would be as weak as other men. Then, said the Philistines, we know where the secret of his strength lies; and the deed was done.

O, the folly and infatuation of the people of the North! For sixty-eight years, we have been telling the slaveholders that we consider the preservation of the American Union paramount to all other considerations! "Do what you will for the extension of slavery, or the subversion of our own rights, there is one thing we mean to do, and that is, *always to stand by the Union!* For that, we will give up everything—conscience, self-respect, manhood, liberty, all!" "We ask nothing more," say the slaveholders; "that is a *carte blanc* in our hands to wield against you with omnipotent effect; it is all we want to know. We will have the Fugitive Slave bill. We know you will wince, and remonstrate, and threaten; but we have only to crack the whip of disunion over your heads, to bring you down on your knees at once. We will repeal the Missouri Compromise. We expect you to rave and resist; but you will yield the point, like whipped spaniels, when we threaten to dissolve the Union. You have agreed that, to save the Union, you will be submissive to the end." And so, all over the North, there is not a political party that does not say, "We are for the Union." The new "fusion" or "republican" party reiterates the cry of the South, "The Union, it must and shall be preserved." What is this but the betrayal of liberty into the hands of the Philistines? Talk about restoring the Missouri Compromise! As well talk of the sun and moon to stand still! Talk of repealing the Fugitive Slave bill! "When the sky falls, we will catch larks." Talk about stopping the progress of slavery, and of saving Nebraska and Kansas!—Why, the fate of Nebraska and Kansas was sealed the first hour Stephen Arnold Douglas consented to play his perfidious part. I hold that any man who talks of a Union with slaveholders, such as they prescribe, has no right to call himself a friend of the slave. In becoming an Abolitionist, I pledged myself to stand by the side of the slave and make his cause my own; and I will not support a Constitution from which he is excluded. I will go in for no Union in which he is doomed to clank his fetters. I will give allegiance to no Government which does not protect his rights with my own. Therefore, I stand outside of this Government, and, by the help of God, I mean to effect its overthrow. That seems to me to be the only consistent course to be taken. "No Union with Slaveholders!" Why? Because they will have no Union with us, unless we will join in their villainy. I do not know what anti-slavery men mean by saying they are opposed to slavery, and yet for preserving the Union. The colored man who glorifies the Union which makes him an outlaw, is beside himself.—Our first duty is to pronounce the American Union accursed to God—to arraign every man who supports it, and tell him, as Jesus told the rich young man in the Gospel, that whatever else he may have done, one thing he yet lacketh: *he must give up his support of the Union.*

Why continue the experiment any longer? It is all madness and delusion. Let this slaveholding Union go; and when it goes, slavery will go down with it. The slaveholders are powerless without us. It is the North, after all, which has done this evil work. Our business is with ourselves. The people of the North hold in their hands the key whereby the dungeon's door may be opened, and the slaves set free. We have little to do with the slaveholders. I do not address myself to them; they are incapable of hearing or understanding our arguments; they are insane men. My appeal is not to them, but to the people of the North, who are the props and the pillars of the slave system. Let our rallying cry be, "No Union with Slaveholders, religiously or politically!" Let us up with the flag of disunion, that we may have a free Northern Republic of our own, by the side of which no slaveholding despotism may exist. And when that hour shall come, God will have made it possible for us to be one people from the Atlantic to the Pacific.

1857

The slavery issue would not be stilled. Neither was it confined to the abolitionist fringe. The United States Supreme Court was drawn into the question when asked to deal with the thorny problem of how to treat runaway slaves: Were they free men if they successfully made it to non-slaveholding states? Or did they remain the property of their masters, chattels forever, subject to retrieval on whim?

Dred Scott was a slave who had been taken by his owner, an army surgeon, into the free state of Illinois, and then into Wisconsin Territory, which had been designated by Congress as a free territory under the terms of the Missouri Compromise of 1820, which barred slavery from all new American states and existing territories in return for Missouri's admission into the Union as a slave state. Scott claimed that once in a free territory he became a free man.

On March 6, 1857, Chief Justice Roger Taney read the court's majority opinion, which concluded that under the terms of the Constitution, "men of African race" could never be citizens, regardless of where they were located. The opinion went on to state that because Congress, which had enacted the Missouri Compromise, did not have the power to grant rights in excess of the property rights conferred by the Constitution, Scott remained the property of his owner.

In covering the Dred Scott decision, the *Washington Evening Star,* on March 7, 1857, provided its readers with the following example of straightforward, concise legal affairs reporting.

The Opinion.—The hour at which we were forced to go to press yesterday, necessarily compelled us to allude very briefly to the opinion of the Supreme Court in the Dred Scott case. We have now to say, that as read by Mr. Chief Justice Taney, it decides that:

1. Negroes, whether slave or free—that is, men of the African race—
    are not citizens of the United States by the Constitution.
2. The ordinance of 1787 had no Independent constitutional force or
    legal effect subsequently to the adoption of the Constitution, and
    could not operate of itself to confer freedom or citizenship within the
    Northwest Territory on negroes not citizens by the Constitution.
3. The provision of the act of 1820, commonly called the Missouri
    Compromise, in so far as it undertook to exclude negro slavery and
    communicate freedom and citizenship to negroes in the northern part
    of Louisiana cession, was a legislative act exceeding the powers of
    Congress, and void and of no legal effect to that end.

In deciding these main points the Supreme Court determined also the following incidental points:

1. The expression "territory and other property" of the Union in the
    Constitution applies in *terms* only to such territory as the Union pos-
    sessed at the time of the adoption of the Constitution.
2. The rights of citizens of the United States emigrating into any Fed-
    eral territory, and the power of the Federal Government there, de-
    pend on the general provisions of the Constitution, which define in
    this, as in all other respects, the powers of Congress.
3. As Congress does not possess power itself to make enactments rela-
    tive to the persons or property of citizens of the United States in
    Federal territory, other than such as the Constitution confers, so it
    cannot constitutionally delegate any such power to a Territorial Gov-
    ernment organised by it under the Constitution.
4. The legal condition of a slave in the State of Missouri is not affected
    by the temporary sojourn of such slave in any other State, but on his
    return his condition still depends on the laws of Missouri.

The delivery of this Opinion occupied about two hours, and was listened
to with profound attention, by a crowded court room; and, whether as a
decision of the Supreme Court or for the constitutional arguments on which
it stands, will work a powerful influence throughout the United States. Its
conclusions were concurred in, we understand, by six of the Justices of the
Court—namely, Justices Taney, Wayne, Catron, Daniel, Grier and Campbell.

Mr. Justice Nelson read an Opinion in which he did not enter into the
constitutionality of the Missouri Compromise, but held, and on that ground
affirmed the judgment of the Court below, that a slave carried into a free
State, whatever might be the laws of that State, remained a slave whenever
returning to the State in which his owner resided.

Mr. Justice Catron also delivered an Opinion in which the freedom of the
Northwest Territory was made to be an act of the State of Virginia, which
was the original proprietor of the Territory, and which alone, and not Con-

gress, had the right to prohibit slavery there. He expressed himself in very decided terms against the constitutionality of the Missouri Compromise.

We are informed that Opinions dissenting from the judgment of the Court will be delivered this morning at 11 o'clock by Justices McLean and Curtis.

1859

Part history, part legend, the story of John Brown's raid on the federal arsenal at Harpers Ferry, West Virginia, is the stuff of an American epic: a picturesque location on the Potomac River, a half-crazed bearded zealot prepared to die for the cause of abolition, a new-fangled, steam-belching railroad, and federal troops, led by the dashing Robert E. Lee, who had been appointed by President James Buchanan to quell the uprising, riding to the rescue.

Although the story was widely reported, perhaps no newspaper covered John Brown's raid better than *The Baltimore Patriot*. The *Patriot* had the ad-

vantage not only of being based in the home city of the Baltimore & Ohio Railroad, whose trains played such a prominent role in the affair, but also the initial point of embarkation for federal troops sent to liberate the West Virginia arsenal.

From the first word received on October 17, 1859, of Brown's entrance into Harpers Ferry the previous evening, until his capture on October 18, the *Patriot* was there, its multiple issues published over the two days providing a professional blend of on-the-scene and local interest reporting to its keenly interested readers.

SECOND EDITION, FIVE O'CLOCK

IMPORTANT FROM HARPER'S FERRY
LETTER FROM A MERCHANT
THE RESIDENTS IMPRISONED —
SEVERAL CITIZENS KILLED

FREDERICK, OCT. 17– The engine and train from here have just returned, being unable to proceed through Harper's Ferry.

Your correspondent has just seen a letter from a merchant of Harper's Ferry, which was sent by two boys over the mountain, and who had to swim the the [sic] river to escape the insurrectionists.

The letter states that most all the leading people of Harper's Ferry are in jail and that several have been killed!

The rioters have all the works in their possession, and have taken the money from the vaults.—The powder house is in their possession, and they won't permit any one to leave the town.

F. Beckham, the Railroad agent was shot twice by the gang. They are said to be disguised—the whites being painted as blacks.

The attack was first made about 12 o'clock last night.

The watchman at the depot was shot dead.

STILL LATER

We learn from the Railroad that the passenger train which left this morning for the West has returned to the city. The Conductor, Capt. Waters—the Brakeman, Mr. Trasher—the Baggage Master, Mr. Simpson, were all arrested and are now in prison. They left the train and went over the bridge to confer with the mob, and met this fate. There are also seven trains of tonnage which started this morning for the West on the road some miles this side the Ferry.

The trains coming East are detained between the Ferry and Martinsburg, not daring to come on, as the banditti have notified them they will all be captured or killed. It is also stated that a number of Slaves on the Maryland side have been captured and taken over to the Ferry and imprisoned.

The Military have gone up well armed, and they with the U.S. Marines will probably put the insurgents to flight, or if they resist they will be, no doubt, shot down as they deserve. It is hoped, however, they may be arrested and punished as the law directs.

The number of our city soldiers reach about 400 arms, under the command of Gen. Egerton.—They will be joined at Relay by the United States Marines and proceed at once to the scene of action, under the charge of Conductor John Snyder. They are well provisioned and provided with every necessity, both of ammunition and provisions. They fill a train of sixteen cars propelled by a tremendous Cammel ten wheel engine.

The greatest excitement prevailed at the depot when the trains left. Many thousands of persons were present, among them a large number of females, weeping at parting from their husbands and brothers, who have gone with the soldiery.

SECOND EDITION, FIVE O'CLOCK

THE INSURRECTION AT HARPER'S FERRY

. . . . .

HARPER'S FERRY, October 18th, 2½ A.M.—The town has been taken possession of by the military from Charlestown, Shepardstown, Va., and Frederick, Md.

The rioters are entrenched in the Armory, and hold Mr. Washington and Mr. Dangerfield as prisoners.

The insurrectionists were commanded by Capt. Brown, of Kansas notoriety, who gave his name as Anderson to conductor Phelps.

They numbered originally seventeen white men and five negroes, but were reinforced during the day.

Several of the military have been shot, including two of the Martinsburg companies, who were shot dead whilst charging on the Armories.

A portion of the insurgents have left under the command of Capt. Bill Cook, with a large party of slaves, all supposed to be moving towards Pennsylvania.

Allen Evans, one of the insurgents, a white man, is lying here dying, with a ball through his breast. He is from Connecticut, but has been in Kansas. He says the whole scheme was got up by Capt. Brown, who represented that the negroes would rise by thousands, and Maryland and Virginia would be made free States.

Colonel Shriver, of Frederick, has just had an interview with Captain Brown, in the Armory. He asked to be allowed to march out with his men, and vowed his intention to defend himself to the last.

The Armory was taken possession of by the rioters about 9 o'clock on Sunday night last, and was so quietly done that the citizens knew nothing of it until the train was stopped.

Col. [Robert E.] Lee has arrived, and thinks that there are abundant troops here to capture the rioters.

It seems perfectly certain that the original number consisted of not more than twenty white men and five free negroes.

Captain Brown has been about here and rented a farm four miles off, which was the rendezvous of the rioters. Captain Cook had also lived in the vicinity, and at one time taught school here. All the other white men are unknown but are supposed to be the men who have been connected with Captain Brown in Kansas. . . .

HARPER'S FERRY, OCT. 18—8 o'clock A.M.—

The Armory has just been stormed and taken by the military, after a determined resistance.

Col. Shutt approached with a flag of truce, and demanded the surrender of all within.

After expostulating for sometime they refused to surrender.

The United States Marines advanced to break the door down with sledge hammers, but they resisted the ponderous blows. A large ladder was then used as a battering ram when the doors partially gave way.

The rioters fired briskly and killed three marines. Marines exchanged shots through the breaches in the door. Very soon the marines forced their way through the break, and in a few minutes all resistance was at an end!

The rioters were now brought out, amidst the most intense excitement, many of the armed militia trying to get a shot at them.

THE RINGLEADER SHOT.

Capt. Brown and his son were both shot, the latter is dead and the former is dying. He now lies on the armory enclosure talking freely. He says he is Old Ossawatimee Brown, whose feats in Kansas have had such a wide notoriety. He says his whole object was to free the slave and justifies his action. He declares he had possession of the town and could have murdered all the people if disposed, and says he has been murdered in return.

Brown's only wound was a sabre cut across his head. Although the wound did not prove fatal, the death sentence handed down after his subsequent trial did.

1861

"The ball is opened. War is inaugurated."

With these words, *The New York World* announced to its readers on April 13, 1861, that hostile shots had been fired at Fort Sumter, in the harbor of Charleston, South Carolina, the previous morning. The *World*'s early view of the opening volley of the Civil War, which would prove to be the bloodiest war in American history, was echoed by partisans everywhere. It would be a "ball."

On the Union side, it was thought that the war would be over in no time, as soon as the "rebels" learned their place. In the South, the war was viewed as an opportunity to teach those "Damn Yan-

kees" a lesson about honor and pride. Both sides saw the war as a sporting contest, but many in the southern states saw it as something more. It was a chance to dress up in military finery, to show off one's horsemanship, to strut and preen for the ladies. The war would be a fine adventure.

The newspapers reporting on the early days of the war reflected these views. Showing little sense of foreboding, they reported the war's opening battles as they would gala county fairs. The lead story of *The Charleston Daily Courier* of April 12, 1861, provides an excellent example of war covered both as spectacle and sporting event.

CONFEDERATE STATES OF AMERICA
SATURDAY MORNING, APRIL 12, 1861

HOSTILITIES COMMENCED
BOMBARDMENT OF FORT SUMTER

At about 2 o'clock, on the afternoon of Thursday, General [Pierre G. T.] Beauregard made a demand on Major [Robert] Anderson for the immediate surrender of Fort Sumter, through his Aids, Col. James Chesnut, Jr., Col. [A.R.] Chisolm and Capt. [Stephen D.] Lee. Major Anderson replied that such a course would be inconsistent with the duty he was required by his Government to perform. The answer was communicated by the General-in-chief to President [Jefferson] Davis.

This visit, and the refusal of the commandant of Fort Sumter to accede to the demand made by General Beauregard, passed from tongue to tongue, and soon the whole city was in possession of the startling intelligence. Rumor, as she is wont to do, shaped the facts to suit her purposes, enlarged their dimensions, and have given them a complexion which they had not worn when fresh from the pure and artless hands of truth.

A half an hour after the return of the orderlies it was confidently believed that the batteries would open fire at eight o'clock, and in expectation of seeing the beginning of the conflict, hundreds congregated upon the Battery and the wharves, looking out on the bay. There they stood, straining their eyes over the dark expanse of water, waiting to see the flash and hear the boom of the first gun. The clock told the hour of eleven, and still they gazed and listened, but the eyelids grew weary, and at the noon of the night the larger portion of the disappointed spectators were plodding their way homeward.

At about nine o'clock, General Beauregard received a reply from President Davis, to the telegram in relation to the surrender of Sumter, by which he was instructed to inform Major Anderson that if he would evacuate the fort he held when his present supply of provisions was exhausted there would be no appeal to arms. This proposition was borne to Major Anderson by the Aids who had delivered the first message, and he refused to accept the condition. The General-in-chief forthwith gave the order that the batteries be opened at half-past four o'clock on Friday morning.—Major Anderson's reply was decisive of the momentous question, and General Beauregard determined to apply the last argument. . . .

The crisis had arrived, and we were fully prepared to meet it. The work that awaited the morrow was of a momentous character, but we had counted the cost, and had resolved to do it or die in the attempt.

At the gray of the morning of Friday the roar of cannon broke upon the ear. The expected sound was answered by thousands. The houses were in a few minutes emptied of their excited occupants, and the living stream poured through all the streets leading to the wharves and Battery. On reaching our beautiful promenade we found it lined with ranks of eager spectators, and all the wharves commanding a view of the battle were crowded thickly with human forms. On no gala occasion have we ever seen nearly so a large number of ladies on our Battery as graced the breezy walk on this eventful morning. There they stood with palpitating hearts and palid faces, watching the white smoke as it rose in wreaths upon the soft twilight air, and breathing out fervent prayers for their gallant kinsfolk at the guns. O! what a conflict raged in those heaving bosoms between love for husbands and sons, and love for our common mother, whose insulted honor and imperilled safety had called her faithful children to the ensanguined field.

At thirty minutes past four o'clock the conflict was opened by the discharge of a shell from the Howitzer Battery on James' Island, under the command of Captain Geo. S. Hames, who followed the riddled Palmetto banner on the bloody battle fields of Mexico.

The sending of this harmful messenger to Major Anderson was followed by a deafening explosion, which was caused by the blowing up of a building that stood in front of the battery.

While the white smoke was melting away into the air another shell, which Lieut. W. Hampten Gibbes has the honor of having fired, pursued its noiseless way toward the hostile fortification.

The honored missive described its beautiful curve through the balmy air, and falling within the hostile fortress, scattered its deadly contents in all directions. Fort Moultrie then took up the tale of death, and in a moment the guns from the redoubtable Gun Battery on Cummings' Point, from Capt. McCready's Battery, from Capt. Jas. Hamilton's Floating Battery, the Enfilade Battery, and other fortifications spit forth their wrath at the grim fortress rising so defiantly out of the sea.

Major Anderson received the shot and shell in silence. And some excited lookers-on, ignorant of the character of the foe, were fluent with conjectures and predictions, that revived the hope fast dying out of their hopeful and tender hearts. But the short-lived hope was utterly extinguished when the deepening twilight revealed the Stars and Stripes floating proudly in the breeze. The batteries continued at regular intervals to belch iron vengeance, and still no answer was returned by the foe. About an hour after the booming began, two balls rushed hissing through the air, and glanced harmless from the stuccoed bricks of Fort Moultrie. The embrasures of the hostile fortress gave forth no sound again till between six and seven o'clock, when, as if wrathful from enforced delay, from casemate and parapet the United States officer poured a storm of iron hail upon Fort Moultrie, Stevens' Iron Battery and the Floating Battery. The broadside was returned with spirit by the gallant gunners at these important posts.

The firing now began in good earnest. The curling white smoke hung above the angry pieces of friend and foe, and the jarring boom rolled at regular intervals on the anxious ear. The atmosphere was charged with the smell of villainous saltpetre, and as in sympathy with the melancholy scene the sky was covered with heavy clouds and everything wore a sombre aspect. . . .

A brisk fire was kept up by all the batteries until about 7 o'clock in the evening, after which hour the guns boomed at regular intervals of twenty minutes.

All the batteries on Morris' Island, bearing upon the channel, kept up a steady fire for some time at the dawn of day. It is reported they threw their shot into the *Harriet Lane,* and that that steamer, having advanced as far as the renowned Star of the West Battery, was crippled by a well aimed shot, after which she deemed it prudent to give up the dangerous attempt, and turned her sharp bow to the sea.

Stevens' Iron Battery played a conspicuous and important part in the brilliant, and as far as our men are concerned, bloodless conflict, which has placed the 12th of April, 1861, among the memorable days. The calibre of its guns, its nearness to Fort Sumter, its perfect impenetrability, the coolness and skill of its gallant gunners, made this fortification one of the most formidable of Major Anderson's terrible opponents. The effect of its Dahlgren's and 64 pounders was distinctly visible at an early stage of the conflict. Clouds of mortar and brick dust arose from the Southwest wall of the fort as the shot hissed on their errand of death. Shot after shot told with terrible effect on the strong wall, and at about three o'clock Major Anderson ceased to return this murderous fire. In the course of the afternoon the joyful tidings that a breach had been effected in that portion of the fortress was borne to the city.

We dare not close this brief and hurried narrative of the first engagement between the United States and the Confederate States, without returning thanks to Almighty God for the great success that has thus far crowned our arms, and for the extraordinary preservation of our soldiers from casualty and death. In the fifteen hours of almost incessant firing, our enemy one of the most experienced and skilful of artillerists, no injury has been sustained by a single one of our gallant soldiers.

The result of the conflict strengthens and confirms our faith in the justness of the course for whose achievement we have suffered obloquy, and dared perils of vast magnitude. At the outset of the struggle we invoked the sanction and aid of that God whom we serve, and His hand has guided and defended us all through the momentous conflict. His favor was most signally, we had almost said miraculously, manifested on this eventful day. We call the roll of those engaged in the battle, and each soldier is here to answer to his name. No tombstone will throw its shadow upon that bright triumphant day. If so it seemeth good in the eyes of Him, in whose hands are the issues of life, we fervently pray that our brave sons may pass unharmed through the perils of the day now dawning.

1861

The first big battle of the War Between the States was fought at Manassas Junction, twenty-five miles southwest of Washington, D.C. Carriages full of senators, congressmen, other government officials, and their ladies, all dressed in their summer best, picnic lunches aboard, followed the Army of the Potomac south on a hot, sultry day in mid-July, 1861, to watch the expected Confederate defeat at Bull Run. Much to their chagrin, the Union troops, singing "John Brown's Body" as they marched toward Richmond, and expecting victory, ran into a stone wall named General Thomas J. Jackson. Ultimately, "Stonewall" Jackson's troops were reinforced by those of General E. Kirby Smith, and the Union soldiers of the proud Army of the Potomac retreated to the banks of its namesake river.

What transpired in the first moments of battle, as reported in the eye-witness account published in the July 20, 1861, edition of *The Richmond Dispatch,* served notice that the country would be at war for a long time to come.

THE FIGHT AT MANASSAS!
BRILLIANT VICTORY!

The Enemy Completely Routed

MANASSAS JUNCTION, July 18—10, P.M.

Victory perches upon our banners. The army of the Potomac, under the command of General [Pierre G. T.] Beauregard, gave battle to the enemy

A Union sharpshooter, as drawn by Winslow Homer and published in a woodcut drawing by Harper's Weekly, *November 15, 1862.* The Library of Congress, Washington, D.C.

to-day, at Bull's Run, four miles from Manassas Junction, in a Northwest direction, and three miles to the left of the Alexandria Rail-Road. The enemy attempted to cross the ford at several points in great numbers, but were repulsed by our brave and determined troops three times, with heavy loss on the enemy's side. The enemy retreated about five o'clock in the afternoon in confusion, two of our regiments pursuing them. A large number of them have been taken prisoners. On our side, the casualties are few.

Yesterday the enemy appeared in force at Fairfax Court House, when, after exchanging a few shots with them, our troops retreated to Bull's Run, General Beauregard preferring to give them battle there. The General was hurriedly sent for and quickly came to the scene of action, when he ordered the retreat, which has proved to be a brilliant strategic movement. At first our troops were much displeased, believing the retreat had been ordered by some junior officer; but when they learned that the order emanated from their General-in-Chief, they were perfectly satisfied, having in him unbounded confidence. The regiments engaged in this brilliant and successful battle were the First Virginia, the Seventeenth (Alexandria) Virginia, the Mississippi and Louisiana.

All of our men behaved with the utmost coolness and fought like the disciplined soldiers of a Napoleon. It would be invidious to single out the troops from any particular State as having exhibited qualities not found in all. The conduct of our gallant little army (never before under fire,) on this occasion surpasses all praise. For steadiness under a most galling fire, indifference to their peril, good order and precision of aim, history may be ransacked in vain for a parallel. The enemy outnumbered them in the proportion of three to one. The Washington Artillery, of New Orleans, were at an early stage of the battle given an opportunity of displaying their high state of efficiency and marksmanship, and they abundantly justified the reputation of the batallion. An eye-witness says at every fire they made a wide gap in the enemy's ranks.

The First Virginia Regiment, (Col. Moore's,) bore the brunt of the action, the killed and wounded on our side being chiefly in that Regiment, as I have already informed you per telegraph. Col. Moore himself was wounded slightly soon after the battle commenced. When being unable to continue at the head of his men, the command devolved upon Lieut. Col. Fry, aided by Major Skinner and Adjutant Mitchell, who inform me that the bullets of the enemy came like hail. He saw eleven of his men wounded at one volley,—Capt. James K. Lee, company B., of same regiment, was mortally wounded. While I write, he is still in life, but not expected to survive the morning.

The following are all members of Colonel Moore's Regiment:

Lieut. H.H. Miles was mortally wounded.

Lieut. W.W. Harris, slightly wounded.

Capt. W.J. Allen, slightly wounded.

Private Reilly, Company E, mortally wounded.

Private Whitaker, Company C, mortally wounded.

Private Diaconte, Company K, instantly killed.

Private Wilkinson, Company G, instantly killed.

Private Mallory, Company C, instantly killed.

Private Allen, Company B, probably killed.

Sargeant Lumpkins, Company B, hand shot off.

Lieut. English, Company C, slightly wounded.

I have not yet been able to learn the killed and wounded in other Regiments. The enemy is variously reported to have lost from five to fifteen hundred—the former probably being nearest the truth. Not having been on the field, I am unable to describe the ground, but am informed the enemy were strongly posted with numerous heavy guns on the embankment which slopes down to the ford, while our troops were in the hollow disputing their advance to the other side.

It has been stated that the enemy threw chain-shot and fired upon our hospital while the yellow flag, which secures immunity in civilized nations, was flying. General Beauregard had a narrow escape, a ball having passed through the kitchen of house where he was partaking of dinner. I need not say the General has displayed qualities of the highest order as a military commander, with, perhaps, the pardonable exception of indifference to his own life, now so valuable to the Confederacy. He exhibited great coolness during the engagement, and was in all parts of the field.

The Alexandria Riflemen are said to have particularly distinguished themselves, having crossed the ford in the face of a terrific fire from the enemy's artillery, and fought hand to hand with the Yankee hirelings.

Capt. Dulany, of the Fairfax Riflemen, was seriously wounded. Lieut. Javins, of the Mount Vernon Guard, of Alexandria, was also seriously wounded. Wm. Sangster, of the Alexandria Riflemen, was killed. One of the enemy's Colonels was killed by a squad of Col. Kershaw's 2d South Carolina Regiment, his horse shot, and $700 in gold found upon his person.

The enemy will doubtless return to-morrow with reinforcements, being exasperated by their humiliating defeat.

I shall probably be able to ascertain additional particulars when the official reports come in.

D.G.D.

1863

As the war wound on, newspapers, while continuing their traditional roles as purveyors of information, also served as morale boosters. Nowhere was this more necessary that in the beleaguered city of Vicksburg, Mississippi. Perched high on a bluff above the Mississippi River, Vicksburg was totally cut off from the outside world for nearly three months as the army of Union General Ulysses S. Grant lay siege to the city. With each successive day, supplies of foodstuffs and water dwindled, until the citizens of Vicksburg were reduced to eating cats and dogs—if they could find them.

J. M. Swords, the publisher of *The* *Vicksburg Daily Citizen* used the pages of his little paper to shore up local spirits as best he could. Alternately engaging in black humor and lecturing his readers on the need not to break ranks, Swords was reduced to printing his newspaper on the reverse sides of wallpaper when newsprint became unavailable.

Defiant to the end, the final regular edition of the *Daily Citizen*, printed on July 2, 1863, made light of General Grant's expressed desire to capture Vicksburg by July 4, so as to celebrate Independence Day by dining in the elusive Confederate city.

We are indebted to Major Gillespie for a steak of Confederate beef *alias* meat. We have tried it, and can assure our friends that if it is rendered necessary, they need have no scruples at eating the meat. It is sweet, savory and tender, and so long as we have a mule left we are satisfied our soldiers will be content to subsist on it.

If aught would appeal to the heart of stone of the extortioner with success, the present necessities of our citizens would do so. It is needless to attempt to disguise from the enemy or our own people that our wants are great, but still we can conscientiously assert our belief that there is plenty within our lines, by an exercise of prudence, to last until long after succor reaches us. We are satisfied there are numerous persons within our city who have breadstuffs secreted and are doling it out, at the most exhorbitant figures, to those who had not the foresight or means at their command to provide for the exigency now upon us. A rumor has reached us that parties in our city have been, and are now, selling flour at five dollars per pound! molasses at ten dollars per gallon! and corn at ten dollars per bushel! We have not yet as proved the fact upon the parties accused, but this allusion to the subject may induce some of our citizens to ascertain whether such prices have been paid, and to whom; and if so, let a brand not only be placed upon their brow, but let it be seared into their very brain, that humanity may scorn and shun them as they would the portals of hell itself.

VICTIMIZED———We learned of an instance wherein a "knight of the quill" and a "disciple of the black art," with malice in their hearts and vengeance in their eyes, ruthlessly put a period to the existence of a venerable feline that has for time, not within the recollection of the "oldest inhabitant," faithfully discharged the duties to be expected to him to the terror of sundry vermin in his neighborhood. Poor, defunct Thomas was then prepared, not for the grave, but the pot, and several friends invited to partake of a nice rabbit. As a matter of course, no one would wound the feelings of another, especially in these times, by refusing a cordial invitation to dinner, and the guests assisted in consuming the poor animal with a relish that did honor to their epicurean taste. The "sold" assure us that the meat was delicious, and that pussy must look out for her safety.

ON DIT.—That the great Ulysses—the Yankee Generalissimo, surnamed Grant—has expressed his intention of dining in Vicksburg on Saturday next, and celebrating the 4th of July by a grand dinner and so forth. When asked if he would invite Gen. Jo. Johnston to join he said, "No! for fear there will be a row at the table." Ulysses must get into the city before he dines in it. The way to cook a rabbit is "first catch the rabbit."

But Grant did take Vicksburg by July 4, when Confederate General John C. Pemberton surrendered to his Union counterpart. Afterwards, a few additional copies of the July 2 edition of the *Daily Citizen* were printed, still on wallpaper, each containing the following story enclosed within a black-border.

NOTE.   JULY 4th, 1863.

Two days bring about great changes; The banner of the Union floats over Vicksburg. Gen. Grant has "caught the rabbit;" he has dined in vicksburg, and he did bring his dinner with him. The "Citizen" lives to see it. For the last time it appears on "Wall-paper." No more will it eulogize the luxury of mule-meat and fricassed kitten—urge Southern warriors to such diet never more. This is the last wall-paper edition, and is, excepting this note, from the types as we found them. It will be valuable hereafter as a curiosity.

1863

The turning point of the war came after three days of savage fighting in July, 1863, between the massed armies of the Union and the Confederacy in the rolling countryside outside of sleepy Gettysburg, Pennsylvania. For the North, Gettysburg was a last stand against the armies of Confederate General Robert E. Lee, pushing ever-northward, fresh on the scent of victory, and seemingly growing stronger and more confident with each passing day. If Lee's forces prevailed, the North would lay open to him. Moreover, he would be in good position to capture Philadelphia, Baltimore, and Washington, D.C., each lying little more than a hundred miles from Gettysburg.

For two days the battle hung in stalemate. But in a last desperate charge on Friday, July 3, 1863, the Confederate advance was halted, and its army routed. The southern wave had crested and ebbed, leaving behind more than 20,000 dead and wounded on Pennsylvania soil. Having lost 23,000 dead and wounded, a wary Union General George Meade failed to pursue the fleeing Army of Northern Virginia. Lee would fight again, but exclusively on southern battlefields.

The July 7, 1863, edition of the Washington, D.C., *National Intelligencer* brought the news of this last Confederate offensive and subsequent Union victory to an anxious nation's capital in a story originally written by *The New York World's* uncredited reporter on the scene.

THE STRUGGLE AT GETTYSBURG
THE BATTLE OF FRIDAY

Special correspondence of the New York World

HEADQUARTERS ARMY OF THE POTOMAC

Friday, July 3—7 1/4 P.M.

The sun of Austerlitz is not more memorable than that which is just flinging its dying rays over the field of this the third day of successful battle. . . . The battles of Wednesday and yesterday were sufficiently terrible, but in that which has raged to day the fighting done, not only by our troops, but by those of Lee's army, will rank in heroism, in perseverence, and in savage energy with that of Waterloo.

The position of Lee at the close of last evening was such that he was forced to day to reduce all his energies into one grand, desperate, and centralized attempt to break through our army. His divisions were so much cut up as to render a pitched battle from wing to wing one of awful hazard. The dilemma was a terrible one, and that the rebel commander fully appreciated all its risks is evinced by the desperation of his onset to-day.

Friday morning found our army reinforced. The reserves of the Sixth corps, Gen. Sedgwick, and the Twelfth, Gen. Slocum, had arrived and taken up strong positions. At the last hour our troops were ranged in line along the Emmetsburg turnpike and the Taneytown road.

The engagement began by an assault by our troops upon some rifle-pits on the extreme right, which were left in the possession of the enemy last evening. Their fire was returned by the rebels, and the fight immediately became general. Until nearly noon the battle raged without intermission, but with no loss to us, when we finally obtained possession of the rifle-pits—the rebel force which had previously held them retreating. The firing then slackened, but at one-o'clock was renewed at different points along the line with a fierceness premonitory of the terrific engagement that ensued.

Several charges were made by the rebels as feints, their troops falling back after the first rush in every part of the field, except that held by their forces under Gen. Ewell, who was seen to concentrate the infantry and artillery together, and who soon opened a murderous fire of cannon on our left centre. Then the engagement began in earnest. The firing became a continuous roar; battery after battery was discharged with a swiftness amazing; yell on yell from the rebels succeeded each gust of shot and shell, until the valley, overhung with smoke from whence these horrible sounds issued, seemed alive with demons. It appeared at times as though not a foot of air was free from the hail of missiles that tore over and through our ranks, thinned but not shaken. Our men stood the shock with a courage sublime—an endurance so wonderful as to dim even the heroic record of the band that fell upon the acre of Tourney. The corps upon which this deadly fire was mainly directed was the Second, the position being commanded by Gen. Hayes.

The artillery fire continued without intermission for three hours, when suddenly, having been formed under cover of the smoke of their own guns, the rebel troops were hurled against our lines by their officers in masses the very tread of whose feet shook the declivity up which they came, with cries that might have caused less dauntless troops than those who waited the onset to break with terror. Not a man in the Federal ranks flinched from his position. Not an eye turned to the right or left in search of security, not a hand trembled as the long array of our heroes grasped their muskets at a charge, and waited the order to fire.

On and up came the enemy, hooting, crowding, showing their very teeth in the venom of their rage until within thirty yards of our cannon. As the turbulent mass of gray uniforms, of flashing bayonets and gleaming eyes, lifted itself in a last leap forward almost to the very mouths of our guns, a volley of shot, shell, shrapnel, and bullets went crashing through it, levelling it as a scythe. Its overwhelming onward rush was in the next instant turned to the hesitating leap forward of a few soldiers more dare-devil than the rest, the wild bounding upwards of more than a few mortally wounded heroes, and the succeeding backward surge of the disjointed remainder, which culminated in a scamper down the slope that was in some instances retarded by the pursuing bullets of our men.

The carnage of this assault among the rebels was so fearful that even the Federal soldiers who rested on their arms triumphant, after the foe had retreated beyond their fire, as they cast their eyes downward upon the panorama of death and wounds illuminated by the sun that shown upon the slope before them, were seen to shudder and turn sickening away.

Then the Third and Fifth Corps joined in the fight. As the rebels rallied for an instant and attempted to make a stand, they were met by such combined volleys as threatened to reduce their columns to fragments. The panic which ensued is unparalleled in any battle in which the Army of the Potomac has ever been engaged. The enemy quailed like ewes before a tempest. Their main line again receded, but numbers, palsied by the horror and tumult, fell upon their knees, upon their breasts, upon their faces, shrieking and lifting up clasped hands in token of surrender and appeal for mercy. Gen. Dick Garnett's brigade surrendered almost entire, but Garnett himself, by the aid of two of his men, succeeded, though wounded, in making his escape. Longstreet, who led the reinforcements which enabled the rebels to make their second brief stand, was wounded, captured, and is now a prisoner.

The musketry firing slowly ceased, and the discharge of artillery continued for a brief period, but even these reverberations finally died away.

Gen. [George] Meade was not deceived in anticipating another onslaught. Lee's columns were collected and reformed with magical haste. Within an hour what seemed to be his whole force was again massed directly in our front, where the contest once more opened. The assault this time was made with a fury even surpassing that of the first. It would seem as if the entire rebel army had resolved itself into a gigantic Forlorn Hope, and bore in its collective bosom the consciousness that the effort now made was the last and the only one that could be made toward retrieving the fortunes of that army, or preventing the inevitable disgrace which hovered over it. Yet the cool and gallant phalanx, secure in its position and confident in its leader, waited with a silence only broken by the occasional roar of the artillery, the approach of the foe, and viewed this onset as calmly and met it as unfalteringly as before. Back, as easily as a girl hurls the shuttlecock, did the soldiers of our gallant army hurl into chaotic retreat the hosts that came on and on, over the stones and ditches, over the bodies of fallen comrades, piling its dead in heaps, and making the soil over which it trod ghastly and alive with struggling wounded.

The firm array of Union soldiers which previously remaining stationary, now bent forward to a charge, and became a pursuing Nemesis to the hordes that in great numbers went reeling westward through the streets of Gettysburg, and beyond, as the brave troops of Reynolds's corps went through them eastward on the previous day but one.

The victory was secure. It was a victory won not without saddening losses— sadder in their comparative extent perhaps than those which have chilled the nation's heart so often before today. Of our actual disasters in killed and wounded it is now impossible to make a just estimate. The same is true of the rebels, though it is positively known from the appearance of the field, and from the acknowledgment of rebel prisoners themselves, that is is far greater than our own.

1863

Ten days after the last shot was fired at Gettysburg, a different kind of battle was fought in the streets of New York City. What had begun as a protest against the military draft by a few dozen impecunious New Yorkers, who, unlike wealthy citizens, could not purchase their way out of military duty, quickly erupted into a full scale urban riot.

Thousands of men, and women, roamed through the streets of Manhattan in an orgy of mindless destruction. The rioters reserved special hostility for black New Yorkers, who, in the mind of the mob, were the reason for the war, and hence, the cause of the hated draft. Ultimately, it took soldiers from General George Meade's command at Gettysburg to quell the disturbances.

As the rioting began, Horace Greeley's *New York Tribune* was there. On July 14, 1863, that paper told its startled readers of a city gone mad.

THE DRAFT

The Riot in the Ninth Congressional District

SOLDIERS MOBBED

PRIVATE HOUSES SACKED

Yesterday morning about 10 o'clock the draft in the Ninth Congressional District of which the headquarters are at the cor. of Third Avenue and Forty-sixth street was resumed pursuant to adjournment. Provost-Marshal Capt Jenkins and other members of the press were present, together with about three hundred spectators. The drawing was commenced about 10-½ o'clock, and from 75 to 100 names had been drawn from the wheel and announced when suddenly the report of a pistol was heard in the street.

This seemed to be the signal for an attack upon the office, for almost upon the instant a perfect shower of brickbats, paving stones and other missiles, were hurled from the street into the building, which, of course, took everyone by surprise. Following the shower of stones came an immense crowd who poured into the office carrying everything before them. The wheel containing the remaining ballots of the 22d Ward was carried by two of the clerks to the top story of the house and placed in a room, the inmate of which refused to have it there, when it was left in the hall. The Provost Marshal, Commissioner, Surgeon, engrossing clerks, with members of the press effected their escape by the back door, Capt. Jenkins clambering a fence and secreting himself in the next house until a favorable moment arrived, when he made his way home.

One of the clerks who endeavored to save some of the papers was seized by the crowd, the papers taken from him by force and torn in pieces. The mob now had possession of the building. In a few moments thereafter a man appeared with a can of turpentine, which he poured on the floor of the office, and, setting fire to it, the room was soon in a blaze. All this time the mob kept breaking up the pavement and pelting the police and men attached to the office with stones. . . .

The fire which had been kindled in the back office spread rapidly to the upper part of the house, the flames in a little time communicating to the three houses adjoining on the North side which were of equal size with the building occupied by the Provost-Marshal.

Around the bell tower in Fifty-first street, the mob had sent their friends to stop the bells from ringing—but when engine No. 33 and Hose 53 were coming down Third avenue, they were cheered by the mob but not allowed to work. . . .

Shortly after 11 o'clock a detachment of the Provost Guard numbering fifteen and a half files belonging to the Invalid Corps left Park Barracks and reached the ground about noon. Upon reaching 34th street the mob began to surround them, hooting, yelling and groaning. The guard formed in line between 44th and 45th streets, but were so closely pressed upon all sides that they were unable to "order-arms." The mob now commenced pushing and jolting the soldiers and throwing stones at them when Lieutenant Reed, who was in command of the guard, ordered his men to load, and immediately after gave the order to "fire," when the soldiers poured a volley into the crowd; but no one, it seems, was hurt. The crowd, who had retreated a short distance when the firing commenced, quickly rallied, and closing upon the guard, wrested their arms from their hands and discharged several of the pieces which had been re-loaded, into the crowd. The soldiers, thus disarmed, quickly retreated, but were pursued by the infuriated throng.

The pursuit was kept up as far as 20th street, when it was abandoned, and a majority of the men escaped; one of the soldiers was pursued up 41st street to 1st avenue, where a crowd of some twenty men surrounded him, knocked him down and beat him until he was insensible. A number of women joined in and one of them endeavored to stab him with a bayonet, but another woman took the weapon out of her hand and carried it off. The soldier was left dead on the walk.

Soon after the defeat of the soldiers a strong squad of police made their appearance in line of battle. As soon as the mob caught sight of them they fired a volley of stones, knocking down two of the officers. The police at once drew their clubs and revolvers, but after a contest of a few minutes they were also forced to retreat, which they did in good order until near Fortieth street, when one of them discharged his revolver four times into the midst of the throng, shooting a horse that was attached to a wagon standing on the corner. A rush was made at once for the officer, who immediately retreated into a store near by, the people of which at once barred the door and endeavored to give him protection. The crowd, however, went to the back of the house, tore down the fence, and rushed into the building, seized the policeman, knocked him down, and beat him in a fearful manner. . . .

Sergt. Kane of the Provost Guard was struck with a paving-stone and knocked senseless.

Private Hobbs was injured in the face, and had his knee-cap fractured.

Private Neill was badly bruised about the face.

Private Horlacker was knocked down, the crowd jumping upon and beating him dreadfully. . . .

No one seem able to tell where the initiatory steps of this movement were taken. In a score of places at once men ceased labor and poured into the streets. . . .

The vast crowd swayed to and fro, racing first in this direction, then in that, attacking indiscriminately every well-dressed man. The general cry was "Down with the rich men." . . .

Immediately after this the leaders of the assaulting party proceeded to a large and beautiful dwelling on the corner of Forty-seventh street and Lexington avenue, followed by an excited crowd, and immediately proceeded to attack the building, for the reason, it was said, that a policemen had taken refuge there.

The mob broke in the doors, which they tore from the hinges, smashed every pane of glass both front and rear, and then commenced to fling out of the windows everything upon which they could lay their hands. Pictures with gilt frames, elegant pier glasses, sofas, chairs, clocks, furniture of every kind, wearing apparel, bed clothes, &c., &c., a whole library was scattered in showers through the windows—they wound up by setting fire to the building, amid the wild cheers, yells and hooting of those who surrounded the house. . . .

About 2 o'clock p.m., a gentlemen connected with the Press, while standing on the corner of Forty-sixth street and Third avenue, was attacked by the crowd, "here's a d—d Abolitionist; let's hang him."

He was seized by the hair and dragged toward an awning post, but fortunately something else diverting the attention of the crowd, he escaped up Third avenue—but only for a short time, for a blow of a paving stone on the back of the head and another one in the face stunned him so, that he lost all consciousness, and while in this state he lost his gold watch and chain, diamond breast-pin and $33 in money. . . .

At about 3 o'clock a procession of about 5,000 people marched up First avenue, all armed with bars, pistols, &c., threatening vengeance on all persons connected with the draft. They halted in front of the Eighteenth ward Station-House in Twenty-second street, yelling in a demoniacal manner.

About 4 o'clock p.m. the rioters, perfectly frenzied with liquor, roamed about in every direction attacking people miscellaneously, and burning every building in which they saw a policeman take refuge. . . .

As if by preconcerted action an attack was made upon colored men and boys in every part of the city during the day, crowds of from 100 to 500 persons hunting them like bloodhounds. Several inoffensive colored men were dragged off the city cars and badly beaten, while a number were taken from carts and drays which they were driving and terribly maltreated. . . .

The Orphan Asylum (in Fifth avenue, near Forty-sixth street), was fired about 5 o'clock in the afternoon. The infuriated mob, eager for any outrage, were turned that way by the simple suggestion that the building was full of colored children. They clamored around the house like demons, filling the air with yells. A few policemen, who attempted to make a stand, were instantly overpowered—several being severely or fatally injured. While this was going on, a few of the less civil disposed gave notice to the inmates to quit the building.

The sight of the helpless creatures stayed, for a moment, even the insensate mob; but the orphans were no sooner out than the work of demolition commenced. First the main building was gutted, the large wing adjoining— used as a dormitory—was stripped, inside and out. Several hundred iron bedsteads were carried off—such an exodus of this article was never witnessed before perhaps. They radiated in every direction for half a mile. . . .

Carpets were dragged away at length; desks, stools, chairs, tables, books of all kinds—everything moveable was carried off. Even the caps and bonnets of the poor children were stolen. The writer picked up fragments of testaments for a quarter of a mile down Fifth avenue. While the rioters stripped the building of furniture, their wives and children, and hundreds who were too cowardly to assist the work of demolition, carried them off. The wing, while yet unburning, swarmed with rioters, who seemed endowed with a demoniacal energy to rend in pieces, rob and destroy. . . .

The fire-engines were there in great numbers, but were not permitted to work, except upon the adjacent buildings. What was very marked, as the destruction proceeded, was the absence of excitement. Things were done as quietly and cooly by rioters as if they were saving instead of destroying property. Mingling with the crows—which amounted, perhaps to 5,000 or 6,000 persons—were many who were evidently not of them; but except in cases of incautious utterances, they were not molested. . . .

While this scene was enacting, a large detachment of rioters ran down to the enrollment rooms corner of Broadway and Twenty-ninth street. The object here was more evidently plunder. The lower part of this fine building was composed of stores, filled with costly goods. Every vestige was carried off. A jeweler's shop was the object of special attention. Gold watches, broaches, bracelets, breast-pins, and all manner of valuable *bijouteria* flew about in the crowd, flashing in the light. The negroes were forgotten in the more congenial business of robbery. . . .

1865

On the morning of April 15, 1865, Charles de Young, the co-owner (with his brother) of a recently established San Francisco theatrical tabloid called *The* *Daily Dramatic Chronicle,* made his regular visit to San Francisco's Western Union office to learn what was happening beyond the still isolated shores of San Francisco Bay. Precisely at that moment, the first news of President Abraham Lincoln's assassination reached the on-duty telegrapher. As soon as a transmission ended, de Young rushed back to his office, and, writing entirely from memory, composed a portion of the following story of Lincoln's murder. Scooping all the other papers in San Francisco by a full day, the *Chronicle's* reputation was established. Today, as the largest circulating daily newspaper in Northern California, it remains in the hands of Charles de Young's descendants. Ironically, de Young himself was shot to death by an assassin in 1880.

ABRAHAM LINCOLN

(FIRST DESPATCH)

Washington, April 15, 1865

Gen. H. W. Carpentier: His Excellency President Lincoln was assinated [sic] at the theatre last night.

(SECOND DESPATCH)

Prsident [sic] Lincoln died at 8:30 this morning, and Secretary Seward a few minutes past 9.

(THIRD DESPATCH)

Reports are contradictory. It is reported that President Lincoln died at 7:22.

DEATH OF THE PRESIDENT

MURDEROUS ATTACK ON MR. SEWARD

Wilkes Booth Supposed to be the Murderer of the President

Washington, April 14.—President Lincoln and his wife, with other friends, this evening visited Ford's Theatre for the purpose of witnessing the performance of the "American Cousin." It was announced in the papers that General Grant would also be present, but that gentleman took a late train of cars for New Jersey. The theatre was densely crowded, and everybody seemed delighted with the scene before them.

During the third act, and while there was a temporary pause for one of the actors to enter, a sharp report of a pistol was heard, which merely attracted attention, but suggested nothing serious until a man rushed in front of the President's box, waved a long dagger in his right hand, exclaiming, *"sic semper tyrannis!"* and immediately leaped from a box which wos [sic] in the second tier of the stage beneath, ran across to the opposite side of the stage, making his escape, amid the bewilderment of the audience, from the rear of the theatre, and, mounting a horse, fled.

The screams of Mrs. Lincoln first disclosed the fact to the audience that the President had been shot, when all dresent [sic] rose to their feet, rushing toward the stage, many exclaiming "Hang him!" The excitement was. of the wildest possible description. Of course, there was an abrupt intermission of the theatrical performance. There was a rush toward the President's box, when cries were heard of "Stand back," "Give him air," "Has anyone stimulants?"

On a hasty examination it was found that the President had been shot through the head above and back of the temporal bone, and that some of the brain was oozing out. He was removed to a private house nearby. The Surgeon-General of the Army and other surgeons were sent for to attend to him. On the examination of the private box, blood was discovered on the back of the cushioned rocking chair on which the President had been sitting, also on the partition, and on the floor; a common single-barreled pistol was found on the carpet.

About 10 o'clock a man rang the bell, and the call having been answered by a colored servant, he said he had come from Dr. Viede, with a prescription, and at the same time holding in his hand a small piece of paper and saying, in answer to a refusal, that he must see the Secretary, as he was entrusted with particular directions concerning the medicine, he insisted on going up. Although repeatedly informed that no one could enter the chamber, he pushed the servant one side, walked heavily toward the Secretary's room, was met there by Mr. Fred Seward, of whom he demanded to see the Secretary making the same representations which he did to the servant. What further passed in the way of colloquy is not known, but the man struck him on the head with a billy, badly injuring the skull, and felling him senseless. The assassin then rushed into the chamber and attacked Mr. Seward, a paymaster in the United States army, and Mr. Hunsell, a messenger of the State Department and two male nurses, disabling them. He then rushed upon the Secretary, who was lying in bed in the same room, and inflicted three stabs in the neck, but severing, it is thought and hoped, no artery, though he bled profusely. The assassin rushed down stairs, mounted his horse and rode off before an alarm could be sounded and in the same manner as the sssassination [sic] of the President. It is believed the injuries of the Secretary are not fatal, nor are those of the others, although both the Secretary and Assistant Secretary are very seriously injured.

1869

The rails of the Pacific Railroad, linking east and west, were joined at Promontory, Utah, on May 10, 1869. However, two days' prior to the ceremonial driving of the last spike, an anonymous correspondent for San Francisco's *Alta*

California, riding eastward on Governor Leland Stanford's special train, painted a colorful picture of the newly settled Utah countryside and a vast western range the new railroad would doom. His words eye view appeared in the paper on May 10, concurrent with the golden spike ceremony nearly a thousand miles away in the desolate wastes of the Salt Lake basin, an account of which followed in the *Alta California* the next day.

FROM THE RAILROAD FRONT

[SPECIAL DESPATCHES TO THE ALTA CALIFORNIA.]

From Promontory to Ogden—
An Excursion—The Scenery—
Incidents—Receptions by the Mormons—Etc.

OGDEN, May 8th—[Received at San Francisco May 9th.]—At 8 o'clock this morning a special train, tendered to Governor Stanford and party by Gen. Casement, of the Union Pacific Railroad, left Promontory Point with a party consisting of Governor Stanford, Doctors Harkness and Stillman, of Sacramento; J. H. Strowbridge, Superintendent of Construction; Mr. Campbell; Judge Sanderson, of the Supreme Court of California; Mr. Tuttle, Col. Lightner, T. P. Woodward, Wm. Sherman, and a number of other Californians. Crossing the long trail of trestle work between Promontory Point and Blue Creek, the train sped gently around the head of Salt Lake. The morning was showery, but the rain was not unpleasant; and as we advanced Eastward, the increasing beauty of the scenery attracted and fixed the attention of the entire party. The rugged barrenness of the hills gradually gave place to more rounded and softened outlines. Broad valleys, covered with luxuriant verdure, took the place of desolate sage-brush plains and inhabitable country of the dreary desert. The wide savannas stretching out on either side of Bear River, green with rank vegetation and intersected with numerous small lagoons, filled with water fowl, reminded one strongly of the shores of the Gulf of Mexico, west of the Mississippi; while the bold, blue Wasatch Mountains, with snowy summits, added an Alpine beauty to the scene.

Corinne, at the crossing of Bear River, is a thriving, bustling town of rough board and canvas houses, located on a flat, muddy plain a few feet above the river's surface. Crossing the stream, the train whirled along through fertile plains like the prairies of Illinois, and from time to time, fields of grain, now but a few inches high, were seen.

Brigham City, a long, straggling town, situated on a beautiful plateau at the mouth of Box Elder Cañon, with a magnificent mountain spur of the Wasatch Range looming up sharp and rugged into the fleecy clouds behind it, lying a mile to the northward of the road, attracted much attention. Here the plain on the left is cut into small farms, bounded by willow hedges and irrigation ditches fed by swift-running mountain streams. Many houses had a comfortable, home-like air, quite refreshing to behold.

The peach trees were in bloom, and everything betokened early spring in a temperate climate. From this point the whole country is less cultivated and farm houses numerous, around many of the latter crops of children of equal age indicated the presence of the peculiar institution of the country unmistakably. As the train whirled along it brought up at Taylor's Mill, a hamlet on the bank of Weber River, which stream is now a turbulent torrent, carrying everything before it. Here dinner was served, and the train started back to Ogden, leaving as the first passenger across the continent, Jenkins of San Francisco, late of Grass Valley, California, to pursue his way eastward from Ogden Station. Ogden City is a place of three thousand inhabitants, a mile from the road, and the party made their way there afoot, passing many quiet residences, surrounded by gardens and blooming shrubbery. The inhabitants hardly manifested so much curiosity as to give the strangers a passing glance. Many houses are double, or treble, each division having a separate outside entrance, evidently occupied by different Mrs. Smiths. The town has a beautiful appearance, resembling San Bernardino in build and location to a wonderful degree, and exhibiting the same general characteristics of inhabitants—something less untidy and shiftless than Arkansas, and something less prim, energetic and thrifty than New England. At the hotel the party met Bishop West, of the Mormon Church, and were cordially but undemonstratively received. At five P.M. the whistle sounded at the depot for the return to Promontory. A more quietly agreeable excursion was never enjoyed anywhere than this, around the green shores of the mountain-girded sea, in the heart of the American continent.

The hoopla over and done, on May 11, 1869, the *Alta California* reflected on the importance of the completion of the Pacific Railroad, not just for California, but for the whole nation.

Nearly a quarter century earlier, *The Baltimore Patriot* had enthused that the use of the telegraph resulted in "the annihilation of space." On the occasion of the joining of the nation by twin ribbons of steel rail, the *Alta California* likewise opined, "space is practically annihilated."

In their day, so must it have seemed.

THE GREAT EVENT CONSUMMATED

"The last rail is laid; the last spike is driven; the Pacific Railroad is completed." In such terse and brief terms as these is the announcement made to the world that the great event of the age is finally accomplished. What seemed an impossibility, has become an established fact. In the face of natural obstacles of the most forbidding character, the shores of the Atlantic and Pacific are at last practically united by an iron highway spanning the continent. During the past few days, we have had a variety of conflicting reports as to the time when the two tracks, pushing from the East and from the West, would unite in the centre of the continent, making complete the iron ligature which binds the hemisphere. But now all the uncertainty which has haunted the public mind, the odd doubts as to the actual completeness of the union of the roads, are dispelled, and, to-day, trains of cars move from the eastern to western terminus of the great trans-continental road without impediment.

It is not possible to make too much of this great event, now so triumphantly consummated. We have already celebrated the practical conclusion of the work, and to-day the world of America congratulates itself on the fact that facile communications between the extremest edges of the Republic is finally and forever established. There will be other Pacific Railroads; other lines of iron will pierce the wastes which lie north and south of the parallel upon which has just been built *the* Pacific Railroad; the continent will be spanned by a vast network of rails where now a slender line only draws its sinuous course across the broad expanse of territory, but we now celebrate the completion of the first line which has bound together the widely separated shores of the Union. The virgin solitude of pathless deserts has been disturbed; the iron messenger which has just reached us from the East is the first that ever burst into the silent sea of natural life which has so long rolled its green waves in the midst of the broad continent. Though other roads may come, and other lines demand the recognition of celebration and welcome, the event which has just been heralded far and wide will never have its fellow. The first road will have heareafter only its limitations in daring and its followers in the general direction already taken.

Heretofore, we have been different from all other portions of the Union in that we were not in direct and rapid connection with the great family of States. The most frequently used line of travel was through a foreign country, and weary weeks of a sea voyage were consumed in a trip from our present abode to the places which we still fondly called home. The difficulties of transportation and intercommunication, despite the passionate love for the Union which has characterized these States of the Pacific, made us a peculiar people, and no artful array of facts or glossing of sentiment could ever disguise the fact that we were provincial, distant, isolated, and, in some sense, a mere appanage [sic] of the Republic. All this is past. The last rail is laid, the last spike is driven in the line of communication which forever changes the ancient order of things and breaks down the barrier which has made the people of the Pacific States a distant people. Space is practically annihilated, and though the peculiar mental characteristics which distinguish us from the other portions of the populations of the Union will not be changed, the blow has been struck at last upon the provincialism which has been the chief distinctive mark of this people. From henceforth we are in the Union and of it, and the great event of the age has brought us all home at last.

1871

The exposure of government corruption, particularly at the local level, long has been a staple of American newspapers. One of the earliest and finest examples of this type of investigative journalism was provided by *The New York Times'* fearless probing of William M. "Boss" Tweed's Tammany Ring in New York City in 1871.

Tweed, a three-hundred pound giant of a man, and his cohorts systematically had been bilking the public treasury of hundreds of thousands of dollars. By controlling the machinery of the Democratic Party in New York City, the denizens of Tammany also controlled elected officials, appointed officials, judges, and civil servants. But the *Times'* edition of July 8, 1871, led to public exposure, trials, and convictions for the miscreants, ushering in a (short-lived) era of responsible government in its home city.

In the following editorial, which ran on the same day, *Times* editors sought to impress upon their readers the seriousness of the Tammany corruption, while at the same time inferring that the silence of competing New York papers on the issue was more than mere coincidence.

MORE RING VILLAINY

Gigantic Frauds in the Rental of Armories

Exhorbitant Prices Given for Regimental Head-Quarters—Stable Lofts at a Premium— Thousands of Dollars Paid for Bare Walls and Unoccupied Rooms—Over Eighty Per Cent of the Money Stolen

Reliable and incontrovertible evidence of numerous gigantic frauds on the part of the rulers of this City has been given to the public from time to time in these columns. Few, if any, of the frauds, however, which have been thus exposed will be found to be of greater magnitude or of a more shameful character than those which are presented in this article. The facts which are narrated are obtained from what we consider a good and trustworthy source, and the figures which help to explain them are transcribed literally from books in the Controller's office. If Controller CONNOLLY can prove them to be inaccurate he is heartily welcome to do so.

The National Guard of this State was organized for the protection of our citizens, but under the baneful influence of the Ring it is made, as far as regards the First Division, an engine of political power, and a source of pecuniary profit to the soulless vampires who now control this City. Nominally, about three-quarters of a million of dollars is annually appropriated for the armories and drill-rooms of the First Division, but this sum forms

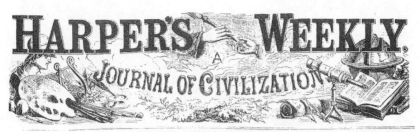

BLINDMAN'S-BUFF.
How long will this Game last?

Famed cartoonist Thomas Nast depicts the ringleader of New York's municipal corruption, William "Boss" Tweed, in the pages of Harper's Weekly, *April 12, 1873.* The Library of Congress, Washington, D.C.

only a small percentage of the amount actually paid out every year, ostensibly for "rents and repairs," but in fact to be divided among the thieves of the Ring and the miserable tools who perform their dirty work. Conspicuous among the latter class is JAS. H. INGERSOLL, who is a partner of WILLIAM M. TWEED in the chair business, and President of an Arms Company (virtually owned by TWEED), the arms of which the Ring are now trying to foist on the National Guard. He is also one of the New Court-House Commissioners, and the confidential agent of "Boss" TWEED in many of the schemes in which the latter is engaged. INGERSOLL was formerly a member of the Seventh Regiment, and an intimate acquaintance of Major JOSEPH B. YOUNG, the Clerk of the Board of Supervisors, when TWEED was president of that immaculate body. He early developed a talent for manipulating jobs, and so commended himself to the favor of TWEED that the latter selected him to look after his (TWEED'S) interests in the division of the spoils accruing from the rental and fitting up of armories. Nor was TWEED mistaken in his man. What had previously been but a bungling, imperfect system was soon reduced to a science, the most elaborate and comprehensive in its details. Buildings that had long remained unoccupied were selected in all parts of the City, without any regard to their adaptability for armory purposes, or any reference to the convenience of the troops that were intended to occupy them. Many of the old armories had been handsomely fitted up, but under the new order of things the substantial black-walnut and oak arm-racks, and the stout servicable chairs, tables and desks, gave place to more pretentious but less substantial furniture and fixtures.

The renting and fitting up of the armories of the First Division National Guard is now under the absolute control of INGERSOLL. He has his runners to find out where there is an empty loft, and to ascertain the best terms that can be made with the party desiring to rent it. When rented he locks it up, takes the keys, and keeps it unoccupied just as long as it suits him, charging the City rent for it all the time. Thus several armories that were rented in May, 1870, have remained unoccupied until May, 1871, while others that were rented at the same time, and still others that were vacated by regiments being moved or disbanded, are yet unoccupied.

During the year 1869, with the exception of the Eighty-fourth, there were no changes made in the location of the different regiments, and but little repairs were attempted, and yet, within thirty days, commencing March 12, 1870, more than HALF A MILLION DOLLARS were paid out of the City Treasury for "repairs on armories and drill-rooms." The checks representing this amount . . . were all returned from the bank bearing the indorsement of JAMES H. INGERSOLL. . . .

Besides this, the yearly rent collected by JAMES H. INGERSOLL, for an armory alleged to be at No. 53 Christy-street, but which never had any existence, is $5,000. The grand total amount, then, drawn from the City Treasury by the Ring as rent for occupied and unoccupied armories, is

$281,100, being an expenditure of just $234,500 more than what should be honestly paid. . . .

Who are responsible for these frauds? First, Mayor HALL and Controller CONNOLLY, who pass upon these claims and sign checks for their payment—knowing them to be fraudulent. Second, WILLIAM M. TWEED and PETER B. SWEENY, who pocket their share of the proceeds—knowing it to be fraudulently obtained. Third, JAMES H. INGERSOLL, JOSEPH B. YOUNG, Clerk to the Board of Supervisors, and STEPHEN C. LYNES, Jr., the present County Auditor, whose agency in these matters is as palpable as it is shameful. . . .

These men are in the position of a gang of burglars, who, having stolen all your silver-ware and jewelry and placed them under lock and key, turn round and challenge you to identify your property. In the case of ordinary burglars, you could summon the Courts to your assistance, arrest the thieves, break open the locks and get a sight of your stolen goods. But the Tammany Ring are a law unto themselves; they are the Government; they control the machinery of justice, and own a large share of the Judges. Hence they defy your efforts to detect their villainy, and laugh at the idea of restitution. But, notwithstanding all these drawbacks and difficulties, the TIMES has succeeded in exposing many frauds upon the City Treasury, and has furnished better vouchers for its bills of indictment that Controller CONNOLLY has furnished for the bills he has drawn on our tax-payers. We apprehend that no one will complain of a lack of facts and specifications in the article to which we now call the reader's attention; and that not even the *Tribune,* or any other of the eighteen daily and weekly papers that have been gagged by Ring patronage, will be able to find an excuse for ignoring the startling record presented elsewhere, on the ground that it is not sufficiently definite.

1876

In the early 1860's, Missourian Samuel L. Clemens set out for the riches to be had digging silver in Nevada's Comstock Lode. Less than successful as a miner, Clemens turned to the Virginia City *Territorial Enterprise* and journalism in 1862. It was a grand match. Both the paper and its new reporter were irreverent, rowdy, and fun-loving. While its prankish nature sometimes led the *Territorial Enterprise* into tongue-in-cheek exaggerations, it was in the city room of that rowdy weekly that Clemens learned the principles of journalism.

Later "known to the police as Mark Twain," or so he put it, Clemens would go on to write for the San Francisco *Alta California,* serve a stint as owner and editor of the *Buffalo Express* and freelance most of his life. His novels brought him fame, but Twain remained a newspaperman. Twain's parody of the long-winded, paid-by-the-inch newswriting of his day appeared nationally; it was rediscovered by social historian Henry W. Splitter in the May 20, 1876, issue of the *Ventura* (California) *Free Press.*

MARK TWAIN WRITES UP ACCIDENT

Mark Twain recently tried his hand writing up a distressing accident for a Boston local paper, and this is how he did it:

"Last evening about 6 o'clock, as Mr. Wm. Schuyler, an old and respected citizen of South Park, was leaving his residence to go downtown, as has been his usual custom for many years, with the exception of only a short interval in the Spring of 1850, during which he was confined to his bed by injuries received in attempting to stop a runaway horse by thoughtlessly throwing up his hands and shouting, which, if he had done so even a single second sooner, must inevitably have frightened the animal still more instead of checking his speed, although disastrous enough to himself as it was, and was rendered more melancholy and distressing by reason of the presence of his wife's mother, who was there and saw the occurrence, notwithstanding it is at least likely, though not necessarily so, that she should be reconnoitering in another direction when incidents occur, not being vivacious and on the lookout as a general thing, but even in the reverse, as her mother is said to have stated, who is no more, but died in the full hope of a blessed resurrection, upwards of three years ago, aged eighty-six, being a Christian woman without guile, as it were, in property, in consequence of the fire of 1849, which destroyed every solitary thing she had in the world. But such is life. Let us all take warning by this solemn occurrence, and let us endeavor to so conduct ourselves that when we come to die we can do it. Let us place our hands upon our hearts, and say with earnestness and sincerity that from this day forth we will beware of the intoxicating bowl."

1876

On July 7, 1876, the 100-year-old nation warmed in the afterglow of a self-congratulatory celebration of a century of progress. The country had come a long way. But however far the raw United States had progressed, it was still a frontier nation—a fact brought home with crushing force with news of Colonel George Armstrong Custer's June 25 defeat on the Little Big Horn River in Montana Territory. The flamboyant civil war veteran and his entire Seventh Cavalry of 265 men rashly had attacked an encampment of Sioux and were cut down in a running fight through the grasslands near the river.

As told by H. M. "Muggins" Taylor, a cavalry scout passing through Bozeman, Montana, following the battle, the scene was one of incredible carnage. Taylor told his story to the *Bozeman Times,* which printed it on July 6, 1876. *The Bozeman Avant Courier,* giving due credit to its rival, printed its version, which appears below, on the next day.

A thousand miles away, also on July 7, back in the civilization that was St. Louis, Missouri, that city's *Republican,* reflected thoughtfully on the meaning of Custer's defeat. Especially noteworthy is the surprisingly enlightened manner in which it assessed blame for the tragedy.

The Indian War

BATTLE OF THE LITTLE BIG HORN!

TERRIBLE CARNAGE

THE GALLANT CUSTER KILLED!

The Seventh Cavalry
Regiment Slaughtered

We give below the report of Mr. H. M. Taylor, bearer of dispatches from Gen. Gibbon to Fort Ellis, substantially as appeared in the Times of yesterday. Mr. Taylor arrived here Monday evening:

A battle was fought 25 miles above the mouth and on the Little Horn river, between General Custer and the Sioux, on 25th day of June, 1876.

The whole force of the command was twelve companies of the Seventh Cavalry. At the head of the five companies Custer charged the center of the Sioux village from the north side of the Little Horn. Major Reno charged the same village at the same time with three companies from the east. Four companies were held on the hill as a reserve and to protect the pack train. The attack was made about three o'clock in the afternoon and lasted about three hours, in the judgment of Major Reno, who heard the first and last volleys of the firing. Custer and his whole command, including sixteen officers, were killed. The attack of Custer on the village seems to have been repulsed, and he fell back to the hill where the dead bodies of the men were found and buried. Two hundred and three dead bodies were found, among them was the whole Custer family, lying close together—the General, his two brothers, a brother-in-law and a nephew—a smooth face boy. Many of the men were horribly mutilated. Some had their heads cut off, some had their legs amputated at the hip joint; some were cut in strips, some had their privates cut off, and some had their entrails taken out. And for the benefit of philanthropists we will mention that those killed in the village were horribly mutilated by the squaws. George Harrington, well known in Bozeman, with an officer and soldier of Reno's command, were cut off and hid in the brush near the village, and saw this performance. The horses were all killed, and to the best of Mr. Taylor's knowledge, there was a dead horse near the corpse of each soldier. Every officer and soldier had been robbed, and much booty in money was secured by the Sioux, the soldiers having been paid off shortly before the battle. . . .

Gen. Custer, prior to attacking the village, had made a forced march of 31 hours following an Indian trail up the Rosebud until two other trails intersected it, and it turned over into the Little Horn, getting fresher all the time. He rested but one hour during the march of 31 hours, and upon coming up to the Indian village immediately attacked it. . . .

The Indian village was four miles long, located in the bottom of the Little Horn; was composed of three streets, and believed to have comprised 2,000 lodges. . . .

The Indians left a vast amount of property . . . without doubt just issued from the agencies. The blankets were of a very fine quality—still packed—having never been used; red in color, and marked "U.S." . . . They took all the arms, ammunition and accoutrements belonging to the dead soldiers. They carried off all of their wounded and most of their dead; the latter they abandoned on their retreat, making an unbearable stench on their route.

A particular feature of the battle with Maj. Reno's command was the fact that, notwithstanding his soldiers had their guns set to carry a bullet 1,300 yards the Indians had guns that proved more effective at that distance, one rifle especially, in the hands of a distinguished Indian, hitting a man or horse at every discharge and Taylor believes it to have been the celebrated needle gun presented by General Grant to Sitting Bull for his friendship and bravery!

There were found on the battle ground fifty or sixty dead Indians—nine of whom were chiefs; men of distinguished note, as was evidence by the fact that horses had been sacrificed to their names; around one chief, particularly, were twelve horses, all artistically arranged—six pintoes and six bays.

About one mile from the battle ground the heart of a man was found.

In an editorial, commenting on the Battle of the Little Big Horn, *The St. Louis Republican* of July 7, 1876, reflected:

. . . . there has been no such a slaughter of regular soldiers in a contest with Indians since BRADDOCK perished with half his army on the banks of the Monongahela a hundred and twenty years ago. . . .

The Indian war, so long talked of, has at last begun. . . . This is not the time to speak of the causes which have brought on the conflict now fully inaugurated. Sufficient to say that we believe it might have been honorably avoided by a strict fulfilment of the treaty obligations of the federal government. But be this as it may, all, we think, will agree with us in declaring that the gold of the Black hills, be it ever so plenty, is not worth the fearful price already paid for it by the sacrifice of CUSTER and his comrades.

1882

They still sing of it, the death of a good man driven outside the law, then shot in the back on April 3, 1882, by a man he had taken into his home. For almost twenty years Jesse James and his brother Frank, with an assortment of sometime accomplices, had staged a long series of bank and train robberies. Not all were successful, yet the James brothers slipped the grasp of sheriffs in half a dozen states; meanwhile his largely undeserved reputation as a Robin Hood grew. Now, after a daring career, Jesse James yearned for peace and a pardon from the governor of Missouri; he found instead betrayal and ironic martyrdom, remembered not for his bloody life, but his bloody death. The coverage in *The St. Louis Post-Dispatch* of April 4, 1882, has become the stuff of legend.

A DASTARD'S DEED.

Cold-blooded Treachery at Last Conquers Jesse James.

The Noted Border Bandit Shot Like a Dog From Behind.

By a Man Who Was Eating His Bread and Was His Friend.

By a Coward Traitor's Hand Missouri Vanquishes Jesse James.

Special to the Post-Dispatch.

St. Joseph, Mo., April 4—Jesse James was shot and killed in his house, on the corner of Fourteenth and Lafayette streets, by Robert Ford at 10 o'clock yesterday morning.

The murderer, in company with his brother Charles, had been hiding with Jesse James for some time past and both were completely in his confidence. A plan had been on foot between the two brothers for some months past to murder James, yesterday morning presenting the first invocable opportunity.

Immediately after breakfast Charley Ford and Jesse James went out into the stable, in the rear yard of the house, for the purpose of currying their horses, to be used that night, as Ford says, in an attempt to rob the bank in Platte City. Upon returning to the house Jesse James divested himself of his coat and vest and his belt, in which were his pistols, and threw them on the bed.

Here was the long looked for opportunity, and as Jesse turned his back to adjust a picture on the wall, Robert Ford,

QUICK AS A FLASH DREW A REVOLVER

and fired, the ball striking the outlaw in the back of the head, penetrating the brain, and coming out through the eye. The ball was fired from a .45-caliber Colt Improved, and death was instantaneous. Mrs. James, hearing the shot, rushed into the room and, putting Jesse's head into her lap, tried to revive him, but without effect.

JESSE JAMES NEVER SPOKE A WORD
after the ball entered his head.

The murderer then ran out of the house, but came back at the request of Mrs. James. He was then accused of the murder, which he strenuously denied, claiming that the pistol had been discharged by accident. The murderer, in company with his brother, then left the house and proceeded to the telegraph office, where Governor Crittenden and Sheriff Timberlake were immediately notified. They then surrendered themselves to await the judicial investigation. . . .

The body was placed in a casket and laid on a table, where in turn the people were allowed to view it. No one recognized the face as familiar, as Jesse had never cultivated anyone, and had remained as secreted as possible. Jesse James was five feet eight inches in stature. The prominence of his chin is mainly noticeable, the eyes are closed, and the firm lips show

THE DETERMINED CHARACTER OF THE MAN.
After the remains were viewed the Coroner, in company with Marshal Craig and the two Ford boys and Mrs. James, she being in company with Marshal Craig, repaired to the Court-house, where the inquest was begun. The

FORD BOYS
testified that they were raised in Ray county, near Richmond, where their father owned a farm. They had been in the confidence of Jesse James ever since the Blue Cut robbery, in which they claimed to have participated. Both young men were allowed to carry their pistols during the inquest. They were strongly guarded by the police and citizens.

At 3 o'clock yesterday afternoon a special train arrived from Kansas City and Cameron, upon which were Sheriff Timberlake, of Clay county, and H.H. Craig, Police Commissioner. Dick Little was also with them, and identified the body of the dead outlaw. He described the scars and marks on Jesse's person to a nicety. James had been living here under the name of Howard for some time past in St. Joseph. Mrs. James strenuously denied the identity of her husband for some time, but finally broke down and acknowledged the truth. Timberlake and Crittenden claimed that they were aware of what was going to happen, which the Fords emphatically deny. Mrs. James denounced the Fords in unmeasured terms and called upon heaven to witness that

SHE WOULD BE REVENGED
as Frank James lived. Mrs. James is a very pleasing lady, slender, light-complexioned, and a perfect blonde. She has two children, one is a girl of seven years, and the other a boy of four.

Upon the officers, searching the house of the outlaw, a perfect armory was discovered. Pistols, shot guns and rifles of the same pattern were found that were identified as having been stolen some weeks ago in Kansas during a horse-stealing raid. Two gold watches were found on the body of James, one said to have been the property of the Governor of Arizona, taken at the Sweet River robbery. The other watch was taken at the time the stage was robbed near Mammoth Cave in Kentucky.

Crittenden's Bargain with Ford

Kansas City, Mo., April 4—The killing of Jesse James at St. Joseph is fully corroborated this morning, and has created much excitement through the county. It is now known that the deed was the fulfillment of a bargain between Governor Crittenden and Bob Ford and that Ford was to receive one-fourth the reward and immunity. In an interview with Dick Little held by a reporter Sunday last the scheme was foreshadowed, but he said it was not to have been accomplished before Wednesday or Thursday, and only then if it was found impossible for Sheriff Timberlake [to take James]. Gov. Crittenden arrived here this morning and immediately telegraphed the authorities at St. Joe to turn the body over to Mrs. James after the inquest, which is now in progress.

In an interview the Governor stated that his first meeting with Ford was at the St. James Hotel, in this city, on the 22nd of February, and that an arrangement by which Jesse James was to be either captured or killed was consummated. He met Little a few days later through an appointment made by Mattie Ford, of Ray County, who called upon him at Jefferson City early in the month. He was non-committal as to the disposition to be made of Ford and Little, but admitted that their ultimate pardon was not improbable.

Sheriff Timberlake, Dick Little and Mrs. Samuels, mother of the dead bandit, passed through this city last night on their way to St. Joe, and have identified the body. . . .

Jesse's Wife and Mother Curse the Traitors

Kansas City, Mo., April 4—The death of Jesse James, the great Missouri bandit, is now beyond question a fact. Governor Crittenden arrived here this morning and said positively that it is he and that his death is the result of an understanding between the authorities and Bob Ford, who killed him, and Dick Little, who surrendered to Sheriff Timberlake at the same time as Ford. The inquest at St. Joe was concluded at noon to-day. Mrs. Samuels, mother of Jesse James, his wife, Dick Little and Sheriff Timberlake identified the body, and during the proceedings Mrs. James and Mrs. Samuels made a highly sensational scene by attacking Dick Little and calling

ALL MANNER OF CURSES DOWN UPON HIM

for having conspired to betray his leader. The Coroner's jury returned a verdict of murder in the first degree against Ford, and the authorities of Buchanan county refuse to give him up. The Governor this morning telegraphed the authorities to turn the body over to Mrs. James when the inquest was concluded, and it will probably be taken to the old farm near Kearney, Clay county, for burial. The confirmation of James' death has

CREATED A PROFOUND SENSATION

in Western Missouri, and farmers near this place and Independence, who have not been in either place for years, rode into town this morning in the rain to investigate the rumor. Some denounce Ford as an assassin whose only object was blood money, while others excuse him upon the ground of expediency. The Governor will not go to St. Joe, but will return to Jefferson City to-night, where some steps will be taken to protect Ford, who is thought to be in danger from the friends of the dead robber. . . .

Jesse James' Career

That Jesse James is dead there is now not the shadow of doubt. In him the master spirit in the train-robbing outrages has been vanquished, and doubtless now the practice of robbing trains in the West will cease.

Jesse James was born in Clay county, Missouri, in 1845. Frank was born in Kentucky in 1841. Rev. Robert L. James, a Baptist minister, was their father. He came to this State in 1843, living here till 1849. He emigrated to California, separating from his wife, their natures being incompatible. Mrs. James (now Mrs. Samuels) is still living, residing on a farm on the Hannibal and St. Joe Railroad, seventeen miles northeast of Kansas City.

Jesse and Frank James first

ENTERED UPON THEIR MURDEROUS CAREER

during the war, when, though mere boys, they joined Quantrell's band of guerrillas, being among the leading spirits of that intrepid band of cut-throats. To give in detail a recital of the hand to hand conflicts, murders and massacres in which the James boys engaged from '61 to '65 would be impossible. Prominent among these bloody events was the massacre at Centralia, Mo., a way-station on the Wabash Railroad September 17, 1864. There Frank and Jesse James and Bill Anderson butchered thirty-two invalid Union soldiers. During the winter of 1865 Jesse James left the guerrillas, and with George Shepherd went to Texas. Frank remained with Quantrell and went with him to Kentucky. By an accident Frank happened to be absent at the fight in Kentucky, in which the guerrillas were almost exterminated and the leader killed.

From 1865 to 1868, nothing was heard of Jesse and Frank James. The first of the series of robberies that have since rendered these boys famous occurred in Russelville, Ky. in 1868 when Jesse James and Cole Younger, Al and George Shepherd and Jon White robbed the bank there of $14,000. George Shepherd was caught soon after the robbery and sentenced to the penitentiary for three years. This time he served.

The first robbery in Missouri occurred in Gallatin. There they robbed the bank and shot and killed Sheets, the cashier.

THE NEXT ROBBERY
occurred in Kentucky, in the town of Columbia, two years afterwards, only $200 being taken there.

In 1873 the Kansas City Fair Grounds ticket office was robbed of $10,000 by Jesse James and two pals in open daylight. Six weeks after the bank at St. Genevieve was robbed of $10,000.

The James boys next came into notoriety in 1873 [sic]. A train on the Chicago, Rock Island and Pacific Railway was wrecked in Clay county, Missouri, and $6,000 taken from the messenger. Next the Iron Mountain train was robbed at Gad's Hill, the total haul there amounting to $10,500.

A train was next robbed at Muncie, near Kansas City, and $25,000 taken. Jesse and Frank James then went to Texas, where the plan for the robbery of the Huntington, W. Va. bank was planned.

This robbery took place in September, 1875, and a haul of $60,000 made. The next train robbery was at Winston on July 15, 1881. There, as will be remembered, Conductor Westfall was killed.

The last two train robberies that characterized the career of the James Boys were the Glendale and the Blue Cut.

Frank James was married in 1875 to Miss Annie Ralston, whose father resided near Independence. She is said to have been a wonderfully beautiful woman, and, being of a romantic disposition, fell in love with Frank, his name having been on the tongue of every inhabitant in that country. They were married clandestinely, the father of the girl objecting emphatically to the union. The marriage of Jesse occurred in 1874, to his cousin, Miss Zeruda Mimms. She was at that time a public-school teacher. Affection of the strongest nature has always existed between the James boys and their wives.

1885

It is, most critics agree, one of the towering achievements of American letters. The usually sour H.L. Mencken judged it the "full equal" of *Don Quixote,* predicting it would be read for generations to come. Ernest Hemingway, probably the most influential of American writers in the 20th Century, concluded that Samuel Clemens's *The Adventures of Huckleberry Finn* was "the best book we've had. All American writing comes from that."

It was not always so. More than a few took offense at what they deemed an uncouth plot, language and theme when *Huck* was first published in the United States on February 18, 1885. The author of such morally impeccable novels as *Little Women,* Louisa May Alcott, sniffed, "If Mr. Clemens cannot think of something better to tell our pure-minded lads and lassies, he had best stop writing for them." *The Boston Transcript* of March 17, 1885, reported the almost predictable result:

The Concord (Mass.) Public Library Committee has decided to exclude Mark Twain's latest book from the library. One member of the committee says that, while he does not wish to call it immoral, he thinks it contains but little humor, and that of a very coarse type. He regards it as the veriest trash. The librarian and other members of the committee entertain similar views, characterizing it as rough, coarse and inelegant, dealing with a series of experiences not elevating, the whole book being more suited to the slums than to intelligent, respectable people.

Within the week *The Springfield* [Massachusetts] *Republican* editorially defended the board. "The trouble with Mr. Clemens is that he has no reliable sense of propriety. . . . [The Tom Sawyer and Huckleberry Finn] stories . . . are no better in tone than the dime novels which flood the blood-and-thunder reading population. . . . Their moral level is low, and their perusal cannot be anything less than harmful."

Twain wrote a tongue in cheek appreciation of the committee's "generous" action. Not only had its ban boosted sales, but . . . "it will cause the purchasers of the book to read it, out of curiosity, instead of merely intending to do so after the usual way of the world and library committees; and then they will discover, to my great advantage and their own indignant disappointment, that there is nothing objectionable in the book, after all."

A century and more since its publication, that great American novel, perhaps the greatest American novel, still runs afoul of Pecksniff and Mrs. Grundy. Somewhere this year a school board or a library committee or a vigilante parents' group will demand that *Huck* be stricken from a reading list or library shelf on the grounds that it is racist, that it encourages youthful rebellion, that it is immoral.

Twain and Huck obviously outlive their critics.

1886

Industrialization and worker unrest grew apace in the last half of the 19th Century. Labor's complaints were many—low wages, virtual servitude in company towns, lack of unemployment insurance or compensation for injuries on the job— but the chief concern was the long working day. Fourteen- and 16-hour days were not uncommon.

Chicago was the very heart of the eight-hour-day movement, according to labor historian Jeremy Brecher. There brewers had won a reduction of hours from 16 to 10 per day, and bakers who worked as many as 18 hours secured 10-hour-days. Other tradesmen and mechanics, as skilled workers were known at the time, gained similar concessions from reluctant managers. Those left out planned a general strike to begin on May Day, 1886, a strike that gathered impetus with each passing day. By May 3, the Chicago correspondent for the labor journal *John Swinton's Paper* exulted, "It is an eight-hour boom, and we are scoring victory after victory. Today the packing houses of the Union Stock Yards all yielded. . . ."

Businessmen and industrialists resisted the labor demands, recruiting local government and the police department as enthusiastic allies. Police first intervened on May 3, firing on a crowd of strikers; four died and a score were wounded.

Workers were bitterly angry; anarchist fliers handed about town urged strikers to take up arms. In that tense atmosphere, labor leaders scheduled a rally in the city's former haymarket to protest the police shootings.

Just as the Haymarket rally was breaking up, police with drawn batons descended on the workers. The militantly anti-labor Chicago *Inter-Ocean* of Wednesday, May 5, 1886, described what happened next.

NOW IT IS BLOOD!

Three Policemen Killed and at Least Thirty Badly Wounded

The Order Is Given to Fire, and Desperate Battle Ensues

It Lasts but a Few Minutes and the Police Conquer

On the Street the Dead and Dying Rioters Are Thickly Strewn

One Corpse at the Desplaines Street Station —Saloons and Drug Stores Full of Wounded

Bloody Work, Bombshells and Bullets

The anarchists of Chicago inaugurated in earnest last night the reign of lawlessness which they have threatened and endeavored to incite for years. They threw a bomb into the midst of a line of 200 police officers, and it exploded with fearful effect, moving [sic] down men like cattle. Almost before the missile of death had exploded the anarchists directed a murderous fire from revolvers upon the police as if their action was prearranged, and as the latter were hemmed in on every side—ambuscaded—the effect of the fire upon the ranks of the officers was fearful. When the police had recovered from the first shock of the attack they gallantly charged upon their would-be murderers, shooting at every step and mowing them down as their fellow officers had been by the bomb. The Anarchists fled in dismay before the charge, but everywhere they turned the withering fire from the revolvers of the policemen followed them and thinned their ranks. The cowardly curs finding that their attack did not completely annihilate the officers and that a force large enough to come with them was left, fled in all directions, seeking the darkness of alleys, hallways, and side streets to escape the revengeful fire of the police.

The collision between the police and the anarchists was brought about by the leaders of the latter, August Spies, Sam Fielden, and A. R. Parsons, endeavoring to incite a large mass-meeting to riot and bloodshed. They gathered on Desplaines street, between Lake and Randolph streets, about 10 o'clock last night in obedience to a call from somebody or something which is known as "the committee." Fielden, Spies, and Parsons were on hand to call the meeting to order, and when there were enough of them to fill up the street, Spies mounted a wagon in front of Crane Brothers' machine shop, on the east side of Desplaines street, and harrangued [sic] the mob to begin at once the annihilation of minions of the law and capitalists. That the mob was in sympathy with his utterances was evinced by the wild applause which was accorded him.

Parsons followed, and his speech was, if possible, even more intemperate and incendiary than that of Spies. When Sam Fielden mounted the wagon and began to tell the howling and exciting anarchists that the only way to evade law and order was to kill off its "minions," the officers who enforce it, the head of a column of police coming from the direction of the station was seen about half a block away. Captain Bonfield and Captain Ward, with nearly two hundred officers and men had been waiting patiently in the station for the socialists to disperse or attempt some act of lawlessness. When the officers who had been sent to mingle with them returned and reported the temper of the anarchists, both Captains came to the conclusion that prompt measures only would avert another serious riot. The order "fall in" went round among the lieutenants with lightning rapidity. It was repeated to the men, and they jumped into their places with accuracy and precision, prepared for the march on the anarchists. . . .

Captains Bonfield and Ward took a position at the head of the line, which was marched to a point almost 100 feet north of Randolph street. Captain Ward raised his club to command the attention of the strikers, and then he ordered them in the name of the people to disperse quietly and peaceably. The order had hardly left his lips when a dark object was thrown from behind a pile of boxes which stood on the sidewalk about one hundred feet from Lake street. It shot over the head of Captain Ward, past the first two companies, and fell hissing at the feet of the men in the front rank of the second company, and exploded with a report which seemede [sic] to shake the earth. Men fearfully wounded and dying fell on all sides, the death-dealing contents of the bomb reaching almost to the rear ranks.

Before the officers had time to realize the destruction and death which had been wrought in their ranks, the crowds of anarchists gathered in front and on either side of them opened fire with their revolvers at almost point blank range. The first volley of the mob was quite as fearful in its effect as was the explosion of the bomb, but the officers did not lose their presence of mind. Orders flew thick and fast from the captains and lieutenants, and within the briefest possible space of time they were charging the murderous assassins on every hand, dealing death and destruction to them with their revolvers. The anarchists did not sustain the charge an instant, but fled as

soon as they could distinguish the blue coats and bright buttons of the officers through the smoke from their revolvers. The cracking of revolvers was
incessant for five minutes, and only once was anything like a volley fired
by either side. This was fired by the anarchists, when the bomb exploded in
the ranks of the police, thus showing that they had been carefully drilled
beforehand to act in concert. When the officers emptied their pistols they
used them as clubs, and it is quite probable that the coroner's jury will
develop that one or more of the strikers came to their death by fractures of
the skull. . . .

After the anarchists had been dispersed the police set to work to look after
their wounded and dying companions. Two of them were found where the
bomb exploded, both so desperately wounded as to be past hope of recov-
ery. About thirty others were found lying on the pavement in the vicinity
and suffering from pistol-shot wounds in their limbs and bodies, and unable
to stir hand or foot. The strikers, too, lay around wounded and dying, but
the officers paid no attention to their sufferings only thinking of their own
fallen companions. They picked them up and bore them who could not walk
or move to the station, and assisted all with slight wounds to walk to their
homes. The drug stores and saloons about the scene of the battle were soon
filled with wounded men, but it was impossible to get even a partial list of
their names. . . .

Scenes at the Station
Dead and Dying

The squad-room in the Desplaines Street Station, half an hour after the
shooting, resembled a charnel-house. Wounded and dying policemen were
lying everywhere. Fifteen wounded officers sat in chairs around the room,
heroically struggling with fearful pains which racked their bodies, waiting
for the arrival of surgeons to dress their wounds. Such a scene is rarely ever
witnessed except on a battle field. Policemen who escaped without injury
were acting as nurses, assisting the few surgeons who reached the station
when the men were brought in. They ministered to the needs of their stricken
fellows with as much care and tenderness as women. . . .

In the cell room of the station lay a dozen wounded strikers. All were
suffering terrible tortures, and as the physicians and surgeons were all busy
above with the wounded officers, they were practically without attention or
care, except from two Catholic priests. Lying the center of the room were
two dead bodies. There was nothing by which to identify them, and their
names will probably not be known until their friends appear at the Coroner's
inquest. . . .

The Haymarket explosion, labor editor John Swinton wrote, "was a godsend to the enemies of the labor movement. They have used it as an explosive against all the objects that the working people are bent upon accomplishing, and in defense of all the evils that capital is bent upon maintaining." For the next fifty years, those enemies of labor included much of the American press.

1887

By the time he was 12, Walt Whitman was working in a newspaper office. In fact, the celebrated poet of *Leaves of Grass* was to hold many jobs in journalism, ranging from positions on the *Brooklyn Daily Eagle* to a stint as editor of the *New Orleans Daily Crescent*. The passionate eye that comes into play in Whitman's verse can be found in his journalism; Whitman viewed the American experience, the daily doings reported by the journalist, as new, raw-boned ritual.

In the following piece, written by the 68-year-old Whitman for the *New Orleans Picayune* of January 25, 1887, the poet recalls his brief sojourn in New Orleans working for the *Crescent*.

NEW ORLEANS IN 1848

Walt Whitman Gossips of His Sojourn Here Years Ago as a Newspaper Writer.

Notes of His Trip Up the Mississippi and to New York.

Among the letters brought this morning (Jan. 15, 1887,) by my faithful post-office carrier, J.G., is one as follows:

"New Orleans, Jan. 11, '87.—We have been informed that when you were younger and less famous than now, you were in New Orleans and perhaps have helped on the Picayune. If you have any remembrance of the Picayune's young days, or of journalism in New Orleans of that era, and would put it in writing (verse or prose) for the Picayune's fiftieth year edition, Jan. 25, we shall be pleased," etc.

In response to which: I went down to New Orleans early in 1848 to work on a daily newspaper, but it was not the Picayune, though I saw quite a good deal of the editors of that paper, and knew its personnel and ways. But let me indulge my pen in some gossipy recollections of that time and place, with extracts from my journal up the Mississippi and across the great lakes to the Hudson. . . .

One of my choice amusements during my stay in New Orleans was going down to the old French Market, especially of a Sunday morning. The show was a varied and curious one; among the rest, the Indian and negro hucksters with their wares. For there were always fine specimens of Indians, both men and women, young and old. I remember I nearly always on these occasions got a large cup of delicious coffee with a biscuit, for my breakfast, from the immense shining copper kettle of a great Creole mulatto woman (I believe she weighed 230 pounds.) I never have had such coffee since. About nice drinks, anyhow, my recollection of the "cobblers" (with strawberries and snow on top of the large tumblers,) and also the exquisite wines, and the perfect and mild French brandy, help the regretful reminiscence of my New Orleans experiences of those days. And what splendid and roomy and leisurely bar-rooms! particularly the grand ones of the St. Charles and St. Louis. Bargains, auctions, appointments, business conferences, &c., were generally held in the spaces or recesses of these bar-rooms.

I used to wander a midday hour or two now and then for amusement on the crowded and bustling levees, on the banks of the river. The diagonally wedg'd-in boats, the stevedores, the piles of cotton and other merchandise, the carts, mules, negroes, etc., afforded never-ending studies and sights to me. I made acquaintances among the captains, boatmen, or other characters, and often had long talks with them—sometimes finding a real rough diamond among my chance encounters. Sundays I sometimes went forenoons to the old Catholic Cathedral in the French quarter. I used to walk a good deal in this arrondissement; and I have deeply regretted since that I did not cultivate, while I had such a good opportunity, the chance of better knowledge of French and Spanish Creole New Orleans people. (I have an idea that there is much and of importance about the Latin race contributions to American nationality in the South and Southwest that I have grown to think highly of and that will never be put with sympathetic understanding and tact on record.)

Let me say, for better detail, that through several months (1848) I work'd on a new daily paper, The Crescent; my situation rather a pleasant one. My young brother, Jeff, was with me; and he not only grew very homesick, but the climate of the place, and especially the water, seriously disagreed with him. From this and other reasons (although I was quite happily fix'd) I made no very long stay in the South. . . .

1888

Whatever the news of June 3, 1888, history has forgotten all but one item— and a fictional one at that. On that slow Sunday in San Francisco, buried on page 4, column 4, William Randolph Hearst's brash *Examiner* introduced an American folk hero, the pride of the Mudville nine, the mighty Casey of "Casey at the Bat." Its author was Ernest Lawrence Thayer, a 25-year-old humor columnist for the *Examiner* who wrote under the penname of "Phin." He got $5 for his epic in 13 stanzas.

Thayer and Hearst had met two years earlier, Thayer as editor of the *Harvard Crimson,* Hearst as the business manager. Thrown out of school for a series of pranks, Hearst first worked on *The New York World* for a year, then moved home to take over management of his father's newspaper. Willie had immediately hired Thayer and a number of other Harvard classmates as writers and editors.

The canonization of "Casey at the Bat" in literary Americana was accomplished by touring vaudevillian William De Wolf

Hopper, a comedian-singer of the day who created a sensation with his melo- dramatic, six-minute recitation of Casey's ignoble defeat.

CASEY AT THE BAT

A Ballad of the Republic
Sung in the Year 1888.

The outlook wasn't brilliant for the Mudville
    nine that day;
The score stood four to two with but one
    inning more to play.
And then when Cooney died at first, and Barrows
    did the same,
A sickly silence fell upon the patrons
    of the game.

A straggling few got up to go in deep despair.
    The rest clung to that hope which springs eternal
    in the human breast;
They thought if only Casey could but get a
    whack at that—
We'd put up even money with Casey
    at the bat.

But Flynn preceded Casey, as did also
    Jimmy Blake,
And the former was a lulu and the latter
    was a cake;
So upon that stricken multitude grim
    melancholy sat,
For there seemed but little chance of Casey's
    getting to the bat.

But Flynn let drive a single, to the wonderment
    of all,
And Blake, the much despis-ed, tore the cover
    off the ball;
And when the dust had lifted, and the men saw
    what had occurred,
There was Johnnie safe at second and Flynn
    a-hugging third.

Then from 5,000 throats and more there rose
    a lusty yell;

It rumbled through the valley, it rattled
   in the dell;
It knocked upon the mountain and recoiled
   upon the flat
For Casey, mighty Casey, was advancing
   to the bat.

There was ease in Casey's manner, as he stepped
   into his place;
There was pride in Casey's bearing and a smile
   on Casey's face.
And when, responding to the cheers, he lightly
   doffed his hat,
No stranger in the crowd could doubt 'twas Casey
   at the bat.

Ten thousand eyes were on him as he rubbed
   his hands with dirt;
Five thousand tongues applauded when he
   wiped them on his shirt.
Then while the writhing pitcher ground the
   ball into his hip,
Defiance gleamed in Casey's eye, a sneer
   curled Casey's lip.

And now the leather-covered sphere came
   hurtling through the air,
And Casey stood a-watching it in haughty
   grandeur there.
Close by the sturdy batsman the ball unheeded
   sped—
"That ain't my style," said Casey. "Strike
   one," the umpire said.

From the benches, black with people, there
   went up a muffled roar,
Like the beating of the storm-waves on a
   stern and distant shore.
"Kill him! Kill the umpire!" shouted some
   one on the stand;
And it's likely they'd have killed him had
   not Casey raised his hand.

With a smile of Christian charity great
   Casey's visage shone;
He stilled the rising tumult; he bade the
   game go on;

He signaled to the pitcher, and once more the
   spheroid flew;
But Casey still ignored it, and the umpire
   said, "Strike two."

"Fraud!" cried the maddened thousands, and
   echo answered fraud;
But one scornful look from Casey and the audience was awed.
They saw his face grow stern and cold, they
   saw his muscles strain,
And they knew that Casey wouldn't let that
   ball go by again.

The sneer is gone from Casey's lip, his teeth
   are clenched in hate;
He pounds with cruel violence his bat upon
   the plate.
And now the pitcher holds the ball, and now
   he lets it go,
And now the air is shattered by the force of
   Casey's blow.

Oh, somewhere in this favored land the sun is
   shining bright;
The band is playing somewhere, and somewhere
   hearts are light,
And somewhere men are laughing, and somewhere
   children shout;
But there is no joy in Mudville—mighty
   Casey has struck out.   —PHIN

1889

After a day of torrential rains, the dam on the Conemaugh River above Johnstown, Pennsylvania, gave way. More than 2,100 drowned in the great wall of water that crashed down upon the narrow valley that Friday evening, May 31, 1889. Property damage, especially in the steel mills of Johnstown, reached a staggering $10 million. The Johnstown flood, later blamed on the shoddy construction of the relatively new dam, remains the worst such disaster in American history. *The Pittsburgh Dispatch* of June 1, 1889, compiled its story from eye-witness accounts telegraphed by stunned reporters.

HORRORS OF HORRORS.

The City of Johnstown Completely Swept Away in an Awful Rush of Waters.

THOUSANDS OF LIVES ARE LOST.

The Dam of South Fork Broken by a Swollen Stream, and an Immense Volume of Water

SWALLOWS EVERYTHING IN ITS REACH.

For Hours Hundreds of People Are Seen Floating Along, Shrieking for Help.

Some of the Scenes Indescribable—The Work of Rescue at all Points—No Trains Able to Reach the Scene of Desolation and All Other Direct Communication Cut Off—The People Warned, but Ineffectually—Familiarity With Their Danger Had Made Them Careless— Touching Incidents of the Work of Rescue at Bolivar, Lockport and Blairsville.

The whole world shudders and sighs this morning.

All the people who have eyes to read or ears to hear the mournful message, as it flies from press to public and from mouth to mouth, will stand appalled as they begin to realize the dire disaster that has befallen one of the most beautiful regions in all the Western Pennsylvania.

When the first news of the Johnstown horror came, it seemed such a pity that fair fields and proud possessions of great extent had suffered devastation by a flood from a lovely little mountain lake, whose clear depths were henceforth to be missed by many a worshipper at one of Nature's sweetest shrines.

That was the thought of property perishing; and it was a deep, an earnest sympathy the thought aroused. . . .

At 2:30 o'clock this morning a bulletin from Bolivar signed by a DIS-PATCH man says a floater rescued from the Conemaugh insists that at least 1,500 persons have perished at and near Johnstown in the flood that floated him thither from that city, and that only two Johnstown dwellings could yet be seen standing. . . .

SCENES OF HORROR.

Women and Children Swept Away—Shrieks
Blend With the Sullen Roar of the
Elements—A Boy Lassoed
Out of the Flood

From a Staff Correspondent

BOLIVAR, PA., May 31.—The water is higher here than was ever known, and two-story houses, barns, stables, whole forests of trees, outhouses, smokehouses, railroad bridges, county bridges, rafts, inverted skiffs and driftwood by the acre are rushing past, from all of which imploring hands were held out to those on the banks willing but impotent to help, and the instability of tracks east of this place renders the only information to be got of a fugitive nature, but for the most part very accurate.

At Lockport, two miles east, the conditions for saving the people are more favorable, and more than 20 persons have been taken from the flood.

The First Great Rush of Water

was observed this evening at 7 o'clock, and this came from the burst dam, just above Johnstown. It came like a frenzied whirlpool, and before the people could realize it they were in its grasp. Fortunately, cool heads and resolute hands were on the alert to save, and before any of the people living on the low-lying ground were caught, all were taken out in skiffs and in the arms of gum-booted and coated men to the high ground. Their furniture was also largely saved, so that the loss will fall upon houses alone, and such live stock as was carried out of the stream.

So terrible was the force of the current that the county bridge over the Conemaugh, apparently a most substantial structure, withstood the rush of waters and the battering of logs for a few minutes, but finally it let go and its parts were cast into the river and part of the debris already choked the waters. As early as 7:30 o'clock a great pile of driftwood that the whirl of waters themselves imported into the drift was swept along and from it.

Shriek upon Shriek

for "help, help for God's sake!" came. The horrified spectators on the shore saw three women, to one of whom were clinging two children, neither of whom was apparently more than an infant. The rapidity of the current and the position of the raft together with the lack of facilities for rescuing precluded the possibility of even thinking of the matter, and the raft passed out of sight. The screams of the women and children, blending in their pleadings for aid, were heard long after their craft was around the bend. The stream then became thickly strewn with men, women and children, clinging to all sorts of temporary means of salvation, and two men and a woman clung madly to the tops of huge trees, the men emulating the females in their shrieks for help that it was not possible to give. . . .

DEATH AND DESOLATION.

The Terrible Warning Came Too Late—
Houses Tossed About as Corks on
the Ocean—The Death Rate
Amounting to Thousands

It was stated in the office of the Pennsylvania Railroad, at an early hour this morning, that the deaths would run up into the thousands rather than hundreds, as it was first supposed. From private dispatches received, it is said that the stream of human beings that was swept before the angry floods was something most pitiful to behold. Men, women and children were carried along frantically shrieking for help, but their cries availed them nothing. Rescue was impossible. Husbands were swept past their wives and children were borne rapidly along, going at a terrible speed to certain death before the eyes of their terrorized and frantic parents. It was said at the depot that it was impossible to estimate the number whose lives were lost in the flood. It will simply be a matter of conjecture for several days as to who were lost or who escaped.

Dispatcher Culp received several telegrams last night, detailing the flood. The recent heavy rains had swollen the old canal reservoir at South Fork, on the Conemaugh river, and fears were entertained for its safety.

Warned to No Purpose.

The basin contained water measuring two miles across by five miles in length, and was 70 feet deep in the deepest place. The people of Johnstown were warned of its possibility of bursting during the morning, but very few, if any, of the inhabitants, took the warning seriously. Shortly after noon the dam gave way about five miles above Johnstown, and sweeping everything before it burst upon the town with terrible force. Everything was carried before it, and not an instant's time was given to seek safety. Houses were demolished, swept from their foundations and carried in the flood to a culvert near the town. Here a mass of all manner of debris soon lodged, and by evening it had dammed the water

Back Into the City,

over the tops of many of the still remaining chimneys. A dispatch to Dispatcher Culp, received about 11 o'clock last night, said the blockade at the Johnstown bridge was three-fourths of a mile long and 40 feet high, and was all on fire. The extent of the damage could not possibly be estimated. . . .

1890

The small town girl from Pennsylvania was plucky. In answer to an editorial in *The Pittsburgh Dispatch* titled "What Girls Are Good For," Elizabeth Cochrane penned a caustic reply that caught the attention of the paper's editors. Not long after, they offered her a reporter's job.

As "Nellie Bly," she wrote widely, earning special recognition for investigative stories that exposed conditions in local jails, and sweatshops. Growing restive, Bly left for New York and a reporter's job on the foremost paper of the day, Joseph Pulitzer's *World*. A string of startling first-person accounts earned the 22-year-old Bly the epithet of "sob sister" (a term coined by humorist-journalist Irvin S. Cobb to denote a female writer who put reporting the news secondary to her emotionally charged telling of the story).

Well-established, on November 14, 1889, Bly set off on her greatest feat: She began a trip around the world challenging the record set by Jules Verne's fictional hero, Phileas Fogg, in *Around the World in Eighty Days*. As Bly made her way easterly, her breathless adventures ran in the *World*. Upon her arrival back on the east coast, 72 days, 6 hours, 10 minutes and 11 seconds after her departure, Bly was wildly welcomed home by New Yorkers with a parade down Broadway. Her concluding account of the journey appeared in the *World* on January 26, 1890.

"FROM JERSEY BACK TO JERSEY."

Nellie Bly's Account of
Her Meteoric Rush
Around the Globe

. . .M. Jules Verne said it could not be done. I have done it. He told me when he met me at Amiens [France] that if the tour was made of the world in seventy-nine days he would applaud with both hands. It has been made in seventy-two days, and M. Verne may now applaud and two hands will not do; he must use four. It was only sixty-eight days from the time I left American soil until I touched it again. During that time I was in many different climes. But only here, in God's own country, have I passed amid fruit and flowers in valley, and over mountain-tops amid snow and frost, all within the space of sixteen hours. In no country save America is the passage from orange groves to snow-crested mountains possible in the same space of time.

I have roasted and I have frozen since leaving home. I have dined on India curry, on Chinese chow and Japanese eel and rice. I have travelled on French and English trains, on French and English boats, on burros, in jin-rickshas, in bullock carts, in catamarans, sampans, gherrys and half a dozen other conveyances peculiar to Eastern countries in my trip around the world.

Everybody knows that the idea was to make a tour of the world in seventy-five days. At many junctures since my departure have I been compelled to face what looked like failure. Did I ever give up hope of success? No, not exactly. Never having failed, I could not picture what failure meant, but I did tell the officers of the Oceanic, when success seemed very, very hazy, owing to the unexpectedly stormy weather, that I would rather go to New York successful and dead than alive and behind time.

When the whistle blew and the steamer Victoria moved off the dock, then for the first time I regretted that I was leaving America. I have already told the story of my trip across the Atlantic. . . .

Miss Jusson, a niece of Carl Schurz, was the only lady besides myself travelling alone. She was going to Germany to her father. There were many bets made on the boat as to whether I would arrive in Southampton in time to catch the India Mail. I took all that were offered me. When we failed to arrive at Southampton at the time the steamer was due I felt a little nervous, but still trusted to my never-failing luck. . . .

NEARLY MISSED THE BOAT TO INDIA.

Then we thought of the ship. "The man said we had but a moment," I cried breathlessly to the guard. I might possibly have missed my ship.

"Come," was all he said as his face paled and we started out of the door and down the narrow, dark street.

"Can you run?" he asked, quietly, and I, feeling the anxiety in his tones, felt myself tremble. "Come, I would not have you lose this boat for £50," he cried, and taking my hand without further words we tore madly through the dark streets and along the water's edge.

A whistle blew!

All power seemed to leave me. We stopped in the middle of the street and looked blankly and hopelessly into each other's faces.

"My boat!" I gasped, while my heart ceased beating. And again we started in a mad race which brought me by a sudden curve breathless at the foot of the plank. I uttered a prayer of thanks when I saw the Victoria still there. The boat bound for Bombay was gone, but I was saved.

SAFE ON BOARD.

I hurried up the gang-plank, leaving the guard to bargain with the vendors of chairs on shore, but I would not stay on land another second. I got my chair, testified my thanks to the guard, and went to bed tired but happy. . . .

AN OFFER OF MARRIAGE.

There was a good deal of curiosity on the Victoria as to who and what I was and what my object was in travelling alone. In a few days some one told me confidentially that it was passed around on board that I was an eccentric American heiress travelling about with a hairbrush and a bankbook. The men on board were very attentive on account of my wealth. One young man whose father boasted of a title, but who is a second son, asked me if I would marry him, and asked me also what I would do with him if I

The star of the first color cartoon strip, Richard F. Outcault's "Down Hogan's Alley," published by the New York World, *February 16, 1896, was The Yellow Kid, who lent his name to the term "yellow journalism."* The Library of Congress, Washington, D.C.

did. I told him I would put him to work, which had rather a dampening effect. When this ceased to be funny I told a man in confidence that instead of being an American heiress I was, in short, a beggar, that my health being bad a few benevolent societies had raised enough money to send me on a long trip, hoping that I would benefit by it. This news he spread about the boat and for several days I was left in peace, while the young men stayed away and regretted that they had spent so much time on a penniless American girl. Making a few pleasant and congenial acquaintances on the boat, I told them of the object of my trip, and it was not long until everybody on the boat knew where I was going and what I was going to do. . . .

ACROSS THE PACIFIC

The trip across the Pacific was very tempestuous. In the first three days we were 110 miles ahead of the Oceanic's last record when she broke the record; but all this and more were lost when we struck the head-winds, which stayed with us the greater part of five days. I cannot say more of the crew than that they were perfect, from the captain down. They did everything for the comfort of the passengers, and strange to say, with all the rough weather, only one or two suffered from seasickness. I could not have felt more grieved over getting into San Francisco one day later than they had expected than did the officers in charge of the Oceanic. How I landed in San Francisco and took THE WORLD'S special train at 9 A.M. Jan. 21, and was whirled across the continent, greeted with kindness and hearty welcomes at every point, has already been told in THE WORLD. NELLIE BLY

1898

With lurid illustrations and even more frenzied headlines, William Randolph Hearst fueled public opinion in the United States against Spanish rule in Cuba. Hardly a broker in truth, Hearst's *New York Journal* screamed of Spanish atrocities perpetuated upon the freedom-loving Cuban peoples. Most Americans remained indifferent. Then the United States battleship *Maine* mysteriously blew up in Havana harbor on February 15, 1898, with the loss of 260 lives. Hearst promised his editors, "This means war." Disregarding evidence to the contrary, the paper's account of February 16, 1898, indicated that the Spanish were to blame for the explosion.

CRISIS IS AT HAND

253 Known to Be Lost

Cabinet in Session

Growing Belief in Spanish Treachery

Maine Destroyed by an Outside Attack, Naval Officers Believe.

Censored Dispatches from Havana Say a Shot Was Heard Before the Ship's Magazines Blew Up.

Washington. Feb. 16.—The President hurriedly called a special meeting of the Cabinet at 11:30 a.m.

While the Cabinet was in session the following cable dispatch from Captain [Charles D.] Sigsbee was handed to the President.

"Advise sending wrecking vessel at once. The Maine is submerged dneep [sic] debris. It is mostly work for divers now. Jenkins and Meritt still missing. There is little hope for their safety. Those known to be saved are: Officers, twenty four; uninjured crew, eighteen. The wounded now aboard steamer, city hospital and at Mascotte Hotel number fifty-nine as far as known.

The destruction of the battle ship Maine aroused great anger and suspicion, as revealed by the front page of the New York Journal.

"All others down on board or near the Maine. Total loss of missing 253. With several exceptions no officer nor man has more than part of a suit of clothing, and that wet with harbor water.

"Ward steamer leaves for Mexico at 2 o'clock this afternoon. Officers saved are uninjured.

"Damage was in compartment of crew. Am preparing to telegraph list of wounded and saved.

"Olivette leaves for Key West at 1 p.m. Will send by her to Key West officers saved except myself, Wainwright, Holman, Heneberger, Ray and Holden. Will turn over three uninjured boats to captain of the port with request for safekeeping. Will send all wounded men to hospital at Havana."

After the Cabinet had been in session an hour and a half Long [John D. Long, Secretary of the Navy] sent this reply:

"Sigsbee, U.S.S. Maine, Havana: The President directs me to express for him and for the people of the United States his profound sympathy with the officers and crew of the Maine, and desires that no expense be spared in providing for the survivors and in caring for the dead."

Secretary Long also announced that an unsigned dispatch from Havana reported the number of dead at 275.

Vice President [Garrett] Hobart was in the Senate chamber at noon when he received a message from the President calling him at once to the White House.

The President and members of the Cabinet were still in conference but the Vice President was at once admitted.

A dispatch was received from General Lee [Fitzhugh Lee, Consul General of Havana], this afternoon, saying "All Quiet. Great Sorrow expressed by authorities. Sigsbee has telegraphed details to Navy Department. Not yet prepared to report cause of explosion."

Public opinion in Washington is rapidly changing. It is now believed that the destruction of the Maine could not have been due to an accident. There is a strong belief in Spanish treachery.

General Blanco has cabled Senor Du Bosc, the Cuban Charge d' Affairs, that a dynamo boiler on the Maine blew up, causing the explosion of the magazine.

Admiral Sicard, of the North Atlantic squadron, will be communicated with at once respecting the sending of another battle ship to Havana.

The lighthouse tenders Fern and Mangrove have arrived at Havana. The coast survey steamer Bache has been ordered there from Key West.

The torpedo boat Ericsson has been dispatched from Key West with orders to Rear Admiral Sicard at the Bay Tortugas.

RUMORS OF DYNAMITE.

Vague rumors reached New York at noon to-day, that the Maine had been blown up by the bumping of a small boat filled with dynamite or other high explosive against the battleship's bows.

The press censorship at Havana had suppressed all but the most meagre news.

Newspapers and private corporations having Cuban interests have made every effort to get dispatches through in plausible cipher.

From a complicated dispatch received by the president of a coast-wise steamship company at noon to-day, the news of a dynamite plot to destroy the Maine was deciphered.

This was the last time the *Journal* would handle the story with any restraint. At "The Chief's" direction, the *Journal* day after day exploited the tragedy, blaming Spain, and selling ever more papers.

Within two months, the United States would be at war, its war cry "Remember the Maine!," yet to this day, the exact cause of the ship's destruction remains uncertain.

1898

It was a most modest debut, staged on the night of March 6, 1898, lest failure attract too much attention. Certainly only the most optimistic or foolish would have shared garage tinkerer Charles B. King's opinion that this coughing, lurching machine "will in time supersede the horse."

The editors of *The Detroit Free Press* tucked a small notice in the paper on the following day to report the appearance of the first automobile on the streets of what would become The Motor City— and got King's initials wrong.

A HORSELESS CARRIAGE

Traveled up and down Woodward Avenue Last Evening.

The first horseless carriage seen in this city was out on the streets last night. It is an invention of S.B. King, a Detroiter, and its progress up and down Woodward Avenue about 11 o'clock caused a deal of comment, people crowding around it so that its progress was impeded. The apparatus seemed to work all right, and went at the rate of five or six miles an hour at an even rate of speed.

1898

For all his foibles, his willingness to sensationalize the news and to pander to the lowest common denominator, William Randolph Hearst could be a surprisingly good newspaperman. Nowhere is this more clear than in the one story to which he put his own by-line in a career that spanned more than six decades. Fill-ing in for his wounded star reporter, James Creelman, editor and publisher Hearst delivered an eye-witness account of the decisive battle of the war he had helped to start. Hearst's story from the Cuban battlefield was published in *The New York Evening Journal* and *San Francisco Examiner* on July 4, 1898.

THE BATTLE OF CANEY—BY W.R. HEARST

The Editor of the Journal Describes the Great Struggle as He Saw It on the Battlefield.

James Creelman, Journal Correspondent, in the Lead of the Awful Charge, Wounded but Captures a Spanish Flag.

Copyright, 1898, by W.R. Hearst
Special Cable to the Evening Journal

With the Army in front of Santiago, July 1, midnight, via Kingston, Jamaica, July 3—To-night, as I write this, the ambulance trains are bringing in the wounded soldiers from the fierce battle around the little inland village of Caney.

Siboney, the base of the army, is a hospital and nothing more. There is no saying when the slaughter will cease. The tents are crowded with wounded, and the hard-working surgeons are busy with their mechanical work. There is an odor of anesthetics and the clatter of ambulances in the one narrow street.

Under the fierce firing of far heavier artillery than it was supposed the Spanish had, the American infantry and dismounted cavalry have done their work, and done it nobly.

I have been at the artillery positions all day to see what our guns could do or could not do. There is no question of the skill or courage of American gunners. Their work was as near perfect as gunnery gets to be, but there was no artillery to speak of.

The War Department has furnished the necessary heavy guns, but they remain in the rear, because of the difficulty of transportation from the coast.

I set out before daybreak this morning on horseback with Honore Laine, who is a colonel in the Cuban Army, and has served for months as the Journal's correspondent to Cuba. We rode over eight miles of difficult country which intervenes between the army base on the coast and the fighting line which is being driven forward toward Santiago.

We arrived at the front on the ridge of Poso, where our batteries were assisting the advance on the line of Santiago's defences.

Poso, as a position for our battery, was ill chosen. The Spaniards had formerly occupied it as a fort, and they knew precisely the distance to it from their guns, and so began their fight with the advantage of a perfect knowledge of range.

Their first shell spattered shrapnel in a very unpleasant way all over the tile roof of the white house at the back of the ridge. It was the doors of this house which we were approaching for shelter, and later, when we came to take our luncheon, we found that a shrapnel ball had passed clean through one of our cans of pressed beef, which our pack mule was carrying. . . .

Heroic Charge to the Hill Fort

Through glasses our infantry could be seen advancing toward this fort. As the cannon at our side would bang and the shell would swish through the air with its querulous, vicious, whining note, we would watch its explosion and then turn our attention to the little black specks of infantry dodging in and out between the groups of trees. Now they would disappear wholly from sight in the brush, and again would be seen hurrying along the open spaces, over the grass-covered slopes or across ploughed fields. The infantry firing was ceaseless, our men popping away continuously, as a string of firecrackers pops. The Spaniards fired in volley whenever our men came in sight in the open spaces.

Many times we heard this volley fire and saw numbers of our brave fellows pitch forward and lie still on the turf while the others hurried on to the next protecting clump of bushes.

For hours the Spaniards had poured their fire from slits in the stone fort, from their deep trenches and from the windows of the town. For hours our men answered back from trees and brush and gulleys. For hours, cannon at our side banged and shells screamed through the air and fall upon fort and town. And always infantry advanced, drawing nearer and closing up on the village, till at last they formed under a group of mangrove trees at the foot of the very hill on which the stone fort stood.

With a rush they swept up the slope and the stone fort was ours.

Then you should have heard the yell that went up from the knoll on which our battery stood. Gunners, drivers, Cubans, correspondents, swung their hats and gave a mighty cheer. Immediately our battery stopped fire for fear we would hurt our own men, and dashing down into the valley hurried across to take up a position near the infantry, who were now firing on Caney from the blockhouse and entering the streets of the town.

The artillery had not sent half a dozen shots from its new position before the musketry firing ceased, and the Spaniards, broken into small bunches, fled from Caney in the direction of Santiago.

Laine and I hurried up the stone fort and found that James Creelman, the

Journal correspondent with the infantry column, had been seriously wounded and was lying in the Twelfth Infantry hospital. . . .

When I left the fort to hunt for Creelman I found him, bloody and bandaged, lying on his back on a blanket on the ground, but shown all care that kindly and skillful surgeons could give him. His first words to me were that he was afraid he could not write much of the story, as he was pretty well dazed, but if I could write for him he would dictate the best he could. I sat down among the wounded and Creelman told me his story of the fight. Here it is:

"The extraordinary thing in this fight of all fights I have seen is the enormous amount of ammunition fired. There is a continuous roar of musketry from 4 o'clock morning until 4 o'clock afternoon. . . .

"The Spaniards fired from loopholes in the stone houses of the town, and furthermore, were massed in trenches on the east side of the fort. They fought like demons.

"From all the ridges around about a stream of fire was kept up on Chaffee's men, who were kept wondering how they were being wounded. For a time they thought General Ludlow's men were on the opposite side of the fort and were firing over it.

"The fact was the fire came from heavy breastworks on the northwest corner of Caney, where the principal Spanish force lay, with their hats on sticks to deceive our riflemen. From this position the enemy poured in a fearful fire. The Seventeenth had to lie down flat under the pounding, but even then men were killed.

"General Chaffee dashed about with his hat on the back of his head like a magnificent cowboy, urging his men on, crying to them to get in and help their country win a victory.

"Smokeless powder makes it impossible to locate the enemy. You wonder where the fire comes from. When you stand up to see you get a bullet.

"We finally located the trenches and could see the officers moving about, urging their men. But one by one their heads went up, while their faces disappeared behind the breastworks. The enemy was making a turning movement to the right.

"To turn the left of the Spanish position it was necessary to get a block house, which held the right of our line. Gen. Chaffee detailed Captain Clarke to approach and occupy this blockhouse as soon as the artillery had sufficiently harried its Spanish defenders.

"Clarke and Captain Haskell started up the slope. I told them I had been on the ridge and knew the condition of affairs, so I would show them the way.

"We pushed right up to the trench around the fort, and getting out our wire cutters, severed the barbed wire in front of it. I jumped over the several strands and got into the trench.

"It was a horrible, blood-splashed thing, and an inferno of agony. Many men lay dead, with gleaming teeth and hands clutching their throats. Others were crawling their [sic] alive.

"I shouted to the survivors to surrender and they held up their hands.

"Then I ran into a fort and found there a Spanish officer and four men alive, while seven lay dead in the room. The whole floor ran with blood. Blood splashed all the walls. It was a perfect hog pen of butchery.

"Three poor wretches put their hands together in supplication. One had a white handkerchief tied on a stick. This he lifted and moved it toward me. The officer held up his hands, while the others began to pray and plead.

"I took the guns from all and threw them outside the fort. Then I called some of our men and put them in charge of the prisoners.

"I then got out of the fort, ran around to the other side and secured the Spanish flag. I displayed it to our troops and they cheered lustily.

"Just as I turned to speak to Captain Haskell I was struck by a bullet from the trenches on the Spanish side."

Such was the graphic story Creelman told as he lay wounded and in pain. . . .

The Spanish flag captured from the Spanish stone fort, I will forward to the Journal by mail.

1900

The history of the American railroad is bespattered with disaster. Wrecks, maimings and, what railroaders called "cornfield meets," derailings, were almost daily occurrences. Yet no accident has been so long remembered as the wreck of the Illinois Central's No. 1 north of Canton, Mississippi, on April 30, 1900. An enginehouse wiper in Vaughan, Wallis Sanders, wrote a song about the wreck and the death of his friend, engineer Luther Jones; that song celebrates the heroism of the man known up and down the line as "Casey" Jones. This was the coverage by *The Jackson* [Mississippi] *Daily Clarion-Ledger* on the afternoon of April 30, 1900, of the most famous of American train wrecks.

A DISASTROUS WRECK ON THE ILLINOIS CENTRAL.

No. 1, the Limited Passenger, Crashes Into a Freight at Vaughan's Station.

Engineer Jones Was Killed.

No. 1, the south-bound limited over the Illinois Central, due in this city at 4:50 o'clock, met with a disastrous wreck at Vaughan's Station, several miles above Canton, about daylight, resulting in the death of one man and the serious injury of two others.

The train was coming into Vaughan's Station a few minutes behind time and was running at a fair rate of speed. On the switch at Vaughan's four freight trains had been sidetracked, and as the switch was not long enough to accommodate the line of freights it was necessary to "see saw" them up and down the track in order to allow the passenger train to get through.

A flagman was started down the main line to signal the engineer on the passenger train, but in some way the engineer failed to catch the signals and did not attempt to bring the train to a stop until several torpedoes that had been placed on the rails were exploded. It was then too late to stop his train and the engine crashed squarely into the end of the caboose of the rear freight. The engine toppled over on one side of the track and the mail and baggage cars were derailed, falling on the other side. Engineer Casey Jones, one of the best known employees of the road, was instantly killed and the fireman who jumped from his cab when the crash came, escaped with several severe bruises. Baggageman Will Miller had two ribs broken and received severe internal injuries.

A panic was created in the coaches when the crash came and several of the passengers were roughly shaken up and all of them badly frightened. Some of the occupants of the sleeping cars were thrown from their berths and several women fainted.

Added to this confusion, two of the freight cars in front of the wreck, laden with hay and grain, caught afire and were extinguished only after considerably difficulty. It appeared for an hour or more that the entire train would be burned.

A wrecking train was sent for and the work of clearing up the track commenced about two hours later. Nearly one hundred yards of track had been torn up by the collision and all trains on the road are delayed for several hours, but the officials say that they will have the usual schedule in operation in time for the night trains. The passengers on the wrecked train were transferred to a local train made up at Canton and run through to New Orleans.

1903

For a half century dreamers and schemers alike had planned to build a canal across the fetid isthmus of Panama, a neglected province of the sovereign nation of Colombia. A French company had gone bankrupt in its effort to build the canal, leaving the way open for President Theodore Roosevelt. The President's ambition stumbled over the refusal of the Colombian government to sell a six-mile-wide canal zone to the United States for an offered $10,000,000.

On October 9 Roosevelt met with a French freebooter who offered to foment a revolution in Panama and set up a friendly government in the ad hoc nation. Philippe Bunau-Varilla asked for a little help: Once he and his cohorts had proclaimed the revolution, United States naval vessels would prevent the Colombian government from landing troops and suppressing the rebellion.

Roosevelt delightedly agreed. Ostensibly, the navy would be on station "to protect American interests and the lives of American citizens if a revolutionary outbreak should occur." Virtually the first act of the new nation of Panama would be to sign a canal treaty with the United States. A week later, the fleet sailed for Panama. On November 4, 1903, *The Washington Post* reported:

REVOLUTION

Independence of the Isthmus of Panama Proclaimed.

United States Ships Sent

Officers of Colombian Army Made Prisoners.

Government to be Formed

State Department Advices Say that Similar Uprising Is Expected in Colon—Conferences Hurriedly Called at the White House—Great Activity at the Navy Department— Official Statement Issued to the Effect that Vessels Have Been Sent to Endeavor to Keep Transit Open and Maintain Order Along the Line of the Railroad.

Panama, Colombia, Nov. 3—The independence of the isthmus was proclaimed at 6 p.m. to-day. A large and enthusiastic crowd of all political parties assembled and marched to the headquarters of the government troops where Gens. Tovar and Amaya, who arrived this morning, were imprisoned in the name of the republic of Panama. The enthusiasm was intense, and at least 3,000 of the men in the gathering were armed.

The battalion of Colombian troops at Panama favors the movement, which is also thought to meet with the approval of at least two of the government transports now here.

The following cablegram was received at the State Department at 10 o'clock last night from the United States consul at Panama:

"An uprising took place at Panama tonight. Independence was proclaimed. The Colombian army and navy officials were made prisoners. A government was to be organized consisting of three consuls and a cabinet. It was rumored at Panama that a similar uprising was to take place in Colon."

The following cablegram has been received at the State Department from United States Consul Malmros at Colon:

"There is every appearance of a revolution here."

An Official Statement

Later the following official statement was made regarding the news from Panama:

"A number of confused and conflicting dispatches have been received from the isthmus indicating rather serious disturbances a both Panama and Colon. The Navy Department has dispatched several vessels to these ports, with directions to do everything possible to keep transit open and maintain order along the line of the railroad."

The sensational advices from the isthmus were not entirely unexpected in view of other advices that had come to the department very recently. The reception of the news caused a sudden outburst of activity at the Navy Department, and at once on President Roosevelt's return he was made acquainted with the situation. Secretary [John] Hay, Assistant Secretary Darling,* Assistant Secretary [Francis B.] Loomis, and a number of others were summoned to the White House hastily and measures were taken at once for protection of American interests at the isthmus. . . .

Canal Believed to be the Cause

The White House conference broke up at about 11 o'clock, but not much beyond the official telegrams received and orders given would be stated by those participating in it. There is a very general belief that the rejection of the Panama canal treaty by Colombia caused the people of the Isthmus to decide to set up a government of their own, but none of the officials of the administration would authorize any statements to the effect that this was the case.

The statement was authorized that the sole purpose of the dispatch of the vessels was the protection of American interests and the maintenance of open transit on the isthmus. The most explicit instructions were cabled last night.

---

*Not listed in official register. This may be a reporter's error.

1903

Now, when as many as 1,000 newsmen and women will cover a space launch, it is difficult to believe that there was nary a reporter on hand to recount man's first powered flight over the sand dunes of Kitty Hawk, North Carolina, on December 17, 1903. The local paper, the *Norfolk Virginian-Pilot,* apparently learned from Coast Guardsmen at a nearby life-saving station of the achievement of the small group of mechanics headed by the two brothers from Dayton, Ohio. The unattributed story, which appeared in the December 18 issue, was based on accounts by the Coast Guardsmen.

FLYING MACHINE SOARS THREE MILES IN TEETH OF HIGH WIND OVER SAND HILLS AND WAVES AT KITTY HAWK ON CAROLINA COAST

No Balloon Attached to Aid it

Three Years of Hard, Secret Work By Two Ohio Brothers Crowned With Success

Accomplished What Langley Failed At

With Man As Passenger Huge Machine Flew Like Bird Under Perfect Control

Box Kite Principle With Two Propellers

The problem of aerial navigation without the use of a balloon has been solved at last.

Over the sand hills of the North Carolina coast yesterday, near Kittyhawk, two Ohio men proved that they could soar through the air in a flying machine of their own construction, with the power to steer and speed it at will.

This, too, in the face of a wind blowing at the registered velocity of twenty-one miles an hour.

Like a monster bird, the invention hovered above the breakers and circled over the rolling sand hills at the command of its navigator and, after soaring for three miles, it gracefully descended to earth again, and rested lightly upon the spot selected by the man in the car as a suitable landing place.

While the United States government has been spending thousands of dollars in an effort to make practicable the ideas of Professor Langley, of the Smithsonian Institute, Wilbur and Orville Wright, two brothers, natives of Dayton, Ohio, have, quietly, even secretly, perfected their invention and put it to a successful test.

They are not yet ready that the world should know the methods they have adopted in conquering the air, but the Virginian-Pilot is about to state authentically the nature of their invention, its principles and its chief dimensions.

The idea of the box kite has been adhered to strictly in the basic formation of the flying machine.

A huge framework of light timbers, thirty-three feet wide, five feet deep, and five feet across the top, forms the machine proper.

This is covered with a tough, but light, canvas.

In the center, and suspended just below the bottom plane, is the small gasoline engine which furnished the motive power for the propelling and elevating wheels.

These are two six-bladed propellers, one arranged just below the center of the frame, so gauged as to exert an upward force when in motion, and the other extends horizontally to the rear from the center of the car, furnishing the forward impetus.

Protruding from the center of the car is a huge, fan-shaped rudder of canvas, stretched upon a frame of wood. This rudder is controlled by a navigator and may be moved to each side, raised, or lowered.

Wilbur Wright, the chief inventor of the machine, sat in the operator's car, and when all was ready his brother unfastened the catch which held the invention at the top of the slope.

The big box began to move slowly at first, acquiring velocity as it went and when halfway down the hundred feet the engine was started.

The propeller in the rear immediately began to revolve at a high rate of speed, and when the end of the incline was reached the machine shot out into space without a perceptible fall.

By this time the elevating propeller was also in motion, and keeping its altitude, the machine slowly began to go higher and higher until it finally soared sixty feet above the ground.

Maintaining this height by the action of the under wheel, the navigator increased the revolutions of the rear propeller, and the forward speed of the huge affair increased until a velocity of eight miles was attained.

All this time the machine headed into a twenty-one-mile wind.

The little crowd of fisherfolk and coast guards, who have been watching the construction of the machine with unconcealed curiosity since September, were amazed.

They endeavored to race over the sand and keep up with the thing in the air, but it soon distanced them and continued its flight alone, save the man in the car.

Steadily it pursued its way, first tacking to port, then to starboard, then driving straight ahead.

"It is a success," declared Orville Wright to the crowd on the beach after the first mile had been covered.

But the inventor waited. Not until he had accomplished three miles, putting the machine through all sorts of maneuvers en route, was he satisfied.

Then he selected a suitable place to land and, gracefully circling, drew his invention slowly to the earth, where it settled, like some big bird, in the chosen spot.

"Eureka!" he cried, as did the alchemists of old.

The success of the Wright brothers in their invention is the result of three years of hard work. Experiment after experiment has been made and failure resulted, but each experiment had its lesson, and finally, when the two reappeared at Kittyhawk last fall, they felt more confident than ever.

The spot selected for the building and perfecting of the machine is one of the most desolate upon the Atlantic seaboard. Just on the southern extremity of that coast stretch known as the graveyard of American shipping, cut off from civilization by a wide expanse of sound water and seldom in touch with the outer world save when a steamer once or twice a week touches at the little wharf to take and leave government mail, no better place could scarcely have been selected to maintain secrecy.

And this is where the failures have grown into success.

The machine which made yesterday's flight easily carried the weight of a man of 150 pounds, and is nothing like so large as the ill-fated *Buzzard* of Potomac River fame.

It is said the Wright brothers intend constructing a much larger machine, but before this they will go back to their homes for the holidays.

Wilbur Wright, the inventor, is a well-groomed man of prepossessing appearance. He is about five feet, six inches tall, weighs about 150 pounds, and is of swarthy complexion. His hair is raven-hued and straight, but a piercing pair of deep-blue eyes peer at you over a nose of extreme length and sharpness.

His brother, Orville, on the other hand, is a blond, with sandy hair and fair complexion, even features, and sparkling black eyes. He is not quite as large as Wilbur, but is of magnificent physique.

The pair have spent almost the entire fall and winter and early spring months of the past three years at Kittyhawk, working upon their invention, leaving when the weather began to grow warm and returning in the early fall to work.

Their last appearance was on September 1, and since then they have been actively engaged upon the construction of the machine which made yesterday's successful flight.

1903

Fires, accidents, disasters of any kind are the great dramatic events of daily journalism, made all the more horrific by their very suddenness. One moment the capacity audience is listening to the double octet singing "Pearly Moonlight." The next, 2,000 are frantically clawing their way to the exits as flames sparked by a broken floodlight burst from the proscenium arch.

The exact death toll at Chicago's Iroquois Theatre on the night of December 30, 1903, will never be accurately known. The city's papers reported more than 500 dead in the wake of the fire. Reference books place the dead variously at 578

and 602. Whatever the count, the Iroquois remains the worst single-structure
fire in American history. In the moralis-
tic, overwrought prose that the 20th Century would eventually sweep aside, the
Chicago *Inter-Ocean* of December 31,
1903, groped to report the tragedy.

HALF A THOUSAND PERISH IN MAD PANIC AT IROQUOIS THEATRE; HUNDREDS INJURED

*Pleasure Seekers, Mostly Women and Children,
Pursued by a Wave of Flame, Struggle Desperately
to Escape from Blazing Playhouse and are Burned
to Death During Terrible Rush for Life*

*Bodies Piled High in Aisles and Exits—Terrified
Women Hurl Themselves from Galleries—Awful
Scenes in Improvised Morgue When Loved Ones
Are Recognized by Relatives and Friends*

By Stanley Waterloo.

Horrors sometimes occur the character of which may not be adequately
described. The quality of the English, or any other language, does not suffice for all the dreadful shadings.

Such an awful happening was that of yesterday afternoon, when the new
and beautiful Iroquois theatre was destroyed, and hundreds of joyous people—men, women and children—were crushed to death, or suffocated, or
consumed by fire.

The police said at midnight that 523 persons were killed.

That tells the story of the awful disaster.

There was a great matinee audience at the theatre, the newest and one of
the finest in Chicago. They were enjoying themselves to the utmost when
death, with unexampled horror, came upon them.

Never came death more suddenly! There was a flash at the stage's front,
scenery in flames, the failure of the falling to its full extent of a fireproof
asbestos curtain, a fierce lap of flame drawn across the face of the theatre
by the draft of the suddenly opened exits, and then such horrors as may not
be all related.

No Escape for Those in Front

For those in the front seats there was no escape and for those farther back
the chances were scarcely better. All, from parquet to gallery, were envel-

oped in a mad rush toward the exits and were swept with it to escape or to death.

It was a wave backward of human beings fighting for the blessing of life. What heroism was shown of man for woman or of woman for children will never be known, for the tragedy was but of minutes.

There was the sweep, the crush, the weak falling and the strong mounting, the inevitable desperate instant which accompanies the grim law of self-preservation; then the horror of flaming death behind crashing death before; then the still outreaching flames, and, finally, a mass of piled-up humanity, a few of the living above and the dead far below. . . .

From the balcony and galleries, where there was no more safety from the flame heat ascending than on the floor below, people hurled themselves downward in their terror. All, or nearly all, of those in the rear met a fearful death. Firemen, the fire practically extinguished, found they were but pouring water on heaps of human beings.

What scenes were found within the heated vault which had been a theater very few of the firemen or policemen who first entered could explain intelligently. Some of them cried and some who did not cry could not talk of anything well. They knew only that they had found the passages to the theatre clogged in front, and upstairs and down, by bodies.

Restaurant Turned Into Morgue

There was no time for conventions. A big restaurant next door became a morgue. The bodies were placed on tables, and later on the floor. At first they came one and one, then by two and two, then by scores.

Horror reigned—literally—among policemen and firemen, but a square was made about the place of death, the wild sightseers were kept back, and the work went on—merely the removing of the dead and wounded from one building to another—but what dead and wounded and what moving!

Soon the restaurant was full, and then, since time had been consumed, came the influx of succoring doctors. The living were laid on the tables and the dead beneath them.

By this time had come the relieving forces. And as the dead were carried out happened before my eyes what I may never see again. I had gone inside and looked on the dead and dying. The former had been selected by the earnest young physicians who came from the adjacent university by scores, and had been laid carefully beneath the tables. It mattered not whether any of these dead were delicate young women or old men or children just old enough to appreciate their first theatrical performance.

The physicians worked on those in whom the breath of life might possibly be preserved. It was a good thing for those who survived that, just to the north of them, lay one of the greatest universities for young physicians, enthusiastic, earnest, and reckless, who could take risks and do things. They themselves saved some of those in peril in the burning theatre. They saved the lives of others by their swift and strenuous attendance.

I stood by the doorway and I saw them carried out. I had seen them within before. I had noted the scene outside after the bodies had been arranged.

Shrieks When Loved Ones Are Found

They lay on the tables of the restaurant, the long rows of the dead, all covered decently and silent, but among and around them was no silence. There would be a lifting of the impromptu shrouds and then either a groan or a shriek as seekers found their own, until the cries of agony seemed blended. I have looked on many ghastly scenes. I was in the midst of the horrors of the greatest of railroad disasters—that at Chatsworth—and I witnessed the burning of the Southern hotel in St. Louis, but I had never witnessed such a scene as this. There was an orderliness to it all that made it more ghastly. It had all occurred so suddenly, in the season of the holidays, in a great city. The happy and the prosperous had gathered to enjoy themselves, and there, all at once, had gone out the call: Come look upon your dead. We have them laid in rows here." . . .

Asbestos Curtain Failed to Work

The failure of the asbestos drop curtain was the cause of the terrible loss of life. Had it worked, or had it been lowered, the flames would have been confined to the stage.

Why the asbestos curtain was not lowered, there seems to be no rational explanation. Some say it was lowered. Others say that it failed to work entirely. And still others claim that it reached within six or seven feet of the stage, and that the frantic efforts of the stage hands to drag it down failed.

In the excitement it must have been forgotten entirely. The frantic rush to safety drove every idea out of the minds of all within the theatre and on the stage except that of personal safety. In the mad dash it was every one for himself. The torn, bleeding, bruised, and blackened corpses bore silent testimony to the terrible conflict that must have been waged for a few minutes within the playhouse.

Solid Sheet of Fire

The construction of the theatre is such that the space between the balcony and gallery seats and the stage is less than fifty feet. With the flimsy scenery of "Mr. Blue Beard" in flames the draft from the stage to the many exits drew a solid sheet of fire on the fleeing spectators. To those in the front rows death was absolutely certain. As the exits became choked and the unfortunate victims were piled up ten and twelve deep, they formed an impregnable wall. With the flames lapping them from behind and the seething, fighting mass choking the doorways, they were overcome.

How these poor unfortunates fought to escape their terrible lacerated and scorched bodies showed after the fire.

Story of the Holocaust
Given in Graphic Words

The theatre was almost in darkness in the second act. The stage was lighted only by the soft artificial beams from the calcium [light], which lent beauty to the scene during the singing of "The Pale Moonlight" by the double sextet.

A flash of flame shot across through the flimsy draperies, started by a spark from the calcium. A show girl screamed hysterically. The singers stopped short, but with presence of mind the director increased the volume of the music. . . .

Eddie Foy rushed from the wings to the footlights, but his words of re-assurance were in vain. Clouds of smoke poured from the stage into the auditorium, enveloping the struggling mass of panic-stricken men, women, and children.

Behind the scenes all was confusion. It required but a moment to perceive that the fire had gone too far to be conquered by the amateur fire brigade formed by the stage hands. . . .

The first seconds of the rush for life were quiet, say those who live to tell the tale. Few if any in that throng realized what was to come. They thought only of themselves and their dear ones as they pushed and struggled for every inch as they advanced toward the exits.

It was but a moment until the stairways leading from the balcony were a mass of struggling humanity, with scores behind constantly pushing closer and fighting to get out. Those in the van, unable to keep their footing, fell headlong. Those behind fell over their prostrate forms, crushing and suffocating them.

The scene was then a veritable bedlam. Women and children were in the majority in the fighting crowd, and their shrieks of agonizing fear mingled with the groans of the dying and the prayers of supplication. In those dark moments poor souls who had perhaps long unheeded religion called upon their God.

Mothers Plead for Babes

Women seized their babes in their arms and frantically clung to them, beseeching ears that were deaf to entreaty to save them from the terrible fate impending. Had the others been so disposed they could not have given the assistance so piteously besought.

In the last hope, born of desperation, scores climbed to the railing and leaned to the pit of the theatre, many feet below. Their mangled bodies were found long afterward when the smoke had cleared away and the firemen could grope their way with lanterns into the grewsome house of death.

The dense smoke quickly rose to the top and added new horror to the ghastly spectacle. To a score of those who had sought to jump from the gallery the smoke was kind, for it brought death more quickly. Their bodies were found hanging over the rail, their faces distorted with agonies of death. . . .

Rush from Orchestra Seats

The great majority of those who had occupied orchestra seats had escaped with their lives, though scores were badly hurt in the rush. Some were knocked down, and, with broken limbs, were unable to rise. They had been left to die with a number of women who fainted from fright. With these bodies were found the corpses of those who had leaped from the balcony and gallery.

In the exits of the balcony and galleries the greatest loss of life occurred. When the firemen went to remove the bodies they found 100 or more piled in indescribable mass in each place. The clothes were torn completely away from some of the bodies. Here and there a jeweled hand protruded from the pile. All the faces were distorted with the death agonies.

Moan from Heap of Dead

From beneath this mangled mass of humanity there suddenly came the moan of a woman. It was a cry of anguish, not of pain. The cry, faint though it was, pierced to the very soul, sounding above the yells of the firemen, the moans of agony from within the smoke-filled auditorium and the shrieks of grief maddened fathers and mothers, sisters and brothers in the street without.

Trembling hands plunged their way into the tangle of human forms, and with a mighty effort pulled to the surface the woman—could such a thing be a human being?—from whose lips had come the cry. The blackened lips parted, and a fireman bent over her to catch the words.

Mother Love is Uppermost

"My child, my poor little boy! Where is he? Oh, do bring him to me."

There in that awful hour, her body bruised beyond recognition in the mad fight for life that followed the first flash of flame across the stage—there was mother love uppermost. Again the trembling lips parted.

"Is he safe? Tell me he is safe and I can die."

"He is safe," the fireman muttered, and all knew his reply was best.

She died, and her body was lifted tenderly with those of the hundred others in that one spot. . . .

1904

It was a stunning accomplishment, the first time in the modern era of the game that a baseball pitcher not only held the opposing team to no hits, but allowed no one to reach base. *The Boston* *Daily Globe* of Friday morning, May 6, 1904, ran its mouth-agape account of Cyrus Denton Young's perfect game against the visiting Philadelphia Athletics on page one.

GREATEST GAME EVER

Young's Feat Unparalleled.

No Quaker Gets As Far As First Base.

Bostons Pound the Mighty "Rube" Waddell Hard.

Game Winds Up With A Score Of 3 To 0.

Only 27 Quakers at Bat.

*Young's Performance Has No Equal
in Baseball History.*

Ten thousand voices, keyed to the highest pitch, went off as if by an electric shock as the last man went out on a fly to "Chick" Stahl, clinching the greatest game ever pitched by mortal man yesterday afternoon at the American grounds, landing Boston a winner over the crack Philadelphia club, 3 to 0.

"Cy" Young, for a score of years the most wonderful slab artist in the business, surpassed all his other achievements, making a new record for pitchers and setting the lovers of the game wild with delight by a phenomenal performance.

It was the treat of a lifetime to see the hard-hitting Athletics, ex-champions of the American league, go down before the masterly performance of the Boston giant. Twenty-seven men walked to the plate, each with his mind bent on reaching that first base, but they returned to the bench in order, each player having three chances and "Rube" Waddell, last on the batting list, closing the game.

Others have shut teams out with no base hits . . . but Young's performance surpassed all, as 27 men went out in order without putting foot on first base. . . .

Both teams were out for the game and advertised Waddell and Young. The crowd was a banner one for the middle of the week, and the day and grounds were ideal for the game—a game that all who attended will long remember and hand down the story of to generations to come; for record breakers come now seldom and are never advertised ahead.

Rube Was Discovered.

"Cy" Young was at his best, having fine speed, good curves and perfect control. He was never forced to shorten his preliminary swing, as there were no bases to watch. Young was out to take the conceit from the "Rube," who had turned the world beaters down twice this season without a run, and the Boston men were confident that the old war horse would land the game.

The eight strikeouts Young had to his account were nothing compared to the work he did when in a hole, after working his man to the limit. When he had to, over went the ball, but with a sharp bend; or at lightning speed, rather close to the man, but over the pan, where umpire Dwyer was doing superb work and giving each man his rights.

Five innings went along without a run for either side, so that Young was forced to keep working. Then with the game practically won, the thought of a shutout for the Quakers was uppermost in the mind of the champions, and finally the vague idea of a no hit game dawned on them—and the crowd, too—until in the last inning came a deathlike silence as each man stood at the plate.

Monte Cross was fanned in fine style. Then came the clever hitter, Schreck, who grounded to Freddy Parent. For a finish appeared at the bat the great Waddell himself. He drove a long fly to Stahl, and, waiting for the catch, the crowd held back. The ball was held by the Boston fielder, and the crowd let itself loose.

Here was a game with not a pass to first by either side, and only one error, made by Davis. Two of the Boston runs were earned, so no blame could be laid to Rube's support.

The Boston boys were not content with doing up the visitors, but they tore the lining out of the Rube's reputation with 10 safe hits. . . . To put it plainly, the Rube was discovered and trimmed for fair.

It Was a Record.

After the game was ended the crowd pressed on the field to look the great Boston pitcher over and congratulate him. One man pressed some money into Young's hands. "Cy" looked it over and handed back one bill. This was a novel sensation for a ball player in a Boston uniform. They have heard of, but never experienced an act of this kind before. "It's a good thing; keep it up," sang out one individual with a straw hat.

The Philadelphia players were among those who congratulated Young. In the dressing room the Boston men were a happy lot. . . .

All over town last night the main topic of conversation was the Young performance, and out-of-town papers wired for special stories about the phenomenal pitching of the live "king of the slab."

To Young the event was nothing out of the ordinary. He was out for the game, as he has been for 100 others, and landed his team a winner. Behind a good cigar, Old Cy enjoyed hearing the fans tell all about it, and retired thinking of that little farm out in Ohio, where he spends his long winters content and happy. . . .

1905

On February 25, 1905, the socialist weekly *Appeal to Reason*, published in | Girard, Kansas, began running Upton Sinclair's powerful serial about the lives of Lithuanian immigrants working in the squalor of "Packingtown." A prolific writer and passionate social reformer, Sinclair had spent six weeks in Chicago gathering material for his novel, interviewing the workers, even touring the packing houses of the companies that controlled the sale of meat in the country.

Reprinted in book form as *The Jungle,* Sinclair's novel became a best seller. After investigators appointed by a skeptical President Theodore Roosevelt validated Sinclair's reporting, Congress in 1906 passed the nation's first laws controlling the quality and content of food and drugs.

Ironically, Sinclair considered his investigative journalism and most famous work a failure. While it had prompted the Pure Food and Drug Act, *The Jungle* had done nothing to improve the horrific working conditions in the fetid slaughterhouses. "I aimed for the heart and by accident I hit the stomach instead," he said ruefully.

This extract from the March 25, 1905, installment of the *Appeal to Reason* serial displays Sinclair's heady mix of factual reporting and fictional narrative. First Jurgis Rudkus, then, in this installment, his father Antanas go to work at Durham's, a great packing plant that resembled the worst of those Sinclair had prowled in Chicago. They and their relatives by marriage, Jonas Lukoszaite and Marija Berczynskas, recount their experiences.

THE JUNGLE
BY UPTON SINCLAIR

. . . Warming to the subject, Tamoszius went on to explain the situation. Here was Durham's, for instance, owned by a man who was trying to make as much money out of it as he could, and did not care in the least how he did it; and underneath him, ranged in ranks and grades like an army, were managers and superintendents and foremen, each one driving the man next below him and trying to squeeze out of him as much work as possible. And all the men of the same rank were pitted against each other; the accounts of each were kept separately, and every man lived in terror of losing his job, if another made a better record than he. So from top to bottom the place was simply a seething cauldron of jealousies and hatreds; there were no loyalty or decency anywhere about it, there was no place in it where a man counted for anything against a dollar. And worse than there being no decency, there was not even any honesty. The reason for that? Who could say? It must have been old Durham in the beginning; it was a heritage which the self-made merchant had left to his son, along with his millions.

Jurgis would find out these things for himself, if he stayed there long enough; it was the men who had to do all the dirty jobs, and so there was no deceiving them, and they caught the spirit of the place, and did like all the rest. Jurgis had come there, and thought he was going to make himself useful, and rise and become a skilled man, but he would soon find out his error—for nobody rose in Packingtown by doing good work. You could lay that down for a rule—if you met a man who was rising in Packingtown, you met a knave. That man who had been sent to Jurgis's father by the boss, *he* would rise; the man who told tales and spied upon his fellows would rise; but the man who minded his own business and did his work—why, they would "speed him up" till they had worn him out, and then they would throw him in the gutter.

Jurgis went home with his head buzzing. Yet he could not bring himself to believe such things—no, it could not be so. Tamoszius was simply another of the grumblers. He was a man who spent all his time fiddling, and he would go to parties at night and not get home till sunrise, and so of course he did not feel like work. Then, too, he was a puny little chap, and so he had been left behind in the race, and that was why he was sore. And yet so many strange things kept coming to Jurgis's notice every day!

He tried to persuade his father to have nothing to do with the offer. But old Antanas had begged until he was worn out, and all his courage was gone; he wanted a job, any sort of a job. So the next day he went and found the man who had spoken to him, and promised to bring him a third of all he earned, and that same day he was put to work in Durham's cellars. It was a "pickle room," where there was never a dry spot to stand upon, and so he had to take nearly the whole of his first week's earnings to buy him a pair of heavy-soled boots. He was a "squeedgie" man; his job was to go about all day with a long-handled mop, swabbing upon the floor. Except that it was damp and dark, it was not an unpleasant job, in summer.

Now Antanas Rudkus was the meekest man that God ever put on earth, and so Jurgis found it a striking confirmation of what the men all said, that his father had been at work only two days before he came home as bitter as any of them, and cursing Durham's with all the power of his soul. For they had set him to cleaning out the traps; and the family sat round and listened in wonder while he told them what that meant. It seemed that he was working in the room where the men prepared the beef for canning, and the beef had lain in vats full of chemicals, and men with great forks speared it out and dumped it into trucks, to be taken to the cooking room. When they had speared out all they could reach, they emptied the vat on the floor, and then with shovels scraped up the balance and dumped it into the truck. This floor was filthy, yet they set Antanas with his mop slopping the "pickle" into a hole that connected with a sink, where it was caught and used over again forever; and if that was not enough, there was a trap in the pipe, where all the scraps of meat and odds and ends of refuse were caught, and every few days it was the old man's task to clean these out, and shovel their contents into one of the trucks with the rest of the meat!

This was the experience of Antanas; and then there came also Jonas and Marija with tales to tell. Marija was working for one of the independent packers, and was quite beside herself and outrageous with triumph over the sums of money she was making as a painter of cans. But one day she walked home with a pale-faced little woman who worked opposite to her, Jadvyga Marcinkus by name, and Jadvyga told her how she, Marija, had chanced to get her job. She had taken the place of an Irish woman who had been working in that factory ever since anyone could remember, for over fifteen years, so she declared. Mary Dennis was her name, and a long time ago she had been seduced, and had a little boy; he was a cripple, and an epileptic, but still he was all that she had in the world to love, and they had lived in a little room alone somewhere back of Halsted Street, where the Irish were. Mary had had consumption, and all day long you might hear her coughing as she worked; of late she had been going all to pieces, and when Marija came, the "forelady" had suddenly decided to turn her off. The forelady had to come up to a certain standard herself, and could not stop for sick people, Jadvyga explained. The fact that Mary had been there so long had not made any difference to her—it was doubtful if she even knew that, for both the forelady and the superintendent were new people, having only been there two or three years themselves. Jadvyga did not know what had become of the poor creature; she would have gone to see her, but had been sick herself. She had pains in her back all the time, Jadvyga explained, and feared that she had womb trouble. It was not fit work for a woman, handling fourteen-pound cans all day.

It was a striking circumstance that Jonas, too, had gotten his job by the misfortune of some other person. Jonas pushed a truck loaded with hams from the smoke rooms to an elevator, and thence to the packing rooms. The trucks were all of iron, and heavy, and they put about threescore hams on each of them, a load of more than a quarter of a ton. On the uneven floor it was a task for a man to start one of these trucks, unless he was a giant, and when it was once started he naturally tried his best to keep it going. There was always the boss prowling about, and if there was a second's delay he would fall to cursing; Lithuanians and Slovaks and such, who could not understand what was said to them, the bosses were wont to kick about the place like so many dogs. Therefore these trucks went for the most part on the run, and the predecessor of Jonas had been jammed against the wall by one and crushed in a horrible and nameless manner.

All of these were sinister incidents; but they were trifles compared to what Jurgis saw with his own eyes before long. One curious thing he had noticed, the very first day, in his profession of shoveler of guts; which was the sharp trick of the floor bosses whenever there chanced to come a "slunk" calf. Any man who knows anything about butchering knows that the flesh of a cow that is about to calve, or has just calved, is not fit for food. A good many of these came every day to the packing houses—and, of course, if they had chosen, it would have been an easy matter for the packers to keep them till they were fit for food. But for the saving of time and fodder, it was the law that cows of that sort came along with the others, and whoever noticed it would tell the boss, and the boss would start up a conversation with the government inspector, and the two would stroll away. So in a trice the carcass of the cow would be cleaned out, and the entrails would have vanished; it was Jurgis's task to slide them into the trap, calves and all, and on the floor below they took out these "slunk" calves, and butchered them for meat, and used even the skins of them.

One day a man slipped and hurt his leg; and that afternoon, when the last of the cattle had been disposed of, and the men were leaving, Jurgis was ordered to remain and do some special work which this injured man had usually done. It was late, almost dark, and the government inspectors had all gone, and there were only a dozen or two men on the floor. That day they had killed about four thousand cattle, and these cattle had come in freight trains from far states, and some of them had got hurt. There were some with broken legs, and some with gored sides; there were some that had died, from what cause no one could say; and they were all disposed of, here in darkness and silence. "Downers," the men called them; and the packing house had a special elevator upon which they were raised to the killing beds, where the gang proceeded to handle them, with an air of businesslike nonchalance which said plainer than any words that it was a matter of everyday routine. It took a couple of hours to get them out of the way, and in the end Jurgis saw them go into the chilling rooms with the rest of the meat, being carefully scattered here and there so that they could not be identified. When he came home that night he was in a very somber mood, having begun to see at last how those might be right who had laughed at him for his faith in America.

1906

The earthquake struck in the early morning of April 18, 1906, shaking San Francisco awake, tumbling cornices and lintels into the street, cracking gas and water mains, then igniting fires that would burn for the next week and destroy half of the city. Stricken residents retreated before the "laughing, roaring, onrushing fire demon" as Army engineers sought to blast a firebreak. Meanwhile, three San Francisco newspapers, their own buildings burning, joined forces in a makeshift city room across the bay to produce a combined edition of *The Call = Chronicle = Examiner* on the morning of April 19. That special edition reported the destruction of a city for those readers lucky enough to get hold of copies.

EARTHQUAKE AND FIRE: SAN FRANCISCO IN RUINS

Death and destruction have been the fate of San Francisco. Shaken by a temblor at 5:13 o'clock yesterday morning, the shock lasting 48 seconds, and scourged by flames that raged diametrically in all directions, the city is a mass of smouldering ruins. At six o'clock last evening the flames seemingly played with increased vigor, threatened to destroy such sections as their fury had spared during the earlier portion of the day. Building their path in a triangular circuit from the start in the early morning, they jockeyed as the day waned, left the business section, which they had entirely devastated, and skipped in a dozen directions to the residence portions. As night fell they had made their way over into the North Beach section and springing anew to the south they reached out along the shipping section down the bay shore, over the hills and across toward Third and Townsend streets. Warehouses, wholesale houses and manufacturing concerns fell in their path. This completed the destruction of the entire district known as the "South of Market Street." How far they are reaching to the south across the channel cannot be told as this part of the city is shut off from San Francisco papers.

After darkness, thousands of the homeless were making their way with their blankets and scant provisions to Golden Gate Park and the beach to find shelter. Those in the homes on the hills just north of the Hayes Valley wrecked section piled their belongings in the streets and express wagons and automobiles were hauling the things away to the sparsely settled regions. Everybody in San Francisco is prepared to leave the city, for the belief is firm that San Francisco will be totally destroyed.

Downtown everything is ruin. Not a business house stands. Theatres are crumbled into heaps. Factories and commission houses lie smouldering on their former sites. All of the newspaper plants have been rendered useless, the "Call" and the "Examiner" buildings, excluding the "Call's" editorial rooms on Stevenson Street being entirely destroyed.

It is estimated that the loss in San Francisco will reach from $150,000,000 to $200,000,000. These figures are in the rough and nothing can be told until partial accounting is taken.

On every side there was death and suffering yesterday. Hundreds were injured, either burned, crushed or struck by falling pieces from the buildings, and one of ten died while on the operating table at Mechanics' Pavilion, improvised as a hospital for the comfort and care of the injured. The number of dead is not known but it is estimated that at least 500 met their death in the horror.

At nine o'clock, under a special message from President Roosevelt, the city was placed under martial law. Hundreds of troops patrolled the streets and drove the crowds back, while hundreds more were set at work assisting the fire and police departments. The strictest orders were issued, and in true military spirit the soldiers obeyed. During the afternoon three thieves met their death by rifle bullets while at work in the ruins. The curious were driven back at the breasts of the horses that the cavalrymen rode and all the crowds were forced from the level district to the hilly section beyond to the north.

The water supply was entirely cut off, and may be it was just as well, for the lines of the fire department would have been absolutely useless at any stage. Assistant Chief Dougherty supervised the work of this men and early in the morning it was seen that the only possible chance to save the city lay in effort[s] to check the flames by the use of dynamite. During the day a blast could be heard in any section at intervals of only a few minutes, and buildings not destroyed by fire were blown to atoms. Through the gaps made the flames jumped and although the failures of the heroic efforts of the

police, firemen and soldiers were at times sickening, the work was continued with a desperation that will live as one of the features of the terrible
disaster. Men worked like fiends to combat the laughing, roaring, onrushing
fire demon.

No Hope Left
For Safety of
Any Buildings

San Francisco seems doomed to entire destruction. With a lapse in the
raging of the flames just before dark, the hope was raised that with the use
of tons of dynamite the course of the fire might be checked and confined to
the triangular sections it had cut out for its path. But on the Barbary Coast
the fire broke out anew and as night closed in the flames were eating their
way into parts untouched in their ravages during the day. To the south and
north they spread; down to the docks and out into the resident section, in
and to the north of Hayes Valley. By six o'clock practically all of St. Ig-
natius' great buildings were no more. They had been leveled to the fiery
heap that marked what was once the metropolis of the West.

The first of the big structures to go to ruin was the Call Building, the
famous skyscraper. At eleven o'clock the big 18-story building was a furnace. Flames leaped from every window and shot skyward from the circular
windows in the dome. In less than two hours nothing remained but the tall
skeleton.

By five o'clock the Palace Hotel was in ruins. The old hostelry, famous
the world over, withstood the siege until the last and although dynamite was
used in frequent blasts to drive the fire away from the swept section toward
Mission street, they [sic] made their way to the point of the hotel until the
old place began to crumble away in the blaze.

The City Hall is a complete wreck. The entire part of the building from
Larkin street down City Hall avenue to Leavenworth, down from top of
dome to the steps is ruined. The colossal pillars supporting the arches at the
entrance fell into the avenue far out across the car tracks and the thousands
of tons of bricks and debris that followed them piled into a mountainous
heap. The west wing sagged and crumbled, caving into a shapeless mass.
At the last every vestige of stone was swept away by the shock and the
building laid bare nearly to its McAllister street side. Only a shell remained
to the north, and the huge steel frame stood gaping until the fire that swept
from the Hayes Valley set the debris ablaze and hid the structure in a cloud
of smoke. Every document of the City government is destroyed. Nothing
remains but a ghastly past of the once beautiful structure. It will be necessary to entirely rebuild the Hall.

Mechanics' Pavilion, covering an entire block, went before the flames in
a quarter of an hour. The big wooden structure burned like tinder and in
less time than it takes to write it was flat upon the ground.

The flames had come from the west, this time fanned by a lively wind. Down from Hayes Valley they swooped, destroying residences in entire rows, sending to cinders the business houses and leaping the gaps caused by the dynamiting of homes. They had stolen their way out from the Mission, while a dense crowd blocked that street. So quickly did they make their way to the north of Market that their approach was not noticed. When it was realized that the danger had come to this particular residence section, the police and the cavalry drove the crowd back in haste to the south and out of harm's way. Down Hayes street playing the cross streets coming on like a demon, the fire swept over St. Ignatious [sic] Church, leveled barns and houses and, as if accomplishing a purpose long desired, blazed down to the front of Mechanics' Pavilion. Only shortly before the patients in this crude hospital had been removed to other hospitals in outlying districts.

From the big shed the flames spread to the north, east, south and west, everywhere. Confusion reigned. Women fainted and men fought their way into the adjoining apartment houses to rescue something from destruction—anything, if only enough to cover their wives and their babies when the cold of the night came on. There was a scene that made big, brave men cry. There were the weeping tots in their mothers' arms wailing with fear of the awful calamity; salesmen and soldiers fighting to get the women out of harm's way through the crowd; heroic dashes in the ambulances and the patrol wagons after the sick and injured, and willing men, powerless as the mouse in the mouth of the lion, ready to fight the destroyer, but driven back step by step while their homes went down before them. . . .

Down in the wholesale district south of the cable and along through the section facing the city's front, the flames appeared. Fire shot into the air from ever[y] corner. Before the first alarm was sent in the fire was beyond control. The city was beyond saving from the time that the first blaze broke toward the heavens.

Gradually the flames stole along Mission and Howard streets, and then rapidly they made their way from building to building until Seventh street was reached. Out in the warehouse district bounded by Sansome on the west and the bay on the north, and west they went. . . .

From Second and Third streets Market street held its own until late in the afternoon. The Call Building was ablaze, but the Examiner Building, the Palace Hotel, the Grand, and the other structures toward Second street stood. Two attempts were made to dynamite the new Monadnock Building when it was seen that the Hearst structure was doomed. And slowly came the blaze from Mission street just below Third, sweeping everything before it and igniting the Examiner Annex. Then the main building took fire and by two o'clock only the Third street wall was standing. Later the Palace took fire in the rear and the flames made quick progress on Market street. By five o'clock, Colonel Kirkpatrick's famous hotel was no more. The Grand went at the same time, and in a few minutes the flames had Market street again. At Sansome they combined with the fire on the north side of the street but the changeable winds kept the fire back from the buildings extending from this point to Kearney street.

At seven o'clock the entire region lying just back of the Hall of Justice was on fire. The dynamite did no good. From the Fairmount Hotel now could be seen the gigantic semicircle of flame extending from the Mission at about Thirteenth street down through the entire southern end of the city proper, along the channel, over the hill, along the waterfront, through the wholesale district and over onto Barbary Coast.

Then the firefighters prepared for the thing they hoped would not happen. It was certain that the fire would spread northward and join the inferno near the Hall of Justice. Dynamite was placed in the Hall of Justice to be sent into the air at the signal. The flames on lower Kearny [sic] street had gained the office buildings on the west side of the street. This foretells the doom of Chinatown. Thousands on thousands of Celestials scurried over Nob Hill to safety.

1909

The scientific quest of the North Pole turned into a hotly contested question of personal integrity when naval commander Robert E. Peary wired *The New York Times* on September 6, 1909, that he had reached the pole on April 6, 1909. But Peary may not have been the first to make the top of the world. Several days before, in an article published in the rival *New York Herald,* explorer Dr. Frederick Cook had asserted that he, accompanied by two Eskimos, had first journeyed to the North Pole on April 21, 1908. Peary countered that two members of Cook's expedition had told him that Cook, once Peary's close friend, had fallen far short of the North Pole.

Though Peary is now generally credited with discovering the pole, the controversy refuses to die. Writing in *National Geographic* in September, 1988, British polar explorer Wally Herbert expressed doubts about whether Peary and his five companions (fellow explorer Matthew Henson and Eskimos Ooqueah, Ootah, Egingwah and Seegloo) actually did reach the pole. According to Herbert, Peary might have been 30 to 60 miles off course. So the arguments, pro and con, continue.

The New York Times, with whom Peary later had an exclusive contract, published on September 7, 1909, the first word that the naval officer had claimed the pole.

PEARY DISCOVERS THE NORTH POLE AFTER EIGHT TRIALS IN 23 YEARS

Notifies The New York Times That He Reached It on April 6, 1909.

HE WIRES FROM LABRADOR

Returning on the Roosevelt,
Which He Reports to
Bridgeman Is Safe.

Is Nearing Newfoundland

Expects to Reach Chateau Bay
To-day, When He Will Send
Full Particulars.

McMILLAN SENDS WORD

Explorer's Companion Telegraphs
Sister: "We Have the
Pole on Board."

SEVEN VAIN EXPEDITIONS

Many Years Consumed in Learning
the Feasible Route—Picked Men
Were His Assistants.

Commander Robert E. Peary, U.S.N., has discovered the north pole. Following the report of Dr. F.A. Cook that he had reached the top of the world comes the certain announcement from Mr. Peary, the hero of eight polar expeditions, covering a period of twenty-three years, that at last his ambition has been realized, and from all over the world comes full acknowledgement of Peary's feat and congratulations on his success.

The first announcement of Peary's exploit was received in the following message to THE NEW YORK TIMES:

Indian Harbor, Labrador, via Cape Ray, N.F. Sept. 6.

THE NEW YORK TIMES, New York:

I have the pole, April sixth. Expect arrive Chateau Bay, September seventh. Secure control wire for me there and arrange expedite transmission big story.

PEARY.

Following the receipt of Commander Peary's message to THE NEW YORK TIMES several other messages were received in this city from the explorer to the same effect.

Soon afterward The Associated Press received the following:

INDIAN HARBOR, via Cape Ray, N.F., Sept. 6.—To Associated Press, New York.

Stars and Stripes nailed to the pole.

PEARY.

To Herbert L. Bridgman, Secretary of the Peary Arctic Club, he telegraphed as follows:

Herbert L. Bridgman, Brooklyn, N.Y.: Pole reached, Roosevelt safe.

PEARY.

This message was received at the New York Yacht Club in West Forty-fourth Street:

INDIAN HARBOR, Via Cape Ray, N. F. Sept. 6—George A. Carmack, Secretary New York Yacht Club:

Steam yacht Roosevelt, flying club burgee, has enabled me to add north pole to club's other trophies.

(signed) PEARY.

Cipher Shows Authenticity.

The telegram to Mr. Bridgman was sent in cipher. The cipher used was a private one and indicated clearly that the dispatch was undoubtedly from Commander Peary.

Commander Peary also sent a message to his wife at South Harpswell, Me., where she has been spending the Summer.

"Have made good at last," said the explorer to his wife. "I have the old pole. Am well. Love. Will wire again from Chateau."

The message was signed simply "Bert," an abbreviation of Robert, Commander Peary's first name. Mrs. Peary sent a wife's characteristic reply, with love and a blessing and a request for him to "hurry home."

By a strange coincidence, Mrs. Frederick A. Cook, too, was in South Harpswell, Me., when she received the first news from her husband. . . .

Follows Cook's Report Quickly.

These messages, flashed from the coast of Labrador to New York and thence to the four corners of the globe while Dr. Frederick A. Cook is being acclaimed by the crowned heads of Europe and the world at large as the discoverer of the north pole, added a remarkable chapter to the story of an achievement that has held the civilized world up to the highest pitch of interest since Sept. 1, when Dr. Cook's claim to having reached the "top of the world" was first telegraphed from the Shetland islands.

The two explorers, Dr. Frederick A. Cook and Commander Robert E. Peary, both Americans, have been in the arctic seeking the goal of centuries, the impossible north pole, whose attainment has at times seemed beyond the reach of man. Both were determined and courageous, and both had started expressing the belief that their efforts would be crowned with success.

Peary the Better Known

Peary was well known to both scientists and the general public as a persistent striver for the honor of reaching the "farthest north." Dr. Cook on the other hand, had held the public attention to a lesser degree. He made his departure quietly and his purpose was hardly known except to those keenly interested in polar research.

Then suddenly, and with no word of warning, a steamer touched at Lerwick, in the Shetland Islands, and Dr. Cook's claim to having succeeded where expedition after expedition of the hardiest explorers of the world had failed was made known. Dr. Cook's announcement was that he had reached the pole on April 21, 1908.

Three days later Dr. Cook arrived at Copenhagen and received a welcome such as no explorer had ever received before.

Peary Announces Success.

Five days after the receipt of the Lerwick message, almost to the hour, came the sensational statement from Indian Harbor, Labrador, that Commander Peary had also been successful on his third expedition to the coveted goal, the date being April 6, 1909.

He filed his brief messages and continued on his way to the south, leaving the world to marvel at a dramatic situation such as has seldom been recorded—the double achievement of a purpose that for almost ten centuries had baffled the endeavor of man and had taken many an explorer to his death in the frozen north.

It is almost certain that Commander Peary did not know of Dr. Cook's announcement when he sent his messages from Indian Harbor.

Under ordinary circumstance Commander Peary's announcement would have evoked world-wide interest, but the existing conditions conspired to add many times the importance of his communication.

According to Dr. Cook's account of his expedition, he buried the American flag at the pole in a metal tube; Peary's words would indicate that the Stars and Stripes were raised by him and left standing.

How the News Came.

The message from Commander Peary to THE NEW YORK TIMES was received in New York at 12:39 yesterday through the Postal Telegraph Company. It was handed in at Indian Harbor, Labrador, and was sent from there by wireless telegraph to Cape Ray, Newfoundland, and from Cape Ray to Port aux Basques by the Newfoundland Government land lines; thence to Canso, Nova Scotia, by cable and to New York from there over the lines of the Commercial Cable Company.

1910

Jack Johnson, world champion heavy-weight boxer, stood larger than life, in and out of the ring. So formidable a figure was Johnson that his presence in the prize fighting game gave rise to not-so-latent racism. Some members of the press and many of boxing's fans were eager for a "Great White Hope" to publicly humiliate this black man, who was living with a white woman, and reclaim boxing's crown for the Caucasian race.

When Jim Jeffries, thirty-five, who had retired from boxing in 1905, announced he was stepping back into the ring to take on Johnson, then thirty-two, the public seized upon Jeffries as the white man's champion. The subsequent match in Reno, Nevada, in which Johnson toyed with his opponent, was a heavily promoted affair that captured the nation's attention.

The New York Herald Syndicate hired Jack London, author of *The Call of the Wild* (1903) and *The Sea-Wolf* (1904), for $100 per day plus expenses to cover the bout. London's story appeared on July 5, 1910.

JOHNSON, IN TAME FIGHT, WHIPS JEFFRIES

Negro, Never in Doubt, Fear or Trouble, Played All the Time, Says Jack London

Jeffries Lost His Old Time Stamina Somewhere Outside the Ring and Did Not Put Up as Strong a Battle as Did "Tommy" Burns.

"GOLDEN SMILE" SHINES ON ADVERSARY, TRAINERS AND 20,000 SPECTATORS

"Did You See That, Jim?" He Asks of Corbett After Landing an Especially Vicious Punch and Clinching with His Adversary—Yellow Streak Question Unsettled.

JEFFRIES, EYE CLOSED, LOSES HIS DEFENCE

First Rounds Were Largely Johnson, Following Ones More Johnson and Close All Johnson— Battered and Staggering, Californian Goes Down Three Times in Last.

FACTS ABOUT BIG FIGHT

John A. Johnson defeated James J. Jeffries in their battle for the world's heavyweight championship at Reno, Nev., yesterday.

The end came in the fifteenth round, when Johnson, after mercilessly battering his opponent, knocked him to the floor three times. The last time at the count of eight Jeffries' seconds rushed over the ring and the referee awarded the fight to Johnson.

It is estimated that 17,000 persons saw the battle, while as many more were unable to obtain entrance to the arena.

The $121,000 purse, which included a $10,000 bonus to each fighter, was divided, sixty per cent to the winner and forty per cent to the loser.

BY JACK LONDON
(SPECIAL DESPATCH TO THE HERALD.)

RENO, Nev., Monday—Once again has Johnson sent down to defeat the chosen representative of the white race, and this time the greatest of them. And as of old, it was play for Johnson. From the opening round to the closing round he never ceased from his witty sallies, his exchanges of repartee with his opponent's seconds and with the audience. And, for that matter, Johnson had a funny thing or two to say to Jeffries in every round.

The "golden smile" was as much in evidence as ever and neither did it freeze on his face nor did it vanish. It came and went throughout the fight spontaneously, naturally.

It was not a great battle after all, save, in its setting and its significance. Little "Tommy" Burns, down in far off Australia, put up a faster, quicker, livelier battle than did Jeffries. This fight to-day, and again I repeat, was great only in its significance. In itself it was not great. The issue, after the fiddling of the opening rounds, was never in doubt. In the fiddling of those first rounds the honors lay with Johnson, and for rounds after the seventh or eighth it was more Johnson, while for the closing rounds it was all Johnson.

Could Afford to Play.

Johnson played as usual. With his opponent not strong in the attack Johnson, blocking and defending in masterly fashion, could afford to play. And he played and fought a white man, in the white man's country, before a white man's audience. And the audience was a Jeffries audience.

When Jeffries sent in that awful rip of his the audience would madly applaud, believing it had gone home to Johnson's stomach, and Johnson, deftly interposing his elbow, would smile in irony at the audience, play acting, making believe he thought the applause was for him—and never believing it at all.

The greatest battle of the century was a monologue delivered to twenty thousand spectators by a smiling negro, who was never in doubt and who was never serious for more than a moment at a time.

As a fighter Johnson did not show himself a wonder. He did not have to. Never once was he extended. There was no need. Jeffries could not make him extend. Jeffries never had him in trouble once. No blow Jeffries ever landed hurt his dusky opponent. Johnson came out of the fight practically undamaged. The blood on his lip was from a recent cut received in the course of training and which Jeffries managed to reopen. . . .

End Begins in Thirteenth.

The thirteenth round was the beginning of the end. Beginning slowly enough, but stung by Corbett [former champion Jim Corbett was Jeffries' manager], Johnson put it all over him in the mouth fighting and all over Jeffries in the out fighting and in fighting. From defence to attack and back again and back and forth Johnson flashed like the amazing fighting mechanism he is. Jeffries was silent and sick, while as the round progressed Corbett was noticeably silent.

A few entertained the fond hope that "Jeff" would recuperate. But it was futile. There was no come back to him. He was a fading, failing, heartsick, heartbroken man.

"Talk to him, Corbett," Jeffries' friends appealed in the fourteenth round. But Corbett could not talk. He had long since seen the end.

And yet through this round Johnson went in for one of his characteristic loafing spells. He took it easy and played with the big gladiator, cool as a cucumber, smiling broadly as ever and yet as careful as ever.

"Right on the hip," he grinned out once as Jeffries, in a desperate, dying flurry managed to land a wild punch in that vicinity. Corbett, likewise desperate, ventured a last sally.

"Why don't you do something?" he cried to the loafing, laughing Johnson.

"Too clever, too clever, like you," was the response.

Round fifteen, and the end. It was pitiful. There happened to Jeffries the bitterness that he had so often made others taste, got which for the first time, per-[sic] he was made to taste himself. He who had never been knocked down was knocked down repeatedly. He who had never been knocked out was knocked out. Never mind the technical decision. Jeffries was knocked out through the ropes by the punch he believed Johnson possessed—by the left and not by the right. As he lay across the lower rope while the seconds were told off, a cry that had in it tears and abject broken pride went up from many of the spectators.

"Don't let the negro knock him out! Don't let the negro knock him out!" was the oft repeated cry.

There is little more to be said. Jeffries did not come back. Johnson did not show the yellow streak. And it was Johnson's fight all the way through. Jeffries was not the old Jeffries at all. Even so, it is to be doubted if the old Jeffries could have put away this amazing negro from Texas, this black man with the unfailing smile, this king of fighters and monologists. . . .

Johnson is a wonder. No one understands him, this man who smiles. Well, the story of the fight is the story of a smile. If ever man won by nothing more fatiging [sic] than a smile Johnson won to-day.

And where now is the champion who will make Johnson extend himself? Who will glaze those bright eyes, remove that smile and silence that golden repartee?

1911

The decision laid out what would later be called the "Rule of Reason." In fact, it was one of the earliest examples of an activist judiciary assuming a legislative role reserved to Congress by the Constitution. Although the Supreme Court held in its 1911 decision that the Standard Oil Company had violated the Sherman Antitrust Act, of 1890, which aimed to prevent the concentration of power in the hands of a few large corporations, Chief Justice Edward D. White's opinion had implications far broader than the predatory practices of Standard's founder, John D. Rockefeller.

In defining a standard of unlawfulness that Congress never intended, the Supreme Court began a power struggle with the legislative branch that would remain a feature of American politics. Henceforth, the high court reserved the discretion to interpret statutes according to its own predilections, rather than in conformity with the meaning of the words of the laws themselves. Only Associate Justice John Marshall Harlan dissented from his brethren's revisionist conclusion, a point duly noted by *The New York Tribune* in its story printed on May 16, 1911.

STANDARD OIL COMPANY ORDERED DISSOLVED; REASONABLE RESTRAINT OF TRADE NOT UNLAWFUL

United States Supreme Court Gives Standard Oil Six Months in Which to Reorganize

Opinion by Chief Justice

The Great Corporation Held to be a Monopoly Within the Letter and the Spirit of the Sherman Anti-Trust Law

Applies "Rule of Reason"

No Precise Definition of the Statute Given— Justice Harlan Would be More Drastic— American Tobacco Case Not Decided

Big Audience in Court

Well Known Men See End of Momentous Legal Battle—New "Rule of Reasonableness" Welcomed by Business Men

Vital Points in Standard Oil Decision

That the Standard Oil Company is a monopoly in restraint of trade.

That the corporation must be dissolved within six months.

Corporations whose contracts are "not unreasonably restrictive of competition" are not affected.

Other great corporations whose acts may be called into question will be dealt with according to the merits of their particular cases.

The court was unanimous as to the main features of the decision, Justice Harlan dissenting only as to a limitation of the application of the Sherman anti-trust law.

Washington, May 15.—The Supreme Court of the United States, by a practically unanimous decision, to-day declared the Standard Oil Company to be a combination in restraint of trade within the meaning of the anti-trust law, and ordered its dissolution within six months. This applies to the Standard Oil Company of New Jersey and thirty-three other corporations, having an aggregate capital of $110,000,000. The court declares that the anti-trust law is clearly intended to prevent monopolies; that the history of this company, the course of its projectors and the results of their acts clearly establish a purpose to monopolize the trade in petroleum, which monopoly is equally clearly a violation of the intent of the statute.

The opinion, which was handed down by Chief Justice White and is regarded as remarkable for the succinctness and the clarity of its reasoning, makes obvious the view of the court that the purpose of the law is to prevent monopoly and indicates that wherever it may be shown that such monopoly exists the court will hold that the statute has been violated.

The Chief Justice rejects the contention of the government that the statute prohibits every case within its letter and language, and holds that in each case presented the judgment of the court must be called into play to determine, first, whether the particular act comes within the prohibition of the statute, and secondly, whether such act causes it to be a restraint within the intendment of the act. Chief Justice White expressly states that the statute is not intended to limit its own scope by precise definition, but that, by defining ulterior boundaries, it does purpose to fix a standard which cannot be transgressed with impunity, thus leaving it to the court to enforce the public policy embodied in the statute and to exercise its judgment in the case of each particular act brought before it.

Justice Harlan Takes More Drastic View

Justice Harlan subscribed to the decision of the court in so far as it applied to the Standard Oil Company, thus making the decision in this case unanimous, but he dissented from the conclusion of the majority that a restraint of trade must be shown to be "undue" in order to come within the purview of the statute, and objected to the extent by which the remainder of the court was guided by the common law in this respect. It was asserted by Justice Harlan that for fifteen years the trusts had sought to have this limitation imposed by legislative amendment, and that they now sought such limitation by judicial determination, whereas, in his opinion, it was the intent of the statute to prohibit all restraint of trade, whether "undue" or otherwise.

Gives No Precise Definition of the Law

The expectation of the Attorney General and of other high legal authorities in the government that the court would refrain from imposing any limitation on its further determination of the law by that "precise definition" which would clearly mark the limits to which restraint might be carried without subjecting its authors to penalty was fully met. The decision, in the opinion of able lawyers, makes it clear that whenever the Supreme Court shall determine, in light of the facts presented, that there has been a successful attempt to create a monopoly, it will adjudge the result to be a violation of the anti-trust law, but that beyond that the opinion does not go, and that the efforts of those who would achieve that end without rendering themselves liable will be attended with as great difficulty in the future as in the past. On the other hand, it is contended that the opinion will serve to relieve from anxiety those whose business operations may to some extent assume the appearance of an effort to create a monopoly, but who may be able to show an entire absence of such intent, and that the restraint achieved is only reasonable.

Standard Oil Purposed to Create a Monopoly

In the case of the Standard Oil Company, the court declares the purpose to create a monopoly to have been so obvious that no unprejudiced person can review its history "without being irresistibly driven to the conclusion that the very genius for commercial development and organization, which it would seem was manifested from the beginning, begot an intent and purpose to exclude others which was frequently manifested by acts and dealings wholly inconsistent with the theory that they were made with the single conception of advancing the development of business power by usual methods, but which, on the contrary, necessarily involved the intent to drive others from the field and to exclude them from their right to trade and thus accomplish the mastery which was the end in view."

Meeting the contention that dissolution of the trust must work inordinate injury to property, the court points out that the stockholders are not restrained from making "normal and lawful contracts," but are restrained from seeking by any device whatever, directly or indirectly, to recreate "the illegal combination which the decree dissolved."

1912

The history of the labor movement in the United States—until the Wagner Labor Relations Act of 1935 fixed in law the right to bargain collectively—is a succession of often bloody defeats. There were few victories for the working man when government, industry, and the press generally opposed even the most modest demands for decent treatment.

The Lawrence, Massachusetts, strike of 1912 would be different from the others. When a new state law reduced the work week from 56 to 54 hours, the owners of the huge American Woolen Mills cut workers' pay, yet increased the speed of the looms to make up for the lost production. The workers rose in a spontaneous, unplanned protest. *The Boston Daily Globe* of January 12, 1912, amply displayed its bias in reporting the outbreak of the strike.

GIRLS BEATEN DOWN BY A LAWRENCE MOB

Two Wounded By Strikers When Several Hundred Storm the Mills.

Clubs and Bobbins Used as Weapons in a Riot Started by Italians and Syrians

Lawrence, Jan. 12—With a nucleus of 400 or 500 operatives of the Washington Mills of the American Woolen Company, a strike was inaugurated this morning which spread to the Wood & Ayer mills of the company, and ended in about 12,000 employees leaving their work, either from inclination or compulsion.

Property and individuals suffered from the violence of a mob, and at 10 o'clock a riot call was sent in on the fire alarm system, calling out the active police force. The Wood & Ayer mills suffered the most from the excited strikers, who were practically all Italians and Syrians.

Power was shut off in both mills, belts thrown from the pulleys and things that were movable overturned. Clubs were used and bobbins and other missiles thrown, to hasten the operatives in leaving their work. It was said that in one instance a revolver was pointed at an employee to enforce a demand of the attacking party.

The situation reached a climax when the strikers attacked the Duck Mill, where a strike was started a few days ago because of dissatisfaction at the wage conditions existing under the new 54-hour law, which was also the cause of today's outbreak. A detail of policemen blocked the entrance to the mill office and stood off the attack of about 50, who broke away from the crowd of several hundred assembled in front of the mill on Union street and attempted to force their way into the mill.

Then the strikers directed their attention to the wagon gate, close by, and one of their number scaled it. Encouraged by his act, others started to follow, and the police brought their clubs into action and blood began to flow.

This attack, which had long been deferred, had its effect, and slowly the mob made its away along ahead of the police, finally dispersing to their homes.

Trouble over the reduction in pay, resulting from the operation of the 54-hour law, has been smoldering among the operatives since the policy of the mills to reduce the time for men and women alike became known, and it had been rumored that the situation would soon reach a climax.

This morning's outbreak was unexpected, however. According to one of the strikers, it had its inception in No. 1 drying room of the Washington plant, and soon spread to No. 2 drying and Nos. 2 and 3 spinning rooms. As soon as the disturbance started word was sent the police for assistance, and this was soon followed by a demand for protection from the Wood mills, toward which the strikers directed their attention after leaving the Washington Mill.

Mob Stormed the Mill

It was then that the riot call was sounded, and night and day patrolmen responded. Gateman Lewis Berry was talking with the watchman at the entrance to the Wood mill when the uproar of the crowd was heard at the doors. He attempted to lock the doors to stay their progress, but his efforts were unavailing.

With force sufficient to break off one of the iron bolts that fastened a door to the frame overhead, the mob made its way into the mill and started through the departments calling upon those at work to quit. Gateman Berry said he endeavored to check the leaders, and a blow was aimed at his head, but did not reach him.

In the excitement he could not estimate the size of the crowd, but he considered that 500 was none too large. Seizing sticks in the picker room, several of the invaders brandished them over the heads of operatives, and some of the latter, who did not move quick enough, received blows from those weapons.

It was claimed others were struck with weights of which the excited foreigners had gained possession. An employee named Richardson, it was said, complied with an order to shut off the power to one of the rooms, and when he attempted to start it again, he was directed to desist at the point of a revolver.

J. Lawson, an employee of the mechanical department, said that he and master mechanic Thomas Somerville tried to stem the tide, but was pushed to one side, and Lawson received a cut on one finger.

Isabelle Cahill of 48 Andover st. was struck by a weight near the ear, and was rendered unconscious, and Lillian Barker of 72 Farnham st., suffered from similar violence. Louise Traverso of 67 Oak st., report had it, was driven from her spinning room by a striker armed with a knife.

Power Shut Down in Mill

Supt. Fred Smith directed that all the power should be shut down, and soon the entire mill, employing about 600 operatives, was in idleness. Serious damage was caused one of the escalators which are operated instead of stairs in this mill.

The man in charge had reserved these to prevent the mob from ascending to the second floor, and evidently some obstacle had been placed in the runway, so that several of the steps were torn from the frames. A sprinkler beneath the escalator was broken and the water poured out into the mill until the flow could be shut off.

Encouraged by their success at the Wood mills, the strikers, headed by leaders, one of whom carried an Italian flag and another an American banner, rushed across South Union st. to the Ayer mill. The iron gates here formed an insufficient barrier to them and they made their way through the various rooms, calling upon the help to leave.

Here too the acts committed in the wood mill, with reference to throwing off the power, were repeated and within a short time nearly all the 3000 operatives had left their work. Many of the employees as they left talked with a few acquaintances regarding the affair, and then departed for their homes, so that at no time was the crowd assembled about the mills with which the police had to contend more than 600 or so.

Added excitement was caused when Asst. Marshal Logan, backed up by several policemen, had a setto with an obstreperous striker. There was an indication that others of the strikers might lend a hand, but they desisted and the incident was closed.

Across the Merrimac River the operatives lingered in front of the Duck mills until a crowd of about 300 had assembled. Shouts were sent up to operatives in the Duck mill to join their ranks, but there was no evidence of activity within the mill.

Mill Windows Are Smashed

Then someone started throwing ice from the streets against the windows, and soon there was a fusillade of ice and snow. Plate glass windows in the office portion of the mill were smashed in, and smaller patches in the other portions of the mill along the street front yielded.

Gradually the leaders assumed still further aggressiveness, and the attack on the entrance followed. After they had been checked a Polander was raised above the heads of the crowd and he told his audience that his fellow countrymen in the mill had already struck, and there was no need of attempting to enter the mill.

He was greeted with cheers and handclapping, but his words had little affect, for soon the attack was resumed and then the police got in their strenuous work.

One of the crowd received a blow on the head, which caused the blood to flow freely. In the scramble to get away from the blows of the police, some of the crowd lost their footing and went down in a heap. After the crowd had moved on one policeman picked up a dinner box, which had been dropped and another a pair of overalls.

Meantime at the Washington mills, all had become quiet, and it was reported at the gate that most of the English-speaking operatives were at work. This mill employs about 6000 operatives.

During the outbreak in front of the duck mill, patrolman Jordan was hemmed in by a group of strikers, and was cut about the face before other officers could come to his assistance. Another patrolman, it is said, also suffered injury.

Maj. Sargent, in command of the local militia, had a conference with Mayor Scanlon and Director of Public Safety Lynch, but it was decided not to call out the militia unless the situation became more serious.

Nearly 11,000 Are Idle

Before the trouble ended several persons had been injured, none seriously, a number of girl operatives had fainted and six arrests had been made by the police. The mill agents hastily looked things over and found that so many operatives had quit work through fear of the angry strikers that it was decided to close down the Wood and Ayer mills at once.

The Washington mills and those of the Lawrence Duck Company, to which the disturbance extended, were kept in operation although 800 operatives at the Washington mills and 400 at the duck mills stopped work after the riot. As the Wood mill employs 600 hands and the Ayer mill 3500, nearly 11,000 operatives were idle this afternoon.

The union leaders were not prepared this afternoon to make any statements as to their probable attitude, but it was evident that the disturbance today had produced a sobering effect. It was generally expected that a meeting would be held soon to decide what action would be taken.

The mill agents intimated that they would open all the mills tomorrow, as usual, including the Wood and Ayer Mills. How many of their operatives will be on hand to go to work cannot yet be foretold.

STATEMENT OF PRES. WOOD

William M. Wood, president of the American Woolen Company, says of the situation at Lawrence:

"Our employes have been led to believe that the reduction from 56 to 54 hours was an act of the manufacturers, whereas the real fact is that the 54-hour law was demanded by certain mistaken labor interests, enacted by the Legislature, and signed by the Governor under pressure from them. Therefore, these labor interests and the law makers, not the manufacturers, are responsible.

"The manufacturers (I say this believing that I express the sentiments of all) are the friends of the employes and greatly regret that the reduction in the hours of work, which the new law has forced, compels their taking home just that much less money. There has been no reduction in the rates of wages; but it cannot be expected that people who work 54 hours should take home the wages equivalent to 56 hours of work.

"I believe that as soon as our employees understand the real issue and where the responsibility actually rests, they will see that their action at Lawrence was hasty and ill-advised. There is no cause for striking, and when the employees find that justice is not on their side the strike cannot possibly be long-lived. I look for an early resumption of work."

It was not so easy as all that. The militant Industrial Workers of the World, the "Wobblies" as they were known scornfully, took up the cause of the poorly organized mill hands. Contrary to their reputation, I.W.W. organizers eschewed violence in Lawrence, even when the increasingly frustrated mill owners attempted to frame them for planting dynamite.

Confronted with the need to support the strikers' families, the I.W.W. decided to house wives and children with sympathetic families in other cities. It was then that the mill owners effectively lost the strike. Their truncheon-swinging strikebreakers, protected by members of the state militia, fell upon the parade of strikers' wives and children marching to the train depot. The naked brutality, the image of bloody women and terror-stricken children, turned public opinion in favor of the strikers. Facing a hostile public and aroused Legislature, the owners yielded, and restored the pay cut in March.

Labor had taken its first small step to the 40-hour week.

1913

On February 13, 1913, the "Armory Show" opened in New York City's Regiment Armory on 69th Street, presenting a bold exhibition of 1,300 works by 300 European and American artists, including some of the most daring and modern. Works by Expressionists, Cubists, and America's own Ash Can painters stunned the critics, most of them academicians who trod safe paths. Most shocking of all was pre-Dadaist Marcel Duchamp's "Nude Descending a Staircase" with its dehumanized portrayal of that beloved art icon, the female nude. More than a few reviewers concluded that much of the new art was bankrupt of reason. However, the Armory Show would permanently redirect American art, despite critics' puzzlement over the radical paintings and iconoclastic sculpture. *The New York Times'* appraisal ran on February 23, 1913.

ART AT HOME AND ABROAD

History of Modern Art at the International Exhibition Illustrated by Paintings and Sculpture.

It cannot be denied that the Post Impressionists and Cubists predominate at the Armory Exhibition.

Can you fill in the blanks in first crossword puzzle?

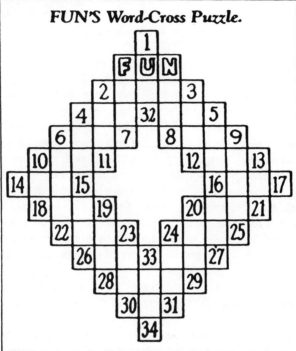

FUN'S Word-Cross Puzzle.

FILL in the small squares with words which agree with the following definitions:

2-3. What bargain hunters enjoy.

4-5. A written acknowledgement.

6-7. Such and nothing more.

10-11. A bird.

14-15. Opposed to less.

18-19. What this puzzle is.

22-23. An animal of prey.

26-27. The close of a day.

28-29. To elude.

30-31. The plural of is.

8-9. To cultivate.

12-13. A bar of wood or iron.

16-17. What artists learn to do.

20-21. Fastened.

24-25. Found on the seashore.

10-18. The fibre of the gomuti palm.

6-22. What we all should be.

4-26. A day dream.

2-11. A talon.

19-28. A pigeon.

F-7. Part of your head.

23-30. A river in Russia.

1-32. To govern.

33-34. An aromatic plant.

N-8. A fist.

24-31. To agree with.

3-12. Part of a ship.

20-29. One.

5-27. Exchanging.

9-25. Sunk in mud.

13-21. A boy.

The first crossword puzzle, as it appeared in the New York World, *December 21, 1913.*   Associated Press/*Los Angeles Herald-Examiner*

Their numbers may not be greater than the combined numbers of the older and more familiar schools, but aggressiveness is of the very essence of their quality, and the size of their separate contributions and the force of their often violent and always powerful color in the same exhibition with the tender shimmer of Monet and Corot gives the impression of an equal number of bass drums and violins playing at the same moment. The exhibition is Wagnerian in scope, and it is Rienzi, not Parsifal. It makes a great deal of noise.

In studying it from the simple point of view of a person who "wants to know," however, it offers an unusual opportunity. We can see, if we care to take the trouble, how the art of painting developed from Ingres down to Seurat, and we can observe the sudden backward jump toward savage art in the work of Matisse and the Cubists. Luckily for the critic, there is no such thing as taking sides. In the presence of such a polyhedron as modern art he would be in trouble enough. He can heartily and with all his emotional being detest the eccentricities of a Matisse, and he can find his soul moved to something approaching ecstacy by the serene and noble rhythms of Puvis de Chavannes, but so can any one of us. His more dispassionate, although less simple, task is to try to discover what addition each of the innovators in the various schools has made to the sum of artistic achievement, what change each one has made in the prevailing taste of his time, and what step he has taken to broaden our perceptions.

Most of us have followed the history of art with any degree of interest are reasonably familiar with earlier work of the men who came immediately after Ingres.

Ingres himself was a great master and a revolutionary, although to-day he seems to the casual observer the embodiment of the academic. So calm, so healthful, so unruffled he is that one properly may apply to him the misused term "classic." He really expressed something of the Greek spirit, something of its love of reality and reasoning. His color was cool and thin but his line pulsated with life. There are a couple of drawings by Ingres in the exhibition which are not yet in place and Whistler's copy of his "Andromeda," a very insufficient representation certainly, but a starting point.

Then came Delacroix, organizing color harmonies and turning the serenity of Ingres into a drama that verges on melodrama. He was tagged "romantic" and he used color to convey emotion.

In Daumier we have the healthfulness of Ingres and the dramatic instinct of Delacroix without the coldness of the former or the unreality of the latter.

In looking now at the work of Daumier and Corot, the likeness of these two friends, at first view so widely separated, becomes apparent. Behind the vaporous atmosphere of Corot lies an appreciation as sound as Daumier's of the solid substance of material things. The plastic effect is always there even when masked by the lightest of tone. And Daumier, so obviously a master of plastic effect, is equally respectful of the envelope of air by which all objects are surrounded, never presenting his forms detached from this envelope. Corot concerns himself most, however, with the movement of air and its delicate elasticity at moments when nature is at peace and Daumier concerns himself most with the mere powerful rhythms of nature and with the full expression of dynamic forces.

Degas leads us quietly enough from these comrades toward the new thought of the Impressionists, but he has more in common with Daumier than with Monet, whose name so often is associated with his. We are fortunate in having two excellent examples of his work in the present exhibition, and it is easy to see in them both his mastery of the line with which Ingres labored and Daumier played, and the effects of light which the later school continually attempted and occasionally achieved. Degas, old and cross, and contented with a manner of life that seems the quintessence of poverty to a New York artist, is known at his true value by the modern connoisseur. Not a pearly flake of his wonderful crayon escapes their acclaim, not a single line of that sullen truth which he tells about humanity as seen by him in all its beauty of ugliness. He is greater than most of the people in this present company, because he is so fierce a critic of himself. With what cold indifference to self-love he has put to himself problems that no one else had solved because he knew that his mind would be forced to independent work thereby. What he could win easily did not interest him. The beautiful contours of the professional model over which Ingres would have lingered with unwearying joy would have seemed to Degas stupid, but his courage rose at sight of the highly developed muscles of a dancing girl, finding in these something upon which to spend original research. Degas, Ingres, and Daumier belong to the limited class of expressionists. They seek in their drawing to reveal every significant feature of their model. In their studies of the figure the contours tell the story of the age, the relaxation or the nervous tension, the race and type and physical training of the model. In their draped figures every fold of the costume has its cause in the pose and gesture of the body. Everything belongs to everything else; no line hangs loose from the general structure. One notes in the drawing of a back by Degas in Gallery R the thickness of the body, the movement of the shoulders, the relationship of the head to the rest of the figure. Nothing has been done according to recipe. It is all first-hand observation and the philosophic sifting of facts for those that express what it is valuable to show. In the same gallery is a nude by Matisse, an early work, we should judge. It tells us that Matisse also knows the trick, so difficult to learn, of placing the limbs in their sockets, so that they may move with the motion of life. He also has studied the muscular development of the body and can give the great twist at the waist which Michael Angelo [sic] taught us to look for and which the weak draughtsmen avoid as they would the plague. But Matisse has put his truly remarkable talent at the services of a schematic art, while Degas has remained free. Hence, we believe, the to [sic] us immense superiority of the earlier man.

Following the people who have used line and mass and color to express personal emotion in the presence of nature, or at least to reproduce those characteristics of nature which heighten emotion in us, come the Impres-

sionists with their objective temper, their clear science, their pursuit of ex-
ternalities. They are the analysts who observe and seek to know through
study rather than intuition. They chase the moment in its flight to record the
exact transition between it and the next moment. They strive to paint mobility from without instead of giving expression to the dynamic force within
that causes mobility. Thus Monet and Pisarro and Sisley and their company
see nature in arrest. With them it is always "I am," not "I am becoming."

This quaintly static art, so nobly pursued, naturally is restful. We see how
restful it is as we pass from the group of Monets in the present exhibition
to the halls beyond, where the air is troubled by the violence of the new
movement. And it is healthy art, just as a soul concerned with its environment rather than with its inner emotions is a healthy soul. And it is a sensitive art, because it seeks to record the most delicate aspects of nature.
Monet was concerned less with the facts of the solid earth than with the
facts of its impalpable envelope of atmosphere, suffused with light. He ana-
lyzed light, and he and his followers resolved the colors of nature back into
the bands of the spectrum, and then reproduced them on the canvas by dots
of pure pigment, and these dots, at suffecent distance, combine their hues in
the eye with the effect of colored light. And Delacroix had done almost this,
with an equally scientific intention, as early as 1825, using little wafers of
color to produce his effect, and experimenting with the reactions of comple-
mentary colors. Probably the science of color relations will not again be
banished from art.

But here, side by side with Monet and Seurat, we find these Post-Impres-
sionists, who are in love with science but not with objective reality, and
who have added to the science of color, which they employ in a different
way from that of the Impressionists, the element of symbolism. Let us turn
back a moment to that quiet room in which Augustus John, the Englishman,
is side by side with Puvis de Chavannes, from whom he has so obviously
derived, and in which, from another corner, Matisee leers, in commingled
savagery and sophistry of mood. Puvis is placed by many historians among
the symbolists, but he is not one. He illustrates legends and decorates spaces.
He wrote once: "A picture should always be looked at from in front, and
peacefully; never from behind, where the painter has hidden nothing." How
can we do otherwise in the case of his Hellenic decoration than look peacefully and be content with what we see? There is no trouble in those large,
wholesome figures. There is no storm brewing in those turquois skies. That
sweet landscape, abounding in all the fair fruits of the earth and in the
daintiest of earth's blossoms, invites us to indolence and bliss. Maurice Denis
is the immediate follower of this "serene and happy sage," but Denis adds
to his master's cheerful pagan art a no less cheerful Christianity. He paints
in a high key, like the Impressionists, and uses purer color than Puvis, and
he paints illustrations to legends in a calm spirit, as Puvis does, but they are
Christian legends, and into his decorations creeps the personal joy in spiritual life of the devout Christian. Denis is well represented in the exhibition,
and the observer, hovering between his old belief in reality and his new

concern with symbolism, will find something comforting in the little ugly, stupid mothers who caress little ugly, stupid children with that passion of maternity which sees no ugliness and feels no lack of wit or grace.

By way of Denis we come reluctantly and holding back, to Matisse. Here we have Post-Impressionism, the expression of movement, the expression of mass, denuded of all that has given joy to past generations in relation of one form to another. We enter a stark region of abstractions that are hideous to our unaccustomed eyes, whatever they may become to the vision of the future. Here and there we see a decorative placing of a great shape of color with another great shape, and see something that would please us in a piece of Indian weaving. But it seems to us to be written in art that a man cannot successfully combine crudity with sophistication. M. Matisse gets back some of the force, some of the decorative value of the work done by savage races, but he presents it with a sophistication that mitigates its effect. He will neither cut loose from nature nor from convention, but his convention is not conventional enough and his nature is not natural enough to reconcile us to his method. What he has added to the art of the present, however, is force of color. It will be long before we can again work with a weak palette.

Matisse has been freely called a charletan, which implies willful eccentricity in pursuit of sensation, but our business is not with his motives. We have not even anything to do with his avowed intentions. All that concerns us is what he has done that is different from the work of his predecessors, and that is at the same time worthy of considerations. We may well say in the first place that his pictures are ugly, that they are coarse, that they are narrow, that to us they are revolting in their inhumanity. His simplications are so extreme that the lines at which he finally stops as expressing the essential contours are to the ordinary observer no more suggestive of the human face and future than the paintings of animals in the palaeolithic age are suggestive of the originals. Nevertheless he has found in the human structure the basic lines which he throws so brutally upon his canvas. They are not created out of nothing, and it is here that we feel their defect most strongly.

Humanity grows richer and more interesting in its complexity as civilization advances. To throw over the complexity, which a great artist like Cézanne synthetizes [sic] into a significant and intense simplicity, in order to return to the primal simplicity empty of spiritual interest which satisfied the savage, seems to us to subtract from the resources of art instead of adding to them. If we look long at caricatures we end by seeing their sources in the faces and forms about us until in time we see nearly everything in terms of caricature—we see it, that is, with the essential forms and idiosyncratic features emphasized and exaggerated. If the caricaturist is a great artist, as Daumier was, he pursues this emphasis and exaggeration only so far as the boundaries of psychological suggestion permit him to go. His human beings remain human beings with interesting minds and souls. Matisse, up to the point of our present familiarity with him, seems to have thrown psychology, the artist's last great opportunity, quite over, or else to have reduced it to a purely animal significance. This seems to us the real reason why his paintings are repellant to us and to many others, the turning of humanity back toward its brutish beginnings. The task, as he has performed it, is not an easy one. He has shown great skill and power, but we do not see before him a goal worth striving for. We repeat, however, that he has made it possible for the young school of artists to revitalize their color and achieve combinations even of pale tints that have force.

What the Cubists are doing is very different from what Matisse is doing. They are asking us to accept a new formula for the representation of nature. And in that formula they insist upon the third dimension and upon angles. Think back. Ingres drew human beings so that we felt their material substance. They had thickness as well as length and breadth. Later generations called that method of painting "vulgar round modeling"; but in the hand of Ingres it was emphatically round. Wherever Ingres could emphasize a curve he did so, and his long, languid curves were a part of the beauty of a painting. But first and foremost he made his figures stand out from their background. When Manet came along, he adopted the flat modeling that he had admired in Velasquez, only, of course, he carried it further than Velasquez had carried it. If his figures seem to have thickness, it is because he so carefully observed and so justly stated the color and tone relations of the various planes, and not because he used light and shade to create the illusion of the third dimension.

Now the Cubists are creating this illusion with cubes and angles. [Francis] Picabia goes further still. He is more scientific in his method and more logical. He does not try at all for representation, but he tries to arrange abstract forms with their appropriate colors in such a way as to convey the same sensation or emotion that is conveyed to him by the reality he starts from. He tries that is, to express the motive power that results in movement without asking us to recognize the moving object. This is very theoretic and an entertaining experiment demanding intellectual activity and balance. But it is terribly confused by the habit which Picabia and Picasso and all the others share, the habit of trying to explain themselves by titles. If their work is music it is programme music, and the programme plays an important part in their conception. Masterpieces are independent of programme, and we see no chance for the new school until it throws over the literary element and stands alone. So long as it prates of people coming down stairs and dancing and walking in procession, it is contradicting itself and inviting ridicule.

The exhibition contains many things of which we have not written in this crude attempt to discriminate its main lines of direction. In the classic phrase of the composing room there is "more to follow."

1914

It was a bold, even startling move, and one that upset many of his fellow industrialists. Henry Ford, the onetime farm boy who had early on experimented with horseless carriages, proposed to double the wages of his skilled employees, to an unheard-of $5 per day. While other businessmen grumbled that Ford's generosity would bankrupt them, the Dearborn, Michigan, auto maker was gambling that high wages would curtail employee turnover and save him the costs of training people for his new assembly line. Further, the workers, once they were better paid, would be able to afford the very automobiles they were producing in record quantities. Thus Ford would doubly profit.

Not all of Ford's employees would qualify for the $5-per-day. Those who did were required to live "moral" lives— and permit Ford's Sociology Department to check up on them. Despite those infringements upon the workers' privacy, the day after Ford announced his offer, *The Detroit News* of January 6, 1914, bannered:

TEN THOUSAND MEN IN BATTLE FOR JOBS AT THE FORD PLANT

POLICE HAVE TO FIGHT BACK MOB TO SAVE DOORS OF FACTORY

Fire Hose Brought Out to Be Used as Last Emergency, But Sight of It Awes Clamoring Mass of Humanity.

Army of Jobless Men Begins to Gather At Plant at 3 O'Clock This Morning

While a police reporter told of efforts to control the mob of job seekers outside the Woodward Avenue factory, a second talked to Ford about his unprecedented plan. That interview ran on page one under the head:

Ford Tells What He Hopes Will Result From His Plans

"We made $25,000,000 last year. We expect to make $30,000,000 to $35,000,000 this year," said Henry Ford in an interview with The News today.

Mr. Ford, as he sat gazing out of the window, spoke nonchalantly of millions as the lesser cogs of industry talk of the weather.

"Why, no, I'm not very busy this morning," said Mr. Ford in answer to a question. "None of us out here is very busy. We all have just a little to do."

Then, making himself comfortable by resting his feet on the radiator, he discussed the plan his company has adopted and some of the criticisms which have been raised against it.

"Every man in our employ over the age of 22 years who is not working on a salary will share in the distribution of profits. The man of minimum wage of $2.34 will receive an additional $2.66 per day semi-monthly and all the men who do the actual work will receive the same increase.

"Foremen and superintendents and all other salaried men will continue to share as usual in the distribution by bonus at the close of the year, based solely on merit. They are passed on by the management. Last year we distributed in bonuses from $200,000 to $300,000 in this way, with about 200 men receiving an average of $1,000 each.

"Do you anticipate even larger profits next year, so that the profit sharing may be even larger?" Mr. Ford was asked.

"Well, as to that, all I can say is, let us hope for better times. Then, you see, of course, there will be greater profits to distribute."

"What effect will your plan have on the other manufacturers of automobiles? Will it injury them in any way?"

"Why, no, I don't think so. But I'll tell you one thing. The successful manufacturer must specialize. No company in the world is big enough to make more than one model. The other manufacturers ought to come to that.

"Now, here is $16,000,000 we are giving to the men who make our cars. We made 200,000 cars last year. That is only $50 a car we are giving back to the men. If the car lasts three years and gives good service, can't our customers afford it? We gave our customers $50 a car last year and took $19,000,000 from profits by cutting the price of the car $50. Leaving the price of the car the same this year we will give the men who do the work that $50."

In reply to the criticism that the Ford plan is likely to disrupt the labor market, Mr. Ford said,

"I do not see how it can. Neither does the plan mean that we intend to displace our employes of foreign birth. We like the foreigners. Every language in the world is represented in our plant. I know the towns and villages in the old country from which many of our foreign workers came. We believe in treating them all alike. This can make no difference.

"Other manufacturers can treat their labor in the same way. Again its up to the management and centralization. All manufacturers ought to manufacture only a small number of articles.

"We expect to make $20,000,000 to $25,000,000 next year. We made $25,000,000 last year. Of course the $15,000,000 remaining after we have given $10,000,000 back to the employes will go back into that fifteen hundred thousand dollar plant out there, new buildings and other improvements being constructed.

"The plan is permanent, but we can't estimate several years in advance how much the distribution each year will amount to.

"It will affect all the workers who work with their hands in the production of the car from the minimum wage man through those on the wage list. The salaried men, all of whom receive a bonus at the end of the year, begin at $100 to $150 a month. The bonus system in the past has included some of the men of the wage list who have made records, as well as salary men. It may be that these, who come under the profit-sharing plan, will be not included in the bonus plan hereafter, but that has not been decided."

"The Men Behind the Guns" Ones to Benefit in Profit-Sharing Plan

The rank and file of the great army of employes of the Ford Motor Co., "the man with the hoe," the shovel, the saw, the worker at the lathe, drill press, the conveyor, the annealing furnace and every man who works with his hands in the production of the Ford car, will derive the greatest benefit from the company's plan to begin Jan. 12, the sharing of profits among all male employes over the age of 23 years.

That the purpose back of the plan as evolved by Henry Ford is to reward the "under dog," the commonest laborer and mechanic who makes the manufacture of the car possible, is made clear by further details of the plan as explained by James Couzens, vice-president and treasurer of the company. Foremen, superintendents and others on high salaries will not be included in the system, but they will share in the usual distributions of bonuses at the end of each year, the amount of the bonus to each man being determined by the officers of the company after examination of his record during the 12 months under consideration. These men, the company believes, are receiving sufficient remuneration to support themselves and their families in comfort and do not need further financial support of the company.

The wages of the lowest laborer will be more than doubled, the minimum wage being increased from $2.34 to $5 a day. This has nothing to do with the length of service and depends only on sobriety and industry while on the job. It means that the worker employed today, tomorrow or next year will receive exactly the same benefits as his companions in his class of labor, who may or may not have been in the employ of the company before the plan was inaugurated.

1915

For ten months Europe heaved with the convulsion of war, Great Britain, France, Italy, and Russia aligned against Germany, the Austro-Hungarian and the

Ottoman Empires. The United States insisted on its neutrality as the fighting on the western front settled into bloody, inconclusive trench warfare. Increasingly anxious, Great Britain sought to enlist America's support for the Allied Powers' war against the "brutal Hun."

Then, on the afternoon of May 7, 1915, two torpedoes from a German submarine ripped into the defenseless British luxury liner *Lusitania*. As reported by the influential *New York Tribune* the following day, Germany had suddenly handed Great Britain a major propaganda coup.

The sinking of the *Lusitania,* with the loss of 1,198 lives, offered terrifying proof that the Teutonic barbarians knew no restraints, and would make war even on innocent civilians. Probably no other act so hardened the United States' attitude and turned popular sentiment against Germany as the sinking of the defenseless liner.

But there was more to the vessel's loss than the press reported. Prior to the attack, Great Britain's First Lord of the Admiralty, Winston Churchill, had withdrawn the liner's destroyer escort and had ordered the ship to reduce speed. The *Lusitania* thus was an easy target. Moreover, the vessel was not quite so blameless as the press portrayed it at the time. Decades later, government archives yielded ship's manifests revealing that the ostensible innocent was, in fact, carrying crates of small arms and ammunition—enough to make it, and its passengers legitimate targets.

1,300 DIE AS LUSITANIA GOES TO BOTTOM; 400 AMERICANS ON BOARD TORPEDOED SHIP; WASHINGTON STIRRED AS WHEN MAINE SANK

Dying and Injured Brought In with Other Survivors to Queenstown—Two Torpedoes Fired, Says Steward.

Few First Class Passengers Saved

Attack Made About Eight Miles from Irish Coast in Broad Daylight and in Fine Weather—Survivor Tells of Bravery of Cunard Officers.

Washington, May 8.—A dispatch to the State Department early to-day from American Consul Frost at Queenstown stated that the total number of survivors of the Lusitania was about 700.

[By Cable to the Tribune.]

London, May 8, 3 a.m.—At least 1,300 lives were lost when the Lusitania was torpedoed without warning in broad daylight yesterday afternoon by a German submarine, according to estimates by survivors. The estimate of First Officer Jones puts the total nearer 1,500.

Only a few of the first class passengers were saved. Most of them remained aboard, thinking the ship would float. Trawlers arriving at Queenstown have a hundred bodies or more.

The "Times" Queenstown correspondent says that some of the survivors who have arrived there report that Alfred Gwynne Vanderbilt was drowned.

At Queenstown there have arrived 647 alive, 40 dead; at Kinsale 11 alive, 5 dead. All boats which went out from Queenstown have now returned, except one trawler. Fishing boats may be bringing more survivors to Kinsdale.

It is believed here that there were about 2,000 persons on board, 1,254 passengers and between 700 and 800 in the crew.

Survivors of the Lusitania who have arrived at Queenstown estimate that only about 650 of those aboard the steamer were saved.

Of the dead, more than two hundred are supposed to be Americans, as it is believed there were about 400 on board.

Lady Macworth, daughter of David A. Thomas, the Welsh "Coal King," and a noted militant suffragist, went down with the liner, but was saved by a life preserver she wore, and later was picked up.

Twenty-two of those landed at Queenstown have since died of their injuries. Nearly all the officers, except Captain Turner and the first and second officers, perished.

A dispatch from Queenstown sent out at midnight says: "Up to the present 520 passengers from the Lusitania have been landed here from boats. Ten or eleven boatloads came ashore, and others are expected."

The Central News says that the number of the Lusitania's passengers who died of injuries while being taken to Queenstown will reach 100. This is believed to indicate that the ship sank much more quickly than was expected, and that the few minutes that elapsed were used in getting into the boats those injured by the explosions.

The motor boat Elizabeth has arrived at Kinsdale and reports that at 3:30 p.m. she picked up two lifeboats containing 63 and 16 survivors of the Lusitania, respectively. A Cork tug took the rescued to Queenstown. They were mostly women and children.

The Lusitania could not launch many of her lifeboats, owing to her list to port.

The tiny hospitals at Kinsale and Clonakilty, and the institutions at Cork and Queenstown are jammed with survivors from the ocean horror, those not actually wounded suffering terribly from shock. The giant Cunarder now rests on the bottom of the ocean, about eight miles off Kinsale Head and twenty miles from the entrance to Queenstown Harbor.

ADMIRALTY GIVES OUT NEWS.

Telegrams have been filtering into London last night and early this morning stating that the rescued are being brought to Queenstown by three steamers. The Admiralty says between five and six hundred have already been landed at Clonakilty and Kinsale, coming into the latter port in a string of boats towed by a Greek steamer. Motor fishing boats hovered near the scene of the wreck, picking up what boats they could and turning them over to the powerful ocean going tug Stormcock.

Huge crowds fill Cockspur Street near the Haymarket, storming the Cunard offices for news. The women, who had been weeping so bitterly, paused for a moment when an agent of the line bellowed through a megaphone the following dispatch:

"Our Liverpool office says First Officer Jones wires from Queenstown he thinks between five hundred and six hundred have been saved. This includes passengers and crew, and is only an estimate.". . .

PASSENGERS WERE AT LUNCHEON.

The tug Stormcock returned to Queenstown, bringing about one hundred and fifty survivors, principally passengers, among whom were many women, several of the crew and one steward.

Describing the experience of the Lusitania, the steward said: "The passengers were at luncheon, when a submarine came up and fired two torpedoes, which struck the Lusitania on the starboard side, one forward and the other in the engine room. They caused terrific explosions.

"Captain Turner immediately ordered the boats out. The ship began to list badly immediately.

"Ten boats were put into the water, and between four hundred and five hundred passengers entered them. The boat in which I was approached the land with three other boats, and we were picked up shortly after 4 o'clock by the Stormcock.

"I fear that few of the officers were saved. They acted bravely.

WENT DOWN BY BOW.

"There were only fifteen minutes from the time the ship was struck until she foundered, going down bow foremost. It was a dreadful sight."

More dispatches brought word that the hotel and lodging houses are being canvassed in an effort to obtain more or less authoritative lists of the survivors. . . .

The Admiralty gave out the official news about midnight that the attack was made in broad daylight and with absolutely no warning.

A Queenstown dispatch to "The Daily Chronicle" says that seven torpedoes were discharged from the German craft and that one of them stuck the Lusitania amidships.

There is no question in anyone's mind that it was a submarine which caused the disaster. There is information at hand that persons on shore near Galley Head did see a submarine yesterday at that point. . . .

The Lusitania was not due, according to the schedule which has been followed since shortly after the war broke out (when her run was lengthened from about four days to seven or more), at the point where she sank until about twenty-four hours later. This indicates that she had put on all her four screws, whereas for many of her trips she has been using only two, in order to save coal.

This would indicate that some attention was paid at least to the more recent threats against the ship in America. The submarine's achievement is considered a wonderful piece of luck, from the German point of view. It has been considered that any ship moving faster than fifteen knots was almost unhitable by the slower moving, clumsy submarine. The German evidently simply lay in wait, gauged the speed of the gigantic liner and at the proper moment let fly.

Naval officers consider that if the Lusitania was making full speed or anywhere near full speed it was almost a miracle that the torpedoes found their mark.

AMERICAN FEELING RUNS HIGH.

American feeling ran high here as soon as the news was received, and Ambassador Page made inquiry immediately at the Foreign Office to learn if any mines had been placed at the spot where the Lusitania sank. He was told definitely there were no mines in the locality, and has forwarded his report to that effect to Washington.

The Cunard company states officially that the ship was sunk without any warning whatever.

The weather off the Irish coast was particularly good yesterday, and the attack took place when the sun was shining.

Capital Aroused, Situation Gravest Yet Faced in War

[From the Tribune Bureau.]

Washington, May 7.—The news of the heavy loss of life on the Lusitania stirred Washington as it has not been stirred since the sinking of the Maine. The earlier reports that both passengers and crew had been landed safely had quieted apprehensions of an immediate crisis in the relations of the United States and Germany. But when it became clear that Americans—undoubtedly a considerable number of them—were to be counted among the victims of German savagery at sea the full significance of the tragedy off Queenstown struck home.

President Wilson made little effort to conceal his feelings. At 8 o'clock to-night the President received the following dispatch from the United States Consul at Cork:

"Lusitania sank at 2:30 o'clock. Probably many survivors. Rescue work proceeding favorably. Shall I send you list of survivors?"

As soon as he read it he put on his hat and walked out of the White House without the knowledge of the Secret Service men who are guarding him. The President walked up Sixteenth Street to Corcoran Street, crossed over to Fifteenth Street and back to the White House, where he went into his study to await further information and to turn over in his mind the message that it is expected he will send to the German Foreign Office as soon as all the details of the disaster are known.

Official Washington has realized the possibility of a clash between our government and the German government ever since the State Department took the stand that Germany must be held to "strict accountability" for any treatment of American citizens and American property not in accordance with existing rules of warfare at sea. . . .

The destruction of the battleship Maine in Havana harbor, though disavowed by the Spanish government, cut American feeling to the quick. It made the preservation of good relations with Spain in Cuba a nearly hopeless task.

The Maine tragedy came without warning. But the Lusitania tragedy comes after a widespread and audacious advertisement of Germany's intention to disregard the protection given to Americans (even when passengers on a British vessel) by the rules of international law. . . .

High officials in the administration declined to-night to discuss the possibility of this country being drawn into the war because of the loss of American lives. They insisted upon taking an optimistic view of the situation and asserted that when the list of survivors was finally made up few would be found to be missing.

That the situation will be acute when loss of American lives is proved is admitted on all sides. No action will be taken by this government until all the details of the torpedoing of the Lusitania are received. There is one thing certain, however, and that it [sic] that Germany will not be allowed to shirk any responsibility for the disaster, should investigation show that the act was performed by a German submarine.

The possibility of the Lusitania having struck a mine was discounted here by the receipt of news that the British Admiralty had given assurances that there were no mines in the neighborhood in which the vessel was blown up.

PROTEST WILL BE VIGOROUS.

Even if no American lives had been lost, the sinking of the Cunard liner by a German torpedo would have been made a part of the most vigorous protest that the American government had yet transmitted to the German Foreign Office. This is the belief of officials high in the administration to-night.

The United States has repeatedly asserted that it recognizes the right of belligerents to visit and search only, and that it will hold the German government to strict accountability for the loss of any American lives through the undersea warfare of the German government.

The United States has no concern over the sinking of the Lusitania itself, but it is gravely concerned over the probable loss of the lives of American citizens through the activity of German submarines in the war zone. In the note of the American government to the German Foreign Office on February 10 it was declared that this country would take any steps it might think necessary to safeguard American lives and property and to secure to American citizens the full enjoyment of their acknowledged rights on the high seas.

It is frankly stated here that there is no doubt that the destruction of the Cunard liner was deliberately planned by the Germans long before it sailed and that the German Embassy's advertisement [warning against sailing on the vessel] was merely a ruse behind which the German government hoped to hide in case there was loss of life. At the time of the publication of the advertisement it was asserted by high officials of the State Department that, so far as this government was concerned, it did not in any way relieve the German government from being held to a strict accountability for the loss of life of any American citizen. . . .

1915

Leo Frank was the outsider, a Jew from Brooklyn, New York, living in hard-shell Baptist Georgia. That was the only reason, his supporters argued, that Frank was accused in April, 1913, of the sexual assault and murder of Mary Phagan. A night watchman had discovered the body of the 12-year-old employee of the National Pencil Company in the Atlanta factory where Frank was plant superintendent. On scant and conflicting evidence, Frank was found guilty and sentenced to be hanged.

The case became at first a local, then a nationwide sensation. A pathetic ballad about "Little Mary Phagan" became a favorite throughout the South. On the other hand, the belief that Frank was convicted only because he was Jewish gained credibility; 100,000 letters from across the country asked Georgia Governor John M. Slaton for clemency on Frank's behalf.

Two days before the scheduled execution, Slaton commuted the death penalty to life imprisonment. An angry mob of 10,000 descended upon the governor's mansion as Frank was transferred to a state prison farm. In July, 1915, another inmate attacked Frank, slitting his throat. He narrowly survived.

Then on the morning of August 17, 1915, *The Atlanta Journal* blared:

LEO FRANK FORCIBLY TAKEN FROM PRISON; HE IS HANGED TO A TREE NEAR MARIETTA; HIS BODY HAS BEEN BROUGHT TO ATLANTA

People Throng to Scene Where Body Dangles from Rope

After Urging the Crowd Not to Indulge in Further Demonstrations, Judge Morris Hurries Frank's Body to Atlanta

Leo M. Frank's dead body, which is now in the hands of an Atlanta undertaker, was found hanging by the neck from the limb of a tree two miles east of Marietta at an early hour Tuesday morning, and the absence of gunshot wounds or other violence indicated that Frank was alive until hanged by the mob that took him from the state prison farm at Milledgeville Monday night.

At the instance of Newt A. Morris, former judge of the Blue Ridge circuit, and a prominent Marietta citizen, the body was cut down and hauled to Marietta in an undertaker's wagon soon after the crowd began to gather around it.

At the outskirts of Marietta, just in front of the National Cemetery, Judge Morris overtook the undertaker's wagon in an automobile, lifted the body in the long basket from the wagon to the automobile, and sped with it to Atlanta at top speed.

BODY BROUGHT TO ATLANTA.

At the outskirts of Atlanta the body was met by an Atlanta undertaker in an automobile ambulance and was again transferred and rushed at top speed to a place which was not disclosed.

About 7 o'clock Tuesday morning W.J. Frey, a former sheriff of Cobb county, who lives two and one-half miles east of Marietta on the Roswell road, saw four automobiles pass along the road in front of his house. They were going like the wind. In the second or third car he recalls seeing a man of Frank's description, wedged between two men in the back seat of the car.

Half an hour later, Mr. Frey drove into Marietta, and there learned that Frank's body had been found handing to a tree in a grove two miles east of Marietta, near the road along which he had driven into town.

BODY IS DISCOVERED.

In company with Gus Benson, a Marietta citizen, and W.W. Yuan, a traveling man from Augusta, Ga., Mr. Frey drove back along the road, and found the body in a grove of young trees on land owned by himself, and within a stone's throw of his gin-house. A number of people had already arrived ahead of them and were viewing the body. The news of the discovery spread like wild fire, and soon the road was full of people coming from both directions.

It appears from the facts known and stated by Mr. Frey that Frank was hanged between 7 o'clock and 7:30 o'clock Tuesday morning. That Mr. Frey did not see the body when he drove by, on his way to Marietta, shows that the men who hanged Frank had done their work and gone, and further shows that the body had not yet been discovered. From the road the body was screened by the leaves of the trees, so that it would not have been noticed unless a passerby had been looking for it.

CROWDS THRONG TO SCENE.

A horrible sight met the eyes of the people who were first to arrive at the grove, and a still more horrible sight met the eyes of later arrivals, who found not only the body swaying in the wind, with the gaping red wound in the throat, but surging around it a closely packed mass of men whose excitement was something fearful.

A grass rope, brown in color, about half an inch in diameter, was thrown over the limb of an oak tree, near the trunk of the tree. One end of this rope was around the neck of Leo M. Frank, tied in hangman's knot, and the other end was tied to the base of a sapling some twenty feet away.

HANDKERCHIEF COVERS FACE.

Frank hung with the top of his head near the limb of the oak tree, his feet about four feet above the ground. A white handkerchief was over his face and the corners knotted at the back of his head. The hangman's knot lay against his right jaw. The wound in his throat, where William Creen attempted to kill him at the state farm a few weeks ago, was pulled open, underneath his left ear. The rope was above the wound underneath his left ear, but toward the front of his throat, where the wound ranged upward, the rope lay in the wound.

Frank's body from the waist up was clothed in a thin, white pajama jacket. Worked in the jacket on the left side of the chest were some letters in red thread, that looked like "L.M.F." The sleeves of the pajama were chipped away by souvenir hunters, wielding their pocket knives, until both sleeves were gone as far up as the elbows.

HANDCUFFS BIND WRISTS.

The arms of the dead man, thus exposed, hung straight and stiff, with the wrists handcuffed in front, and the arms and hands and fingers were blue, while the left thumb showed the healing cut where Frank defended himself from Creen's knife attack at the state farm.

The body from the waist down was wrapped in a dirty piece of brown cloth that looked like khaki. It was stretched across the front like a skirt drawn tight, and tied together by the corners behind, somewhat toward the left hip. The edges of the cloth, just barely meeting on the left side, would flap open in the wind as the body swayed back and forth, exposing the leg of the dead man from the knee down, blue and stiff like the arm.

Around the ankles was tied a piece of grass rope, about the same size of the rope Frank was hanged with, and this rope was cut from around the ankles by souvenir hunters soon after the crowd gathered. . . .

WOMEN AND CHILDREN SWELL THE THRONG.

The crowd gathered with the rapidity that only intense curiosity and intense excitement can produce. They swarmed the road from both directions. They seemed to rise up out of the ground, so fast they came. The automobiles came careening, recklessly disregarding life and limb of occupants. Horse-drawn vehicles came at a gallop. Pedestrians came running.

The vehicles stopped in the road at the grove and soon packed the road and overflowed into the fields. As the vehicles would stop, their occupants would jump out and run to the grove, bending forward, panting, wild-eyed.

Women came. Children came. Even babes in arms. The sight of the body, swaying in the wind, with the red gaping wound in the throat, made some of the women sick, and they would utter little shrieks and groans and turn their heads away. Other women walked up to the packed mass of men and pushed their way into the pack, and looked on the dead body without the quiver of an eyelash.

FRENZIED MAN SHAKES FISTS AT BODY.

Excitement began to manifest itself as soon as the crowd began to gather, and as the crowd increased the excitement increased.

One of the first arrivals was a man in a wild frenzy of passion. He was bareheaded, coatless, his eyes blazing like the eyes of a maniac. He ran through the crowd, ran up to the body, threw up his hands and clenched his fists and shook them at the body. Then his hands would open and his fingers would writhe, and his fists would close again, and he would shake them at the body.

"Now we've got you!" he screamed. "You won't murder any more little innocent girls! We've got you now!! We've got you now!!!"

His voice would rise to a shrill high note, and then it would drop off and become hoarse, and he would chant his words in a kind of sing-song, repeating one imprecation over and over.

And every once in a while, when he paused, some man in the crowd would give a yell, and the crowd would join in the yell, and it would grow and get higher and higher, and the sound of it would fill the little grove and echo back and forth.

These demonstrations seemed to fan the fury of the man by the body. His gesticulations became more violent, his raving words came faster and faster from his mouth, pouring out of him like a torrent.

"They won't put any monument over you!" he cried. "They are not going to get you! They are not going to get a piece of you as big as a cigar!!"

The crowd yelled and packed closer.

JUDGE MORRIS PLEADS.

At this juncture, a short, thick-set man, with blue eyes gleaming, ran up to the crowd, jostled his way through the crowd, and pushed up to a place beside the man who was cursing the body. He climbed up on something so that he could see over the heads of the crowd. "Men, hear me," he said.

It was Newt A. Morris, former judge of the Blue Ridge circuit, who had just arrived in an automobile from Marietta with Attorney John Wood, of Canton. They were attending Alpharetta court, heard the news early Tuesday morning, and come [sic] at top speed to the scene.

"Hear me, men," said Judge Morris. The crowd got quiet, except for a mumbling in an undertone by the man beside the body.

"Citizens of Cobb county, listen to me, will you?" said Judge Morris. They gave a murmur of assent.

"Who ever did this thing—"

The man beside the body broke in with a shout.

"God bless him, whoever he was!" shouted the man.

Judge Morris laid his hand on the man's shoulder and asked him please to be quiet for a few minutes.

"Whoever did this thing," said Judge Morris, "did a thorough job."

The crowd whooped.

"They 'shore' did," chorused the crowd.

LEFT NOTHING MORE TO DO.

"Whoever did this thing," said Judge Morris, "left nothing more for us to do. Little Mary Phagan is vindicated. Her foul murder is avenged. Now I ask you, I appeal to you, as citizens of Cobb county, in the good name of our county, not to do more. I appeal to you to let the undertaker take it."

The man by the body broke in again.

"We are not going to let the undertaker have it!" he shrieked. "We are not going to let them erect a monument over that thing! We are not going to let them have a piece of it as big as a cigar! We are going to burn it! That's what we are going to do! We are going to burn it! Come on, boys! Let's burn the dirty thing!". . . .

Judge Morris got down and ran back through the crowd and began to call for an undertaker. While he was calling, somebody laid a knife on the rope and Frank's body dropped to the ground with a thud, and the crowd packed around it in a solid mass, with the excited man standing at the head.

A negro ran up to Judge Morris. "Here I am, Judge," he said. "Here's the wagon."

Judge Morris gave orders, and the negro and another negro opened the back end of the wagon and pulled out a long undertaker's basket, and started with it toward the body.

"Bring the body on, men," shouted Judge Morris. "Bring it on. Quick, for God's sake!"

But none of them would pick it up, and Judge Morris, beckoning to the negroes, wedged in and worked his way toward the body, until the negroes finally got hold of it and started toward the undertaker's wagon.

HEEL CRUNCHES INTO FLESH.

The man [beside the corpse] reached out and struck at the body, and the negroes dropped it, and when it hit the ground the man stamped upon the face, and ground his heel into the dead flesh, and stamped again, and again, until the crowd, stricken silent and motionless by the horror of the sight, could hear the man's heel as it made a crunching sound.

Again and again, as a man grinds the head of a snake under his heel, did the man in the awful frenzy drive his heel into the face of Leo M. Frank, grinding the black hair of the dead body into the black dirt and dead black leaves.

"Stop him! For God's sake, stop him!" cried Judge Morris, and ran up to the man and begged him to stop.

And while the judge begged and pleaded with him, the negroes, at an order from the undertaker, seized the body again and ran with it to the basket, and seized the basket and ran with the body in the basket to the wagon, and shoved the body with mad haste into the wagon, snapped down the door and leaped to the seat and drove towards Marietta running on a dead run.

Judge Morris and Attorney Wood broke and ran for their automobile, and got in and started after the undertaker's wagon. . . . [T]he judge seized the first favorable opportunity and jerked the long basket out of the undertaker's wagon and laid it across the back seat of Attorney Wood's car. Then, jumping in beside the attorney, Judge Morris said, "Now, John drive like hell to Atlanta.". . .

Leo Frank's mutilation—the *Journal* only discreetly hinted at it—and death at the hands of what historian John Caughey has called "His Majesty, the Mob," was only one of hundreds of lynchings in the United States in the first years of the 20th Century. His case was unusual only in that he was a Jew; most often the victims were black, like John Riggins, lynched in Decatur, Georgia, the day after Frank's death, for allegedly assaulting a white woman.

According to a member of the lynch mob, identified only as a Marietta resident and "a clansman," Frank maintained his innocence to the end. A hint of the truth would only come seven decades later, when an elderly man, a former janitor at the Atlanta factory of the National Pencil Company, reluctantly revealed that he had seen the night watchman carrying Mary Phagan's limp body through the basement of the factory. The guilt-ridden janitor had not come forward earlier because he was black and the watchman, long since dead, was white.

1918

Twice in the 20th Century the United States has found itself dragged into world wars, wars it considered not of its concern and certainly not of its making. Both times American presidents sought to shape the peace that American arms would win and both times they failed. Indeed, had Woodrow Wilson succeeded in putting over his fourteen-point plan when the peace treaty was written, the world might have averted a second world war.

Having campaigned for reelection in 1916 on the slogan "He kept us out of war," Woodrow Wilson was loathe to lead the United States into the three-year-old stalemate in France. But a succession of German submarine attacks on United States vessels carrying war materiel to Great Britain roused American public opinion. Cannily fanned by British propagandists, that sentiment led a reluctant Wilson to ask Congress for a declaration of war against Germany and its allies in April, 1917.

Five months before United States troops actually entered combat in France, the President laid out his idealistic war aims. *The Washington Post* of January 9, 1918, reported Wilson's address to Congress, in a separate box summarizing the fourteen points:

WHAT THE UNITED STATES IS FIGHTING FOR CLEARLY STATED BY PRESIDENT WILSON IN HIS ADDRESS TO CONGRESS YESTERDAY

In his address to Congress yesterday, President Wilson set forth as the chief war aims of the United States:

No secret diplomacy.

Freedom of the seas in peace and war.

Equality of trade conditions among nations.

Reduction of national armaments.

Independent existence for Russia.

Fair adjustment of colonial claims.

Evacuation, restoration and sovereignty of Belgium.

Restoration to France of Alsace-Lorraine and all invaded territory.

Readjustment of Italian frontier.

Evacuation and restoration of Roumania, Serbia and Montenegro.

Sovereignty of Turkish portions of Ottoman empire.

Security of other nationalities now under Turkish control.

Freedom of the Dardanelles to commerce of all nations.

Freedom for Poland and access to the sea.

Political independence and territorial integrity of great and small states alike.

FREEDOM OF WORLD IS U.S. AIM IN WAR, WILSON TELLS CONGRESS; TO STAND BY ALLIES TO THE END

By Albert W. Fox.

America's peace terms, and the terms of the entente allies as well, were given to the world yesterday by President Wilson.

In an address to Congress in joint session, as remarkable as it was unexpected, the President removed for all time uncertainty and doubt as to what the war program of the coalition powers against German militarism must achieve before the conflict is ended. And he makes it clear to all that no cost or sacrifice must be considered in bringing the announced terms to fulfillment.

Fourteen Concrete Proposals

Nothing approaching the President's outline in definiteness or detail has appeared since the war began. Fourteen concrete proposals are laid down with unmistakable clearness. For the allies and the United States they are the final goal of peace. For the enemy they are the handwriting on the wall.

They show, first of all, that the President in the role of leader for democracy's cause yields not an inch from the path of justice and right to German autocracy. The terms he outlines provide no loophole of escape for Germany, as typified by the aspirations of her military masters. They are, in their detailed form, more uncompromising than the interpretations which have been read into previous general statements. No one thinks they bring peace nearer now.

Salient Features in Address

Epitomized, the President's outline of terms and his accompanying address brings out these salient features:

It meets the German drive for an insincere premature peace discussion with a fearless and detailed announcement of the real terms which must prevail.

It places the United States squarely on record as a full-fledged ally with a program indorsed by all.

It pledges the nation to "right the wrong" done to France, when Germany military power wrested away Alsace-Lorraine.

Italian Aspirations Supported

It support's Italy's aspirations for freedom of territory from military dominance.

It recognizes the sincerity of the bolsheviki and pledges continued support to the Russian people, whether their present leaders desire it or not.

It supports Lloyd George's program with respect to conquered German colonies.

It virtually pledges the nation against a separate peace.

"Together to the End"

"We cannot be separated in interest or divided in purpose," the President said. "We stand together to the end."

Any single one of these statements would have sufficed to stamp the President's address as a momentous announcement of policy. Taken together they have come with less startling effect, for it is realized at last that the moment of open, above-board frankness in discussing international questions is here and that President Wilson himself has been largely instrumental in bringing it about.

Comes Without Warning

The President's appearance before the joint session of Congress came with less than an hour's warning. . . .

The fact that there were few in the galleries partly accounted for the lack of pronounced applause when the President entered the chamber, after having waited several minutes in the ante room while Speaker [Champ] Clark named the committee to usher him in. There was a feeling that something important to the fate of the nation was certainly involved and vociferous applause seemed out of harmony with the solemnity of the occasion. Perfunctory handclapping alone greeted the President when he took his place at the Speaker's rostrum.

The President's opening sentence gave a clew at once as to what was coming. There had been hints of a statement or restatement of war aims, and it was evident that the time for it had come. . . .

It was after the President had begun enumerating the 14 specific terms that his hearers began voicing pronounced approval, in spite of a certain effort at restraint. When the President mentioned Alsace-Lorraine, restraint was thrown to the winds and pandemonium reigned for several minutes.

"All French territory should be freed and the invaded portions restored, and the wrong done to France by Prussia in 1871 in the matter of Alsace-Lorraine—."

The President got no further. There was a spontaneous outburst of applause, mingled with shouts and yells of approval, which grew in volume and intensity. Senators and representatives rose in chorus, some climbed on chairs and waved their arms. The President waited patiently and then smiled as the uproar continued. When he had completed the sentence, applause broke out afresh.

Is America's Battle Cry

The voice of approval was not altogether prompted by unanimous bonds of friendship and sympathy for France. It was realized that the President has never before mentioned Alsace-Lorraine specifically and that now he was taking the bull by the horns and stating frankly and with unmistakable clearness that France's battle for Alsace-Lorraine is our battle, and that this is one of the terms we will fight for to the end.

It is known that Germany is on record squarely as opposing the return of Alsace-Lorraine or any compromise which would take the fate of this province from German domination. . . .

Diplomatists here regard the President's present differentiation between the military minority and the [elected] reich majority as much more forceful than his previous attempts to place the German government and the German people in distinct classes. There is logic, too, in the manner in which the President warned the German people in advance of the role the military masters would necessarily assume when it came time to talk of peace.

"We wish her (Germany) only to accept a place of equality among the peoples of the world—the new world in which we live, instead of a place of mastery.

Must Know Huns' Spokesmen.

"Neither do we presume to suggest to her any alteration or modification of her institutions. But it is necessary, we must frankly say, and necessary as a preliminary to any intelligent dealing with her on our part, that we should know whom her spokesmen speak for when they speak to us, whether for the reichstag majority or for the military party and the men whose creed is imperial domination."

When the time comes for Germany, through the weight of power against her, to talk peace seriously or sue for peace, this question will come before the German people with particular significance. The President makes it clear that the trustworthiness of the German representations and their bona fide characters as spokesmen for the German people—instead of an autocratic military system—must be established "as a preliminary" requisite. In other words, Germany cannot even get to the stage of "intelligent dealings" with the United States until the people are supplied with representative spokesmen. This is another way of stating that the Hohenzollern military system as it now is must go.

Are Really War Terms.

There is little thought wasted here as to whether Germany will receive the President's terms in a favorable mood. Admittedly terms which demand evacuation of Russia, France, Belgium, &c., together with restoration and the relinquishing of Alsace-Lorraine and the surrender of the German contention concerning colonies, will be viewed in Germany as "war terms and not peace terms." President Wilson, [British Prime Minister David] Lloyd George and other leaders fully anticipate this.

It is clearly indicated that both President Wilson and Lloyd George have had a full understanding prior to the war aims speeches begun by the British premier and now followed up, more definitely and in more official form, by President Wilson. . . .

1918

Ernest Hemingway's seven-month stint at the *Kansas City Star* served as an important apprenticeship for the eighteen-year-old cub reporter.

One of the *Star* stories now attributed to Hemingway (who was paid $15 a week) described soldiers enjoying themselves at a local dance while outside a prostitute paces wet city streets. Indeed, according to Charles Fenton in *The Apprenticeship of Ernest Hemingway,* this story won the fledgling newsman praise in the city room.

The story, which ran on April 21, 1918, contains a number of attributes marking the later, mature Hemingway style of spare, muscular language that avoids easy romanticism and suggests, rather than states, emotion.

Hemingway was to take to heart in his novels the rules advanced by the *Star's* style sheet—"Use vigorous English. Be positive, not negative. Avoid the use of adjectives."—rules that yielded groundbreaking fiction tempered by the lessons of reporting.

MIX WAR, ART AND DANCING

Outside a woman walked along the wet street-lamp sidewalk through the sleet and snow.

Inside in the Fine Arts Institute on the sixth floor of the Y.M.C.A. Building, 1020 McGee Street, a merry crowd of soldiers from Camp Funston and Fort Leavenworth fox trotted and one-stepped with girls from the Fine Arts School while a sober faced young man pounded out the latest jazz music as he watched the moving figures. In a corner a private in the signal corps was discussing Whistler with a black haired girl who heartily agreed with him. The private had been a member of the art colony at Chicago before the war was declared.

Three men from Funston were wandering arm in arm along the wall looking at the exhibition of paintings by Kansas City artists. The piano player stopped. The dancers clapped and cheered and he swung into "The Long, Long Trail Awinding." An infantry corporal, dancing with a swift moving girl in a red dress, bent his head close to hers and confided something about a girl in Chautauqua, Kas. In the corridor a group of girls surrounded a tow-headed young artilleryman and applauded his imitation of his pal Bill challenging the colonel, who had forgotten the password. The music stopped again and the solemn pianist rose from his stool and walked out into the hall for a drink.

A crowd of men rushed up to the girl in the red dress to plead for the next dance. Outside the woman walked along the wet lamp lit sidewalk.

It was the first dance for soldiers to be given under the auspices of the War Camp Community Service. Forty girls of the art school, chaperoned by Miss Winifred Sexton, secretary of the school and Mrs. J. F. Binnie were the hostesses. The idea was formulated by J. P. Robertson of the War Camp Community Service, and announcements were sent to the commandants at Camp Funston and Fort Leavenworth inviting all soldiers on leave. Posters made by the girl students were put up at Leavenworth and on the interurban trains.

The first dance will be followed by others at various clubs and schools throughout the city according to Mr. Robertson.

The pianist took his seat and the soldiers made a dash for partners. In the intermission the soldiers drank to the girls in fruit punch. The girl in red, surrounded by a crowd of men in olive drab, seated herself at the piano, the men and the girls gathered around and sang until midnight. The elevator had stopped running and so the jolly crowd bunched down the six flights of stairs and rushed waiting motor cars. After the last car had gone, the woman walked along the wet sidewalk through the sleet and looked up at the dark window of the sixth floor.

1918

The German army had been relentlessly advancing south in a drive against the French. On May 30, 1918, the Germans reached the Marne River near Château Thierry, a communications center about 40 miles northeast of Paris. Hastily thrown into the line, one untested division of General John J. Pershing's American Expeditionary Forces stood between the Germans and the great prize, Paris. Under heavy artillery shelling from the enemy on the river's northern bank, United

States soldiers and marines turned rip-
ening wheat fields into a killing ground.
Wilbur Forrest, one of a group of Amer-

ican correspondents to gain celebrity status in France, reported on the battle in
The New York Tribune of June 6, 1918.

AMERICAN FIRE SPREAD HAVOC IN FOE'S LINES

U.S. Machine Gunners at
Chateau Thierry Inflicted
Heavy Losses

By Wilbur Forrest
(Special Cable to The Tribune)

With The Allied Armies Between Rheims and Soissons,
June 5.—The Americans have repeatedly distinguished themselves in the
terrific fighting of the last three days. In the defence of Veuilly Wood and
in their counter charge a mile to the north they won the praise of their allies
by their smashing blows.

But more dramatic was their resistance to the German attempts to drive
them back at Château Thierry and to force a crossing of the Marne there.

Throughout the fighting the Americans were under the enemy's rifle and
machine gun fire from the north side of the river. Some actually experienced
the novelty of seeing their first hostile German and of being under fire for
the first time in their lives simultaneously.

Under Heavy Fire
They were subjected to shell fire as they entered Château Thierry, which
the enemy had been bombarding all day long. On the following evening
about 9 o'clock the enemy again filtered into the western suburbs and followed the banks of the Marne into the city, while his artillery subjected the
streets to the most intense bombardment.

In addition to the semi-darkness the Germans used smoke grenades to
obscure their movements and also to hamper machine gun fire.

American gunners held the south approach of the main bridge which the
enemy reached from the opposite bank. The bridge had been mined in the
centre and the Germans, though under a deluge of American machine gun
bullets, attempted to rush the structure.

Bridge is Blown Up
When many had reached the middle span, it was blown up and German
bodies went hurtling through the air with the debris. Those who approached
the southern bank were made prisoners.

The machine guns spat precise streams of lead at the enemy troops which
had crowded onto the north approach of the bridge in the attempt to cross.

Throughout the night the American guns on the left bank commanded the river and frustrated every enemy attempt to repair the footbridges. They constantly enfiladed the streets leading to the bridges, making the vicinity perilous for the Germans.

The American losses were more than repaid in the losses they inflicted on the enemy, not to mention the admiration they inspired among the French Colonials, with whom bravery is commonplace.

For a month Germany had teetered on the brink of anarchy, its people no longer willing to bear the horrific toll of the Kaiser's war. Kaiser Wilhelm II vacillated between abdication and fighting on despite the growing strength of the Allies—Great Britain, France, and the newly armed United States. Finally, the Kaiser conceded defeat, and negotiators hammered out an armistice. On the eleventh hour of the eleventh day of the eleventh month, after four years and three months of war, after 15 million dead and 20 million more wounded, it was over.

The Hearst newspapers, which had opposed American entry into the war nineteen months before, celebrated the Armistice with patriotic fervor. William Randolph Hearst's own favorite, the *Los Angeles Evening Herald,* on November 11, 1918, blared:

TERMS OF ARMISTICE

CONDITIONS OF PEACE LEAVE HEART OF FOE COUNTRY WIDE OPEN

Washington, Nov. 11—The German army must evacuate the left bank of the Rhine and leave the gateway to the very heart of the nation open to the allies.

This is the crux of the terms of the armistice, which were made public by President Wilson this afternoon.

The whole world waited with abated breath to learn the stringent ruling which Gen. [Ferdinand] Foch and Admiral [Sir Rosslyn] Wemyss had decreed would "pull the teeth" of Germany and put her out of the war for keeps.

Early today President Wilson announced that he would go before Congress at 1 o'clock and make known the terms which the German envoys had signed in order to gain a cessation of hostilities.

Severity of Terms

It was known in advance that these terms were severe for all nations among the allies had agreed that nothing but an armistice which would put the Teutons effectually out of the action could be considered and the matter of their final drafting was left to Foch and Wemyss in order that nothing of military importance would be overlooked.

President Wilson first learned that the armistice had been signed when he was awakened at 4 o'clock this morning by Joseph P. Tumulty, his secretary, who imparted to him the welcome news.

Informed Over Phone

Tumulty was informed by telephone by Philip Patchin, chief of the division of the foreign intelligence of the state department, who made the first announcement of the news here. . . .

The President was all smiles when he went from his bedroom to his office later in the morning and began to receive the congratulations of those about him on the glad tidings from overseas.

President Wilson appeared on the steps of the White House shortly after noon and waved gaily in response to repeated cheers of marchers who halted in front of the executive mansion.

The parade, an impromptu one, was organized by the war trade board employees and was headed by the chairman, Vance McCormick. Later, fuel administration workers, carrying flags of all the allied countries, joined in the demonstration.

First Appearance

It was the President's first appearance since the announcement of the signing of the armistice was made.

The joint session to hear President Wilson outline the armistice terms was arranged for 1 o'clock by Majority Leaders Kitchin and Martin. . . .

"There is no comment to make. None is necessary."

Broadly smiling Secretary of State [Robert] Lansing made this remark when asked by the International News Service as to the end of the war.

The secretary on arrival at his office said that he would make public the terms of the armistice "as soon as details could be arranged."

Though nothing official was given out in advance, it was known that the terms of the armistice were so drastic in their nature as to preclude the possibility of Germany re-entering the war.

The acceptance by Germany of these terms amounted practically to unconditional surrender.

It required 47 hours for the courier to reached German headquarters with the terms of the armistice and some additional time was consumed before the German acceptance could be wirelessed back to the delegates who waited at allied headquarters and who were empowered officially to affix their signatures to the document.

The official act of signing took place at midnight and the war ended at 11 o'clock Paris time, or 6 o'clock Washington time.

The preliminaries to the final act were long drawn out. The German envoys, headed by Mathias Erzberger, the Centrist leader, met Gen. Foch and the terms were read to them. Then they sent a courier back into the German lines bearing the text and their recommendations.

Meanwhile, certain changes had taken place in the German government and delay was caused in order to bring out official action. Finally the wireless message came for the envoys to sign the terms.

The pens with which the delegates affixed their signatures will be distributed among the national museums of the allies.

LATEST NEWS
More Armistice Terms Announced

Washington, Nov. 11—Additional armistice terms as announced by President Wilson are: "All German troops in any territory which before the war belonged to Russia, Rumania or Turkey shall withdraw within the frontiers of Germany as they existed on August 1, 1914. Evacuation by German troops to begin at once and all German instructors, prisoners and civilian, as well as military agents, now on the territory of Russia (as defined before 1914), to be recalled. . . .

1919

It would come to be known as the "Red Summer," the summer of 1919 during which twenty-five race riots swept cities north and south. The underlying causes were deep-rooted social problems—competition for scarce jobs, overcrowded living conditions and brutal police repression of blacks, among other evils. The immediate cause, as in Chicago on July 26 when 15 whites and 23 blacks died and 500 blacks were injured, was often trivial. There, two blacks sought to go swimming at a Lake Michigan beach, and were attacked by angry whites.

The city editor of *The Chicago Daily News* assigned Carl Sandburg—a bright young reporter who had begun to make a name for himself as a promising young poet—to look into the true causes of the riot the day and night before. This was Sandburg's story, run on July 27, 1919.

SAYS LAX CONDITIONS CAUSED RACE RIOTS

Dr. George C. Hall Blames Politicians for State of Affairs

No Protection Is Given

By Carl Sandburg

Charges that colored officials have not properly protected their race and have permitted lax conditions which resulted in the race riots of to-day and yesterday were made to-day by Dr. George C. Hall, 3488 South Park avenue, one of the best known colored men of the city.

Dr. Hall declared that an unwise police policy was at the bottom the cause of the outbreaks. He said that a serious political situation exists in the ward by reason of the fact that the two colored aldermen are responsible to white politicians, rather than to the voters who elected them.

Deplores Segregation

"In the first place, the police had no business to undertake segregation of bathers with no ordinance or warrant of law or any form of consultation of the people concerned," said Dr. Hall. "The action of the police in this instance may be traced back to the same conditions that permit gambling to flourish at the present time to an extent never before known in recent years. The segregation line on the bathing beach was drawn by the police. Then when a boy got over the line and trouble arose, the police immediately spread their men out through the district. Wherever colored people were in the habit of congregating peacefully squads of policemen were placed. They drew the color line and followed a policy precisely as the authorities do in Georgia.

"The colored people have simply been sold out by colored leaders. Our leaders are in the hands of white politicians. That is the whole situation to a nutshell. We need representatives who are strictly representative, who are responsible first of all to the people of the ward."

Ministers to Meet Aldermen

The two colored aldermen from the 2d ward, Maj. R. R. Jackson and Louis B. Anderson, have been invited to appear before a joint meeting of Baptist and Methodist colored ministers this afternoon. There will be a discussion and an inquiry as to responsibility for the affair of yesterday.

In several churches in the colored residence district of Chicago the congregations were dismissed last night without services being held. The cabarets and clubs, however, did business up to the limit of 1 o'clock in the morning. Dreamland, 3618 South State street; the De Luxe, upstairs at 3503 South State street; the Entertainers at 209 East 35th street, and the old Elite at 3030 South State street, all had bright lights and big crowds. At 12:30 Monday morning two white men and three white women in various stages of intoxication made merry for the squads of police at 35th and State streets. Complaints made to the police that the action of mounted police squadrons patrolling the colored district was not having a quieting effect apparently had results, as at 3 a.m. the mounted squadrons were withdrawn.

Sent Parishioners Home

"When I went to my church I saw squads of police officers on the streets and learned there was trouble," said the Rev. J. F. Thomas, pastor of the Ebenezer church, 3629 Vernon avenue. "I was a little fearful of what might happen after dark and told the members of my church to go to their homes while it was still daylight and to be quiet.

"To me and to most of my people this trouble comes very suddenly. Among our people and over the city in general, as we knew about it, we did not expect an outbreak of violence. On Sunday, just a week ago I preached a sermon on a circular issued by the I.W.W. [Industrial Workers of the World]. I told my people we must stand against violence in every form, that we must stand by law and order no matter what happens. I don't care what the past has been; it won't help us to jump in for revolutionary ideas."

Dr. L. K. Williams, pastor of the Olivet church, at 31st and South Park avenue, where squads of mounted police clattered by while religious services were being conducted, said that attendance was the smallest last night of any night in the last year. A joint meeting of Baptist and Methodist colored ministers from the entire city is being held this afternoon at the old First Church of the Olivet congregation, at 27th and Dearborn streets. They represent 35,000 church members.

Caused by Race Prejudice

"It appears to me that the best information at hand indicates that this whole affair of yesterday and last night had its origin in or was occasioned by the same old thing, race prejudice, race restriction, which essayed to express itself by stopping two colored boys from bathing or swimming in a certain locality supposed to be pre-empted by white bathers," said Dr. Williams to-day. "It was but another expression of force to take away from the members of my race the right granted to us by law. Let the best white and colored people come together and form a program that will protect us all and save this city's fair name."

Charles E. Fox, president of the Kenwood and Hyde Park Property Owners' association, which has been dealing with problems in connection with the influx of colored people in the white residence districts of the south side, prepared the following statement on the recent occurrences: "The rioting of yesterday emphasizes the need of intelligent co-operation on both sides. Both can be blamed for this unfortunate occurrence. Violence will not help to solve the problems of the races. Some real constructive action at this time tending toward the creation of a commission to adjudicate differences arising from time to time will do much toward solving the problem. Both races have rights and the rights of each should be respected by the other."

1920

In the wake of the first world war, political and social unrest swept the nation. Reports of race riots and industrial strikes—including one by Boston police—filled the daily papers. Led by radical union organizers, workers had struck United States Steel, demanding an end of the seventy-four hour, $28 work week. Authorities uncovered a number of bombs mailed to Wall Street investors.

His eye on the presidency, the ambitious attorney general of the United States, A. Mitchell Palmer, aligned himself with the industrialists and local political leaders who felt threatened by the social upheaval. In a series of speeches, Palmer inveighed against subversives, deliberately whipping up a Red Scare that galvanized the nation's press. On January 1–2, 1920, Palmer capped the alarm with a coordinated round-up in 33 cities of "Reds," "anarchists," and assorted other "Unamericans." Eventually some 700 aliens, whose only offense was that their political beliefs offended the majority, would be deported.

Associated Press provided both city- by-city coverage and a national round-up story of the Palmer raids. Significantly, the story reports no actual crimes committed—by the Reds—whose activities were ostensibly protected by the First Amendment. This version appeared in *The Washington Post* of January 3, 1920.

U.S. AGENTS CAPTURE 2,500 "REDS" IN NATION-WIDE RAID; 4,000 WARRANTS OUT; WIDE SOVIET PLOT IS FOUND

Greatest Movement Yet Against Lenine Groups.

GET EVIDENCE IN PAPERS

Documents Show Conspiracy to Overthrow Government

Net From Coast to Coast

Object of Captures, Assistant Attorney General Garvan Says, Is to Obtain Data for Department of Labor to Deport Large Numbers of Most Dangerous Anarchists and Radical Agitators— Officials Tell of Menacing Propaganda Among Negroes, From Which Trouble May Yet Develop.

(By the Associated Press.)

The greatest roundup of radicals in the nation's history was conducted last night by the government acting through Department of Justice agents in cities stretching from coast to coast. Latest reports indicated that 2,500 members of the communist and communist labor parties, against whom the raids were directed, were in custody, and Department of Justice officials expressed the opinion that daylight would see a far larger number behind the bars. Altogether 4,000 warrants have been issued.

Sought With Goods On.

Not alone was the round-up the largest yet conducted by the government in its effort to rid the country of radicalism, but in the view of officials it was the most thoroughly carried out. Department of Justice agents had been instructed several days ago, and at 9 o'clock last night the move was begun on the radical headquarters, whether in Portland, Me., or in Portland, Ore.

Department of Justice operatives were directed to catch the radicals "with the goods on," and that these directions were carried out was evidenced in reports, particularly from New York, where the offices of communist newspapers were raided, and from New England, where considerable literature prepared for dissemination by the two parties was seized.

The primary object of the raids, Assistant Attorney [General Francis P.] Garvan announced, was the obtaining of evidence upon which the Department of Labor might proceed with the deportation of undesirables.

Round-Up Widest Yet.

The general charge of attempting to overthrow the government by force and violence was placed against the persons arrested during the raids. Officials declared they believed that several hundred members of the communist and communist labor parties would be behind bars before morning.

Officials here declared the nation-wide round-up was the most completely planned and the machinery was the best oiled for this of any raids launched against the radical element in this country. It was arranged some ten days ago that the raids should take place last night and confidential communications were sent to department of Justice representatives and United States attorneys in the 33 cities.

Secret Documents Sought.

Department of Justice agents desired most of all to capture incriminating documents, not so much of the literature and propaganda but papers showing details of the communist organizations in each city.

It was indicated that if such evidence were obtained, deportations of the persons concerned would be an easy matter. As in the case of the members of the Union of Russian Workers, seven score of whom were aboard the transport Buford, which sailed from New York ten days ago, membership cards in the organization were regarded by officials as constituting the best documentary evidence on which to base deportation cases.

Officials said the only difference between the communist party and the communist labor party was one of leadership. Both have been endeavoring to bring about the establishment of a soviet form of government in this country since their organization last September, according to officials.

Soviet Government's Aim.

Documents gathered by Federal agents recently show conclusively, it was said, that plans were drawn up by the leaders of each of these parties to develop a score or more of soviets through the country.

These were to be merged under a soviet council similar to that which now exists in Russia, according to Mr. Garvan.

The department revealed last night activities of these two organizations among the negroes. Their attempts to organize the negroes in support of plans to overthrow the present political and economic system were carried far, and officials admitted that this propaganda had gone to such a length that trouble may yet be expected in certain negro communities.

Mr. Garvan made public information gathered by the Federal agents showing the nature of the work done among the negroes.

Text of One Document.

One document contains the following:

"In close connection with the unskilled workers is the problem of the negro. The negro represents a political and economic problem. The racial oppression of the negro is simply the expression of his economic bondage and oppression, each intensifying the other. This complicates the negro problem, but does not alter its proletarian character. The communist party will carry on agitation among the negro workers to unite them with all class-conscious workers."

The communist party recently spread broadcast among its adherents a "manifesto" setting forth its views and plans. While officials have been unable to obtain a similar document from the communist labor party, they asserted that its views were not unlike those of the communist party as disclosed in the manifesto.

Would End Capitalism.

"The communist party of America is the party of the working class," the manifesto says. "The communist party of American proposes to end capitalism and organize a workers' industrial republic. The workers must control industry and dispose of the products of industry. The communist party is a party realizing the limitations of all existing workers' organizations, and proposes to develop the revolutionary movement necessary to free the workers from the oppression of capitalism. . . ."

Advance information on the activities of the communist party revealed its emissaries were in many cities boring into labor organizations which hitherto have been noted for their conservatism.

Literature obtained by Federal agents made it apparent that the communist leaders were concentrating on plans to obtain control of well-founded labor groups.

Through this method they were to exert their power politically and to put forward candidates which could be regarded by government officials as nothing more than destructive elements within the present government.

The communist labor group is said to have directed its propaganda more generally among the foreign element of citizenry.

Appealing to Foreign Workers.

From several sources Federal agents gleaned information that the communist labor party was appealing to the foreign workers with the argument that the present government was unfriendly to them and that their rights would never be respected by the appointed authorities. The insertion of the word "labor" in the name of the party was regarded by officials as only a subterfuge, the leaders realizing that it would lend strength for their argument among foreigners.

Assistant Attorney General Garvan expressed the opinion that the leaders of the two parties had a "working agreement" and planned eventually to bring all the radicals under one communist party and thereby amass enough strength to upset the constituted government.

Suspect a Higher Power.

Officials are working on the theory that a higher power is directing the work of both organizations and that the leaders who are behind this directing hand only recently have come to this country from Russia. This belief, they said, was supported by evidence gathered by representatives of this and the allied governments in the heart of Soviet Russia.

It is known that agents of the allied nations have been working for nearly two years among the followers of Lenine and Trotzky [sic] and their efforts have resulted in connecting links in the chain of soviet propaganda in this country and the soviet leaders in Russia.

1920

How long they had waited, patiently and impatiently. For a century American women had petitioned their unheeding government for the most basic of all freedoms, the right to vote. The suffrage movement produced a succession of vital leaders—Elizabeth Cady Stanton, Lucretia Mott, Lucy Stone (and their husbands), Susan B. Anthony, Victoria Woodhull Claflin, and Carrie Chapman Catt—but not until 1920 did Congress and 35 of the necessary 36 states ratify an amendment granting women the vote. *The Knoxville* [Tennessee] *Journal and Tribune* of August 19, 1920, reported as the last of the required state legislatures approved a resolution in favor of what would become the 19th Amendment to the Constitution of the United States.

TENNESSEE'S LEGISLATURE RATIFIES AMENDMENT GIVING SUFFRAGE TO WOMEN

Suffrage Vote Was 50 To 46

Tennessee is Thirty-sixth State To Ratify

By The Associated Press

Nashville, Tenn., Aug. 18.—Tennessee today ratified the federal woman suffrage amendment, the lower house of the legislature by a vote of fifty to forty-six concurring in the action of the senate which last Friday adopted the ratification resolution by a vote of 25 to 4.

Although it was the thirty-sixth state to act favorably and the amendment should become effective as soon as certified by Brainbridge Colby, secretary of state, whether 17,000,000 women of the country would vote in the presidential election in November remained to be determined. . . .

The end came with dramatic suddenness. Debate on the motion to concur had been in progress little more than an hour and there was no indication a vote was imminent when Speaker [Seth] Walker called Representative Overton to the chair and took the floor to reply to a suffragist who had charged that special interests were at work to defeat ratification.

Walker Makes Speech

"The battle has been won and the measure has been defeated," Mr. Walker said.

"I resent the iniquitous remarks that special interests are alone against this measure. I resent this on behalf of the womanhood that is both for and against suffrage, Mr. Speaker," he shouted. "I move that this measure goes where it belongs, to the table."

Chamber in Uproar

Instantly the chamber was in an uproar. Suffragists clamored for recognition while a chorus of "second the motion" came from the antis. Mr. Overton, however, refused to recognize any one and ordered the roll call and at the conclusion many spectators, members and newspapermen who had kept tally had a total of 49 in favor of the motion and 47 against it. An equal or greater number declared the vote was 48 to 48 and an appeal to the clerk developed that his tally also showed a tie.

Another Roll Call

Pandemonium reigned, members leaving their seats and crowding around the speaker's stand, many demanding another roll call, others declaring it unnecessary. Mr. Overton, who occupied the chair during the remainder of the session managed to restore order and instructed the clerk to proceed with a second roll call in order that there might be no doubt.

The second ballot showed a tie of 48 to 48 and the speaker declared the motion lost for want of majority.

A Crucial Moment

Instantly the anti suffragists demanded a vote on the original motion to concur in the senate action. It was a crucial moment. The motion to table had just been lost through a tie vote and if the opposing forces held together and another tie resulted it meant rejection of the amendment.

When Speaker Walker put the motion hundreds of suffragists regarded the battle as lost.

Burn Changes Vote

The vote at the outset was on partisan lines but when the name of Representative Harry T. Burn, Republican, of McMinn county, was called he voted "aye." The opposition then virtually conceded defeat for Mr. Burn had voted with them to table the resolution and his change gave the suffragists the needed majority.

The stand of members was unchanged as the clerk ran down the list until the name of Representative B. P. Turner, Democrat, of Gibson county was reached. Turner passed and instantly there was a shout of satisfaction among the antis. He had voted against the motion to table and his failure to vote on ratification balanced the loss incurred through Mr. Burn's vote for the amendment. The pleasure experienced by the antis was shortlived, however, for Mr. Turner, just before the end of the roll call requested the clerk to record him as voting "aye."

Mr. Turner had said repeatedly that he would vote neither for nor against ratification unless it was evident that his vote was needed for passage or rejection and that if such an occasion arose he would vote for the amendment.

Big Demonstration

Suffragists everywhere launched an uproarious demonstration before the clerk announced the vote for there was no question suffrage had won. The chamber became a bedlam of cheers and shouts, women screamed at the top of their voices, scores placed their arms around the necks of those nearest them and danced, so far as it was possible to do so, in the mass of humanity. Hundreds of suffrage banners were waved wildly and many removed the yellow flowers they had been wearing and threw them upward to meet a similar shower from the galleries.

No Time for Weeping

There were few tears of joy shed by the suffragists. Some wiped their eyes but on the whole they considered it no time for weeping. Their happiness was far beyond that stage.

A motion to adjourn until 10 o'clock tomorrow morning was offered after the official vote was announced but in the uproar it was doubted whether any members heard it or whether it was seconded. The speaker put the question, called for the "ayes" and "noes" and announced gravely that the motion had carried unanimously.

1920

From the stirrings of organized games, the press has portrayed sports in America as the essence of purity, of nobility, and of patriotism. Athletes, even professionals, represented the best in us, or that which Americans hoped to be. Hence the shock when eight superlative ballplayers, mainstays of the Chicago White Sox baseball team that won the American League championship in 1919, were indicted for deliberately losing the world series to the Cincinnati Red Sox. White Sox owner Charles Comiskey promptly suspended the eight "Black Sox" and a powerful commissioner of baseball was installed to restore confidence in the game, but baseball and sport in general had lost its claim to ironclad morality.

The Chicago Daily News of September 28, 1920, reported the Grand Jury's indictments of the eight players and their immediate suspension. (Though never convicted, the eight players suffered lifetime bans from major league baseball.)

EIGHT OF WHITE SOX INDICTED COMISKEY SUSPENDS 7; CICOTTE AND JACKSON TELL THE JURY ALL

Jackson, Cicotte, Felsch, Weaver, Williams, Risberg, McMullin and Gandil Are the Men Accused in True Bills.

Star Batter and Pitcher Said to Have Admitted Their Share in Loss of World's Series—Jackson Breaks Down and Weeps.

True Bills for 8 White Sox

Seven White Sox players and one former member of the team including some of the most famous members of the American league team, were named in true bills following a reported statement by Eddie Cicotte involving all of them in a conspiracy to "throw" the world's series of last fall.

Admits Getting $10,000.

Cicotte, it is learned, confessed that he received $10,000, and said that [Joe] Jackson asked for $20,000, but received only $5,000.

"I refused to pitch a ball until I got the money," Cicotte said. "It was placed under my pillow in the hotel the night before the first game of the series. Every one was paid individually, and the same scheme was used to deliver it."

"Chick" Gandil, former first baseman for the Sox, who is now playing outlaw ball in Idaho, Cicotte said, acted as the chief go-between in all the money deals. He is reported to have received $30,000 for his part in fixing the series.

Jackson, in his statement to the jury, is reported to have told the same story Cicotte told.

Cicotte Admits Throwing Game?

Cicotte is said to have admitted that during the first game of the world series last year he lost the game for the Sox by purposely intercepting a throw from the outfield which would have caught a Red player at home and that later he made a wild throw which allowed another runner to score. This game was lost 2 to 1.

He confessed also, it is said, that the accusations of Ray Schalk, Sox catcher, that Cicotte and [Claude] Williams double-crossed him on signals are true.

According to Attorney Austrian, Jackson made a "full, free and complete statement to Judge McDonald." After listening to his story Judge McDonald advised him to repeat it to the grand jury, Attorney Austrian said.

Following a conference between Judge McDonald, Attorney Austrian and Jackson, Assistant State's Attorney Replogle was called and the ball player went directly to the grand jury room. He refused to talk after he had been in conference with Judge McDonald, but his lawyer said that he had decided to go before the grand jury and tell the whole truth.

"This 'blowoff' is due to Mr. Comiskey's action," said Attorney Austrian; who said that he had prepared the evidence at his client's orders, taken Cicotte to the grand jury and was adopting the same course in reference to Jackson.

"As soon as he knew what the state of affairs was he ordered me to go ahead. We rushed the evidence to the grand jury and are now having Jackson tell what he knows of the affair.

"This is due to Mr. Comiskey's desire to get at the bottom of the scandal and to have the matter cleared up at once."

The players named in the indictments are:

    ARNOLD ("CHICK") GANDIL
    FRED MCMULLIN
    OSCAR ("HAPPY") FELSCH
    CHARLES ("SWEDE") RISBERG
    EDDIE CICOTTE
    CLAUDE WILLIAMS
    JOSEPH JACKSON
    GEORGE ("BUCK") WEAVER

Gandil is the ex-member of the team.

Seven Sox Players Suspected.

Within a few minutes after the true bills had been announced, Charles A. Comiskey, owner of the White Sox, issued through his secretary a statement indefinitely suspending seven players. "I take this action," the statement said, "even though it costs Chicago the pennant." That it does cost whatever chance Chicago had of getting the pennant is conceded. The statement follows:

"To Charles Risberg, Fred McMullin, Joe Jackson, Oscar Felsch, George Weaver, C. P. Williams, and E. V. Cicotte:

"You and each of you are hereby notified of your indefinite suspension as a member of the Chicago American league baseball club (the White Sox).

"Your suspension is brought about by information which has just come to me directly involving you and each of you in the baseball scandal (now being investigated by the present grand jury of Cook county) resulting from the world's series of 1919.

"If you are innocent of any wrong doing you and each of you will be reinstated; if you are guilty you will be retired from organized baseball for the rest of your lives, if I can accomplish it.

"Until there is a finality to this investigation it is due to the public that I take this action, even though it costs Chicago the pennant.

"Chicago American League Baseball Club.
BY CHARLES A. COMISKEY."

Charged with Conspiracy.

All are charged with conspiracy to violate a state law. More specific charges, it was stated, will be made against them later. . . .

Cicotte, according to one of the grand jurors, broke down in the middle of the examination. When he resumed tears were streaming down his face.

"I'd give anything" he is reported as saying, "if I wasn't mixed up in this business."

The voting of bills against the eight players is the first time that such a thing has occurred in the history of American baseball. It follows long and costly efforts by Charles A. Comiskey, owner of the White Sox, to run down charges that his team had "thrown" the 1919 world series—rumors which arose during the series.

It is understood that the information in the hands of the grand jury supports the story told by "Billy" Maharg, Philadelphia gambler and baseball enthusiast, involving Bill Burns, a former White Sox and Cincinnati pitcher, and Abe Attell, ex-featherweight champion. According to the story, Attell and Burns "framed" with Eddie Cicotte and other White Sox players the throwing of the series to the Cincinnati "Reds." For this the players in the deal were to have received a lump sum of $100,000. Instead, the gamblers are said to have "double crossed" their co-conspirators and paid them only $10,000.

The names of all those indicted have been mentioned repeatedly in connection with the investigation.

Indictments are a Surprise.

The true bills came almost as a complete surprise. It had been announced this morning that the jury would not resume the inquiry until 3 o'clock this afternoon, when John J. McGraw, manager of the New York Giants, was to have been the first witness. However, the announcement merely served to cover up the jury's actual proceedings. What happened was quite different.

First, after reading over the statement of Maharg, Chief Justice Charles

A. McDonald and Assistant State's Attorney Hartley Replogle went into conference with Alfred Austrian, attorney for the White Sox. It is believed it was agreed at this conference that Cicotte should be brought to the jury room and urged to tell all he knew about the gambling deals in return for a promise of immunity.

Foreman Calls Reporters.

Cicotte, at any rate, was taken to the jury room about 10:30 o'clock. About 1 o'clock it became known that "something big" was happening in the jury room. At 2 o'clock Henry H. Brigham, foreman of the grand jury, sent for newspaper men, and in the presence of the jury announced the voting of the bills and the names of the players.

A little later Cicotte was seen being smuggled from the grand jury room on the sixth floor to an office on the fourth floor.

"Did you get a bath, Eddie?" a friend called, referring to an "immunity bath."

Only the Beginning.

Cicotte grinned sheepishly and made no reply. He was later conducted out of the Criminal Court building by Detective Sergeant "Billy" Sullivan, attached to the state's attorney's office.

"This is only the beginning," said Assistant State's Attorney Replogle in commenting on what had happened. "So far there has been too much talk and not enough action. From now on the grand jury is going to take things in its own hands and see that the truth is brought out.". . .

McGraw arrived in the outskirts of Chicago this morning resolved to be taciturn regarding baseball scandals, but he broke his resolve of reticence a few minutes after the Twentieth Century left the Englewood union station.

"I am willing to do anything I can to clean up the game," declared the fighting manager of the Giants.

"You can know that, because McGraw is coming here of his own free will and also because he was the first to nail players who weren't square," broke in Judge Francis X. McQuade, treasurer of the Giants, who accompanied Mr. McGraw to Chicago, as legal chaperon.

Prefers Poor Players to Crooks.

"I think it is the duty of managers to clean up their own clubs," continued McGraw. "I don't know anything about the fixing of the White Sox in last year's world series, except what I have read in the newspapers."

"You yourself would prefer an inferior team of honest players to a high class team of crooked ones, wouldn't you?" was asked.

"Certainly," he answered.

"In the event that the state's attorney's office does not find sufficient legal basis for prosecution, do you favor having all the managers put in possession of the facts, so that they can throw out any crooks who may be in the game?". . . .

1924

It is probably the most famous lead, or opening paragraph, of an American sports story ever written, a touchstone of journalism classes decades after Grantland Rice, in the press seats of New York's Polo Grounds, first tapped it out for *The New York Herald-Tribune* of October 19, 1924. Never mind that Rice was, in the style of the day, overwriting; after all, a final score of 13–7 hardly suggests cataclysmic defeat by a cyclone or otherwise. Never mind that Rice mixes his metaphors beyond reason. His opening image echoes through the ages, gracing an otherwise routine account of a routine football game.

NOTRE DAME'S CYCLONE BEATS ARMY, 13 TO 7

Fleet, Powerful Western Backs and Hard Charging Line March Down Field for 2 Touchdowns

Cadet Score Comes on Brilliant Fake

55,000 at Polo Ground See West Point Lose Gamely to Better Team

By Grantland Rice

Outlined against a blue-gray October sky, the Four Horsemen rode again. In dramatic lore they are known as Famine, Pestilence, Destruction and Death. These are only aliases. Their real names are Stuhldreher, Miller, Crowley and Layden. They formed the crest of the South Bend cyclone before which another fighting Army football team was swept over the precipice at the Polo Grounds yesterday afternoon as 55,000 spectators peered down at the bewildering panorama spread on the green plain below.

A cyclone can't be snared. It may be surrounded, but somewhere it breaks through to keep on going. When the cyclone starts from South Bend, where the candle lights still gleam through the Indiana sycamores, those in the way must take to storm cellars at top speed. Yesterday the cyclone struck again, as Notre Dame beat the Army, 13 to 7, with a set of backfield stars that ripped and crashed through a strong Army defense with more speed and power than the warring cadets could meet.

Marvelous Backfield

Notre Dame won its ninth game in twelve Army starts through the driving power of one of the greatest backfields that ever churned up the turf of any gridiron in any football age. Brilliant backfields may come and go, but in

Stuhldreher, Miller, Crowley and Layden, covered by a fast and charging line, Notre Dame can take its place in front of the field.

Coach McEwan sent one of his finest teams into action, an aggressive organization that fought to the last play around the first rim of darkness, but when Rockne rushed his Four Horsemen to the track they rode down everything in sight. It was in vain that 1,400 gray-clad cadets pleaded for the Army line to hold. The Army line was giving all it had, but when a tank tears in with the speed of a motorcycle, what chance has flesh and blood to hold?. . . .

At the game's start Rockne sent in almost entirely a second string cast. The Army got the jump and began to play most of the football. It was the Army attack that made three first downs before Notre Dame had caught its stride. The South Bend cyclone opened like a zephyr.

And then, in the wake of a sudden cheer, out rushed Stuhldreher, Miller, Crowley and Layden, the four star backs who helped to beat the Army a year ago. Things were to be a trifle different now. After a short opening flurry in the second period, Wood, of the Army, kicked out of bounds on Notre Dame's 20-yard line. The cloud in the west at this point was no larger than a football. There was no sign of a tornado starting. But it happened to be at just this spot that Stuhldreher decided to put on his attack and begin the long and dusty hike.

Dynamite Goes Off

On the first play the fleet Crowley peeled off fifteen yards and the cloud from the west was now beginning to show signs of lightning and thunder. The fleet, powerful Layden got six yards more and then Don Miller added ten. A forward pass from Stuhldreher to Crowley added twelve yards and a moment later Don Miller ran twenty yards around the Army's right wing. He was on his way to glory when Wilson, hurtling across the right of way, nailed him out of bounds. Crowley, Miller and Layden—Miller, Layden and Crowley—one or another, ripping and crashing through, as the Army defense threw everything it had in the way to stop this wild charge that had now some seventy yards. Crowley and Layden added five yards more and then, on a split play, Layden went ten yards across the line as if he had just been fired from the black mouth of a howitzer.

In that second period Notre Dame made eight first downs to the Army's none, which shows the unwavering power of the Western attack that hammered relentlessly and remorselessly without easing up for a second's breath. The Western line was going [doing?] its full share, led by the crippled Walsh with a broken hand.

But always there was Miller or Crowley or Layden, directed through the right spot by the cool and crafty judgment of Stuhldreher, who picked his plays with the finest possible generalship. The South Bend cyclone had now roared eighty-five yards to a touchdown through one of the strongest defensive teams in the game. The cyclone had struck with too much speed and power to be stopped. It was the preponderance of Western speed that swept the Army back.

The next period was much like the second. The trouble began when the alert Layden intercepted an Army pass on the 48-yard line. Stuhldreher was ready for another march.

Once again the cheering cadets began to call for a rallying stand. They are never overwhelmed by any shadows of defeat as long as there is a minute of fighting left. But silence fell over the cadet sector for just a second as Crowley ran around the Army's right wing for 15 yards, where Wilson hauled him down on the 33-yard line. Walsh, the western captain, was hurt in this play, but soon resumed. Miller got 7 and Layden got 8 and then, with the ball on the Army's 20-yard line, the cadet defense rallied and threw Miller in his tracks. But the halt was only for the moment. On the next play Crowley swung out around the Army's left wing, cut in and then crashed over the line for Notre Dame's second touchdown. . . .

The sudden change came late in the third quarter, when Wilson, raging like a wild man, suddenly shot through a tackle opening to run thirty-four yards on to midfield before he was finally collared and thrown with a jolt. A few moments later Wood, one of the best of all the punters, kicked out of bounds on Notre Dame's 5-yard line. Here was the chance. Layden was forced to kick from behind his own goal. The punt soared up the field as Yeomans called for a free kick on the 35-yard line. As he caught the ball he was nailed and spilled by a Western tackler, and the penalty gave the Army fifteen yards, with the ball on Notre Dame's 20-yard line.

At this moment Harding was rushed to quarter in place of Yeomans, who had been one of the leading Army starts. On the first these plays the Army reached the 12-yard line, but it was now fourth down, with two yards left to go. Harding's next play was the feature of the game.

As the ball was passed he faked a play to Wood, diving through the line, held the oval for just a half breath and then, tucking the same under his arm swung out around Notre Dame's right end. The brilliant fake worked to perfection. The entire Notre Dame defense had charged forward in a surging mass to check the line attack and Harding, with open territory sailed on for a touchdown. He traveled those last twelve yards after the manner of food shot from guns. He was over the line before the Westerners knew what had taken place. It was a fine bit of strategy, brilliantly carried out by every member of the cast.

The cadet sector had its chance to rip open the chilly atmosphere at last, and most of the 55,000 present joined in the tribute to football art. But this was the Army's last chance to score. From that point on it was see-saw, up and down, back and forth, with the rivals fighting bitterly for every inch of ground. It was harder now to make a foot than it had been to make ten yards. Even the all-star South Bend cast could no longer continue a romp for any set distances, as Army tacklers, inspired by the touchdown, charged harder and faster than they had charged before.

The Army brought a fine football team into action, but it was beaten by a faster and smoother team. Rockne's supposedly light, green line was about as big as the Army's and every whit as aggressive. What is even more important, it was faster on its feet, faster in getting around.

It was speed that beat the Army, speed plus interference. And when a back such as Harry Wilson finds few chances to get started you can figure upon the defensive strength that is barricading the road. Wilson is one of the hardest backs in the game to suppress, but he found few chances yesterday to show his broken field ability. You can't run through a broken field until you get there.

One strong feature of the Army play was its headlong battle against heavy odds. Even when Notre Dame had scored two touchdowns and was well on its way to a third, the Army fought on with fine spirit until the touchdown chance came at last. And when this chance came Coach McEwan had the play ready for the final march across the line. The Army has a better team than it had last year. So has Notre Dame. We doubt that any team in the country could have beaten Rockne's array yesterday afternoon, East or West. It was a great football team brilliantly directed, a team of speed, power and team play. The Army has no cause for gloom over its showing. It played first class football against more speed than it could match. Those who have tackled a cyclone can understand.

1925

There in the sweltering courtroom in Dayton, Tennessee—the proceedings later moved outside to accommodate the curious—goodness and evil, science and religion, the 19th and the 20th Centuries clashed. John T. Scopes, a young biology teacher, had volunteered to be the defendant in a test case challenging a new state law that prohibited the teaching of Darwinian theory of evolution in the classroom. To his defense came a team of American Civil Liberties Union attorneys, Arthur Garfield Hays, Dudley Field Malone, and John Randolph Neal, headed by the foremost criminal lawyer of this day, Clarence Darrow. Opposing Darrow, an affirmed atheist, stood the Great Commoner, William Jennings Bryan, once the Boy Orator of the Platte, a three-time Democratic presidential nominee, and a stout religious fundamentalist prepared to argue, to prove the literal truth of the Bible.

For ten days the nation followed the "Monkey Trial" in tiny Dayton, amused and appalled by turns. Darrow finally called as a witness the weary Bryan himself, as an authority on the Good Book; Darrow's scathing examination left Bryan befuddled, hopelessly overmatched. (The exhausted Bryan was to suffer a cerebral hemorrhage and die five days later.)

No matter. A jury of Dayton's good citizens was out only a few minutes. *The Chattanooga Daily Times* of July 22, 1925, reported the outcome of the trial in the tiny mountain town of Dayton, Tennessee.

JURY FINDS EVOLUTION TEACHER "GUILTY"

Scopes Fined $100

Dayton Trial Ends Suddenly After Testimony of Bryan Stricken

Charge, In Effect, Instructed Jury

Darrow Tells Jurymen He Could Not Ask for An Acquittal.

Good Humor Marks Final Hour of Session

Attorneys Exchange Compliments and Sermon Is Delivered By Trial Judge—Both Sides See Victory—Jurors Deliberate Only Two or Three Minutes—Scopes Makes Bond.

By Staff Correspondent.

DAYTON, July 21—With the jury's verdict of "guilty," and assessment by the court of a fine of $100, the trial here of John T. Scopes suddenly ended today. But the trial of evolution has just begun, say Darrow, Hays, Malone and Neal.

The prosecution won the Scopes case at Dayton, but it seems that the first round of the evolution case has been won by the defense. Defense counsel claim they have accomplished their purpose in coming to Dayton. In the words of Arthur Garfield Hays, of the defense: "If we had arranged every step in the case, it could not have been better. We have got our case before the country. That is where the great issue will be decided, and not down here in this court."

And in the language of the Dayton attorney, Gordon McKenzie, of prosecution counsel, replying to statements of the defending lawyers after Scopes had been fined:

"On behalf of Rhea county and Gen. Steward and on behalf of the prosecution I desire to say to the gentlemen who have just made their statements that we are delighted to have had you with us. We have learned to take a broader view of life since you came * * * We people here want to be more broadminded than some have given us credit for, and we appreciate your coming, and we have been greatly elevated, edified and educated by your presence."

The end of the twelve-day trial came at noon, to the disappointment of a great gathering of the curious, who had settled down to listen to another day of debate on the Bible or Bryan oratory. The abrupt ending was due to the unexpected announcement of Judge Raulston, immediately after the morning session opened, that he feared that he had been in error in permitting, on the day before, the examination of Mr. Bryan by Mr. Darrow. The court ordered stricken from the record the testimony of the great defender of fundamentalism.

"I feel that the testimony of Mr. Bryan can shed no light upon any issues that will be pending before the higher courts," said the judge, and Mr. Bryan, thereby, was saved from being required to give further evidence of what he does not know about evolution and the Bible.

This ruling of the court operated to prevent also the questioning of Mr. Darrow by Mr. Bryan, which had been anticipated, and, as the court further held that the only issue to be determined was whether or not Scopes taught that man descended from a lower order of animals, the charge of the court to the jury was, in effect, instruction to bring a verdict of guilty, as there has been no question as to Scopes' teaching the theory of evolution . . . down in the textbook given him by the state authorities.

So the jury brought in the verdict of "guilty" just as soon as the twelve men could walk right out, turn around and walk right back again. During the twelve-day trial the jury had been in the courtroom, altogether, approximately three hours. Their "deliberation," after they had been told by Mr. Darrow that they could not, under the definition of the issues as given by the court, ask for a verdict of not guilty, lasted only two or three minutes. The jury was given the case, without argument, at 11:20 a.m., and the verdict was read at 11:29, most of the time having been consumed in leaving and reentering the crowded courtroom. The jurors didn't even sit down to think it over, but stood huddled together in the hallway of the courthouse for the brief interval they were deciding to do what everybody who has followed the trial knew they would do.

"We have found for the state—found the defendant guilty," announced Foreman Thompson when the jury returned. There was no demonstration. The crowd apparently attached less importance to what the foreman of the jury had said than to stirring remarks by counsel during the long trial. Scopes made a brief statement, calling the law unjust and the court then fixed the penalty.

After the defense had gone through the formalities incident to their preparation for an appeal to the supreme court and Scopes had arranged bond of $600, an extraordinary court scene was enacted. It was like home-coming week—or the closing hours of a big convention, when resolutions are adopted thanking everybody and everything from the press to the chairman of the ladies' committee on palm leaf fans. It was a great mixture of preaching, praying, laughing, handshaking, back-slapping and exchange of compliments. Everybody seemed anxious to "kiss and make up." The lawyers exchanged compliments, newspapermen expressed their gratitude, and the volunteer speakers were legion.

Judge Raulston delivered another sermon in which he defined a great man as one "who possesses the wisdom to know the truth and has the courage to declare it in face of all opposition.'' The judge, in his remarks, again tied together the north and the south, rent asunder so frequently by Gen. McKenzie with his ranting about the ''furrin'' lawyers.

It was a free-for-all speechifying. When no one had the floor for the moment, the judge would ask, ''Any one else?''

And the Scopes trial, which opened Friday, July 10, with prayer, closed Monday, July 21d with prayer. The final chapter is pictured as follows:

The Court (Referring to the Visiting Attorneys)—I am glad to have had these gentlemen with us. This little talk of mine comes from my heart, gentlemen. I have had some difficult problems to decide in this lawsuit, and I only pray to God that I have decided them right. If I have not the highest courts will find the mistake. But if I failed to decide them right, it was for the want of legal learning, and legal attainments, and not for the want of a disposition to do everybody justice. We are glad to have you with us.

(Applause)

Mr. Hays—May I, as one of the counsel for the defense, ask your honor to allow us to send you the ''Origin of Species and the Descent of Man,'' by Charles Darwin?

(Laughter)

The Court—Yes. Yes.

(Laughter and applause). . . .

The Court—We will adjourn. And Brother Jones will pronounce the benediction.

Dr. Jones—May the grace of our Lord Jesus Christ, the love of God and the communion and fellowship of the Holy Ghost abide with you all. Amen.

The Court—The court will adjourn sine die.

1925

Celebrity as a newspaperman first came to Ring Lardner as a sports writer and then columnist for the *Chicago Tribune*. With publication in 1916 of his first collection of short stories, *You Know Me, Al: A Busher's Letters,* Lardner won accolades as one of America's foremost humorists—yet one whose writing was tinged with a hint of melancholy. A letter to the editor of *The New York World* on November 1, 1925, manifests Lardner's singular, sardonic spirit.

Ring Lardner's Tips on Horses

To the Editor of The World:

Once in every so often the undersigned receives a circular from the Horse Breeders ass'n of America or something, along with a request to give same all possible publicity to the end that people's interest in horses will be revived and roused up and not allow the genius equine to become extinct in our land from lack of attention. And just as often as one of these literary broadsides hits my happy home just so often do I feel it incumbrance on myself to come out flat-footed and open and above the boards and state my attitude towards what is known in exclusive livery stable circles as his highness le Horse.

Children, dogs and horses is regarded in this country as sacred items and it is considered pretty close to a felony to even make a face when any of the 3 is mentioned. Well, I am fond of children, at least four of them and can tolerate a few dogs provided they keep their mouths shut and ain't over a ft. high. But irregardless of less majesty and the deuce with same, I can't help from admitting at this junction that the bear mention of a horse has the same effects on me like red flags to a bull or gingerale to an Elk.

A horse is the most overestimated animal in the world with the possible exception of a police dog. For every incidence where a horse has saved a human life I can dig you up a 100 incidences where they have killed people by falling off them or trampling them down or both. Personally, the only horse who I ever set on their back throwed me off on my bosom before I had road him 20 ft. and did the horse wait to see was I hurt, no.

Devotees of horse flesh is wont to point out that King Richard the 3rd once offered his kingdom for one of them but in the 1st place he was not the kind of man who I would pin any faith on his judgement of values and in the 2nd place the kingdom had been acquired by a couple of mild little murders and it was a case of easy come, easy go.

A study of some of the expressions in usage at the present day will serve to throw light on the real personality of a horse. Take for example the phrase "eat like a horse." The picture you get from this phrase is the picture of somebody eating without no regard to ethics or good manners, the picture of a person who you would as leaf have a horse at the table as they.

Or take "horse laugh." This indicates the coarsest, roughest kind of a laugh and a person of breeding and refinement would pretty near as soon have their friends give them a head cold as the horse laugh. Or "Horse play." How often you hear theater goers complain that such and such a comedy has got too much horse play or observe parents order their kiddies to cut out the horse play. The answer is that a horse can't play nice like kittens or oxen or even wolfs, but has got to be ribald and rough in their sports as in everything else.

Defenders of le horse will no doubt point to the term "good, common horse sense," or the simile "work like a horse" as being proof of the beast's virtues, but if a horse has got such good common sense why do they always half to have a jockey show them the way around a fenced in race track where you couldn't possibly go wrong unless you was dumb, and as for working like a horse, I never met a horse who worked because he thought it was fun. They work for the same reason the rest of us works.

I will pass over what different horses has done to me in places like Saratoga, Belmont, Havana and New Orleans. Suffice it to say that none of them ever lived up to what I had been led to believe. And one day just last month I had to walk across 34th Street in N.Y. City and dodge my way amongst taxicabs, trucks and street cars and was just congratulating myself on making the trip unscathed when a horse reached out and snapped at me, a stranger.

Horses ain't been no good in battle since trench warfare came into its own and besides you never heard of a horse volunteering for any army. . . . And do you think Paul Revere would of even looked at a horse if all the taxis hadn't been engaged with the theater crowds that night?

Last, but not lease, have you ever been hit by a horsefly, which never would of been thought of only for his highness le horse.

RING LARDNER

1926

Rudolph Valentino reigned as one of the great romantic stars of the silent screen, the dark and dashing lover of everywoman's secret dreams. His role in *The Sheik* started a national craze for things Arabic; in fact, "sheik" became the male counterpart to the Roaring Twenties' devil-may-care "flapper."

Regardless of his public image, Valentino was a bewildered figure trying to keep afloat in a sea of adoration. Columnist Henry L. Mencken recognized this in his *Baltimore Sun* column of August 30, 1926, published a week after Valentino's death at 31 of a ruptured appendix.

VALENTINO

By H. L. MENCKEN

By one of the chances that relieve the dullness of life and make it instructive, I had the pleasure of dining with this gentlemen in New York a week or so before his fatal illness. I had never met him before, nor seen him on the screen; the meeting was at his instance, and, when it was proposed, vaguely puzzled me. But soon its purpose became clear enough. Valentino was in trouble and wanted advice. More, he wanted advice from an elder and disinterested man, wholly removed from the movies and all their works. Something that I had written, falling under his eye, had given him the notion that I was an enlightened and judicious fellow. That part, of course, didn't surprise me.

So, the night being infernally warm, we stripped off our coats, and came to terms. I recall that he wore suspenders of extraordinary width and thickness—suspenders almost strong enough to hold up the pantaloons of Chief Justice Taft. On so slim a young man they seemed somehow absurd, especially on a hot summer night. We perspired horribly for an hour, mopping our faces with our handkerchiefs, the table napkins, the corners of the tablecloth, and a couple of towels left by the waiter. Then there came a thunderstorm, and we began to breathe. There was a hostess at the party, a woman as tactful as she is charming. She disappeared mysteriously and left us to commune.

The trouble that was agitating Valentino turned out to be very simple. The ribald New York papers were full of it, and that was what was gravelling him. Some time before, out in Chicago, a wandering reporter had discovered, in the men's washroom of a gaudy hotel, a slot machine selling talcum powder. That, of course, was not unusual, but the color of the talcum powder was. It was pink. The news made the town giggle for a day, and inspired an editorial writer on the eminent Chicago *Tribune* to compose a hot-weather editorial. In it he protested humorously against the effeminization of the American male, and laid it light-heartedly to the influence of Valentino and his sheik movies. . . .

Suddenly it dawned on me—I was too dull or it was too hot for me to see it sooner—that what we were talking about was really not what we were talking about at all. I began to observe Valentino more closely. A curiously naive and boyish young fellow, certainly not much beyond thirty, and with a disarming air of inexperience. To my eye, at least, not handsome, but nevertheless immensely attractive. There was an obvious fineness in him; even his clothes were not precisely those of his trade. He began talking of his home, his people, his early youth. His words were simple and yet somehow very eloquent. I could still see the mime before me, but now and then, briefly and darkly, there was a flash of something else. That something else, I concluded, was what is commonly called, for want of a better name, a gentleman.

Valentino's agony, in brief, was the agony of a man of civilized feelings thrown into a situation of intolerable vulgarity, destructive alike to his peace and his dignity—nay, into a whole series of such situations. It was not that trifling Chicago episode that was riding him; it was the whole grotesque futility of his life. He had achieved, out of nothing, a vast and dizzy success? Then that success was hollow as well as vast—a colossal and preposterous nothing. Was he acclaimed by yelling multitudes? Then every time the multitudes yelled he felt himself blushing inside.

In other words, the old story of Diego Valdez, but with a new poignancy in it. Valdez, at all events, was High Admiral of Spain. But Valentino, with his touch of fineness in him—he had his commonness too, but there was that touch of fineness—Valentino was only the hero of the rabble. Half-wits surrounded him in a dense herd. He was pursued by women—but what women! (Consider the sordid comedy of his two marriages—the brummagem, star-spangled passion that invaded his very deathbed!) The thing, at the start, must have only bewildered him. But in those last days, unless I am a worse psychologist than even the professors of psychology, it was revolting him. Worse, it was making him afraid.

I incline to think that the inscrutable gods, in taking himself off so soon and at a moment of fiery revolt, were very kind to him. Living, he would have tried inevitably to change his fame—if that is what it is to be called—into something closer to his heart's desire. That is to say, he would have gone the way of many another actor—the way of increasing pretension, of solemn artiness, of hollow hocus-pocus, deceptive only to himself. I believe he would have failed, for there was little sign of the genuine artist in him. He was essentially a highly respectable young man, which is the sort that never metamorphoses into an artist. But suppose he had succeeded?

Then his tragedy, I believe, would have only become the more acrid and intolerable. For he would have discovered, after vast heavings and yearnings, that what he had come to was indistinguishable from what he had left. . . .

Here, after all, is the chiefest joke of the gods; that man must remain alone and lonely in this world, even with crowds surging about him. Does he crave approbation, with a sort of furious, instinctive lust? Then it is only to discover, when it comes, that it is somehow disconcerting—that its springs and motives offer an affront to his integrity. . . . I confess that the predicament of poor Valentino touched me. It provided grist for my mill, but I couldn't quite enjoy it. Here was a young man who was living daily the dream of millions of other young men. Here was one who was catnip to women. Here was one who had wealth and fame, both made honorably and by his own effort. And here was one who was very unhappy.

1927

The image flickered and wavered. But nothing less than a technological triumph was occurring. U.S. Secretary of Commerce Herbert Hoover, speaking in Washington, D.C., simultaneously appeared before a group of reporters in New York City, thanks to an invention called television.

However, on this April day in 1927, television's demonstration looked more novelty than epiphany. Executives of American Telephone and Telegraph, the parent company of Bell Laboratories conducting the broadcast, doubted television's commercial viability. *The New York Times* of April 8, 1927, covered television's city-to-city debut.

FAR-OFF SPEAKERS SEEN AS WELL AS HEARD HERE IN A TEST OF TELEVISION

Like a Photo Come to Life

Hoover's Face Plainly Imaged as He Speaks in Washington.

The First Time in History

Pictures are Flashed by Wire and Radio Synchronizing With Speaker's Voice.

Commercial Use in Doubt

But A.T.&T. Head Sees a New Step in Conquest of Nature After Years of Research.

Herbert Hoover made a speech in Washington yesterday afternoon. An audience in New York heard him and saw him.

More than 200 miles of space intervening between the speaker and his audience was annihilated by the television apparatus developed by the Bell Laboratories of the American Telephone and Telegraph Company and demonstrated publicly for the first time yesterday.

The apparatus shot images of Mr. Hoover by wire from Washington to New York at the rate of eighteen a second. These were thrown on a screen as motion pictures, while the loud-speaker reproduced the speech. As each syllable was heard, the motion of the speaker's lips and his changes of expression were flashed on the screen in the demonstration room of the Bell Telephone Laboratories at 55 Bethune Street.

When the television pictures were thrown on a screen two by three inches, the likeness was excellent. It was as if a photograph had suddenly come to life and begun to talk, smile, nod its head and look this way and that. When the screen was enlarged to two by three feet, the results were not so good.

Phone Hides His Face.

At times the face of the Secretary could not be clearly distinguished. He looked down, as he read his speech, and held the telephone receiver up, so that it covered most of the lower part of his countenance. There was too much illumination also in the background of the screen. When he moved his face, his features became clearly distinquishable. Near the close of his talk he turned his head to one side, and in profile his features became clear and full of detail.

On the smaller screen the face and action were reproduced with perfect fidelity.

After Mr. Hoover had spoken, Vice President J.J. Carty of the American Telephone and Telegraph Company and others in the demonstration room at Washington took his place and conversed one at a time with men in New York. The speaker on the New York end looked the Washington man in the eye as he talked to him. On the small screen before him appeared the living face of the man to whom he was talking.

Time as well as space was eliminated. Secretary Hoover's New York hearers and spectators were something like a thousandth part of a second later that the persons at his side in hearing him and in seeing changes of countenance.

The faces and voices were projected from Washington by wire. It was shown a few minutes later, however, that radio does just as well.

Similar Test by Wireless.

In the second part of the program the group in New York saw and heard performances in the Whippany studio of the American Telephone and Telegraph Company by wireless. The first face flashed on the screen from Whippany, N.J., was that of E. L. Nelson, an engineer, who gave a technical description of what was taking place. Mr. Nelson had a good television face. He screened well as he talked.

Next came a vaudeville act by radio from Whippany. A. Dolan, a comedian, first appeared before the audience as a stage Irishman, with side whiskers and a broken pipe, and did a monologue in brogue. Then he made a quick change and came back in blackface with a new line of quips in negro dialect. The loudspeaker part went over very well. It was the first vaudeville act that ever went on the air as a talking picture and in its possibilities it may be compared with the Fred Ott sneeze of more than thirty years ago, the first piece of comedy ever recorded in motion pictures. For the commercial future of television, if it has one, is thought to be largely in public entertainment—super-news reels flashed before audiences at the moment of occurrence, together with dramatic and musical acts shot on the other waves in sound and picture at the instant they are taking place at the studio. . . .

The demonstration of combined telephone and television, in fact, is one that outruns the imagination of all the wizards of prophecy. It is one of the few things that Leonardo da Vinci, Roger Bacon, Jules Verne and other masters of forecasting failed utterly to anticipate. Even interpreters of the Bible are having trouble in finding a passage which forecast television. H.G. Wells did not rise to it in his earlier crystal-gazing. It is only within the last few years that prophets have been busy in this field. Science has moved ahead so rapidly in this particular line that one of the men, who played a major part in developing the television apparatus shown yesterday, was of the opinion four years ago that research on this subject was hopeless. More than twenty years ago, however, Dr. Alexander Graham Bell, the inventor of the telephone, predicted at a gathering in the tower of the Times Building that the day would come when the man at the telephone would be able to see the distant person to whom he was speaking.

Light Squares Put on Wire.

The demonstration began yesterday afternoon at 2:15 with General Carty at the television apparatus in Washington. As he held the transmitter in his hand and talked the light of an arc lamp flickered on his face. Small circles of light were moving across his face, one after another, but they were traveling at such high speed that they seemed to bathe his face in a uniform bluish light. By a complicated process these lights were dividing his face into fine squares. Each square traveled as a telegraph signal from Washington to New York. Here, with inconceivable rapidity, these squares were assembled as a mosaic. Each square differs in its amount of illumination. These differences of illumination traced the countenance in light and shadow and registered the least changes of expression. The squares rushed across the wire from Washington at the rate of 45,000 a second. The face was done over every eighteenth part of a second. About 2,500 squares—or "units," as they are called—make up each picture.

As General Carty talked his face was thus dissected by light in Washington and reconstructed on the small screen in New York. President Walter S. Gifford of the American Telephone and Telegraph Company was on the New York end of the wire.

"How do you do, General? You are looking well," said Mr. Gifford.

The face of General Carty smiled and his voice inquired after the health of the speaker on the New York end.

"I am instructed to make a little conversation," said President Gifford, "while they are getting the loudspeaker ready. They are having a little power trouble."

"We are all ready and waiting here," said General Carty. "Mr. Hoover is here."

"You screen well, General," said Mr. Gifford. "You look more handsome over the wire."

"Does it flatter me much?" General Carty asked.

"I think it is an improvement," was the reply. . . .

1927

The word "Runyonesque" has become part of the language, a term describing someone resembling the New York City-Broadway characters created by Damon Runyon.

"Harry the Horse," "Big Butch" and "Milk Ear Willie," fictional gangsters and deadbeats, are now firmly established American literary archetypes. However, it was from real life that Runyon, a habitué of Manhattan's speakeasies, drew his guys and dolls during the 1920s and '30s.

One of them was Ruth Snyder, portrayed in the opening installment of Runyon's coverage of the Snyder-Henry Judd Gray murder trial. It appeared on April 19, 1927, in *The New York American* and also was carried on Hearst's International News Service.

CAN'T AGREE ON SNYDER JURY

50 talesmen retired after trial starts

Widow's Attorney Indicates She Will Not Take Stand to Defend Self in Slaying

Gray's Mother Grimly Faces His Former Paramour, but Couple Ignore Each Other

By Damon Runyon

A chilly looking blonde with frosty eyes and one of those marble, you-bet-you-will chins, and an inert, scare-drunk fellow that you couldn't miss among any hundred men as a dead set-up for a blonde, or the shell game, or maybe a gold brick.

Mrs. Ruth Snyder and Henry Judd Gray are on trial in the huge weather-beaten old court house of Queens County in Long Island City, just across the river from the roar of New York for what might be called for want of a better name, The Dumbbell Murder. It was so dumb.

They are charged with the slaughter four weeks ago of Albert Snyder, art editor of the magazine, *Motor Boating,* the blonde's husband and father of her nine-year-old daughter, under circumstances that for sheer stupidity and brutality have seldom been equalled in the history of crime.

Stupid Slaying

It was stupid beyond imagination, this slaughter, and so brutal that the thought of it probably makes many a peaceful, home-loving Long Islander of the Albert Snyder type shiver in his pajamas as he prepares for bed.

They killed Snyder as he slumbered, so they both admitted in confessions—Mrs. Snyder has since repudiated hers—first whacking him on the head with a sash weight, then giving him a few whiffs of chloroform, and finally tightened a strand of picture wire around his throat so he wouldn't revive.

This matter disposed of, they went into an adjoining room and had a few drinks of the whiskey used by some Long Islanders, which is very bad, and talked things over. They thought they had committed "the perfect crime," whatever that may be. It was probably the most imperfect crime on record. It was cruel, atrocious and unspeakably dumb.

They were red-hot lovers then, these two, but they are strangers now. They never exchanged a glance yesterday as they sat in the cavernous old court room while the citizenry of Long Island tramped in and out of the jury box, and the attorneys tried to get a jury of twelve men together without success.

Plumbers, clerks, electricians, merchants, bakers, butchers, barbers, painters, salesmen, machinists, delicatessen dealers, garage employes, realtors and gardeners from the cities and the hamlets of the County of Queens were in the procession that marched through the jury box answering questions as to their views on the death penalty, and their sympathies toward women, and other things.

Selection Slow

Out of fifty men, old and young, married and single, bald and hairy, not one was found acceptable to both sides. Forty-three were excused, the State challenged one peremptorily, the attorneys for Mrs. Snyder five, and the attorneys for Gray one. Each defendant is allowed thirty peremptory challenges, the State thirty against each defendant.

At this rate, they may be able to get a jury before the Long Island corn is ripe. The State is asking that Mrs. Snyder and her meek looking Lothario be given the well-known "hot seat" in Sing Sing, more generally know as the electric chair, and a lot of the talesmen interrogated today seemed to have a prejudice against that form of punishment.

Others had opinions as to the guilt or innocence that they said they couldn't possibly change. A few citizens seemed kindly disposed toward jury service, possibly because they haven't anything at hand for the next few weeks, but they got short shrift from the lawyers. The jury box was quite empty at the close of the day's work.

Mrs. Snyder, the woman who has been called a Jezebel, a lineal descendent of the Borgia outfit, and a lot of other names, came in for the morning session of court stepping along briskly in her patent-leather pumps, with little short steps.

Wears Clothes Well

She is not bad looking. I have seen much worse. She is thirty-three and looks just about that, though you cannot tell much about blondes. She has a good figure, slim and trim, with narrow shoulders. She is of medium height and I thought she carried her clothes off rather smartly. She wore a black dress and a black silk coat with a collar of black fur. Some of the girl reporters said it was dyed ermine; others pronounced it rabbit.

They made derogatory remarks about her hat. It was a tight-fitting thing called, I believe, a beret. Wisps of her straw-colored hair straggled out from under it. Mrs. Snyder wears her hair bobbed, the back of the bobbing rather ragged. She is of the Scandinavian type. Her parents are Norwegian and Swedish.

Her eyes are blue-green, and as chilly looking as an ice cream cone. If all that Henry Judd Gray says of her actions the night of the murder is true, her veins carry ice water. Gray says he dropped the sash weight after slugging the sleeping Snyder with it once and that Mrs. Snyder picked it up and finished the job. . . .

Mother in Court

Gray's mother and sister, Mrs. Margaret Gray and Mrs. Harold Logan, took seats in the courtroom just behind Mrs. Snyder. At the afternoon session, Mrs. Gray, a small, determined-looking woman of middle age, hitched her chair over so she was looking right in Mrs. Snyder's face. . . .

There was a rather grim expression in Mrs. Gray's eyes. She wore a black hat and a black coat with a fur collar, a spray of artificial flowers was pinned to the collar. Her eyelids were red as if she had been weeping.

The sister, Mrs. Logan, is plump and pleasant looking. Gray's wife has left him flat in the midst of his troubles and gone to Norwalk, Conn., with their nine-year-old daughter. She never knew her husband was playing that Don Juan business when she thought he was out peddling corsets. That is she never knew it until the murder.

Turns From Lover

Gray, a spindly fellow in physical build, entered the court room with quick, jerky little steps behind an officer, and sat down between his attorneys, Samuel L. Miller and William L. Millard. His back was to Mrs. Snyder who sat about ten feet distant. Her eyes were on a level with the back of his narrow head.

Gray was neatly dressed in a dark suit, with a white starched collar and subdued tie. He has always been a bit to the dressy side, it is said. He wears big, horn-rimmed spectacles and his eyes have a startled expression. You couldn't find a meeker, milder looking-fellow in seven states, this man who is charged with one of the most horrible crimes in history.

He occasionally conferred with his attorneys as the examination of other talesmen was going forward, but not often. He sat in one position almost the entire day, half slumped down in his chair, a melancholy looking figure for a fellow who once thought of "the perfect crime."

Mrs. Snyder and Gray have been "hollering copper" on each other lately, as the boys say. That is, they have been telling. Gray's defense goes back to old Mr. Adam, that the woman beguiled him, while Mrs. Snyder says he is a "jackal," and a lot of other things besides that, and claims that he is hiding behind her skirts.

Blame Each Other

She will claim, it is said, that while she at first entered into the conspiracy to kill her husband, she later tried to dissuade Gray from going through with it, and tried to prevent the crime. The attorneys will undoubtedly try to picture their respective clients as the victims of each other.

Mrs. Snyder didn't want to be tried with Gray, but Gray was very anxious to be tried with Mrs. Snyder. It is said that no Queens County jury ever sent a woman to death, which is what the State will ask of this jury, if it ever gets one. The relations among the attorneys for the two defendants are evidently not on the theory of "one for all and all for one." Probably the attorneys for Gray do not care what happens to Mrs. Snyder, and probably the attorneys for Mrs. Snyder feel the same way about Gray.

Edgar Hazelton, a close trimmed dapper looking man, with a jutting chin and with a pince-nez balanced on a hawk beak, who represents Mrs. Snyder, did most of the questioning of the talesmen for the defense. His associate, Dana Wallace, is a former district attorney of Queens County, and the pair are said to be among the ablest lawyers on Long Island. It is related that they have defended eleven murder cases without a conviction going against them.

Supreme Court Justice Townsend Scudder is presiding over the courtroom, which has a towering ceiling with a stained glass skylight, and heavy dark oak furniture with high-backed pews for the spectators. Only no spectators were admitted today because the room was needed for the talesmen. . . .

Microphones Used

Microphones have been posted on the tables, and amplifiers have been rigged up on the walls, probably the first time this was ever done in a murder trial, but the apparatus wasn't working any too well today, and one hundred and twenty newspaper writers scattered around the tables listened with their hands cupped behind their ears.

Here is another record, the number of writers covering the trial. We have novelists, preachers, playwrights, fiction writers, sports writers and journalists at the press benches. Also we have nobility in the persons of the Marquis of Queensbury and Mrs. Marquis. The Marquis is a grandson of the gent whose name is attached to the rules governing the manly art of scrambling ears, but the young man wore a pair of fancy-topped shoes yesterday that surprised me. It isn't done you know, really! . . . .

Philosophers Also

There were quite a number of philosophers. I have been requested by my Broadway constituency to ascertain if possible what, if anything, philosophy suggests when a hotsy-totsy blonde with whom a guy is enamoured tells him to do thus and so. But then a philosopher probably never gets tangled up with blondes, or he wouldn't be a philosopher.

Mrs. Snyder showed signs that might have been either nervousness or just sheer impatience during the day. Her fingers constantly toyed with a string of black beads at her throat. Her entire get-up suggested mourning. She has nice white hands, but they are not so small as Gray's. His hands are quite effeminate.

In fact, the alienists who examined Gray and pronounced him quite sane say he is effeminate in many ways. Gray showed no signs of nervousness or any particular animation whatever. He just sat there. It must be a strain on a man to sit for hours knowing the eyes of a woman who is trying to get him all burned up are beating against the back of his neck and not turn around and give her at least one good hot glare. . . .

Oddly enough, there was but a small crowd in front of the towering old brick and stone courthouse, probably because the populace knew there was no chance for a peek at the defendants. The county jail adjoins the courthouse, and Mrs. Snyder and Gray were taken from one to the other by a passageway that keeps them concealed from public view. . . .

State Maps Case

As soon as court adjourned until 10 o'clock tomorrow, Mrs. Snyder and Gray were hurried back to the jail house. Their guardians somewhat considerably permit a lapse of time between their respective arrivals and departures that prevents them from coming face to face.

It probably would make no difference. Mrs. Snyder says she hates Gray now, for all she was his "momsie" and he was her so and so, whatever it was. In the meantime poor Albert Snyder, who had done them no harm, lies a-mouldering in his grave.

1927

American journalists discovered the power of the press to create national celebrities in the 1920s. A succession of heroes and villains, movie stars and sports figures paraded across the front pages during this gaudy era of "jazz journalism." Still no athlete, no actor captured the public's fancy as did a 25-year-old air mail pilot, Charles Augustus Lindbergh.

Shy, boyishly handsome, Lindbergh was determined to win a $25,000 prize posted by French hotelier Raymond Orteig for the first to fly the Atlantic non-stop. (French aviators Charles Nungesser and Francois Coli had been lost over Newfoundland on May 10 attempting to win the prize.) Contrary to the myth that has grown up around the

Lindbergh—in no small measure because of the publicity given him—the "Lone Eagle" was not a lone wolf in his effort to best four other American teams planning transatlantic flights in the next months. He was well-financed by corporate sponsors quick to advertise that Lindbergh had used their products, and by the City of St. Louis Chamber of Commerce, which demanded the Ryan monocoupe be dubbed "The Spirit of St. Louis." In the swelter of publicity, Lloyd's of London posted odds of 10 to 3 and *The New York Times* bought exclusive rights to Lindy's story.

On May 21, 1927, the *Times'* Paris correspondent, Edwin L. James, was on hand at Le Bourget airfield, near Paris, to cover Lindbergh's arrival.

LINDBERGH DOES IT! TO PARIS IN 33 1/2 HOURS; FLIES 1,000 MILES THROUGH SNOW AND SLEET; CHEERING FRENCH CARRY HIM OFF FIELD

Crowd Roars Thunderous Welcome

Breaks Through Lines of Soldiers and Police and Surging to Plane Lifts Weary Flier from His Cockpit

Aviators Save Him From Frenzied Mob of 100,000

Paris Boulevards Ring with Celebration After Day And Night Watch—American Flag is Called For and Wildly Acclaimed

By Edwin L. James
Special Cable to the New York Times

Paris, May 21.—Lindbergh did it. Twenty minutes after 10 o'clock to-night suddenly and softly there slipped out of the darkness a gray-white airplane as 25,000 pairs of eyes strained toward it. At 10:24 the Spirit of St. Louis landed and lines of soldiers, ranks of policemen and stout steel fences went down before a mad rush as irresistible as the tides of the ocean.

"Well, I made it," smiled Lindbergh, as the white monoplane came to a halt in the middle of the field and the first vanguard reached the plane. Lindbergh made a move to jump out. Twenty hands headed for him and lifted him out as if he were a baby. Several thousands in a minute were around the plane. Thousands more broke the barriers of iron rails round the field, cheering wildly.

Lifted from His Cockpit

As he was lifted to the ground Lindbergh was pale and with his hair unkempt, he looked completely worn out. He had strength enough, how-ever, to smile, and waved his hand to the crowd. Soldiers with fixed bayo-nets were unable to keep back the crowd.

United States Ambassador Herrick was among the first to welcome and congratulate the hero.

A New York *Times* man was one of the first to reach the machine after its graceful descent to the field. Those first to arrive at the plane had a picture that will live in their minds for the rest of their lives. His cap off, his famous locks falling in disarray around his eyes, "Lucky Lindy" sat peering out over the rim of the little cockpit of his machine.

Dramatic Scene at the Field

It was high drama. Picture the scene. Almost if not quite 100,000 people were massed on the east side of Le Bourget air field. Some of them had been there six and seven hours.

Off to the left the giant phare [sic] lighthouse of Mount Valerien flashed its guiding light 300 miles into the air. Closer on the left Le Bourget Light-house twinkled, and off to the right another giant revolving phare sent its beams high into the heavens.

Big arc lights on all sides with enormous electric flares were flooding the landing field. From time to time rockets rose and burst in varied lights over the field.

Seven thirty, the hour announced for the arrival, had come and gone. Then 8 o'clock came, and no Lindbergh; at 9 o'clock the sun had set but then came reports that Lindbergh had been seen over Cork. Then he had been seen over Valentia in Ireland and then over Plymouth.

Suddenly a message spread like lightning. The aviator had been seen over Cherbourg. However, remembering the messages telling of Captain Nungesser's flight, the crowd was skeptical.

"One chance in a thousand!" "Oh, he cannot do it without navigating instruments!" "It's a pity because he was a brave boy." Pessimism had spread over the great throng by 10 o'clock.

The stars came out and a chill wind blew.

Watchers are Twice Disappointed

Suddenly the field lights flooded their glares onto the landing ground and there came the roar of an airplane's motor. The crowd was still, then began to cheer, but two minutes later the landing glares went dark for the searchlight had identified the plane and it was not Captain Lindbergh's.

Stamping their feet in the cold, the crowd waited patiently. It seemed quiet apparent that nearly every one was willing to wait all night, hoping against hope.

Suddenly—it was 10:16 exactly—another motor roared over the heads of the crowd. In the sky one caught a glimpse of a white gray plane, and for an instant heard the sound of one. Then it dimmed, and the idea spread that it was yet another disappointment.

Again landing lights glared and almost by the time they had flooded the field the gray white plane had lighted on the far side nearly half a mile from the crowd. It seemed to stop almost as it hit the ground, so gently did it land.

And then occurred a scene which almost passed description. Two companies of soldiers with fixed bayonets and the Le Bourget field police, reinforced by Paris agents, had held the crowd in good order. But as the lights showed the plane landing, much as if a picture had been thrown on a moving picture screen, there was a mad rush.

Soldiers and Police Swept Aside

The movement of humanity swept over soldiers and by policemen and there was the wild sight of thousands of men and women rushing madly across half a mile of the not too even ground. Soldiers and police tried for one small moment to stem the tide, then they joined it, rushing as madly as anyone else toward the aviator and his plane.

The first people to reach the plane were two workmen of the aviation field and half a dozen Frenchmen.

"Cette fois, ça va!" they cried. (This time, it's done.)

Captain Lindbergh answered:

"Well, I made it."

An instant later he was on the shoulders of half a dozen persons who tried to bear him from the field.

The crowd crushed about the aviator and his progress was halted until a squad of soldiers with fixed bayonets cleared a way for him.

It was two French aviators—Major Pierre Weiss and Sergeant de Troyer—

who rescued Captain Lindbergh from the frenzied mob. When it seemed the excited French men and women would overwhelm the frail figure which was being carried on the shoulders of a half dozen men, the two aviators rushed up with a Renault car and hastily snatching Lindy from the crowd, sped across the field to the commandant's office.

Then followed an almost cruel rush to get near the airman. Women were thrown down and a number trampled badly. The doors of the small building were closed, but the windows were forced by enthusiasts, who were promptly ejected by soldiers.

Five Minutes of Cheering for Nungesser

Spurred on by reports spread in Paris of the approach of the aviator, other thousands began to arrive from the capital. The police estimate that within half an hour after Captain Lindbergh landed there were probably 100,000 storming the little building to get a sight of the idol of the evening.

Suddenly he appeared at a window, waving his helmet. It was then that, amid cheers for him, came five minutes of cheering for Captain Nungesser. . . .

Not since the armistice of 1918 had Paris witnessed a downright demonstration of popular enthusiasm and excitement equal to that displayed by the throngs flocking to the boulevards for news of the American flier, whose personality has captured the hearts of the Parisian multitude.

Thirty thousand people had gathered at the Place de l'Opera and the Square du Havre, near St. Lazare station, where illuminated advertising signs flashed bulletins on the progress of the flier. In front of the office of the Paris Matin in the Boulevard Poissonniere the crowds quickly filled the streets, so that extra police details had the greatest difficulty in keeping the traffic moving in two narrow files between the mobs which repeatedly choked the entire street.

From the moment when the last evening editions appeared at 6:30 o'clock, until shortly after 9 there was a curious reaction, due to the fact that news seemed to be at a standstill. The throngs waited, hushed and silent, for confirmation. . . .

Wait Tersely for News

During a long, tense period no confirmation came. The people stood quietly, but the strain was becoming almost unbearable, permeating through the crowd. Pessimistic phrases were repeated. "It's too much to think it possible." "They shouldn't have let him go." "All alone, he has no chance if he should be overcome with exhaustion."

To these comments the inevitable reply was, "Don't give up hope. There's still time."

All this showed the French throng was unanimously eager for the American's safety and straining every wish for his ultimate victory.

A French woman dressed in mourning and sitting in a big limousine was seen wiping her eyes when the bulletins failed to flash confirmation that

Lindbergh's plane had been sighted off Ireland. A woman selling papers near-by brushed her own tears aside exclaiming:

"You're right to feel so, Madame. In such things there is no nationality—he's some mother's son." . . .

Something of the same despair which the crowds evinced two weeks ago spread as an unconfirmed rumor was circulated that Lindbergh had been forced down. Soon after 9 o'clock this was turned to a cheering, shouting pandemonium when Le Matin posted a bulletin announcing that the Lindbergh plane had been sighted over Cherbourg.

Crowd Delirious with Joy

The crowd applauded and surged into the street, halting traffic in a series of delirious manifestations which lasted for ten minutes with cries of "Vive Lindbergh, Vive l'Americain." The news was followed by a general rush for taxicabs and subway stations, thousands being seized simultaneously with the idea of going to Le Bourget to witness the arrival of the victorious airman.

All roads leading toward the air field were jammed with traffic, though thousands still clung to their places before the boulevard bulletin boards. Other throngs moved toward the Etoile, limiting ways of access to the hotel where it had been announced the American's rooms were reserved, in the hope of catching a glimpse of the international hero, the first to make Paris from New York by air, as he passed in triumph from the airdrome.

Landing Excites Crowd to Frenzy

Ovation after ovation followed the news of Lindbergh's startling progress through France, the crowds steadily augmenting until they filled the entire block. The throng was estimated at 15,000 people. After Cherbourg word was flashed that the plane had traversed Louvirs, then the outskirts of Paris.

In a perfect frenzy the huge crowd hailed the announcement that Lindbergh had landed at Le Bourget. Straw hats sailed in the air, handkerchiefs fluttered and a roar of cheers and clapping spread through the throng and was carried along down the boulevards, where the crowds seated in the cafe terraces rushed into the streets and joined in the demonstration. The cheering was renewed again and again. . . .

1927

Five months after Attorney General Palmer began his nationwide round-up of Reds, two Italian immigrants, both professed anarchists, were arrested for the murders of a paymaster and guard during the April 15, 1920, robbery of a $16,000 shoe factory payroll in South Braintree, Massachusetts. Amid an atmosphere of barely contained hysteria and self-righteous patriotism, the two were tried, convicted, and, on July 14, 1921, sentenced to death in the electric chair.

For the next six years, Nicola Sacco and Bartolomeo Vanzetti fought for their lives. Charging bias against their clients, attacking what they claimed was scant or faulty evidence, attorneys representing the convicted radicals managed to place the American system of justice itself on trial.

The case became an international *cause célèbre;* there were demonstrations in support of the two prisoners throughout Europe and in South America. Protestors, including a large part of America's intel- ligensia, raised money, marched, and solicited support for the two condemned men.

It was to no avail. Their appeals turned aside by the United States Supreme Court and the governor of Massachusetts, Sacco and Vanzetti, along with a third man, Celestino Madeiros, condemned for a separate offense, went to the electric chair on the night of August 22/23, 1927. *The Boston Daily Globe* story appeared the morning of the 23rd.

MADEIROS, SACCO, VANZETTI DIED IN CHAIR THIS MORNING

Electrocuted in That Order Soon After Midnight —All Reject Religious Consolation to the Last— Two Make Statements

Madeiros in Stupor—Other Two Face Death Calmly

Judges Holmes, Anderson and Lowell Refuse Final Appeals

Vanzetti Forgives, Sacco Says Goodbye

Nicola Sacco and Bartolomeo Vanzetti are dead.

Between midnight and 12:30 this morning, at the Charlestown State Prison, they paid with their lives for a crime of which they had been convicted by a jury of their peers.

Sacco marched to his death at 12:11:12 with defiance on his lips for the social order which executed him, and a farewell for his family and friends. He was dead seven minutes and 50 seconds later. Vanzetti's last words were a cry of innocence and forgiveness. He was brought into his death chamber at 12:20:38, and was dead at 12:26:55. . . .

The final chapter in a drama which has stirred the entire world was written in an obscure corner of a prison over which hung the stillness of death. Outside, the tramp of guards, the impatient clatter of the hoofs of mounted troops and the occasional rattle of rifle or accoutrements were the only audible evidence of the regiment which had been thrown about the prison as a protection against the attack which was feared from partisans of the condemned men.

No such demonstration occurred. The explosions and outbreaks which occurred in many lands while the legal battle to free the men was being carried unsuccessfully to the highest courts and executive power in the land had no echo when Sacco and Vanzetti paid for the crime which turned them from humble immigrants to world figures.

Madeiros First to Go

Madeiros was first to die. The legal witnesses left the office of Warden William Hendry on the stroke of 12. Their short walk to the death house was completed in less than two minutes and at 12:02:47 Celestino Madeiros had walked the 13 steps from cell No. 1 to the door of the execution chamber.

The two guards on his right and left led him to the electric chair.

Looking at nobody, saying nothing, Madeiros sat down stolidly. He was unmoved while the guards went swiftly about their work of applying the electrodes. At 12:03:37 the executioner, Robert Elliott, threw on the current of 1400-1900 volts. Three times the current was thrown on and off, and at 12:09:35, four examining physicians declared officially that Celestino Madeiros was dead.

Sacco Walks Firmly

The guards returned to the death house, and returned with Sacco at 12:11:12. Despite his hunger strike, Sacco walked firmly. He was pale, but his pallor was no greater than could be expected after his long imprisonment. The guards led him directly to the chair, and he sat down without protest.

As the guards swung about to adjust the straps, Sacco sat bolt upright in the chair of death. Casting about wildly with his eyes, he cried in Italian "Long live anarchy." Then he calmed himself, and in a quieter tone added in English "Farewell, my wife and child and all my friends."

Then, seeming to become cognizant of the witnesses as individuals, rather than as an audience, he went on politely, "Good evening, gentlemen." With this the guards had completed their work of adjusting the straps and electrodes and slipped the mask over his eyes.

His last cry, as the current was thrown on was "Farewell, my mother." The farewell was in English, the rest, "mia matre," in his native tongue.

Current was administered at 12:13:10, an extra heavy current being applied in Sacco's case, the voltage being 1800 to 2000. He was pronounced dead at 12:19:02.

The guards quickly went to the cells for the last time, unlocked cell 3, and escorted Vanzetti over the 20 short steps to the door of the death chamber. He was very cool, and not at all belligerent. His manner belied his fierce mustaches, when having been led to the electric chair, he paused a moment to shake hands cordially with three of the guards, who had befriended him in prison.

Then he was urged toward the chair, and sat down obediently. Once seated, he began to speak, slowly and coolly in English. "I wish to tell you I am innocent,'' he began. ''I never committed any crime but sometimes some sin. I thank you for everything you have done for me. I am innocent of all crime, not only of this one, but all. I am an innocent man. I wish to forgive some people for what they are now doing to me.''

The guards lingered with their work to permit him to finish. When he paused, as though he had done, they slipped the blindfold over his eyes and current was applied at 12:26:33, five minutes and five seconds after he stepped into the death chamber. As in the case of Madeiros, 1400 to 1800 volts were sufficient and death was pronounced at 12:26:55. . . .

Men Told Their Fate

The three condemned men were told their fate just after 8:40. Word had come to the prison that Judge Lowell of the Federal District Court had denied a petition for a writ of habeas corpus, and with this news it became apparent that the last hope of life had died. Accompanied by Rev. Michael J. Murphy, Catholic chaplain of the prison, Warden Hendry left his office and made his way through the prison yard to the death house—a low, grim structure at the far end.

The culmination of the bitter battle for the life of Sacco and Vanzetti had little of the dramatic, unless it was dramatic in its very simplicity. As Warden Hendry and the priest stepped into the death house the two guards, who had been seated at a table facing the cells, rose. The condemned men made no move. . . .

''I am sorry,'' began Warden Hendry, ''but it is my painful duty to inform you that you have to die tonight. Your lawyers have exhausted their efforts.''

Madeiros blinked uninterestedly with the faint air of irritation of a man who had been roused to be given some unimportant message. Without a word of acknowledgement or disappointment, he rolled over toward the wall of the death chamber. He was once more asleep in but a few minutes.

Fr. Murphy stepped to the cell door to offer condolences and to plead, almost for the last time that Madeiros accept the consolation of the church of his baptism. The condemned man might have been deaf, for all the attention he paid, and Fr. Murphy gave up his task as hopeless.

Sacco Writing Father

Next Warden Hendry stepped to cell number 2. Sacco sat at the table, writing busily, facing the side wall, his left side toward the door. ''I am sorry,'' began Warden Hendry again, and again he repeated the same phraseology: ''It is my painful duty to tell you that you have to die tonight. Your lawyers have exhausted their efforts.''

At the words, Sacco stopped writing, and looked over his left shoulder at the warden. He apparently had not overheard Warden Hendry's message to Madeiros, for his countenance fell. He appeared greatly dejected. For a few moments he said nothing, but sat staring at the writing in front of him. Then he turned to face Warden Hendry once more and said: "I would like to be sure that this, my last letter, which I am writing to my father in Italy, will be mailed."

"I will come down myself between 11 and 11:30," replied the warden, "and I will personally make sure that it is mailed." Sacco then rose, and in somewhat halting style expressed his gratitude to Warden Hendry for this and other kindnesses which he had shown during Sacco's confinement at the State Prison. The warden briefly acknowledged the thanks and stepped on to the next cell. . .

Vanzetti, less absorbed than Sacco, appeared to have gathered the news from Warden Hendry's murmured conversation at the next cell. He, too, appeared shocked to find that his last hope of life no longer existed. For a brief period he stood staring at the floor, then he flung his arms wide and cried, dramatically, "We must bow to the inevitable."

Sacco shook his head. He said he had appreciated Fr. Murphy's interest in him, and that he had enjoyed his talks with the chaplain, but he reiterated that he had no belief in the orthodox Creator and that he had no intention of embracing any religion at the last moment. The man was obviously firm, and Fr. Murphy did not press the matter when Sacco turned back to his writing.

Meanwhile, at the last cell, Warden Hendry was repeating his fateful message for the last time. He found, when he reached the door of the cell, that Vanzetti was pacing about, door to wall, wall to door, and repeat. The man stopped his pacing to face the warden through the bars of the door.

Vanzetti Thanks Warden

He turned away to resume his pacing, turning back once more to thank the warden for his efforts to make the life of a condemned man as pleasant as possible. Warden Hendry bowed, and made way for Fr. Murphy, who went over with Vanzetti, the same ground he had covered with Sacco and Madeiros. Vanzetti's response was similar to Sacco's. . . .

At about 10 o'clock Chief Electrician Greenough of the State Prison, accompanied by his assistant, John Mulaney, went to the death chamber for a final test of the chair. Using a resistance board of electric lamps as the subject of the test, the electricians connected the electrode and shot through the current, in the presence of the executioner, Robert Elliott of New York. The apparatus was found to be in good condition.

Message Sent to Men

During the evening several messages were received at the prison for the prisoners. One sent from New York and signed Epstein, which was not shown to Sacco, to whom it was addressed, urged the condemned man to keep up his courage, and added: "It is justice that dies, Sacco and Vanzetti will live in history." . . .

1927

He was surely the most beloved of baseball players of his time, perhaps of all time. After all, when his 1927 record of 60 home runs in a single season was finally broken by Roger Maris in 1961, the panjandrums of organized baseball insisted that an asterisk follow the new mark, since it was set in a season eight games longer than George Herman Ruth played. Thus the "Babe's" awesome record endures, protected by an asterisk.

New York sportswriters who covered the Yankees that year seemed to take the Bambino's accomplishment in stride. Ruth had set the earlier home run record in 1921 with 59. He had led the league in home runs six times in his career. Such feats were expected of him. And these Yankees were the stuff of legend. Five of the starters hit over .300 that year; the team won a record 110 games during the season, losing but 44.

The New York Times story of October 1, 1927, probably written by John Drebinger, reported Ruth's feat—off of pitcher Tom Zachary—in the jargon-laden style then popular among the scribes of the sporting press.

HOME RUN RECORD FALLS AS RUTH HITS 60TH

Ruth Crashes 60th
To Set New Record

Babe Makes it a Real Field Day
by Accounting for All Runs
In 4-2 Victory.

1921 Mark of 59 Beaten

Fans Go Wild as Ruth Pounds
Ball Into Stands With One
On, Breaking 2-2 Tie.

Connects Last Time Up

Zachary's Offering Converted Into
Epochal Smash, Which Old Fan
Catches—Senators Then Subside.

Babe Ruth scaled the hitherto unattained heights yesterday. Home run 60, a terrific smash off the southpaw pitching of Zachary, nestled in the Babe's favorite spot in the right field bleachers, and before the roar had ceased it was found that this drive not only had made home run record history but also was the winning margin in a 4 to 2 victory over the Senators. This also was the Yanks' 109th triumph of the season. Their last league game of the year will be played today.

When the Babe stepped to the plate in that momentous eighth inning the score was deadlocked, Koenig was on third base, the result of a triple, one man was out and all was tense. It was the Babe's fourth trip to the plate during the afternoon, a base on balls and two singles resulting on his other visits plateward.

The first Zachary offering was a fast one, which sailed over for a called strike. The next was high. The Babe took a vicious swing at the third pitched ball and the bat connected with a crash that was audible in all parts of the stand. It was not necessary to follow the course of the ball. The boys in the bleachers indicated the route of the record homer. It dropped about half way to the top. Boys, No. 60 was some homer, a fitting wallop to top the Babe's record of 59 in 1921.

While the crowd cheered and the Yankee players roared their greetings the Babe made his triumphant, almost regal tour of the paths. He jogged around slowly, touched each bag firmly and carefully and when he imbedded his spikes in the rubber disk to record officially Homer 60 hats were tossed into the air, papers were torn up and tossed liberally and the spirit of celebration permeated the place.

The Babe's stroll out to his position was the signal for a handkerchief salute in which all the bleacherites, to the last man, participated. Jovial Babe entered into the carnival spirit and punctuated his Ringly Strides with a succession of snappy military salutes.

Ruth 4, Senators 2.

Ruth's homer was a fitting climax to a game which will go down as the Babe's personal triumph. The Yanks scored four runs, the Babe personally crossing the plate three times and bringing in Koenig for the fourth. So this is one time where it would be fair, although not original, to record Yankee victory 109 as Ruth, 4, Senators, 2.

There was not much else to the game. The 10,000 persons who came to the Stadium were there for no other purpose than to see the Babe make home run history. After each of Babe's visits to the plate the expectant crowd would relax and wait for his next effort. They saw him open with a base on balls, follow with two singles and then clout the epoch-making circuit smash.

The only unhappy individual within the Stadium was Zachary. He realized he was going down in the records as the historical home run victim, in other words, the goat. Zachary was one of the most interested spectators of the home run flight. He tossed his glove to the ground, muttered to himself, turned to his mates for consolation and got everything but that. There is no denying that Zachary was putting everything he had on the ball. No pitcher likes to have recorded after his name the fact that he was Ruth's victim on the sixtieth homer.

The ball that the Babe drove, according to word from official sources, was a pitch that was fast, low and on the inside. The Babe pulled away from the plate, then stepped into the ball, and wham! According to Umpire

Tabloid journalism at its most graphic: the death by electrocution of convicted murderer Ruth Snyder at New York's Sing Sing Prison, January 13, 1928. Copyright by the *New York Daily News*

Bill Dinneen at the plate and Catcher Muddy Ruel the ball traveled on a line and landed a foot inside fair territory about half way to the top of the bleachers. But when the ball reached the bleacher barrier it was about ten feet fair and curving rapidly to the right.

Fan Rushes to Babe With Ball.

The ball which became Homer 60 was caught by Joe Forner of 1937 First Avenue, Manhattan. He is about 40 years old and has been following baseball for thirty-five, according to his own admission. He was far from modest and as soon as the game was over rushed to the dressing room to let the Babe know who had the ball. . . .

1929

A sensation-hungry press has often heaped adulatory attention on a number of otherwise undistinguished people with no greater talent than the ability to excite public curiosity and sell newspapers. None were less deserving of the gee-whiz coverage than the small-time thugs who took advantage of the passage of the Prohibition Amendment to go into business supplying the illicit liquor America suddenly craved. In time, the fawning coverage of men like Alphonse Capone, Legs Diamond, George Moran and Dion O'Banion changed—as *The Chicago Herald Examiner* of February 15, 1929, makes clear in reporting what has come to be known as the St. Valentine's Day Massacre.

SEVEN LINED UP AND SLAIN BY GANGLAND FIRING SQUAD

Machine Guns Wipe Out
North Side 'Mob'; Killers
Disguised as Policemen

O'Banion Remnants Assassinated by
One Volley at Garage; Moran Feared
Kidnaped; Uniformed Gunmen Fled
in Auto; Sirens Clear Path for Flight

Chicago gangsters graduated yesterday from murder to massacre.

They killed seven men in a group. There were just a few seconds of machine gun and shotgun fire. Then six of them lay dead and the seventh was dying.

It was like the precise work of an execution squad of the Mexican army, like the assassination of Czar Nicholas and his family.

The seven victims were slain in the garage of the S.M.C. Chicago Company, 123 N. Clark St. . . .

Executioner Snaps Order;
Guns Bark; Seven Die

The leader of the massacre squad gave an order, the machine guns clattered, and all was over.

That brief blaze of bullets almost wiped out the Moran gang, which was the rallied remnant of the men-at-arms led by the late, assassinated Dion O'Banion.

The victims were:

CLARK, JAMES, 32; brother-in-law of George ("Bugs") Moran, and his associate since early gang days.

SCHWIMMER, DR. R.H., Parkway Hotel, with offices in the Capitol Building.

GUSENBERG, FRANK, 38; known as "Hock," member of North Side gang formed by O'Banion, Moran and others, and Moran's lieutenant.

GUSENBERG, PETER, 36; known as "Goosey," member of Moran gang for three years.

HEYERS, ADAM, alias Frank Schneider, 29; business man of the gang.

MAY, JOHN, 30; a North Side gangster with a lengthy police record.

WEINSHANK, ALFRED, 35; cleaning and dyeing emissary for the gang.

If Moran is alive, it is because he has influenza and was too ill to be with his men. Willie Marks, his right-hand man, is like his shadow. He goes everywhere with his chief. Therefore, he, too, may have escaped.

But one theory is that the assassins kidnaped Moran and perhaps Marks also and killed them afterward. This is predicated upon the idea that the shooting was in reprisal for some hijacking of whisky from a rival gang. The slayers might have expected Moran to tell where the liquor was hidden.

A widespread search was being made last night for Moran and Marks.

Reconstruct the scene and the action, as the police have done, from their own deductions and inferences and the stories of witnesses:

Six of the seven men who are to die are in a group, talking. The seventh, May, is at work on a truck. The police think that truck was used in booze running.

Mystery Phone Call
Seals Doom of All

The telephone rings. One answers. The call is for Weinshank. He answers, but is told "the party has hung up." Probably the call sealed the doom of all, probably the assassins were making sure of their prey.

The police know that there was such a call because a phone operator recalled it.

Moran's men resume their talk. A police dog, chained to the truck, dozes with his nose on his paws. All quiet.

Then four men walk in through the front door. The two leaders wear the uniforms of police, though no stars appear. They carry packages, paper wrapped.

Their victims regard them without much interest—apparently just a police squad, scouting around.

The wrappers come off the packages. Machine guns come into view. Suddenly, the seven become apprehensive. Too late.

"Line against the wall! Hands up!"

Four stand. Three remain seated. All lift their hands.

The chief executioner says something. The victims hear their death sentence.

The bullets splatter through the human flesh. They crash against the brick wall. They splinter and riccochet.

The men tumble down, sprawled about in the awful, grotesque attitudes of sudden death. Wounds gape. Blood flows upon the floor, bright in the white light of an overhead electric light.

Victim Stumbles to
Chair in Last Fight

One man—Frank Gusenberg—is not quite dead. He stumbles, reaches for the wall, slithers down, clutches at a chair, clinging to life, fighting for it.

The place is a shambles.

The police dog comes to life, furious, courageous, but helpless. He growls and springs. His collar brings him up sharp, half choked from the tug at his throat. He tries again. He barks and howls in his thwarted ferocity.

The execution squad turns about and walks out the way they entered. But their order is changed. The men garbed as civilians lead now. The uniformed men follow, prodding them with the machine gun muzzles.

That is camouflage. Persons who see it think two police have arrested two hoodlums.

Uniformed Men Take
"Prisoners" Outside

The four step into an automobile. Witnesses notice the car resembles those used by the detective bureau. There is even a gong on the side.

The start of the flight is made slowly, sedately. A corner is turned, the car's speed quickens. It roars out of sight.

Thus Chicago gangland, long master of murder, matriculates in massacre.

Some who heard the rattle of gunfire thought of an automobile backfiring, but others thought of guns.

Woman Sounds Alarm;
Passerby Calls Police

One of the latter was Mrs. Jeanette Landsman, 2124 N. Clark St. She ran toward the garage. Afraid to enter, she notified a passerby. He hurried in, then he hurried out. He telephoned police.

The police arrived, singly, in twos, in squads, as the magnitude of the slaughter became apparent.

So soon did the first reach the scene that blood still drained from the wounds. Gusenberg still struggled to keep a hold on life.

"The worst sight I ever saw," said policeman after policeman. And there were those among them, of course, who had seen war.

Too awful to look at—but they had to look. They had to move Frank Gusenberg to a hospital, where he died a little later, with never a word as to the identity of the slayers or their motive.

They had to scan every detail of the scene for clues. They had to photograph the bodies from many angles, to record them in all the horrid postures of sudden death.

And, of course, they had eventually to remove them, to take them first to an undertaking parlor and later to the county morgue, in which charnel house they now lie, side by side, awaiting the formal gesture of interest by a coroner's jury.

Hysterical Dog's
Frenzy Adds Horror

It was much too terrible for humans. It was too terrible for the police dog.

The animal was veritably hysterical. He pointed his nose toward the ceiling, and howled. And the way he howled was ghastly in the presence of that wholesale death.

From time to time he lunged toward the police, as they moved about the dead.

His frenzy became monumental when the officers touched the bodies.

The police feared his neck would snap as he tried to prevent their search of the pockets of the dead men, extracting among other things the "rolls" characteristic of gangsters—$800 here, $600 there, $1,300 from this pocket, and $400 from that.

Throng Rushes to
Scene; All 'Witnesses'

While police surged about inside, a tremendous crowd formed outside, some who had heard the shots, others who already had heard fragments of the story, still others that came from afar, drawn by the strange magnetism of morbidity.

Witnesses developed mysteriously, persons who knew all about it, who saw it, who could identify the killers, etc.

But as the police questioned them, the great majority of their stories dwindled pitifully. They didn't know; they had "just heard" some one say something.

There were two eye witnesses—Frank Gusenberg and the dog.

While he lived Gusenberg could probably have told. But he wouldn't. He just looked stolidly at the questioners, while death galloped toward him.

The dog would have told. But he couldn't. He just howled.

George "Bugs" Moran escaped his hunters, but the destruction of his gang reduced him to petty burglaries during the 1930's. He served a ten-year term in Ohio, was released in 1956, and imme- diately rearrested by federal agents on longstanding bank robbery charges. Convicted once more, he died, peacefully, of lung cancer in Leavenworth prison in February, 1957.

1929

Studio boss Louis B. Mayer wanted to improve Hollywood's flamboyant, sometimes tawdry image. From a banquet meeting hosted by Mayer grew the notion of an Academy of Motion Picture Arts and Sciences, and an annual awards ceremony to honor film's best. The first such presentation was held in the Blossom Room of the Hollywood Roosevelt Hotel on May 16, 1929. And here the statuette later known as "Oscar" made its debut.

The Los Angeles Times of May 17, 1929, tersely reported this first Academy Awards ceremony, avoiding the fawning saturation coverage accorded the awards more recently.

FILM—MERIT TROPHIES AWARDED

Recognition Bestowed for Notable Achievements

In the presence of more than 400 notables of the motion-picture world the awards for outstanding individual performances were presented formally last night at the annual banquet of the Academy of Motion Picture Arts and Sciences in the Roosevelt Hotel. This was the second anniversary of the formation of the academy.

The award for the best acting performances of the year were given to Janet Gaynor for her performance in "Seventh Heaven" and other photoplays, and Emil Jannings for performances in "The Way of All Flesh" and "The Last Command." The first award for directorial work was given Frank Borzage for his direction of "Seventh Heaven." The award for the best comedy picture went to Lewis Milestone for "Two Arabian Knights." Benjamin Glazer will receive first prize for his adaptation of "Seventh Heaven." The title-writing award went to Joseph Farnham. Charles Rosher and Karl

Struss received the first award for cinematography of "Sunrise." Struss accepted the award for both of them as Rosher is in England. The art direction award was given William C. Menzies for art direction of "The Tempest."

The first prize for engineering effects was given Roy Pomeroy for his work in "Wings." Pomeroy was not present.

Paramount Famous-Lasky Corporation received first prize for the production of the most outstanding picture during the year, which was "Wings." Adolph Zukor made the acceptance speech for the corporation by means of a talking film. He is now in New York. The Fox company received the highest award for the production of the most unique and artistic picture, "Sunrise." The acceptance was made by Winfield Sheehan, vice-president and general manager.

Special first awards were made to Warner Brothers for producing "The Jazz Singer," pioneer talking picture. Acceptance was made by Darryl Zanuck, associate executive of the company, on behalf of the late Sam Warner, who had charge of its first Vitaphone development. A special first award was given to Charles Chaplin for writing, acting, directing and producing "The Circus."

Douglas Fairbanks, the president of the academy, introduced William C. De Mille, who acted as master of ceremonies in awarding the prizes which were statuettes gold and bronze. Certificates were given to those honored in addition to the trophies. More than thirty certificates of honorable mention were given to persons for outstanding work in various branches of the industry during the year.

Short speeches were made by Prof. Walter Richard Miles, head of the department of psychology, Stanford University; Sir Gilbert Parker, and several others.

1929

On September 3, 1929, stock prices soared to an all-time high. Seven weeks later, the market paused in its decade-long climb, slipped slightly, then plummeted into a sickening free fall historians have yet to explain adequately.

Investors lost billions of dollars with the stock market's collapse on October 24, 1929. In all, nearly 13,000,000 shares were traded that "Black Thursday" while brokers scrambled to save something, anything from the ruins of the market.

But worse was to come. Five days later, on October 29, "Black Tuesday," more than 16,000,000 shares changed hands. Panicked investors, most of whom had bought on credit, confronted "calls" for immediate payment from equally frightened brokerages. Investors and brokers alike dumped stocks in a frenzied attempt to recoup whatever they could. The panic mounted.

Taking their cue from the nation's captains of industry and finance—who outwardly maintained unshakeable optimism in the face of the catastrophe—many newspapers adopted an air of blithe reassurance. Matters were not as grave as events would indicate, they insisted. Again and again the press quoted industrialists' assurance that the basic economy of the country was sound, that the market would soon right itself, that the bull market would surely return to Wall Street.

Such misplaced optimism gripped *The Wall Street Journal* of October 30, 1929, as it reported the worst day in market history, and the beginning of the Great Depression.

STOCKS STEADY AFTER DECLINE

Bankers State Support Continues— Spokesman Expresses View Hysteria is Passing

Record Trading Volume

The stock market passed through its record day of business on Tuesday with the general level of prices reaching new lows. There were signs of support buying, however, as well as investor purchases having some effect on checking the widespread break.

Large banking group [sic] which has been working to stabilize market conditions since the break last Thursday was again an active factor in the situation.

It held to sessions, one early in the day and the other after the close. Following the second meeting, a partner of J.P. Morgan & Co., acting as spokesman for the group, officially stated that the group had been supporting and would continue in a cooperative way to support the market and had not been a seller of stocks. This banker took occasion again to note that the group was not seeking to put stocks up but to help out a situation where hysteria was reigning.

Richard Whitney, vice president of New York Stock Exchange, issued the following statement: "The meeting of the board of governors of the New York Stock Exchange considered carefully the present situation, but felt no action was necessary and adjourned to its regular meeting Wednesday afternoon."

More Hopeful About Conditions

There was no doubt that the banking group felt much more hopeful about conditions. Discussing the situation following the afternoon meeting, the spokesman pointed out that a canvass of the situation indicated that the hysteria of the past few days seemed to be passing and the public gradually coming to its senses. That, he added, was the consensus the banking group obtained in its survey of the Street after the day's session.

The more sensible state of mind, he pointed out, was shown by the fact that a very considerable amount of first class investment buying was in the market Tuesday; further, that a number of corporations were known to be buyers of stocks on a considerable scale for their employe [sic] stock ownership and similar funds. Many large capitalists, likewise, were hunting bargains and buying stocks.

The situation, in the opinion of the spokesman, indicated "that people are taking the blinders off their eyes and looking more at the facts."

Trading in Record Volume

Though trading volume of 16,410,000 shares exceeded last Thursday's record by some 3,000,000 shares, the tape was not nearly as late recording prices, the last sale being printed at 5:32 p.m., against 7:03 p.m. on the smaller business Thursday.

Furthermore, the average decline in prices was less than the previous day, Tuesday's closing finding the Dow-Jones industrial average down 30.57 points compared with 38.33 points on Monday. . . .

Statement from J.P. Morgan

Following the afternoon conference of the banking group in the office of J.P. Morgan & Co., one of the partners of that firm, acting as a spokesman of the group said:

"I want to take occasion tonight to explain again, as heretofore, that the banking group was organized to offer certain support in the market and to act as far as possible as somewhat of a stabilizing factor," the spokeman for the banker's group said.

"It was not an attempt of the group to maintain prices but to maintain a free market. In other words, to correct the conditions that prevailed last Thursday.

"The group has continued and will continue in a cooperative way to support the market and has not been a seller of stocks. . . .

1931

New York City's Empire State Building dwarfed all other structures. Constructed for $52,000,000 in midtown Manhattan on the former site of the old Waldorf-Astoria Hotel, this office tower was to reign as the world's tallest building for almost four decades.

When the Empire State Building opened on May 1, 1931, an elaborate ceremony marked the occasion. President Herbert Hoover in Washington, D.C., pressed a button, switching on the building's lights. Then several hundred invited guests joined former New York City Governor Alfred E. Smith, who was president of Empire State, Inc., to see the city from a new, lofty perspective.

A *New York Times* reporter recorded his impressions for the May 2, 1931, edition.

PANORAMA VIEWED FROM 85TH STORY

Vast Area of Shimmering Water,
Tall Buildings and Homes
Seen from Empire State.

SHIPS VISIBLE ON OCEAN

Other Skyscrapers are Dwarfed—
At Night a Million Lights
Change the Scene.

A new view of the metropolitan district—a vast panorama of shimmering water, tall towers, quiet suburban homes and busy Manhattan streets—was unfolded yesterday to visitors who ascended to the observatory above the eighty-fifth floor of the Empire State Building.

From the highest vantage point steamers and tugs, which appeared to be little more than rowboats, could be seen far up the Hudson and the East River. Down by the bay, beyond the Narrows and out to sea a ship occasionally hove into view or faded in the distance.

For miles in every direction the city was spread out before the gaze of the sight-seers. To the north the apartment houses of the Bronx were plainly visible. To the east and southeast lay the green residential sections, the business and factory districts and shorelines of Long Island and dBrooklyn [sic]; beyond the bay, the hills of Staten Island, and to the west, the smoke of Jersey's industries with wooded slopes hiding a thousand dwellings.

In Manhattan the tall buildings, which from the streets below appeared as monsters of steel and stone, assumed a less awe-inspiring significance when viewed from above. Fifth Avenue and Broadway were little more than slender black ribbons which had cut their way sharply through masses of vari-colored brick. Along them lilliputian vehicles jockeyed for position, halting or moving forward in groups, often like a processional. From a height of more than 1,000 feet pedestrians were little more than ants and their movements cardly [sic] could be detected.

Central Park appeared as a flattened rectangle of earth and turf, a welcome relief from the stern irregularity of the skyline and the buildings which hemmed in its lake and trees. The new apartment houses along the East River were pierced by the spire of the Chrysler tower. Some of the modern skyscrapers of white brick and stone stood out in sharp contrast to the darker edifices surrounding them and to the rows of brownstone homes which are rapidly giving way to taller residential buildings.

At night the scene was hardly recognizable as the same which greeted the daytime visitors. Beyond the immediate shadows of midtown Manhattan on the south a million windows glowed with light from the towers of the financial district, although the darkened outline of some of these skyscrapers showed that they had become deserted with the coming of night. Lines of lights and the dim, errant flicker from motor vehicles marked the streets with Broadway as a kaleidoscope of flickering color. Brief rows of brightness, or slight lights, moved slowly up and down the waters around the island.

The observatory will be open daily from 9 A.M. to 10 P.M. and also for a few hours every Sunday.

1932

For almost a half-century Walter Lippmann reigned as the foremost geopolitical commentator in the United States. First in the pages of *The New Republic,* then on the editorial pages of *The New York World* (with novelist James N. Cain), finally as proprietor of *The New York Herald-Tribune*'s widely syndicated column "Today and Tomorrow," Lippmann rendered Olympian judgments of the works of presidents, prime ministers and sundry politicians.

Despite his considerable reputation, however, Lippmann could be spectacularly wrong headed. He privately considered Franklin Delano Roosevelt, then governor of New York, no more than "a kind of amiable boy scout" and in his column of January 8, 1932, with a despairing nation in the very pit of the Depression, Lippmann dismissed FDR as unfit for the presidency. Roosevelt would never forget the slur, and the haughty Lippmann would rue that column until FDR died.

TODAY AND TOMORROW
BY WALTER LIPPMANN

The Candidacy of Franklin D. Roosevelt

It is now plain that sooner or later some of Governor Roosevelt's supporters are going to feel badly let down. For it is impossible that he can continue to be such different things to such different men. He has, at the moment, the highly preferred candidate of left-wing progressives like Senator Wheeler of Montana and of [William Jennings] Bryan's former secretary, Representative Howard of Nebraska. He has, at the same time, received the enthusiastic support of "The New York Times."

Senator Wheeler, who would like to cure the depression by debasing the currency, is Mr. Roosevelt's most conspicuous supporter in the West, and Representative Howard has this week hailed the Governor as "the most courageous enemy of the evil influences" emanating from the international bankers. "The New York Times," on the other hand, assures its readers that "no upsetting plans, no Socialistic proposals, however mild and winning in form," could appeal to the Governor.

The Roosevelt bandwagon would seem to be moving in two opposite directions.

There are two questions raised by this curious situation. The first is why Senator Wheeler and "The Times" should have such contradictory impressions of their common candidate. The second, which is also the more important question, is which has guessed rightly.

The art of carrying water on both shoulders is highly developed in American politics, and Mr. Roosevelt has learned it. His message to the Legislature, or at least that part of it devoted to his Presidential candidacy, is an almost perfect specimen of the balanced antithesis. Thus at one place we learn that the public demands "plans for the reconstruction of a better ordered civilization" and in another place that "the American system of economics and government is everlasting." The first sentence is meant for Senator Wheeler and the second for "The New York Times."

The message is so constructed that a left-wing progressive can read it and find just enough of his own phrases in it to satisfy himself that Franklin D. Roosevelt's heart is in the right place. He will find an echo of [Wisconsin] Governor LaFollette's recent remarks about the loss of "economic liberty." He will find an echo of Governor LaFollette's impressive discussion about the increasing concentration of wealth and how it does not guarantee an intelligent or a fair use of that wealth. He will find references to "plans." On the other hand, there are all necessary assurances to the conservatives. "We should not seek in any way to destroy or to tear down"; our system is "everlasting"; we must insist "on the permanence of our fundamental institutions."

That this is a studied attempt to straddle the whole country I have no doubt whatever. Every newspaper man knows the whole bag of tricks by heart. He knows too that the practical politician supplements these two-faced platitudes by what are called private assurances in which he tells his different supporters what he knows they would like to hear. Then, when they read the balanced antithesis each believes the half that he has been reassured about privately and dismissed the rest as not significant. That, ladies and gentlemen, is how the rabbit comes out of the hat, that is how it is possible to persuade Senator Wheeler and "The New York Times" that you are their man.

In the case of Mr. Roosevelt, it is not easy to say with certainty whether his left-wing or his right-wing supporters are the more deceived. The reason is that Franklin D. Roosevelt is a highly impressionable person, without a firm grasp of public affairs and without very strong convictions. He might plump for something which would shock the conservatives. There is no telling. Yet when Representative Howard of Nebraska says that he is "the most dangerous enemy of evil influences," New Yorkers who know the Governor know that Mr. Hoard does not know the Governor. For Franklin D. Roosevelt is an amiable man with many philanthropic impulses, but he is not the dangerous enemy of anything. He is too eager to please. The notion, which seems to prevail in the West and South, that Wall Street fears him, is preposterous. Wall Street thinks he is too dry, not that he is too radical. Wall Street does not like some of his supporters. Wall Street does not like his vagueness and the uncertainty as to what he does think, but if any Western Progressive thinks that the Governor has challenged directly or indirectly the wealth concentrated in New York City, he is mightily mistaken.

Mr. Roosevelt is, as a matter of fact, an excessively cautious politician. He has been Governor for three years, and I doubt whether anyone can point to a single act of his which involved any political risk. Certainly his water power policy has cost him nothing, for the old interests who fought [former Governor Al] Smith have been displaced by more enlightened capitalists quite content to let the state finance the development. I can think of nothing else that could be described as evidence of his willingness to attack vested interests, and I can think of one outstanding case in which he has shown the utmost reluctance to attack them. I refer to his relations with Tammany.

It is well known in New York, though apparently not in the West, that Governor Roosevelt had to be forced into assisting the exposure of corruption in New York City. It is well known in New York that, through his patronage, he has supported the present powers in Tammany Hall. It is well known that his policy has been to offend Tammany just as little as he dared in the face of the fact that a investigation of Tammany had finally to be undertaken. It is true that he is not popular in Tammany Hall, but, through they do not like him, they vote for him. For there is a working arrangement between him and Tammany. That was proved last November when the Tammany organization went to the polls for the amendment which Smith opposed and Roosevelt sponsored. Tammany had no interest in that amendment. It dealt with reforestation hundreds of miles from the sidewalks of New York. Yet it was the Tammany machine which gave the Governor his victory.

I do not say that Mr. Roosevelt might not at some time in the next few months fight Tammany. I do say that on his record these last three years he will fight Tammany only if and when he decides it is safe and profitable to do so. For Franklin D. Roosevelt is no crusader. He is no tribune of the people. He is no enemy of entrenched privilege. He is a pleasant man who, without any important qualifications for the office, would very much like to be President.

It is meaningless for him to talk about "leadership practical, sound, courageous and alert." He has been Governor in the community which has been the financial center of the world during the last year of the boom and the two years of the depression. The Governor of New York is listened to when he speaks. Can any one point to anything Mr. Roosevelt has said or done in those three years to provide the leadership we should all so much like to have had? I do not think any one can. He has carefully refrained during these years from exerting any kind of leadership on any national question which [sic] was controversial. That was probably shrewd politics. It has helped his candidacy. But as a result of his strategic silence nobody knows where he stands on any of the great questions which require practical, sound, courageous and alert leadership. And those who think he can supply such leadership next year are playing their hunches.

Lippmann, of course, blamed Roosevelt for the misperceptions of his supporters. Hardly a revolutionary, FDR managed to save the free enterprise, capitalistic system from its own mistakes, while instituting a broad range of new programs that addressed the needs of the people. It was that very skill at balancing water on both shoulders that made FDR one of the great presidents in American history, both in war and peace.

1932

They were American's golden couple, he the modest, shy Lone Eagle who had bravely flown the Atlantic alone, she a talented writer, the beautiful daughter of a Wall Street financier and diplomat. Their courtship and marriage, then the birth of their son, Charles A. Lindbergh, Jr., were the stuff of drug store romances. If America had a royalty, then Charles and Anne Morrow Lindbergh were the stalwart prince and his beautiful princess.

The fantasy crashed to a terrible end on the night of March 1, 1932, when their 20-month-old son was kidnaped from his crib. The press descended upon Hopewell, New Jersey, creating what would come to be called a "media circus," setting up a ghoulish death watch, transmitting lengthy, often sensational stories even when there was little to report. For 72 days the world held its breath, and the family waited anxiously for some word of the boy. It came on Friday, May 13, 1932. *The New York Herald-Tribune*, one of the best papers in the country, managed to retain its sense of restraint.

LINDBERGH BABY IS FOUND SLAIN NEAR HOPEWELL; KILLED SOON AFTER KIDNAPPING, FLUNG INTO THICKET

Covered by Leaves, Skull Fractured

Body, Found by Negro Truck Helper, Identified by Shirt, Flannel Band, Hair, Teeth, Overlapping Toes

News Finds Colonel
Absent on Vain Lead

Tragic Denouement of 72-Day Hunt
Around the World Comes Five Miles
From Nursery Where It Began

Charles A. Lindbergh jr., kidnapped on the night of March 1 from the crib of his parents' Sourland Mountain home near Hopewell, N.J., was found dead at 3:15 o'clock yesterday afternoon in a thicket at Mount Rose, N.J., just off the Hopewell-Princeton highway and approximately five miles southeast of the Lindbergh estate.

The child had been murdered and abandoned to the elements soon after the kidnapping, it was announced last night after an autopsy at an undertaking establishment in Trenton, to which the body was taken from the thicket. Death was attributed to a fractured skull due to external violence.

Parents Accept the Identification

Identification of the body was stated as a fact by Colonel H. Normal Schwarzkopf, Superintendent of the New Jersey State Police, who has been in charge of the kidnapping investigation, and Dr. Charles A. Mitchell, County Physician, who performed the autopsy. . . .

Discovery of the body of the kidnaped child who had been the object of world-wide search in which many noted detectives participated came about accidentally. A Negro helper on a lumber truck, William Allen, of Trenton, spied the body in the rain-soaked woods. He notified Hopewell police, who passed the word along to New Jersey State troopers quartered in the large garage attached to the Lindbergh residence.

After nearly three hours had elapsed, during which the body had been identified to the satisfaction of the authorities, reporters were summoned to the Lindbergh garage from their posts in Hopewell and Trenton. To the reporters Colonel Schwarzkopf read a typewritten statement.

Lindbergh Baby, Says Nursemaid

Colonel and Mrs. Lindbergh were not present when the news was given to the press, but Colonel Schwarzkopf indicated the parents were convinced the identification was authentic. Any doubt on this score was removed late last night when the child's nursemaid, Betty Gow, identified the body at the Trenton morgue. Miss Gow visited the morgue accompanied by two state troopers and departed quickly.

Thus ended the hopes of millions who have followed the case that the son of one of the world's great figures would be returned alive and well, even if at an enormous price of ransom.

Mysterious negotiations which have been in progress "for the baby's return" and which have cost Colonel Lindbergh $50,000 outright and additional large expenses now appear to have been the forlorn response to plotters who had no baby to deliver. The mystery of who seized the child and killed it by intent or by throwing it from an automobile in fright remains to be solved.

Ransom Gangs Revealed as Frauds

News of the identification of the child's body as that of the Lindbergh baby brought expressions of sympathy from President [Herbert] Hoover, Governor Moore of New Jersey, Mayor Walker and many others prominent in public life. Coupled with some of the messages of condolence was the expressed determination that the slayer or slayers must be tracked down with all possible vigor of the New Jersey and New York police. As long as there had been hope that the child was alive the authorities were disposed to seek the child rather than the abductors, but now, it is understood, no quarter will be shown.

Up until the hour of the finding of the body Colonel Lindbergh had not given up hope that his son would be returned alive. Through intermediaries at Norfolk, Va., he had been negotiating in recent weeks with the supposed kidnapers, and before that he had paid the $50,000 in the Bronx to a man who failed to keep a promise to return the child. . . .

Colonel Schwarzkopf's Statement

Colonel Schwarzkopf said:

"We have to announce that apparently the body of the Lindbergh baby was found at 3:15 p.m. today by William Allen, Negro, of Trenton, who was riding on the Mount Rose Road toward Hopewell.

"He was riding with Orville Wilson on a truckload of lumber. They stopped the truck so he could answer a call of nature.

"He went into the woods for this purpose on the Mount Rose Hill, in Mount Rose, N.J. Going under a bush he lowered his head, and as he raised his head he saw a skeleton on the ground. He says in his statement that what he saw had a person's foot on it. He called back to Mr. Wilson. Mr. Wilson ran into the woods, saw what it was and decided to go to Hopewell and get the police." . . .

Colonel Lindbergh Absent From Home

Colonel Lindbergh, who has been away from home much of late while carrying on negotiations with the supposed kidnapers, was not home when the body was found, but Mrs. Lindbergh and her mother, Mrs. Dwight W. Morrow, were, according to a supplementary statement issued by Colonel Schwarzkopf.

The statement follows:

"A preliminary telephone report from the county physician indicates that a number of positively identifying characteristics have been discovered in the body found today which would identify it as being the body of the Lindbergh baby.

"Betty Gow (the baby's nursemaid) has positively identified the garments found on the body discovered today as being the garments in which the Lindbergh baby was clothed on the night of the kidnapping. The sleeping suit was not on the baby, but the two shirts on the body have been positively identified by Betty Gow. Mrs. Morrow and Mrs. Lindbergh were at the Hopewell home when it became known that the baby found today was the Lindbergh baby. . . ."

Death Due to External Violence

The autopsy report by Dr. Mitchell dwelt upon the decomposed state of the body but did not speculate as to whether the skull fractures were caused by a club, a bullet or some other form of violence.

"Diagnosis of the cause of death is a fractured skull due to external violence," said the report.

Speaking informally to reporters after his autopsy report had been made public, Dr. Mitchell said: "The death could have been caused by a bullet, by the child having been banged against a tree, by an automobile, or hit with a club or other instrument. At any event the death was caused by a fractured skull. The baby had been dead about two months."

Allen, the Negro who found the body, told the following story at his home, 45 Roosevelt Avenue, Trenton.

"I went into the woods and I saw a skull lying in a hole. I walked closer and then I called Wilson. I said 'that's a baby.'

"Its ribs were exposed and there was some blond hair lying on the ground. I told Wilson that I was going to Hopewell to tell Charlie Williamson (Assistant Chief of Police). We both went to Hopewell. I found Williamson. I told him about finding the baby's body. . . ."

Allen and Wilson found the body near Montrose Road, one and a half miles southeast of Hopewell, and nearly seventy-five yards west of the road. It lay on a slope. From the road at the top of the hill, near the spot, the Lindbergh house is clearly seen. . . .

Spot is Owned by Orphanage

The land where the baby was found is known as the "old John Van Dyke property" and is owned by St. Michael's Orphanage of Hopewell. The 500 children at the orphanage had been praying daily that the kidnaped child might be left unharmed at the door of the institution. In their anxiety to speed the return of the child, the orphans and the nuns in charge hurried to the orphanage steps every morning. This morning the children will learn there is no more hope that their prayers will be answered. . . .

Discovery of the body so close to the home bore out the ideas given voice from time to time by the Hopewell police and county detectives, who intimated that a more extensive search should have been made of the Sourland Mountain region and less attention paid to running down city gangsters and faraway clans.

The Lindbergh home was brightly lighted last night. Colonel Lindbergh, whose recent movements have been enveloped in mystery, was expected momentarily, but where he had been during the day was not revealed. Mrs. Lindbergh and her mother, Mrs. Dwight W. Morrow, had returned to the Hopewell estate Wednesday night after passing several days at the Morrow family residence in Englewood while Colonel Lindbergh was away on a last vain quest for his son.

Informed of the child's death, Mrs. Lindbergh and Mrs. Morrow bore up with "characteristic equanimity," according to Dr. John Grier Hibben, president of Princeton University, who is a close friend of the family.

Sourlands Never More Dreary

It had been raining most of the day and the desolate Sourlands mountain region was never more dreary. Hopewell police had been observed going to and from the Lindbergh estate during the afternoon, but no particular significance was attached to this until word was sent to press headquarters at Hopewell and Trenton that an important announcement awaited them at the Lindbergh garage. Over the muddy and rocky roads dashed forty reporters and photographers to the private gateway, through which they climbed up a narrow, winding lane to the Lindbergh grounds.

The newspaper men, barred from the premises the day after the kidnapping, were welcomed silently into the garage, which had been converted into emergency police headquarters. Early arrivals from Hopewell were kept fidgeting for an hour until their colleagues from Trenton arrived.

Reporters Storm Locked Door

Then Colonel Schwarzkopf, a stiff, military figure, took up his position at the center of a long table and read his statement on the finding of the child's body. The doors were locked. The silence was oppressive until he reached the words: "Body . . . was found." Instantly, there was a rush to the doors as some of the reporters sought to break through to telephone their offices.

"No, no," protested Colonel Schwarzkopf. "Not a man will leave this room until I have read all of my statement." He read on and on.

"That's all, boys," he said finally. He refused to answer any questions. The doors were unlocked, and the reporters ran to their cars parked in the Lindbergh yard. Then began a race back to Hopewell, where telephones and telegraph instruments were available.

On September 28, 1934, authorities arrested Bruno Hauptmann, an illegal immigrant from Germany, charging him with the kidnaping and murder of the Lindbergh child. Colonel Lindbergh testified that Hauptmann's was the voice he, Lindbergh, had earlier heard on the telephone while setting up an abortive $50,000 ransom. In Hauptmann's home, forensic examiners testified at the trial, was some of the money from the ransom attempt, as well as wood matching that used in the makeshift ladder by which the kidnaper climbed into the second floor nursery.

Despite the apparent misgivings of some members of the jury, Hauptmann was convicted and sentenced to death. Post-trial investigations indicated grave flaws in the prosecution's case, yet the United States attorney general refused to reexamine the Federal Bureau of Investigation's evidence. On April 3, 1936, still protesting his innocence, Hauptmann was executed.

1935

Cowboy, movie actor, political humorist and newspaper columnist, Will Rogers was as celebrated a figure as his times knew. Like so many Americans in the years between the wars, Rogers doted on fliers and flying; unlike most, millionaire Rogers had the money to indulge himself with such stunts as flying over Alaska with his close friend and fellow Oklahoman, the record-breaking aviator Wiley Post.

The death of Will Rogers and Wiley Post on April 15, 1935, was certainly a major news story. But for the tabloid *Los Angeles Illustrated Daily News,* the death of the beloved Rogers held special meaning. He had long made Beverly Hills his home and hometown heroes deserved special attention.

PLANE BRINGING BODIES OF ROGERS, POST HOME

POINT BARROW, Alaska, Aug. 16—(U.P.)—Will Rogers and Wiley Post, two of aviation's greatest boosters, were dead tonight—victims of one of aviation's most tragic failures.

They died instantly last night when the motor of Post's new streamlined monoplane missed fire a few minutes after take-off from an Eskimo village, 15 miles from Point Barrow, and the pontoon-equipped ship plunged into the boggy tundra.

Always close friends, they had gone on a flying vacation trip prior to Post's projected flight to Siberia.

Rogers, the part-Cherokee Indian boy from Oklahoma who became America's beloved humorist, philosopher and character actor, was hurled from the cockpit as the ship somersaulted among the hummocks near the river they had just left.

Post, the one-eyed Oklahoman who had skyrocketed to aviation's pinnacle, dared death scores of times and came through with greater glory, perished in the wreckage—pinned among the shattered controls by the thrust-back motor.

Natives said the men had paused at the Eskimo village of Walkpi while Post tinkered with the sputtering motor. While the big shiny airplane bobbed at anchor, Rogers and Post ate dinner on the river bank with the wondering tribesmen.

Apparently convinced the engine would take them the few remaining miles to Point Barrow, the men climbed aboard and roared off in a heavy fog.

Natives said the ship soared easily to 50 feet. Then the motor began missing. Post banked hard to the right in a terrific effort to glide back to the river.

But the heavy ship lost flying speed and dived earthward with terrific force. It struck the rough terrain near the river bank and bounded over. The pontoons collapsed. The motor crashed back into the cockpit atop the fuselage.

Rogers was catapulted into the open.

Gasoline leaked out and burned around the wreck, but the bodies were not seared.

Eskimos said a herd of reindeer, browsing on the river bank, dashed in panic from the spot as the plane lunged downward. Most of the tribesmen covered their faces with their hands in terror as the craft crashed into the tundra and the gasoline ignited.

Post's watch stopped at 8:18 p.m. Rogers' watch was still running when the bodies were found.

Sergt. Stanley Morgan of the U.S. Signal Corps, Point Barrow, brought the bodies out in a whaleboat manned by Eskimos.

It was necessary to tear the wreckage apart to reach Post's body.

The bodies were wrapped in blankets and placed in the whaleboat for the return trip. They were turned over to Dr. Henry Griest, superintendent of the Presbyterian Mission Hospital . . .

Many hours after the crash, bits of wreckage were seen floating downstream toward the Arctic ocean.

Sergeant Morgan filed a complete report of the crash to officials at Washington. It follows:

"At 10:00 p.m. a native runner reported a plane had crashed 15 miles south of Point Barrow. I immediately hired a fast launch and proceeded to the scene. I found the plane a complete wreck and partially submerged in two feet of water.

"I recovered the body of Rogers and then found it necessary to tear the plane apart to extract the body of Post from the water.

"Brought the bodies to Barrow and turned them over to Dr. Griest. Also salvaged the personal effects, which I am holding.

"Advise relatives and instruct this station fully as to procedure.

Engine Misfires

"Natives camping on the small river 15 miles south of here say Post and Rogers landed, asked their way to Barrow, and on taking off, the engine misfired on a right bank when only 50 feet over the water. The plane went out of control, crashed, tearing the right wing off and toppling over, forcing the engine back through the body of the plane.

"Both apparently were killed instantly."

Dr. Griest said both Rogers' legs were broken, his face and head cut badly and his skull crushed. Post's body was crushed and his legs and arms broken.

In the halls of Congress, when the news was broken, were many personal friends of America's foremost political humorist and the Oklahoma aviator. Vice-President John N. Garner, host to Rogers at a dinner last winter, was stunned.

"I can't talk about it," he said. "Rogers was one of the best friends I had. Two mighty good men have been lost to the world."

The cowboy-humorist and the aviator had been on a rambling trip. It started at Los Angeles and there was a lengthy stop at Seattle while the retractable landing wheels were replaced by pontoons for Arctic travel.

After several hunting and fishing expeditions, on one of which Post received a ducking when he fell from a slippery pontoon, the men visited the Government's farm colonization project in the Matanuska Valley.

They returned to Fairbanks yesterday, and set out for Point Barrow.

Army officials sent word of the tragedy to Rogers' family and to Mrs. Post, who originally had intended to make the trip, but changed her mind in Seattle.

1935

Franklin Delano Roosevelt's New Deal transformed the United States physically, socially, and economically, and nowhere more so than with the pioneering Social Security Act of 1935. Shaped by a number of committees and guided by University of Wisconsin Professor of economics Edwin Witte, this bold legislation established for the nation a "safety net" or minimal standard of subsistence. More important, the act's passage proclaimed that henceforth the well-being of the people was to be the business of government, that the poor amongst us were not to be ignored. A half-century later, it remains the great monument to F.D.R. and the greatest accomplishment of his New Deal.

The Christian Science Monitor, one of the better papers in the United States from its founding in the early years of the century, provided some of the best coverage of the 14-month effort to draft what was first known as the "Economic Security Act." That paper reported the bill's signing on Thursday, August 15, 1935.

U.S. TAKES BIG STEP IN SOCIAL AID

Signing of Security Act by President Opens Way to Aged and Needy

States Must Do Part

By a Staff Correspondent

Washington, Aug. 15—The way is open today for the greatest measure of social protection to American citizens ever afforded by their government. Late yesterday President Roosevelt signed the Social Security Act in the presence of the key individuals who helped carry through the most momentous measure of the 1935 session. In a few days he will appoint the three administrators who will put the act into operation.

The Social Security Act throws an anchor of safeguard to about 30,000,000 Americans. It directly affects three groups: the aged, the unemployed, and women and children. Old people have under its provision a system of pensions and a system of insurance.

States Must Now Act

Unemployed will have a form of insurance against joblessness just as fast as state legislatures adopt their own measures of meeting the federal provisions. Through an enormous expansion of federal services, aid to children and to mothers will be available on an unprecedented scale.

The first year's cost will run to $100,000,000, but by 1950 a pay-roll tax is expected to channel annually about $2,700,000,000 into a vast stabilizing fund intended to reduce the pinch of depressions and give every worker a reserve upon which he can fall when the specter of unemployment descends.

The entire system, in President Roosevelt's words on signing the bill, is part of a structure ". . . that will take care of human needs and at the same time provide for the United States an economic structure of vastly greater soundness."

President Defines Intent

The President's statement follows:

Today a hope of many years' standing is in large part fulfilled. The civilization of the past hundred years, with its startling industrial changes, has tended more and more to make life insecure. Young people have come to wonder what would be their lot when they come to old age. The man with a job has wondered how long the job would last.

The Social Security measure gives at least some protection to 30,000,000 of our citizens who will reap direct benefits through unemployment compensation, through old-age pensions and through increased services for the protection of children and the prevention of ill health.

We can never insure 100 percent of the population against 100 percent of the hazards and vicissitudes of life, but we have tried to frame a law which will give some measure of protection to the average citizen and to his family against the loss of a job and against poverty-ridden old age.

The German zeppelin Hindenburg *explodes while landing at Lakehurst, N.J., as captured by a photographer from the* Philadelphia Public Ledger, *May 7, 1937.* Copyright by AP/Wide World Photos

This law, too, represents a cornerstone in a structure which is being built but is by no means complete, a structure intended to lessen the force of possible future depressions, to act as a protection to future administrations of the government against the necessity of going deeply into debt to furnish relief to the needy, a law that will take care of human needs and at the same time provide for the United States an economic structure of vastly greater soundness.

Thanks All Who Helped

I congratulate all of you ladies and gentlemen, all of you in the Congress, in the executive departments and all of you who came from private life, and I thank you for your splendid efforts in behalf of this sound, needed and patriotic legislation.

If the Senate and the House of Representatives in their long and arduous session had done nothing more than pass this bill, the session would be regarded as historic for all time.

Signing Made a Ritual

The bill's signature was marked by one of the few signing ceremonies of the session. A score or more of contributing guests were present—guests who have fought for social security. Among them were Frances Perkins, Secretary of Labor; Senator Robert F. Wagner (D) of New York and Representative David J. Lewis (D) of Maryland, the two sponsors of the bill who have worked tirelessly for such legislation for years.

Members of the Senate Finance and House Ways and Means Committees were there and a total of 30 officials, all of whom received a pen used in signing the bill. President Roosevelt's pen-distributing feat was one of the most notable in White House history, since he apparently used more than one pen for writing of each letter in his name.

The Practical Side

But of greater interest to everybody is how the bill will work—how elderly Mr. and Mrs. X in South Bend will avail themselves of its needed protection, how Pete in Binghamton can get protection for his job, how the slum children in Pittsburgh and their mothers will find things better.

Well, the bill first sets up an entirely independent organization in Washington, and will begin establishing its agents in all parts of the country. Of course, pensions will not be paid out as from tomorrow, it will take time to get the structure going and much is dependent upon state laws.

How It Will Work Out

However, 36 states have already exacted old-age pension laws to fit in with the federal structure. In any of these commonwealths, with varying dates and terms, Mr. and Mrs. X may make their application for a pension.

They, or one of them, must have reached the age of 65. They are without other income or means of support. They will get up to $15 a month from the Federal Government, the same amount from the State or as much more as their State has decided to grant.

In some cases partial payments may be made to aged who have other but inadequate means of support, less than the federal maximum.

Fund Open To All

Then young and old will have available an annuity pension plan—old-age insurance. Anybody can start making contributions to a fund to be available to them when they reach 65. Employers and employees jointly contribute. Regardless of other income, workers will get benefits from this fund if they have contributed.

As for the unemployed, they will have to wait until their states enact necessary legislation, for only New York, California, New Hampshire, Washington, Utah and Wisconsin have already done so. The first four have pooled funds for the State as a whole, the latter two permit separation through individual company reserves.

Tax On Employers

In states not having legislation, employers will also be compelled to pay a 1 per cent pay roll tax in 1936, 2 per cent in 1937 and 3 per cent in 1938 and thereafter. If they already pay into state funds, employers will get a 90 per cent refund. The pay roll tax is expected to hasten passage of state laws.

Once the system is in widespread operation, with wide latitude allowed between different states, any unemployed man from the contributing groups—which exclude, for instance, farm labor—will be able to draw on the funds for varying amounts of financial aid.

A Case For New York

In New York State, for instance, a worker must wait for a three-week unemployed period, and then he will receive insurance benefits up to $15 a week for a maximum period of 16 weeks. In Wisconsin he would get $10 a week for 10 weeks.

Pete Scolnik, therefore, must consult his state laws to determine his status, but in the fortunate commonwealths he will shortly have an insurance fund instead of a dole to assist him when hard luck comes.

As mothers and children, they will look to already established—or new—state offices in their community. These state bureaus will be enormously assisted by the new resources at Washington, and an expansion from one third upward of existing facilities is expected.

The bureaucratic machine in Washington will admittedly be heavy. In other countries, existing administrative bureaus are generally used. Here much of the work will be from the ground up. But there has already been created a system of national employment exchanges spreading over the country, and these will be utilized as a great constructive aid not to relief, not to made work, but to jobs in private industry.

Such, in rough outline, is the structure now available to Americans, and estimated ultimately to aid 30,000,000 of them. Difficulties of administration are frankly expected to be encountered and perhaps ironed out by future amendment. Great responsibility devolves upon the states.

Jobless Fund a High Light

The unemployment insurance feature is the most drastic in the bill, the old-age insurance one of the most hopeful. All industrial wage-earners will be expected to contribute to the latter fund, after pay roll payments begin in 1937.

Pensions will vary according to salary received and length of service and will range from $17.50 to $81.25 a month. Co-ordination of the scheme with plans already in operation in private industry is an important feature.

But in the words of even the most drastic critics of the New Deal, "a long-needed reform has been effected."

"The United States joins the roster of other advanced countries—Great Britain, Scandinavia, the British Commonwealth, Germany" and so on.

1935

"Porgy and Bess," the 1935 opera based upon a play by Du Bose and Dorothy Heyward, has become a capstone of American musical theater. The music by George Gershwin and lyrics by his brother Ira Gershwin and Du Bose Heyward have been celebrated for their original use of American idiom.

Despite favorable reviews, "Porgy and Bess" was not an immediate hit. Only after revivals of the work in revised form were well received did "Porgy and Bess"

establish itself as a staple for theatergoers. "Porgy and Bess" proved to be Gershwin's farewell to Broadway; he and Ira left New York for Hollywood in 1936.

Brooks Atkinson's incisive review in *The New York Times* of October 11, 1935, exemplifies the writing that would make him the dean of American theater critics. Later, Atkinson would equally distinguish himself as a war correspondent for the *Times*.

'Porgy and Bess,' Native Opera, Opens at the Alvin; Gershwin Work Based on Du Bose Heyward's Play

Dramatic Values of Community Legend Gloriously Transposed in New Form With Fine Regard for Its Verities.

By BROOKS ATKINSON.

After eight years of savory memories, "Porgy" has acquired a score, a band, a choir of singers and a new title, "Porgy and Bess," which the Theatre Guild put on at the Alvin last evening. Du Bose and Dorothy Heyward wrote the original lithograph of Catfish Row, which Rouben Mamoulian translated into a memorable work of theatre dynamics. But "Porgy and Bess" represents George Gershwin's longing to compose an American folk opera on a suitable theme. Although Mr. Heyward is the author of the libretto and shares with Ira Gershwin the credit for the lyrics, and although Mr. Mamoulian has again mounted the director's box, the evening is unmistakably George Gershwin's personal holiday. In fact, the volume of music he has written during the last two years on the ebony fable of a Charlestown rookery has called out a whole brigade of Times Square music critics, who are quite properly the masters of this occasion. Mr. Downes, soothsayer of the diatonic scale, is now beetling his brow in the adjoining cubicle. There is an authoritative ring to his typewriter clatter tonight.

In these circumstances, the province of a drama critic is to report on the transmutation of "Porgy" out of drama into music theatre. Let it be said at once that Mr. Gershwin has contributed something glorious to the spirit of the Heywards' community legend. If memory serves, it always lacked glow of personal feeling. Being a fairly objective narrative of a neighborhood of Negroes who lived a private racial life in the midst of a white civilization,

"Porgy" was a natural subject for theatre showmanship. The groupings, the mad fantasy of leaping shadows, the panic-stricken singing over a corpse, the evil bulk of the buzzard's flight, the screaming hurricane—these large audible and visible items of showmanship took precedence over the episode of Porgy's romance with Crown's high-steppin' gal.

Whether or not Mr. Gershwin's score measures up to its intentions as American folk opera lies in Mr. Downes's bailiwick. But to the ears of a theatre critic Mr. Gershwin's music gives a personal voice to Porgy's loneliness when, in a crowd of pitying neighbors, he learns that Bess has vanished into the capacious and remote North. The pathetic apprehension of the "Where's My Bess" trio and manly conviction of "I'm On My Way" adds something vital to the story that was missing before.

These comments are written by a reviewer so inured to the theatre that he regards operatic form as cumbersome. Why commonplace remarks that carry no emotion have to be made in a chanting monotone is a problem in art he cannot fathom. Even the hermit thrush drops into conversational tones when he is not singing from the topmost spray in a tree. Turning "Porgy" into opera has resulted in a deluge of casual remarks that have to be thoughtfully intoned and that amazingly impede the action. Why do composers vex it so? "Sister, you goin' to the picnic?" "No, I guess not." Now why in heaven's name must two characters in an opera clear their throats before they can exchange that sort of information? What a theatre critic probably wants is a musical show with songs that evoke the emotion of situations and make no further pretensions. Part of the emotion of a drama comes from the pace of the performance.

And what of the amusing little device of sounds and rhythms, of sweeping, sawing, hammering and dusting, that opens the last scene early one morning? In the program it is solemnly described as "Occupational Humoresque." But any music hall would be glad to have it without its tuppence colored label. Mr. Mamoulian is an excellent director for dramas of ample proportions. He is not subtle, which is a virtue in showmanship. His crowds are arranged in masses that look as solid as a victory at the polls; they move with simple unanimity, and the rhythm is comfortably obvious.

Mr. Gershwin knows that. He has written the scores for innumerable musical shows. After one of them he was presented with the robes of Arthur Sullivan,* who also was consumed with a desire to write grand. To the ears of a theatre critic there are intimations in "Porgy and Bess" that Mr. Gershwin is still easiest in mind when he is writing songs with choruses. He and his present reviewer are on familiar ground when he is writing a droll tune like "A Woman Is a Sometime Thing," or a lazy darky solo like "I Got Plenty of Nuttin'," or made-to-order spirituals like "Oh, de Lawd Shake de Heaven," or Sportin' Life's hot-time number entitled "There's a Boat That's Leavin' Soon for New York." If Mr. Gershwin does not enjoy his task most

---

*Sir Arthur Seymour Sullivan, composer of comic light operas with W. S. Gilbert.

in moments like this, his audience does. In sheer quality of character they are worth an hour of formal music transitions. . . .

1936

In the summer of 1936, in the depths of the Depression, a *San Francisco News* editor, George West, assigned a young writer he met at the home of retired muckraker Lincoln Steffens to do a series of articles about white migrant workers flooding into California looking for work. John Steinbeck spent weeks bucketing up and down U.S. 99 through the San Joaquin Valley, gathering material in Hoo-vervilles and hoboes' camps, seeing the plight of those dust bowl refugees preyed upon by farm labor contractors. The hungry Okies and Arkies whom Steinbeck met that summer would come to life three years later as Tom Joad, his family, and friends in Steinbeck's great novel, *The Grapes of Wrath*. The first of the articles that gave rise to the novel ran in the *News* on October 5, 1936.

THE HARVEST GYPSIES

Beaten, Bewildered and Half-Starved, They Wander the Trails of the Fruit Season: What Can be Done to Aid Them?

John Steinbeck, author of "Tortilla Flat" and other books, followed the people who follow the crops in California, to see their working and living conditions. He tells his story at first hand. Migrant labor is at once the salvation of the fruit and vegetable farmer, and the most important social-economic problem faced by the state.

—The Editor.

By John Steinbeck

At this season of the year, when California's great crops are coming into harvest, the heavy grapes, the prunes, the apples and lettuce and the rapidly maturing cotton, our highways swarm with the migrant workers, that shifting group of nomadic, poverty-stricken harvesters driven by hunger and the threat of hunger from crop to crop, from harvest to harvest, up and down the state and into Oregon to some extent, and into Washington a little. But it is California which has and needs the majority of these new gypsies. It is a short study of these wanderers that these articles will undertake. There are at least 150,000 homeless migrants wandering up and down the state, and that is an army large enough to make it important to every person in the state.

To the casual traveler on the great highways, the movements of the migrants are mysterious if they are seen at all, for suddenly the roads will be filled with open rattletrap cars loaded with children and with dirty bedding, with fire-blackened cooking utensils. The boxcars and gondolas on the railroad lines will be filled with men. And then, just as suddenly, they will have disappeared from the main routes. On side roads and near rivers where there is little travel and squalid, filthy squatters' camps will have been set up, and the orchards will be filled with pickers and cutters, and driers.

Needed and Hated

The unique nature of California agriculture requires that these migrants exist and requires that they move about. Peaches and grapes, hops and cotton cannot be harvested by a resident population of laborers. For example, a large peach orchard which requires the work of 20 men the year around will need as many as 2,000 for the brief time of picking and packing. And if the migration of the 2,000 should not occur, if it should be delayed even a week, the crop will rot and be lost.

Thus, in California we find a curious attitude toward a group that makes our agriculture successful. The migrants are needed, and they are hated. Arriving in a district they find the dislike always meted out by the resident to the foreigner, the outlander. This hatred of the stranger occurs in the whole range of human history, from the most primitive village form to our own highly organized, industrial farming. The migrants are hated for the following reasons, that they are ignorant and dirty people, that they are carriers of disease, that they increase the necessity for police and the tax bill for schooling in a community, and that if they are allowed to organize they can, simply by refusing to work, wipe out the season's crops. They are never received into a community nor into the life of a community. Wanderers in fact, they are never allowed to feel at home in the communities that demand their services.

Just Who Are They?

Let us see what kind of people they are, where they come from, and the routes of their wanderings. In the past they have been of several races, encouraged to come and often imported as cheap labor; Chinese in the early period, then Filipinos, Japanese and Mexicans. These were foreigners, and as such they were ostracized and segregated and herded about.

If they attempted to organize they were deported or arrested, and having no advocates they were never able to get a hearing for their problems. But in recent years the foreign migrants have begun to organize, and at this danger signal they have been deported in great numbers, for there was a new reservoir from which a great quantity of cheap labor could be obtained.

The drouth in the middle west has driven the agricultural population of Oklahoma, Nebraska and parts of Kansas and Texas westward. Their lands are destroyed and they can never go back to them.

Thousands of them are crossing the borders in ancient rattling automobiles, destitute and hungry and homeless, ready to accept any pay so that they may eat and feed their children. And this is a new thing in migrant labor, for the foreign workers were usually imported without their children and everything that remains of their old life with them.

Beaten, Bewildered

They arrive in California usually having used up every resource to get here, even to the selling of the poor blankets and utensils and tools on the way to buy gasoline. They arrive bewildered and beaten and usually in a state of semi-starvation, with only one necessity to face immediately, and that is to find work at any wage in order that the family may eat.

And there is only one field in California that can receive them. Ineligible for relief, they must become migratory field workers.

Because the old kind of laborers, Mexicans and Filipinos, are being deported and repatriated very rapidly, while on the other hand the river of dust bowl refugees increases all the time, it is this new kind of migrant that we shall largely consider.

The earlier foreign migrants have invariably been drawn from a peon class. This is not the case with the new migrants.

They are small farmers who have lost their farms, or farm hands who have lived with the family in the old American way. They are men who have worked hard on their own farms and have felt the pride of possessing and living in close touch with the land.

They are resourceful and intelligent Americans who have gone through the hell of the drouth, have seen their lands wither and die and the top soil blow away; and this, to a man who has owned his land, is a curious and terrible pain.

And then they have made the crossing and have seen often the death of their children on the way. Their cars have broken down and been repaired with the ingenuity of the land man.

Their Blood is Strong

Often they patched the worn-out tires every few miles. They have weathered the thing, and they can weather much more for the blood is strong.

They are descendants of men who crossed into the middle west, who won their lands by fighting, who cultivated the prairies and stayed with them until they went back to desert.

And because of their tradition and their training, they are not migrants by nature. They are gypsies by force of circumstances.

In their heads, as they move wearily from harvest to harvest, there is one urge and one overwhelming need, to acquire a little land again, and to settle on it and stop their wandering. One has only to go into the squatters' camps where the families live on the ground and have no homes, no beds and no equipment; and one has only to look at the strong purposeful faces, often filled with pain and more often, when they see the corporation-held idle lands, filled with anger, to know that this new race is here to stay and that heed must be taken of it.

It should be understood that with this new race the old methods of repression, of starvation wages, of jailing, beating and intimidation are not going to work; these are American people. Consequently we must meet them with understanding and attempt to work out the problem to their benefit as well as ours.

It is difficult to believe what one large speculative farmer has said, that the success of California agriculture requires that we create and maintain a peon class. For if this is true, then California must depart from the semblance of democratic government that remains here.

Good Old Names

The names of the new migrants indicate that they are of English, German and Scandinavian descent. There are Munns, Holbrooks, Hansens, Schmidts.

And they are strangely anachronistic in one way: Having been brought up in the prairies where industrialization never penetrated, they have jumped with no transition from the old agrarian, self-containing farm where nearly everything used was raised or manufactured, to a system of agriculture so industrialized that the man who plants a crop does not often see, let alone harvest, the fruit of his planting, where the migrant has no contact with the growth cycle.

And there is another difference between their old life and the new. They have come from the little farm districts where democracy was not only possible but inevitable, where popular government, whether practiced in the Grange, in church organization or in local government, was the responsibility of every man. And they have come into the country where, because of the movement necessary to make a living, they are not allowed any vote whatever, but are rather considered a properly unprivileged class.

Where the Fruit—!

Let us see the fields that require the impact of their labor and the districts to which they must travel. As one little boy in a squatters' camp said, "When they need us they call us migrants, and when we've picked their crop, we're bums and we got to get out."

There are the vegetable crops of the Imperial Valley, the lettuce, cauliflower, tomatoes, cabbage to be picked and packed, to be hoed and irrigated. There are several crops a year to be harvested, but there is not time distribution sufficient to give the migrants permanent work.

The orange orchards deliver two crops a year, but the picking season is short. Farther north, the Kern County and up the San Joaquin Valley, the migrants are needed for grapes, cotton, pears, melons, beans and peaches.

In the outer valley, near Salinas, Watsonville and Santa Clara there are lettuce, cauliflowers, artichokes, apples, prunes, apricots. North of San Francisco the produce is of grapes, deciduous fruits and hops. The Sacramento Valley needs masses of migrants for its asparagus, its walnuts, peaches, prunes, etc. These great valleys with their intensive farming make their seasonal demands on migrant labor.

A short time, then, before the actual picking begins, there is the scurrying on the highways, the families in open cars hurrying to the ready crops and hurrying to be first at work. For it has been the habit of the growers associations of the state to provide by importation, twice as much labor as was necessary, so that wages might remain low.

Trailed by Starvation

Hence the hurry, for if the migrant is a little late the places may all be filled and he will have taken his trip for nothing. And there are many things that may happen even if he is in time. The crop may be late, or there may occur one of those situations like that at Nipomo last year when twelve hundred workers arrived to pick the pea crop only to find it spoiled by rain.

All resources having been used to get to the field, the migrants could not move on; they stayed and starved until government aid tardily was found for them.

And so they move, frantically, with starvation close behind them. And in this series of articles we shall try to see how they live and what kind of people they are, what their living standard is, what is done for them and to them, and what their problems and needs are. For while California has been successful in its use of migrant labor, it is gradually building a human structure which will certainly change the State, and may, if handled with the inhumanity and stupidity that have characterized the past, destroy the present system of agricultural economics.

1938

Jazz, it must be said, had a poor reputation in polite circles during the first decades of the century. Critics dismissed the music as a noisy and certainly undisciplined product of nightclubs, saloons, and even worse. It might serve for dancing, but one did not truly listen to it.

On Sunday night, January 16, 1938, a bespectacled clarinetist by the name of Benny Goodman would change all that, introducing jazz into that holy of concert holies, Carnegie Hall. The concert was not only historic; the music was excellent, as *The New York Sun*'s perceptive music critic Irving Kolodin noted in his review the following day. (A recording of the concert, made almost as an afterthought, remains a staple in music stores a half-century later.) Jazz had arrived as a serious American art form.

SWING CONCERT FILLS CARNEGIE

Goodman Orchestra and Soloists Heard.

By Irving Kolodin

Whether the local seismographs record it or not, an earthquake of violent intensity rocked a small corner of Manhattan last night as swing took Carnegie Hall in its stride. However, when the tremor had subsided, with midnight not far away, the only perceptible damage was to those who had brought musical preconceptions into the hall with them. With Benny Goodman and his orchestra as hosts, and a variety of jazz celebrities as additional performers, an audience that filled seats, standing room and as much of the stage as was not required for actual performance, tapped and swayed to a swing program that ran the gamut several times. Since this was purely a jazz program, with no other pretensions, ordinary concert hall criteria did not apply. Informality reigned supreme, with the knowing ones in the audience (and there was an abundance of them) applauding their favorite soloists during the progress of a number, matching the spontaneity of the players with immediate response to their efforts.

Probably the most remarkable of the evening's spectacles was the interest that attended the eighteen-minute jam (or improvising) session, in which were enlisted such able performers as William (Count) Basie and Lester Young, Buck Clayton, Fred Green and Walter Paige of his orchestra; Johnny Hodges and Harry Carney of the Ellington orchestra, and the Messrs. Goodman, [Gene] Krupa, [Harry] James and [Vernon] Brown of the presiding body. Though there was perhaps too much solo playing for the best simulation of what an actual jam session is like, it was remarkably accomplished, considering the surroundings. Since the initial occurrence of the set tune was somewhat skeletonized, it may be well to record that it was Fats Waller's "Honeysuckle Rose." The subtlety and skill with which the improvisation was carried on found honors about even for all the participants. Wisely, no encore was attempted.

In deference to the fact that this was the first swing concert in formal surroundings, the program included a section entitled "Twenty Years of Jazz," in which the characteristic styles of various jazz personalities were set forth. Included in the progression was the Dixieland Band of hallowed memory ("Sensation Rag"), Leon (Bix) Beiderbecke (with Bobby Hackett as cornet soloist), Ted Lewis (the Goodman clarinet mimicking his "When

My Baby Smiles at Me''), Louis Armstrong (Harry James performing a chorus of "Shine"), and Duke Ellington. For "Blue Reverie," by the last of these, Cootie Williams, Johnny Hodges, and Harry Carney of the Ellington orchestra were imported to give authenticity to the proceedings. The series was brought up to date with the Goodman orchestra performing the violent "Life Goes to a Party," by its own Messrs. James and Goodman. Each of the sections was avidly applauded by an audience extremely aware of what was going on.

Though not actually so designated, each of the two appearances of the remarkable Goodman trio and quartet (with Teddy Wilson, piano, Gene Krupa, drums, and Lionel Hampton, vibraphone, added to Mr. Goodman's clarinet) was in effect a miniature jam session of its own. They presented, in their highly individual manner, a variety of jazz tunes, including "Body and Soul," "Avalon," "The Man I Love," "I Got Rhythm," "China Boy," and "Stompin' at the Savoy." Added to these was a still untitled work of their own composition.

Surrounding these several specialities, the Goodman orchestra exhibited its discipline, virtuosity and spirit in a variety of pieces ranging from Basie's "One O'Clock Jump," to the currently popular "Loch Lomond" and "Bei Mir Bist du Schoen," with Martha Tilton as vocal soloist. Along the way points touched were Sampson's "Don't Be That Way" and the Henderson arrangements of Youman's "Sometimes I'm Happy," Berlin's "Blue Skies," and Rodgers' "Blue Room." The formal program concluded with the Goodman traditional, "Sing, Sing, Sing," with an especially fine piano solo by Jess Stacy, but the audience demanded two encores before Mr. Goodman brought the concert to an end by walking off the stage, followed by his band. For the connoisseurs, the high points of the evening were his finely restrained and inventive solos in "One O'Clock Jump" and "Life Goes to a Party," and his skillful management of the unboundedly enthusiastic audience.

1938

It was over in round one. Joe Louis, son of a sharecropper, and Detroit's "Brown Bomber," launched a savage set of punches, sending Germany's Max Schmeling to the canvas for the third time. Soon after, the referee stopped the fight. Louis's triumph amounted to the settling of a score: Schmeling had knocked out Louis two years earlier. Moreover, with Hitler and national Socialism on the rise, Louis was also symbolically waging a fight against the Nazi notion of the supremacy of the Caucasian race.

Jimmy Cannon's sketch for *The New York Journal and American* of June 23, 1938—the champ cornered in his dressing room at Yankee Stadium after his victory—thrusts the reader into setting and scene.

LOUIS TELLS CANNON HE MADE SCHMELING QUIT

Joe Recalls Pre-Battle Promise; Max Didn't Land Hard Blow

By James Cannon

Max Schmeling hasn't hit Joe Louis yet. That's Joe's story, and Schmeling's obituary.

"Smellin' never teched me," drawled the saffron sand man five minutes after he had cured Schmeling's insomnia with a murderous mixture of knuckles and leather. "He never teched me one little bit."

Louis lay full length on a rubbing plank in the strangely dim dressing room under the Yankee Stadium stands.

Flashlights blinked and glittered like a neurotic's eyes. Police shoved and panted in roaring aimlessness. Julian Black and John Roxborough [Louis's seconds] squirmed and hopped at opposite ends of the plank like hysterical book-ends. But Louis was cool.

TOUCH OF A FLY

"What about that right hand Schmeling may have landed?" I asked.

"I pulled away from that right hand," said Louis without pride, without malice, without boasting but more in the manner of a man who eats in a new restaurant and says the food is good and he is satisfied with it. "It teched me the way a fly teches me. Punches, they hurt. But this one it don't hurt. It was just like a little fly teches me on the jaw."

The showers were splashing, the crowd was beating at the rickety door, a beaten fighter was weeping in a corner and you could barely hear Joe's soft mumbling voice.

"I say," he said and again there was no excitement in that hazy voice, only the drowsy tone of a man who might be lying in the sun with no place to go. "That I make Smellin' quit and I make him do that."

I asked him what he thought when the towel rose and fell in the ring like a clay pigeon of mercy.

"They do that out West," he said. "I say maybe I'm out West again."

Joe chuckled and wriggled his bare toes and sat up, pushing away the crowd which pressed against him.

"The punch I get him going on his way with is that right hand I hit him in the ribs with," he said, jerking open the white terry cloth bath robe which was streaky with sweat stains. "I bend him over. I see him bend over. I say I got that man. The last punch I hit Smellin', and the best one I hit him, was a right hand punch right on his jaw."

Mayor Richard Reading, Governor Frank Murphy of Michigan, and Jimmy Braddock reached hands over the crowd.

"Joe, you old son of a gun," the mayor shouted and Governor Murphy said good-luck and Braddock was laughing and winking as though he had won back the title he lost to Joe.

"I warmed up myself in the dressing room," Joe rambled, "not much. Just a little bit. Three minutes like. Not very long. When I know I had the man. I know I knock out that Smellin' when I signed the contracts. Chappie, you want to know how many punches I throw? I throw them so fast I couldn't count 'em. I bet Smellin' couldn't count them either."

Some one shouted back in the surging crowd asked if this was the softest touch Louis ever had.

"This fight was all right." Louis said in that disinterested tone. "So was the fight with King Levinsky. I guess this fight with Smellin' and the one with Levinsky were bout as all right as any."

1938

Director-actor Orson Welles was looking for something unusual to celebrate Halloween on the regularly scheduled Sunday evening broadcast of his Mercury Theater on the Columbia Broadcasting System. At the last minute Welles settled on a radio adaptation by writer Howard Koch of H.G. Wells' 50-year-old novella, *The War of the Worlds*. To add just a bit of authenticity, Welles and Koch interspersed their drama with purported news bulletins reporting the landing of death-dealing Martians in Grovers' Mill, New Jersey. Welles announced this was a dramatization at the 8 p.m. beginning of the hour-long program. But a number of listeners who tuned in at 8:30, after the popular NBC program featuring Charlie McCarthy and Edgar Bergen went off the air, failed to hear Welles' cautionary announcements.

Because of the three-hour time differential between the east and west coasts, *The San Francisco Chronicle* of October 31, 1938 was able to include in its morning edition of October 31, 1938, a more or less complete wire service account of the audience reaction to the Welles broadcast.

THE GREAT RADIO SCARE

U.S. Terrorized By Radio's 'Men From Mars'

NEW YORK, Oct. 30 (AP)—Hysteria among radio listeners throughout the nation and actual panicky evacuations from sections of the metropolitan area resulted from a too-realistic radio broadcast tonight describing a fictitious and devastating visitation of strange men from Mars.

Excited and weeping persons all over the country swamped newspaper and police switchboards with the question:

"Is it true?"

FALLING METEORS

It was purely a figment of H.G. Wells' imagination with some extra flourishes of radio dramatization by Orson Welles. It was broadcast by the Columbia Broadcasting System.

The broadcast was an adaptation of Wells "War of the World" [sic] in which meteors and gas from Mars menace the Earth.

New York police were unable to contact the CBS studios by telephone so swamped was its switchboard and a radio car was sent there for information.

A woman ran into a church in Indianapolis screaming: "New York destroyed. It's the end of the world. You might as well go home to die. I just heard it on the radio." Services were dismissed immediately.

Five boys at Brevard (N.C.) college fainted and panic gripped the campus for a half hour with many students fighting for telephones to inform their parents to come and get them.

PLEA FOR REASSURANCE

At Fayette, N.C., people with relatives in the section of New Jersey where the mythical visitation had its locale, went to a newspaper office in tears, seeking information.

Many New Yorkers seized personal effects and raced out of their apartments, some jumping into their automobiles and heading for the wide open spaces.

A message from Providence, R.I., said:

"Weeping and hysterical women swamped the switchboard of the Providence Journal for details of the massacre and destruction at New York and officials of the electric company received scores of calls urging them to turn off all lights so that the city would be safe from the enemy."

At Concrete, Wash., women fainted and men prepared to take their families into the mountains for safe-keeping when electric power failed during the radio dramatization.

At a highly effective dramatic high in the radio program when all sorts of monsters were flocking down on New Jersey from the planet Mars, lights went out in most of the homes of the town of 1000. For a time the village verged on mass hysteria.

Because of the power failure, many persons actually thought the invasion had reached Washington State.

Elsewhere in the Northwest calls poured into newspaper and press association offices by the thousands.

The Boston Globe told of one woman who "claimed she could 'see the fire' and said she and many others in her neighborhood were 'getting out of here.' "

PHONE BOARDS DELUGED

Minneapolis and St. Paul police switchboards were deluged with calls from frightened people.

In Atlanta there was worry in some quarters that "the end of the world" had arrived.

It finally got so bad in New Jersey that the State police put reassuring messages on the state teletype instructing their officers what it was all about.

And all this despite the fact that the radio play was interrupted four times by the announcement: "This is purely a fictional play."

The Times-Dispatch of Richmond, Va., reported some of their telephone calls came from people who said they were "praying."

The Kansas City bureau of the Associated Press received queries on the "meteors" from Los Angeles, Salt Lake City, Beaumont, Texas, and St. Joseph, Mo.

One telephone informant said he had loaded all his children into his car, had filled it with gasoline and was going somewhere.

"Where is safe?" he wanted to know.

Residents of Jersey City, N.J., telephoned their police frantically, asking where they could get gas masks. In both Jersey City and Newark hundreds of citizens ran out into the streets. . . .

In Birmingham, Ala., people gathered in groups and prayed, and Memphis had its full quota of weeping women calling in to learn the facts.

SYSTEM'S STATEMENT

In later broadcasts tonight the Columbia system announced:

"For the listeners who tuned to Orson Welles' Mercury Theater of the Air, broadcast from 8 to 9 p.m. Eastern standard time, tonight and did not realize that the program was merely a radio adaptation of H.G. Wells' famous novel 'The War of the Worlds,' we are repeating the fact, made four times on the program that the entire content of the play was entirely fictitious."

The Columbia System also issued a formal statement which said in part:

"Naturally it was neither Columbia nor the Mercury Theater's intent to mislead anyone, and when it became evident that part of the audience has been disturbed by the performance five announcements were made over the network later in the evening to reassure those listeners.". . .

The program which brought such unexpected developments opened with a regular announcement that another of the Mercury Theater of the Air's radio dramatizations—H.G. Wells' novel—was about to be presented.

The drama began with dance music, which was interrupted after a few seconds with a breath-taking announcement in news broadcast tempo.

"We interrupt our program of dance music to bring you a special bulletin from the Intercontinental Radio News," it said. "Twenty minutes before 8, Professor Farrell of the Mt. Jennings Observatory, Chicago, Ill., reports observing several explosions of incandescent gas occurring at regular intervals on the planet Mars."

An object was reported "moving toward the Earth with enormous velocity, like a jet of blue gas shot from a gun.

"We return you now to our New York studios," the drama continued.

After a few more bars of music, the scene shifted to an observatory at Princeton, N.J., for an interview with an astronomer about the phenomenon just reported.

After some routine astronomical questions, the "announcer" in the drama asked the scientist about the possibility of life on Mars. The actor replied the chances were a thousand to one against it, noting that Mars was 40,000,000 miles away.

INTENSE SHOCK

. . . . The scene shifted back to the New York studios; whereupon there was an announcement that a meteorite had struck at "Grovers Mill, New Jersey," and that a mobile broadcasting unit was being rushed there for a description.

There was 30 seconds more of music, and the broadcast from the supposed scene started. The announcer described huge men, like octopuses, emerging from the meteorite. Just as they were starting to wield a death-dealing "heat ray," his description broke off.

The program returned to New York "because of circumstances beyond our control" and a few seconds later there a came a "telephone bulletin" from the scene reporting that the bodies of more than 40 people had been found there. This program ended a few seconds later.

Orson Welles' Halloween prank had frightened the nation; a few citizens were actually terrified by the broadcast. As a result, the Federal Communications Commission slapped a prohibition on all such realistic-sounding, if fictional news broadcasts and bulletins in the future.

1939

The Great Depression of the 1930s lay as a pall on the nation when an engineer, Joseph F. Shagden, proposed to a group of New York City businessmen that the city sponsor a world's fair to spur the local economy. "Building the World of Tomorrow" became the theme of the New York World's Fair of 1939–40. And in the radiant architecture and inspired design by visionaries such as Norman Bel Geddes, Raymond Loewy, Walter Dorwin Teague, and Henry Dreyfuss, a stunning view of the American future took shape in Flushing, Queens. At a cost of close to $160 million, the fair and its symbols—the 700-foot-tall Trylon and the 200-foot-diameter Perisphere—exuberantly proclaimed a perfect tomorrow. Still, with the world lurching toward global war, *The New York Daily News* story of

May 1, 1939, reporting the fair's opening the previous day conveyed a sense that

tomorrow might not be as rosy as predicted.

HISTORY'S MOST COSTLY EXHIBITS SHOWN AT FAIR

By LEO CASEY.

The hundreds of thousands of people from all over the United States who tramped Flushing Meadows yesterday saw the biggest most costly fair ever held. With its 1,216 acres, it is three times the size of the current San Francisco Fair. Its cost—$157,000,000—dwarfs the $33,000,000 spent on the 1933–34 Century of Progress Exposition.

The vast expanse of the World of Tomorrow is divided into three general areas or zones—The Exhibit Area, with the displays of the country's great industries; the International Zone, with the exhibits of sixty nations and most of the States, and the Amusement Area.

The Transportation Zone is a sub-division of the Exhibit Area, and it contains the buildings of the great automobile manufacturers and the utilities. In this area also is the New York City building, the United States Post Office exhibit, as well as the Hall of Pharmacy and the building which houses some of the most magnificent art treasurers of the ages.

By far the most impressive exhibits of the Fair were the 700-foot Trylon and 200-foot Perisphere—the spike and ball, to less reverent New Yorkers. According to Grover Whalen, their significance is mathematical—the triangle and sphere.

Inside the eighteen-story Perisphere, in an auditorium twice the size of Radio City Music Hall, thousands rode on two moving balconies and looked down on "Democracity," a mammoth model of the city of tomorrow—a city of broad streets, many parks, and huge buildings. Choral and symphonic music, dazzling lighting effects—these brought the continuous six-minute show to an end.

New words were coined to name both structures. Trylon came from "tri" (three-sided) and "pylon" (gateway). Perisphere came from "peri," meaning "beyond, all around, about," and "sphere," describing its shape.

Millions in Jewels.

You might want to start your trip at the House of Jewels. Many did yesterday. There, millions of dollars worth of precious stones, both rough and polished, are on display. A spiral tower provides the illusion of rough diamonds rising from a volcano and settling on a platinum globe as glittering gems. The biggest bauble—your ring, girls, is a beauty if it's one carat—is a yellow diamond, 128½ carats.

In one of the tobacco buildings, 1,000,000 cigarets are turned out every day. In another display, the world's largest steam locomotive, 130 feet long, weighing 519 tons, keeps running at 75 miles an hour. But it doesn't get any place, it's mounted on friction bearings and does not move an inch, simply marks time at tremendous speed.

In the Westinghouse Building, there's a robot—an eight-foot metal man who talks, sees, smells, sings and counts with his fingers. An ingenious arrangement of photo-electric cells enables him to do thirty different things.

In all, the wonders of modern science, the farm is not forgotten. Cows are milked by machine. Electricity has erased need for the old-fashioned milk maid. . . .

A shot rings out. A man is murdered—several times a day in fact. It's all a part of the New York City police exhibit. Theses "crimes" are immediately solved through fingerprints and all sorts of scientific clues at the police laboratory.

Gruesome Cards.

If you are interested in card games you may view the "Devil's Picture Books," the most complete collection of cards in the world. In it is a deck made 300 years ago, and it is fashioned from the scalps of human beings.

The Hall of Man, a vast cathedral-like chamber, is one of the medical and public health exhibits. As you enter the gloom of the great room, you are aware of a large figure of Man, which dominates one end of the Hall. A pulsating heart shines blood red in his breast. A system of electric lights, synchronized with a transcribed record, explains the construction and functions of the twenty main organs of the human body.

You close your eyes for a moment. When you open them prepare for a shock. Comes next a moving, walking skeleton and then the Parade of the Translucent Men, exhibiting the separate organs of the human body. They have real organs and real bones made translucent by the Spalteholz process of immersion in oil.

You may even see in the Hall of Man how the world looks to those less fortunate than you—the color-blind, the nearsighted, the far-sighted. Just peek through the varied lenses in a huge false eye.

Dawn and dusk—thunderstorms rumbling through the city—are portrayed in the exhibit of one of the great utility companies. You get a twenty-four-hour picture of a metropolis. Miniature trains speed in subways, elevators rise and descend in skyscrapers, automobiles travel across suspension bridges. The only trouble with this exhibit is that Junior will probably ask you to buy it for him and take it home.

The glassware you buy at the dime store or in Fifth Avenue's swankiest jewelry stores is made before your eyes in the Glass Exhibit. There are furnaces containing molten glass and skilled glass-blowers forming all sorts of creations out of glass.

At the axis of the Hall of Electrical Power and the Hall of Electric Living is the "Immortal Well"—the Time Capsule buried in its depths. The Time Capsule contains millions of pages of microfilm, designed to provide a comprehensive cross-section of today's civilization for the world 5,000 years from now.

For the World of Today there are enough restaurants on the grounds to feed 250,000 persons in one day. Yesterday, however, there wasn't enough food prepared to go around. The statisticians did a little figuring the other day, and they estimated that 15,00,000 [sic] hamburgers and 15,000,000 hotdogs will be sold before Grover Whalen greets the last distinguished visitor next Friday.

Five hundred moving pictures will be run off daily in fifty auditoriums. Among them will be full length features, animated cartoons, scenic and industrial films.

If you long for a sight of old Ireland, you need travel no father than Flushing Meadows. Ireland's exhibit, in a shamrock-shaped building, has transplanted chunks of the "ould sod" for its lawns. There's a miniature River Shannon and lakes of Killarney and the water in them came right from the Shannon and Killarney.

If you want to see a lock of George Washington's hair, there is one on exhibit in the Venezuela building. In Great Britain's display you see the Magna Charta, the original manuscript from Lincoln Cathedral, guarded carefully under glass. Mummies 1,300 years old stare at you in Peru's exhibit. Diamond cutters and polishers from famed Antwerp work at their trade in Belgium's exhibit.

Caviar, rare cheeses, wines from countries that the average man visits only in his imagination are set out before World's Fair visitors at a modest price.

The Court of States is one of the most interesting of the Fair's many exhibits. In the Illinois Building there is a scale model of Chicago.

A huge fishing schooner is part of New England's display. A reproduction of Independence Hall in Philadelphia features Pennsylvania's display.

Celebrated musicians from the United States and abroad play the world's largest carillon in Florida's building. An entire orange grove has been transplanted to the Fair and will bloom and bear fruit throughout the summer.

In all the wonders of the World of Tomorrow, there are a few nostalgic reminders of these staid old days of 1939. It is the year 6939 in the Hall of Pharmacy. Tots get their ABC's and college men their calculus by hypodermic injection. Traffic cops get after the erring motorists in rocket shoes, but they still serve him on rye at the soda fountain.

The Avenue of Tomorrow in the Electric Utilities Pavilion is a gorgeous thoroughfare, but Little Old New Yorkers may drop a tear or two for the Street of Yesterday, right alongside it. It is gas-lighted. A horse-drawn street car and an ice wagon clang over its cobblestones. The dudes of the day are resplendent in their high collars, and there's even a bicycle built for two.

1939

Louis "Lepke" Buchalter helped establish the national crime syndicate. A poor boy from Manhattan's Lower East Side, Lepke first took to crime in 1913, robbing pushcarts in his neighborhood. Two decades later he was pulling in nearly $50 million a year as boss of New York's rackets, drug smuggling operations, and the nation's most feared "removal service," Murder, Inc.

Lepke's surrender to widely read newspaper columnist Walter Winchell was a carefully choreographed move by the crime chief. Fellow jobster Moey "Dimples" Wolinsky had urged Lepke to surrender to police, saying that was the wish of the syndicate's leadership. Wolinsky told Lepke that things had been fixed so Lepke would only be jailed for narcotics violations and would not be prosecuted on long-standing murder charges. Unfortunately for Lepke, Wolinsky had double-crossed him; there was no fix. Lepke and two henchmen went to the electric chair on March 4, 1944.

Winchell wrote his version of Lepke's surrender for *The New York Daily Mirror* of August 26, 1939.

The Inside Story: How Lepke Gave Up to Winchell

By WALTER WINCHELL

. . . The surrender of Public Enemy "Lepke" Buchalter to the Government Thursday night took place while scores of pedestrians ambled by and two police radio cars waited for the lights to change, near 28th St. and 5th Ave.

The time was precisely 10:17 p.m. and the search for the most wanted fugitive in the nation was over. The surrender was negotiated by this reporter, whom G-man John Edgar Hoover authorized to guarantee "safe delivery."

'Drops Out of Sky'

After a series of telephone talks with persons unknown and with the head of the FBI, Lepke appeared to drop out of the sky, without even a parachute. The time was 10:15. The scene was Madison Square between 23rd and 24th St., where we had halted our car as per instructions.

The following two minutes were consumed traveling slowly north on 4th Ave. and west on 27th St. to 5th Ave., where the traffic lights were red—and to the next corner at 28th St., where Mr. Hoover waited alone, unarmed and without handcuffs, in a Government limousine. Hoover was disguised in dark sun glasses to keep from being recognized by passerby [sic].

The presence of two New York police cruisers, attached to the 14th Precinct, so near the surrender startled Hoover as well as Lepke. The G-man later admitted he feared "a leak." Lepke, who was calmer than this chauffeur, was on the verge of rushing out of our machine into Hoover's arms.

$50,000 Saved

The police cruisers, ironically, were the first observed by this reporter in two hours of motoring to complete the surrender. Not until the final seconds was there a sign of uniformed law. But it was too late. The long arm of the government had reached out and claimed another enemy. The Federal Bureau of Investigation and the City of New York had saved $50,000—the reward offered.

While pausing alongside one police car at the 27th St. intersection for the lights, Lepke, who was wearing spectacles as part of his disguise, threw them to the corner pavement. They crashed noisily. Two passerby [sic], middle-aged men with greying temples, stopped and looked up at a building. Apparently they thought a window had broken above. They never realized that the man for whom every cop in the land was searching—was within touching distance.

'Glad to Meet You'

After parking our car behind a machine which was parked behind Hoover's, we shut off the ignition and escorted Lepke into Hoover's car.

"Mr. Hoover," we said, "this is Lepke."

"How do you do," said Mr. Hoover affably—instead of punning. "Lepke call you sweetheart." But G-men rarely go in for levity.

"Glad to meet you," replied Lepke, "let's go."

"To the Federal Building at Foley Square," commanded Hoover. His colored pilot turned swiftly south.

Lepke was a little excited. He seemed anxious to talk—to talk to anybody new—after being in the shadows for over two years with so many other hunted men.

"You did the smart thing by coming in, Lepke," comforted Hoover.

"I'm beginning to wonder if I did," Lepke answered. "I would like to see my wife and kids, please."

Mr. Hoover arranged for them to visit him shortly after he was booked, fingerprinted and kodaked. He had $1,700 on him. He gave $1,100 to the boy and $600 to the jailer—for "expenses."

When the Government car reached 14th St., we got out and went to the first phone to notify our editor, who groaned:

"A fine thing! With a World War starting!" . . . .

1939

Atlanta was a city gone mad, intoxicated with the fabled glamour of Hollywood. But then the motion picture premiering on Friday night, December 15, 1939, turned on a pivotal moment in the history of the city, and the film was based on a book by Atlanta's own Margaret Mitchell. *The Atlanta Constitution* devoted virtually its entire front page the following morning to the premiere of what remains probably the most widely seen motion picture of all time, *Gone*

With the Wind.* The *Constitution*'s Willard Cope began his story with an imaginary report written as if *GWTW* were premiering 70 years earlier.

"GONE WITH THE WIND" ENTHRALLS AUDIENCE WITH MAGNIFICENCE

Epochal Picture
Made by Crowd
At First Showing

Two Brilliant Shows
Presented—One Within
Theater, the Other a
Colorful Drama Outside

The company of ladies and gentlemen, including the city's elite, assembled in De Give's Opera House last evening for the first showing of a cinematograph film named "Gone With the Wind," whose subject matter was the experiences of this city and immediate section during the recent outrageous assault upon southern rights which is euphemistically termed in some quarters "The Civil War." The entertainment attracted the beauty and chivalry not only of our own people but those from other sections, including the north. It was received with enthusiasm. The picture, or series of pictures in motion, was based upon a book written by one of our talented young matrons, Mrs. John Marsh, nee Margaret Mitchell, who drew from our glory and tragedy a most arresting novel.

By WILLARD COPE

Even if "Gone With the Wind" had been contemporary with the scenes it depicts, and its review had appeared as this imagined quotation from an issue of The Constitution of the '70s, its premier still would have been the greatest possible news story in Atlanta since Sherman.

In brilliance, in color, in distinction, in action and in plot the premiere last night evidenced what a quiet, bright-eyed somewhat mouselike young feminine person can do in drawing to her home city the notables of America. It was merely one aspect of her remarkable one-book literary career.

Apt Commentary.

If ever there was an apt physical commentary upon an event, it was the presence of the greatest known peacetime concentration of lights—five 800-million candlepower army searchlights—in front of the theatre.

They will be talking about the premiere, and its divers eye-arresting, pulse-quickening, heart-warming details when the last small boy there, is an old, old boy indeed, biting toothlessly into his porridge.

There was build-up. There was timing. But through it all ran a comforting, kindly, pleasant, even sentimental thread, or strain. The whole brilliant scene had reality.

Held Together.

All present—in an assemblage which drew from every important region and stratum of American life—were held together by the sense of sharing in a common, and most historic, experience.

Sitting with them in seats about the theatre were Miss Mitchell, the author; David O. Selznick, the producer; such stars as Gable, Leigh, de Havilland, Munson, Rutherford, Keyes and Crews; the head of the publishing house which brought out the original book, and its associate editor, Lois Dwight Cole, lifelong friend of the author, who might justly have been termed co-author since it was she, as the story runs, who insisted that a literary scout for her firm should look up Miss Mitchell on a now historic southern trip.

It was as if two shows were being presented simultaneously—the fictional "Gone With The Wind" on the screen and the factual "Biography of 'Gone With the Wind' " in the seats and aisles, as well as upon the screen, of the theatre.

History Made.

News, history, was being made, and everybody knew it.

The "four hundred" of America, numbering 2,031, were all there, literature, the theatrical arts, journalism, banking, politics, society, each had a large, even generous quota of representatives.

Every person attending was a potential celebrity, at least to strangers, and this fact had a way of putting electricity into the air. The whole crowd, spiritually, were moving about upon a stage.

It was Hollywood, but it was also Atlanta. It was theatre, but also life.

Before Appointed Hours.

The premiere began far before the appointed hour of 8:30 o'clock. It began when, about 6 o'clock, the area before the theatre, formed of the meeting of Carnegie way, Forsyth, Peachtree and Pryor streets, was closed to general traffic to become, for the moment. "Celebrity Square." . . .

The cars drew toward the theatre slowly through narrow lanes of humanity created by the actual linking of guardsmen together along the route, each gripping a short loop of strong rope in each hand, and each loop being shared with a neighboring soldier. People pressed solidly against the guardsmen, but not too strenuously.

There was great good humor among the spectators. They stared and smiled and commented on the appearance of passing groups or individuals and occasionally burst into cheers and applause as somebody among the notable visitors was recognized. They were having a party on their own and enjoying it.

Piercing Lights.

For this aspect of the premiere the piercing aerial lights, rotating according to a fixed pattern, provided the most dramatic element. In such a setting, even [the] commonplace, would have become romantic, and there was little of the commonplace even about standing in a crowd in a somewhat chill evening at such a time.

These patient, happy watchers had their moment of moments later, however—in fact, a series of them—when the stars came by the same route to the theatre. Each was recognized, each was advanced in his or her vehicle through a continuing wave of cheers, and each found it very pleasing. Gable, as has become the Atlanta custom, received the greatest volume of plaudits, received them with his easy, winning smile and wave of the hand.

At the entrance to the theatre the glamor began in earnest. The facade was given over to a reproduction of a stately, columned manor house. Above it hung a very large cameo of Rhett and Scarlett. The whole was bathed in roving lights, so bright that the reflection almost was blinding. . . .

It was the sense of participating in a show as it was being written and enacted which [sic] gave the premiere the most remarkable quality.

Restlessness Sweeps.

Restlessness, however, swept through the observers as the hour of 8 o'clock approached—the hour for most patrons to be seated so that the stars and other celebrities could be admitted with a minimum of distraction.

Somewhat reluctantly, the marquee and its immediate environs were abandoned for the approach through the beautifully decorated lobby to the ushers—and seats. Once established, the spectators began an anxious watching of aisle entrances to be sure no one of the stars would pass undiscovered.

Soon enough the parade began. There were bursts of applause as each came down the aisle to the appointed seat. The "names" came, one after the other, with Gable last, of course, and receiving the greatest applause of any of the actors.

Miss Mitchell Enters.

But the entrance of Miss Mitchell—her mere coming down the aisle, smiling on the arm of her tall, prematurely white-haired husband, John Marsh—brought a spontaneous ovation which exceeded the greeting given any other.

It was her night, even more than Gable's, and the assemblage realized and paid tribute alike to her and to the occasion. Dressed in a costume which seemed something like a wedding dress, she smiled brightly, yet shyly, and it might have been suspected that she was a trifle frightened. Her husband smiled jovially, both performed a sort of bow-in-motion, and an usher escorted them to a haven of temporary obscurity.

This was the high moment, recognizably so, and the audience soon relaxed for the beginning of the first public exhibition of the film so long awaited and so animatedly discussed. . . .

1941

He played in a record 2,130 consecutive league games, four times won the most-valuable-player award, and posted a lifetime batting average of .340 during his nearly 15 years in baseball.

On July 4, 1939, it ended. "Iron Horse" Lou Gehrig retired, an occasion marked by a special ceremony at Yankee Stadium. The worsening effects of a crippling disease that eventually was to kill Gehrig forced him to leave the game he loved. But on that July day in 1939, Gehrig,

choking back tears, told the crowd of 61,808 fans he was "the luckiest man alive."

Gehrig, who was elected to the Baseball Hall of Fame in 1939, spent the last two years of his life as a parole commissioner in New York City, despite the ever increasing toll of his illness. Gehrig died on June 2, 1941.

Stanley Frank of *The New York Post* remembered the Yankee first baseman in a column the day after Gehrig died.

STANLEY FRANK REPORTS:

Gehrig Was Game, Grand Character

This is the story we have been dreading for two years. And now that it is necessary to record, with terrible and tragic finality, that Lou Gehrig is dead, mere words on perishable paper are hopelessly inadequate.

Those of us who knew Lou Gehrig cannot express our sorrow. The language does not yet include the words we need. Only in our hearts can we give full and complete expression of our grief, the shocking sense of personal loss, left there by the passing of the grandest fellow and the most admirable character baseball was privileged to see during its first century.

Elsewhere you will read the sincere tributes paid by men in high places to the memory of Lou Gehrig, to his skill and his endurance and his utter dependability as a ball player. The little man knows Lou Gehrig was immeasurably more than a ball player.

Lou Became an Inspiration to Others

He was a man, and I tell you his true stature could not be appreciated unless you knew him as a favored few of us knew him.

You will read of Lou Gehrig's epic achievements. Of his incredible record of 2,130 consecutive games over a span of 14 years and 11 months; of his .361 batting average in seven World Series; of his 494 home runs, four in one game and 23 with the bases filled; of his 184 runs-batted-in for one season.

And I tell you mere statistics, which will be inscribed in record books as long as baseball is played, cannot begin to tell of Lou Gehrig's infinite courage and his tremendous inspirational force as competitor.

[Yankee manager] Joe McCarthy said everything, simply and succinctly, when he called Lou Gehrig the most valuable ball player of all time.

It is monstrously unfair that Lou Gehrig should be dead in his 38th year. Indestructible Gehrig, the living, breathing symbol of endurance and strength, is no more and his passing makes a hollow mockery of all our man-made rules of good, clean living.

But today I want to remember Lou Gehrig as I will see him always. I want to remember him as a magnificent athlete, a professional playing his game more cleanly and gallantly than any amateur played any game and, above all, as a man I was lucky to call a friend.

I want to remember Lou Gehrig wearing pajamas and sitting in a dark hotel room in Cleveland one night and telling, with eloquent simplicity, why he loved baseball . . . How he owed everything worthwhile in life to the game which enabled him to give his folks security in their old age.

Always Had Word of Encouragement

I want to reconstruct the picture of Lou Gehrig, at his first training camp in 1923, walking six miles through New Orleans to and from the ball park every day to save the dime carfare he didn't have . . . And bringing his lunch in a brown paper bag to the Yankee Stadium when he was learning the game he was to play so well.

I want to listen to him gagging with Lefty Gomez . . . telling Babe Ruth stories . . . telling the gang to lay off Lyn Lary for pulling the boner which cost him the home run championship in 1931 . . . berating himself as a dumb Dutchman when he made a mistake . . . laughing uproariously at the timeless baseball stories they tell in Pullman cars . . . arguing with Bill Dickey over the bridge table . . . thanking the awe-struck people who besieged him for autographs . . . yelling encouragement and thumping his glove when a pitcher was faltering . . . giving a pep talk to a teammate in a slump . . . shouting hello the first time he saw you in the locker room at St. Pete . . . and meaning it.

I want to keep before me the unforgettable picture of Lou Gehrig putting his great shoulders into a pitch when the Yankees needed a base-hit in the clutch . . . the ball etched high against the sky when he met the ball on the sweet spot of his bat . . . the way he drew back his arm and let the ball go . . . his hand-to-hand fights with bad throws at first base . . . the look of intense concentration on his face when the Yankees were losing . . . and his happy smile when they won. . . .

Yankees Always Came First With Him

I want to remember Lou Gehrig coming back after getting knocked unconscious by a pitch in Norfolk seven years ago and hitting three triples in Washington the next day . . . I want to remember him disregarding broken fingers, broken toes, broken ribs, ugly spike wounds because he remembered he had a job to do . . . I want to recapture the thousand thrills he gave me.

They say Lou Gehrig is dead. I say Lou Gehrig always will be with us who know him as an enduring, shining symbol of devotion to duty, pride of achievement and worthwhile friendship.

I hope there is a uniform with a No. 4 on the shirt, a bat, a ball, a pitcher and a rightfield fence where Lou Gehrig has gone. He would like that.

1941

Almost half a century after the young Joe DiMaggio set it, the record for the longest hitting streak in baseball history stands. Beginning May 15, 1941, through 56 baseball games, the New York Yankee centerfielder got at least one base hit until stopped by the Cleveland Indians on July 17. *Cleveland Plain Dealer* sportswriter Gordon Cobbledick, perhaps caught up in his passion for the home team, rather downplayed the end of the streak in favor of the Indians' premature demise in the pennant race. His story appeared Friday morning, July 18, 1941.

DIMAGGIO STOPPED, BUT YANKEES WIN

67,468 set record for night game

Joe's Batting Streak Ends at 56; Tribe Loses, 4-3, Trails by 7

By Gordon Cobbledick

The greatest crowd in the history of night baseball—67,468 fans—saw the Indians virtually eliminated from the pennant race in a bitter battle with the Yankees at the stadium last night.

Beaten, 4 to 3, when a ninth-inning rally died with the tying run on third base and none out, the tribe was dropped seven games behind the league leaders—and seven games behind such a team as the Yankees is more than any rival can afford to be at this stage of the race.

It was hard to say whether the huge throng that filled all but a few remote corners of the stadium was more interested in the outcome of the game or in the fact that Joe DiMaggio's record-shattering hitting streak was ended after 56 games.

The great Yankee slugger failed to get the ball out of the infield in three official times at bat against Al Smith and Jim Bagby, although on each attempt he hit it more solidly than he has on many of the occasions when he has driven it into safe territory.

Double Play Stops Joe

Ken Keltner made a great backhanded stop behind third base to rob him in the first inning. In the fourth he walked after fouling off a three-and-two pitch. In the seventh he hit sharply to Keltner again, and was thrown out. And in the eighth, with Bagby in the box and the bases full, he grounded into a double play.

That ball, a sizzler to Lou Boudreau, nearly continued DiMag's streak, for it took a bad hop just as Lou set himself to field it. But the Cleveland shortstop handled it cleanly and a record that far exceeds anything of the kind in all baseball history had come to an end.

DiMaggio started his streak on May 15, after Mel Harder had held him hitless the previous day. Thus the last two times he has failed to get at least one hit in a game have been against Cleveland pitchers.

In the 56 games in which he hit safely he went to bat 223 times, made 91 hits for a total of 160 bases. Among them were 16 doubles, four triples and 15 homeruns. He scored 56 runs and batted in the same number. His batting average for the period of his epochal performance was .408. . . .

1941

Homing in on the dance music broadcast over radio station KGMB, the first of the 350 fighters and bombers swept out of the clouds over Battleship Row in Pearl Harbor. It was shortly before 8:00 a.m. on Sunday, December 7, 1941—in Franklin D. Roosevelt's phrase, "a date that will live in infamy."

There, literally on the doorstep, was the biggest story of their lives for newsmen on *The Honolulu Star-Bulletin*. A story of global importance it might be, yet for them it was a breaking, local story.

Those who made their way to the city room put out a series of extra editions that day, reporting the opening battle of the war as best they could from fragmentary reports by frightened civilians. Perhaps fearing they would reveal military secrets, they failed to report the scope of the American defeat; five battleships and a score of smaller vessels rested on the muddy bottom of the oily harbor. Two hundred military aircraft lay burning; more than 2,000 soldiers and sailors were dead.

WAR!

(Associated Press by Transpacific Telephone)
SAN FRANCISCO, DEC. 7.—President Roosevelt
announced this morning that Japanese planes
had attacked Manila and Pearl Harbor.

OAHU BOMBED BY JAPANESE PLANES

SIX KNOWN DEAD, 21 INJURED
AT EMERGENCY HOSPITAL

Attack Made
on Island's
Defense Areas

WASHINGTON, Dec. 7.—Text of a White House announcement detailed the attack on the Hawaiian islands is:

"The Japanese attacked Pearl Harbor from the air and all naval and military activities on the island of Oahu, principal American base in the Hawaiian islands."

Oahu was attacked at 7:55 this morning by Japanese planes.

The Rising Sun, emblem of Japan, was seen on plane wing tips.

Wave after wave of bombers streamed through the clouded morning sky from the southwest and flung their missiles on a city resting in peaceful Sabbath calm.

According to an unconfirmed report received at the governor's office, the Japanese force that attacked Oahu reached island waters aboard two small airplane carriers.

It was also reported that at the governor's office either an attempt had been made to bomb the USS Lexington, or that it had been bombed.

CITY IN UPROAR

Within 10 minutes the city was in an uproar. As bombs fell in many parts of the city, and in defense areas the defenders of the islands went into quick action.

Army intelligence officers at Ft. Shafter announced officially shortly after 9 a.m. the fact of the bombardment by an enemy but long previous army and navy had taken immediate measures in defense.

"Oahu is under a sporadic air raid," the announcement said.

"Civilians are ordered to stay off the streets until further notice."

CIVILIANS ORDERED OFF THE STREETS

The army has ordered that all civilians stay off the streets and highways and not use telephones.

Evidence that the Japanese attack has registered some hits was shown by three billowing pillars of smoke in the Pearl Harbor and Hickam field area.

All navy personnel and civilian defense workers, with the exception of women, have been ordered to duty at Pearl Harbor.

The Pearl Harbor highway was immediately a mass of racing cars.

A trickling stream of injured people began pouring into the city emergency hospital a few minutes after the bombardment started.

The U.S.S. Shaw *explodes during the Japanese bombing of Pearl Harbor, Hawaii, December 7, 1941.* The Library of Congress, Washington, D.C.

Thousands of telephone calls almost swamped the Mutual Telephone Co., which put extra operators on duty.

At the Star-Bulletin office the phone calls deluged the single operator and it was impossible for this newspaper, for sometime, to handle the flood of calls. Here also an emergency operator was called.

HOUR OF ATTACK—7:55 A.M.

An official army report from department headquarters, made public shortly before 11, is that the first attack was at 7:55 a.m.

Witnesses said they saw at least 50 airplanes over Pearl Harbor.

The attack centered in the Pearl Harbor.

Army authorities said:

"The rising sun was seen on the wing tips of the airplanes."

Although martial law has not been declared officially, the city of Honolulu was operating under M-day [Mobilization Day] conditions.

It is reliably reported that enemy objectives under attack were Wheeler field, Hickam field, Kaneohe bay and naval air station and Pearl Harbor.

Some enemy planes were reported shot down.

The body of the pilot was seen in a plane burning at Wahiawa.

Oahu appeared to be taking calmly [sic] after the first uproar of queries.

ANTIAIRCRAFT GUNS IN ACTION

First indication of the raid came shortly before 8 this morning when antiaircraft guns around Pearl Harbor began sending up a thunderous barrage.

At the same time a vast cloud of black smoke arose from the naval base and also from Hickam field where flames could be seen.

BOMB NEAR GOVERNOR'S MANSION

Shortly before 9:30 a bomb fell near Washington Place, the residence of the governor. Governor [Joseph P.] Poindexter and Secretary Charles M. Hite were there.

It was reported that the bomb killed an unidentified Chinese man across the street in front of the Shuman Carriage Co. where windows were broken.

C.E. Daniels, a welder, found a fragment of shell or bomb at South and Queen Sts. which he brought into the City Hall. This fragment weighed about a pound.

At 10:05 a.m. today Governor Poindexter telephoned to The Star-Bulletin announcing he has declared a state of emergency for the entire territory.

He announced that Edouard L. Doty, executive secretary of the major disaster council, has been appointed director under the M-Day law's provisions.

Governor Poindexter urged all residents of Honolulu to remain off the street, and the people of the territory to remain calm.

Mr. Doty reported that all major disaster council wardens and medical units were on duty within a half hour of the time the alarm was given.

Workers employed at Pearl Harbor were ordered at 10:10 a.m. not to report at Pearl Harbor.

The mayor's major disaster council was to meet at the city hall at about 10:30 this morning.

At least two Japanese planes were reported at Hawaiian department headquarters to have been shot down.

One of the planes was shot down at Ft. Kamehameha and the other back of the Wahiawa courthouse.

DAMAGE DONE AROUND THE CITY

At 9:38 a.m. a live wire was reported down at Richards and Beretania Sts.

At 9:42 a.m., Nuuanu above Vineyard, a gas line was leaking.

At 9:44 a.m., at 2840 Kalihi St., a bomb in the road. There was a mysterious Japanese in a tent camped near there.

At 9:45 a.m., at 2683 Pacific Heights Rd., a bomb struck a house.

REPORT AIRPLANE CRASHES, WAHIAWA

It was reported that an airplane (nationally undisclosed) crashed near the Hawaiian Electric Co. plant at Wahiawa. It was destroyed by fire as were two houses near which it fell. The army and police flung a guarding cordon around the location and civilians were kept at a distance.

MANY INJURIES ARE REPORTED

An unidentified army witness arriving at Hawaiian department headquarters about 9:30 reported that two oil tanks at Pearl Harbor were ablaze.

A bomb was reported to have struck at 9:25 this morning near 624 Ala Moana.

At 8:35 a.m. the police department broadcast a statement to all officers to warn persons to leave the streets and return to their homes.

All soldiers, sailors and marines off duty were ordered to report at once to their respective posts and stations.

Residents were ordered by radio not to use their telephones.

At 8:17 a.m. a Honolulan at Pearl Harbor gate heard marines ordered out.

1942

December 7, 1941, and the attack on Pearl Harbor struck panic on the Pacific Coast. Fearing invasion, fearing foreigners, fearing especially the Japanese amongst them, various groups began clamoring for the removal of all those of Japanese ancestry from their homes in so-called "sensitive" areas. The military commander of the Western Command, Lieutenant General John DeWitt, dismissed those who argued there was not a single instance of sabotage. "The very fact that no sabotage has taken place to date is a disturbing and confirming indication that such action will be taken."

Military security was an excuse. As a representative for the Salinas Grower-Shipper Association told Congress, "We're charged with wanting to get rid of the Japs for selfish reasons. We might as well be honest. We do. It's a question of whether the white man lives on the Pacific Coast or the brown men. They came into this valley to work, and they stayed to take over." Disregarding the fact that the majority of the 115,000 Japanese-Americans were citizens, the federal government bowed to political pressure. Thus began a mass evacuation of people of Japanese descent and a confinement in concentration camps that ignored civil liberties and human decency.

While the actual evacuation order would not be issued for another month, there is a sense of impending tragedy in the report of General DeWitt's first proclamation that appeared in the Japanese American Citizen League's weekly *Pacific Citizen* of March 1, 1942. That issue was the last the *Pacific Citizen* would publish during the war.

WEST HALF OF WASHINGTON, OREGON, CALIFORNIA, SOUTHERN ARIZONA DESIGNATED AS MILITARY AREAS

Proclamation Merely Sets Prohibited Region; Future Rulings to Order Gradual Evacuation

Acting under an Executive order directing designated military commanders to prescribed "military areas" from which any and all persons may be excluded, Lieutenant General John L. DeWitt, commanding general of the Western Defense Command and Fourth Army, issued proclamation No. 1 from his headquarters, establishing military area No. 1—including approximately the west half of Washington, Oregon, and California, and the south half of Arizona—from which "such persons or classes of persons as the situation may require will by subsequent proclamation be excluded."

All portions of Washington, Oregon, California and Arizona not included in military area No. 1 are embraced in military area No. 2. Persons in the same category can be excluded from certain portions of this second area.

General DeWitt's proclamation establishes the military areas. It does not order any evacuations.

"The Government is fully aware," the General said, "of the problems involved, particularly with respect to property, resettlement and relocation of those groups to be affected. Since the issuance of the Executive order, all aspects of the various problems have been subject to careful study by appropriate agencies of the Federal government.

"Plans are being developed to minimize economic dislocation and the sacrifice of property rights. Military necessity is the most vital consideration but the fullest attention is being given the effect upon individual and property rights."

The proclamation also imposes restrictions on persons within the military areas announced. Any Japanese, German or Italian alien, or person of Japanese lineage changing his place of habitual residence either from one place to another within the military area, or by leaving the area, is required to register the change.

Post offices have been designated as the places where this registration will be made. General DeWitt said arrangements were being made to have registration forms issued these offices as rapidly as facilities permit.

In speaking of his proclamation, the General indicated that future proclamations forthcoming shortly would affect five classes of people. These are:

Class 1, all persons who are suspected of espionage, sabotage, fifth-column or other subversive activity;

Class 2, Japanese aliens;

Class 3, American-born persons of Japanese lineage;

Class 4, German aliens;

Class 5, Italian aliens.

Persons in class 1 are being apprehended daily by the Federal Bureau of Investigation and other intelligence services.

"Evacuation from military areas will be a continuing process," General DeWitt declared. "Persons in classes 2 and 3 will be required by future orders to leave certain critical points within the military areas first. These areas will be defined and announced shortly.

"After exclusion has been completed around the most strategic area, a gradual program of exclusion from the remainder of military area No. 1 will be developed."

The General stated that German and Italian aliens of 70 years of age or over would not be required to move except when individually suspected, and that families, including parents, wives, children, sisters and brothers, of Germans and Italians in the armed forces would not be moved unless for some specific reason.

Specifically directing his comments toward predictions of immediate mass evacuation from Pacific coastal areas, General DeWitt said:

"Immediate compulsory mass evacuation of all Japanese and other aliens from the Pacific coast is impracticable.

"Eventually, orders will be issued requiring all Japanese including those who are American-born, to vacate all of military area No. 1.

"Those Japanese and other aliens who move into the interior out of this area now will gain considerable advantage and in all probability will not again be disturbed."

1942

From the first days of war in September, 1939, the Axis knew only success. German, Italian and Japanese armies and navies swept through Europe, the Soviet Union and the Far East. But the tide was running, and on June 4–6, 1942, two elements of the U.S. Pacific Fleet under Admirals Raymond Spruance and Frank Fletcher intercepted a Japanese invasion fleet near Midway Island. In the ensuing two-day battle, the Japanese would lose four carriers and 332 aircraft, the very core of their First Air Fleet. The United States lost one carrier, the *Yorktown*.

The U.S. Navy's first announcement of the battle was extravagant in its claims of Japanese ships sunk, claims the *San Diego Tribune-Sun*, published in the home port of the Pacific Fleet, was happy to pass on to readers. But for all the exaggeration, and the tincture of wartime propaganda (the Battle of the Coral Sea was at best a standoff) in its report on Saturday, June 6, 1942, what the *Trib* could not know, and what would not be clear to the Navy for months to come was that the Japanese had shot their bolt. The Battle of Midway had turned the tide in the Pacific.

JAP FLEET REELING UNDER U.S. BLOWS

Eight Enemy Ships
Victims in Fight;
Disaster Hinted

By The Associated Press

America's wasp-nest defense of Midway island sent the Japanese fleet staggering in retreat today as Adm. Chester W. Nimitz dramatically summarizing the three-day-old battle, declared: "While it is too early to claim a major Japanese disaster, the enemy appears to be withdrawing, but we are continuing the battle. It may be conservatively stated that the United States control remains firm in the Midway area." A communique issued at U.S. naval headquarters, Pearl Harbor, Honolulu, said the powerful Japanese naval squadron was limping away with at least eight warships and transports damaged by American bombers and submarines.

The communique indicated American forces were pursuing the battered invaders after beating off the initial onslaught in a victory possibly surpassing the Allied triumph in the Battle of the Coral Sea.

Nimitz said latest reports showed that "the enemy damage is very heavy, indeed," with crippling blows inflicted on several ships in each of the aircraft carrier, battleship, cruiser and transport classes.

The crushing defeat of the Japanese armada, the biggest enemy naval force ever to penetrate so far eastward toward American shores, came even as Tokyo newspapers boasted that their navy's latest exploits had "established complete Japanese domination of the Pacific and Indian oceans."

Helpless Fliers Machinegunned

Nimitz, commander in chief of the U.S. Pacific fleet, said the Japanese had machinegunned United States fliers forced to bail out in parachutes during dogfights.

Americans adrift in rubber boats received the same ruthless treatment, he declared.

Acknowledged American losses were confined to planes and aviation personnel, alert and fully prepared, who carried the brunt of the attack. Their apparent rout of the first major attempt to invade the strategic mid-Pacific island, which has weathered five previous assaults, wrote another shining page in their brilliant defense of America's island outposts.

Threat to Hawaii Repulsed

The Japanese attack carrying with it a threat to Hawaii and even the United States mainland struck the tiny island 1150 miles northwest of Honolulu at 6:25 a.m. Thursday and in the opening phases of the battle ran into heavy blows to a battleship, airplane carrier and other craft.

"One carrier already damaged by air attack, was hit by three torpedoes fired by a submarine," Nimitz reported.

As the battle continued, other Japanese capital ships suffered heavy damage and by last night apparently turned in flight.

Surprised Completely

"The damage is far out of proportion to that which we have received," said Nimitz.

"The Japanese have not followed up their initial air attack on Midway island except for a few ineffectual shots from a submarine during last (Thursday) night."

The size of United States forces involved in the battle was veiled by military secrecy, but apparently the Japanese were taken by complete surprise. The mention of troop transports indicated that the enemy expected to subdue the small island garrison quickly by aerial assault and then send landing parties to take over control.

Two Carriers Used

Instead, the island suddenly erupted with violent counter-attacks sufficient to beat off the invaders in short order.

At least two Japanese aircraft carriers, each carrying 20 to 30 planes, were included in the big armada.

Meanwhile, a Tokyo naval spokesman, Capt. Hideo Hiraide [sic], asserted that "our imperial navy, which has placed the eastern half of the Indian ocean under its control, is now operating along the eastern coast of Africa in swift pursuit of British warships."

Imperial Tokyo headquarters claimed four Allied submarines had been sunk in Japanese waters in the last few weeks, one of them in Tokyo Bay.

1943

Opened at the St. James Theater on March 31, 1943, the musical play *Oklahoma!* was both a moment out of war and a landmark of the American stage. Here was the first Broadway "musical" to integrate successfully book, music, lyric, and dance into a seamless drama. New York critics such as the *Herald Tribune*'s Howard Barnes immediately recognized the show's appeal. Barnes even seemed to sense that the musical he had seen just an hour before writing his review for the April 1st paper would become an enduring piece of American theater.

THE THEATER

By Howard Barnes

Lilacs to "Oklahoma"

Songs, dances and a story have been triumphantly blended at the St. James. "Oklahoma!" is a jubilant and enchanting musical. The Richard Rodgers score is one of his best, which is saying plenty. Oscar Hammerstein 2d has written a dramatically imaginative libretto and a string of catchy lyrics; Agnes de Mille has worked small miracles in devising original dances to fit the story and the tunes, while Rouben Mamoulian has directed an excellent company with great taste and craftsmanship. Is it any wonder, then, that this Theater Guild production is one of the most captivating shows of the season?

Plots are generally a nuisance in musical comedies, but the narrative line in "Oklahoma!" is arresting and even dramatic. It is based on the Lynn Riggs play of a dozen years ago, "Green Grow the Lilacs." That work, as I remember it, was lean on substantial subject matter for a straight play, but it has been transmuted into a brilliant frame for songs and dances. The melodrama which Rigs invented for the Indian Territory at the turn of the century has been given exciting elaboration at the St. James, with the vocalists and the dancers picking up the threads of the fable unerringly.

The point is that everybody concerned with this new offering has conspired to make it a striking piece of theatrical Americana as well as a series of musical-comedy numbers. The songs stick to the outline of the frontier tale in both theme and mood. The ballets and production numbers give it an irresistible flavor. "Oh, What a Beautiful Mornin'," "People Will Say" and "Out of My Dreams" are going to be heard a lot, but less-featured Rodgers tunes, such as "Pore Jud" and "All 'er Nothin'," keep the proceedings at the St. James tremendously refreshing.

So many scenes are so good after "Oklahoma!" gets off to a rather slow start that it is difficult to single out any one of them for special commendation. The ballet at the end of the first act, when the heroine dreams of a fight between her cowboy lover and the smokehouse villain who has what were known in 1900 as designs on her pretty person, is a superb piece of musical choreography. That between the hero and the villain in the smokehouse is brilliant short dramatic scene with a perfect song for the incident. The "Oklahoma" number of the climax is a knockout and a picnic tableau is something to see.

There are no particularly well known performers in the piece, but that is all to the good in a show which has inherent theatrical excitement. Alfred Drake is first rate as the cowpuncher and Howard da Silva is equally fine as the smokehouse skunk. Joan Roberts makes an attractive heroine and Betty Garde is splendid as her rough-and-ready aunt. Meanwhile, Joseph Buloff has some wonderfully funny scenes as a Persian peddler in the western wilds and Marc Platt is particularly striking among the dancers. Lemuel Ayers has designed exactly the right settings for the production. They had to be good to go with this superb musical.

1944

There are three ways to cover a war, each requiring different skills, each, oddly enough, reporting a different war entirely. There is the story at the geopolitical level, the affairs of state and government that shape the strategy of war itself. There is the tactical war of armies attacking and divisions advancing, of ground taken and victories reported. Then there is the real war, the war of the fighting man and woman, a story whose scope is limited from one foxhole to the next, and where survival that day is victory enough. No one captured that last struggle, the terribly personal war of the foot soldier, as did soft-spoken Ernest Taylor Pyle, whose column ran in more than 400 newspapers across the country. Pyle, bone-weary, hating the assignment but unable to let go, was killed by a sniper on the tiny Pacific island of Ie Shima on April 18, 1945.

Pyle's most famous column recounted the death of Captain Henry T. Waskow during the fighting in the Italian campaign in January, 1944. Pyle's moving story served as the basis for one of the few Hollywood films of the era to accurately convey something of what combat was truly like, *The Story of G.I. Joe.* Scripps-Howard syndicated the column for release on January 10, 1944.

By Ernie Pyle

In this war I have known a lot of officers who were loved and respected by the soldiers under them. But never have I crossed the trail of any man as beloved as Captain Henry T. Waskow, of Belton, Texas.

Captain Waskow was a company commander in the Thirty-sixth Division. He had led his company since long before it left the States. He was very young, only in his middle twenties, but he carried in him a sincerity and a gentleness that made people want to be guided by him.

"After my father, he came next," a sergeant told me.

"He always looked after us," a soldier said. "He'd go to bat for us every time."

"I've never known him to do anything unfair," another said.

I was at the foot of the mule trail the night they brought Captain Waskow down. The moon was nearly full, and you could see far up the trail, and even partway across the valley below.

Dead men had been coming down the mountain all evening, lashed onto the backs of mules. They came lying belly-down across the wooden pack-saddles, their heads hanging down on one side, their stiffened legs sticking out awkwardly from the other, bobbing up and down as the mules walked.

The Italian mule skinners were afraid to walk beside dead men, so Americans had to lead the mules down that night. Even the Americans were reluctant to unlash and lift off the bodies when they got to the bottom, so an officer had to do it himself and ask others to help.

I don't know who that first one was. You feel small in the presence of dead men, and you don't ask silly questions.

They slid him down from the mule, and stood him on his feet for a moment. In the half-light he might have been merely a sick man standing there leaning on the others. Then they laid him on the ground in the shadow of the stone wall alongside the road. We left him there beside the road, that first one, and we all went back into the cowshed and sat on water cans or lay on the straw, waiting for the next batch of mules.

Somebody said the dead soldier had been dead for four days, and then nobody said anything more about it. We talked soldier talk for an hour or more; the dead man lay alone, outside in the shadow of the wall.

Then a soldier came into the cowshed and said there were some more bodies outside. We went out into the road. Four mules stood there in the moonlight, in the road where the trail came down off the mountain. The soldiers who led them stood there waiting.

"This one is Captain Waskow," one of them said quietly.

Two men unlashed his body from the mule and lifted it off and laid it in the shadow beside the stone wall. Other men took the other bodies off. Finally, there were five lying end to end in a long row. You don't cover up dead men in the combat zones. They just lie there in the shadows until somebody comes after them.

The unburdened mules moved off to their olive grove. The men in the road seemed reluctant to leave. They stood around, and gradually I could sense them moving, one by one, close to Captain Waskow's body. Not so much to look, I think, as to say something in finality to him and to themselves. I stood close by and I could hear.

One soldier came and looked down, and he said out loud, "God damn it!"

That's all he said, and then he walked away.

Another one came, and he said, "God damn it to hell anyway!" he looked down for a few last moments and then turned and left.

Another man came. I think he was an officer. It was hard to tell officers from men in the dim light, for everybody was bearded and grimy. The man looked down into the dead captain's face and then spoke directly to him as though he were alive, "I'm sorry, old man."

Then a soldier came and stood beside the officer and bent over, and he too spoke to his dead captain, not just in a whisper but awfully tenderly, and he said, "I sure am sorry, sir."

Then the first man squatted down, and he reached down and took the captain's hand, and he sat there for a full five minutes holding the dead hand in his own and looking intently into the dead face. And he never uttered a sound all the time he sat there.

Finally he put the hand down. He reached over and gently straightened the points of the captain's shirt collar, and then he sort of rearranged the tattered edges of the uniform around the wound, and then he got up and walked away down the road in the moonlight, all alone.

The rest of us went back into the cowshed leaving the five dead men lying in a line end to end in the shadow of the low stone wall. We lay down on the straw in the cowshed, and pretty soon we were all asleep.

1944

Long awaited, the Allied invasion of France came as the fulfillment of a promise to the embattled Soviet Union and the enslaved nations of Europe. From England on that fateful day of June 6, 1944, sailed an awesome armada of 6,483 vessels from battleships to landing craft while thousands of aircraft swept the skies over the English Channel. By the end of the day, the allies had ensured the success of one of the most daring feats of arms in World War II, landing 150,000 men. Though their way would be bitter, they had sealed the doom of Hitler's Third Reich.

No newspaper was better situated to

cover the march of events than the GI's own *Stars and Stripes,* written and edited by a staff of professional journalists few peacetime newspapers could match. This was *Stars and Stripes'* report of the biggest story of the war in Europe on the morning of June 7, 1944:

ALLIES DRIVING INTO FRANCE

Opposition Less Than Expected; Troops 10 Mi. In

Allied armies, supported by more than 4,000 ships and 11,000 warplanes, stormed the northern coast of France in the dark hours of yesterday morning to open the decisive battle for the liberation of Europe, and by nightfall had smashed their way ten miles inland to Caen, between the vital ports of Cherbourg and Le Havre. Enemy radio stations said heavy street fighting was in progress.

By reaching Caen, the invasion forces may have cut the railway running from Paris to Cherbourg, main route for the supply of Hitler's troops on the peninsula.

German opposition in all quarters—sea, air and land—was less than expected, according to information reaching supreme headquarters and losses appeared to be astonishingly light.

American naval losses were only two destroyers and one LST (landing ship, tank) craft, while American air losses were kept to one per cent, President Roosevelt revealed in Washington on the basis of a noon dispatch from General Eisenhower. The President said operations were "up to schedule."

Losses of troop-carrying aircraft were extremely small, although more than 1,000 of such planes were used, headquarters disclosed. The airborne troops themselves were "well established," Prime Minister Churchill had announced earlier.

And as for the forces which landed on the beaches, Adm. Sir Bertram Ramsay, Allied naval commander-in-chief, reported that "naval ships landed all their cargoes 100 per cent." He added that there was "slight loss in ships, but so slight that it did not affect putting armies ashore. We have got all the first wave of men through the defended beach zone and set for the land battle."

Along a front described by the Germans as 80 miles long—from the mouth of the Seine River at Le Havre to the tip of the Cherbourg peninsula—American, British and Canadian troops landed on French soil from the choppy waters of the English Channel and from the storm-studded skies.

From 600 naval guns, ranging from four to 16 inches, and from massive fleets of supporting planes, ton upon ton of high explosives thundered into the concrete and steel of the West Wall which Hitler erected to guard his conquered countries.

The actual landings took place in daylight after an aerial assault on the coastal defenses which lasted from before midnight to dawn, a communique disclosed late last night. The airbourne troops, however, had landed behind enemy positions during the darkness.

Between 6:30 and 7:30 two naval task forces—one commanded by Rear Adm. Sir Philip Vian, aboard HMS Scylla, and the other by Rear Adm. Alan Goodrich Kirk, aboard the U.S.S. Augusta—launched their assault forces at enemy beaches.

It was on the cruiser Augusta that President Roosevelt and Prime Minister Churchill signed the Atlantic Charter in August, 1941.

The mightiest air and sea armadas ever assembled pave the way for the successful landings. American warships participating included battleships, cruisers and destroyers, as well as hundreds of smaller craft and troopships.

Thirty-one thousand Allied airmen, not counting airborne troops, made a continuous road through the night in the skies over France. Between midnight and 8 a.m. more than 10,000 tons of high explosives were hurled upon the Normandy invasion area by Allied aircraft, which flew 7,500 sorties.

Against this aerial might the Luftwaffe was able to mount only 50 sorties, despite an order of the day from Goering that [the] "invasion must be beaten off even if the Luftwaffe perishes." Allied fighters swept 75 miles inland without opposition.

After an initial communique made the momentous announcement of the landings, Prime Minister Churchill gave the first word that the assault had been successful. To a cheering House of Commons he announced shortly after noon that landings were proceeding according to plan, that sea obstacles planted by the Nazis had been less serious than had been feared, that the fire of shore batteries had been largely quelled, and that airborne landings had been effected successfully behind the enemy lines.

Later, after visiting Gen. Eisenhower's headquarters with King George VI, Churchill said that "many dangers and difficulties which appeared at this time last night to be extremely formidable are behind us. The passage of the sea has been made with far less than we apprehended." . . .

It was left to the Germans to give most of the details, and all day long came a steady stream of reports from German agencies of new airborne and sea landings, most of them between Le Havre and Cherbourg and some airborne landings southwest of Boulogne.

Enemy radio stations late last night painted a picture of growing Allied successes, with new beachheads established and a general spreading out from positions on coastal stretches already occupied.

German Overseas News Agency said fierce fighting was in progress along the whole 19-mile stretch of road between Carantan and Valognes on the Cherbourg peninsula. Paratroops established themselves on both sides of the road and later were reinforced by glider troops, the agency added.

Vichy radio said Allied reinforcements were pouring into the beachheads and "it must be admitted that the Allied landing area has been considerably extended."

"Cherbourg Battle Grows"—Paris

Despite fierce German resistance, Paris radio—less than 100 miles from the fighting—said that the battle for the Cherbourg peninsula was "widening in depth."

A steady stream of Allied troops continued to pour onto the beaches in the vicinity of the bathing resort at Arromanches at noon, Berlin reported, with light tank formations also ashore.

The invasion force was the greatest ever used in amphibious operations. Commanding it under the supreme leadership of Gen. Eisenhower, was Gen. Sir Bernard L. Montgomery. There was unconfirmed reports that Hitler himself was rushing to France to take charge of Axis forces.

The weather, which had caused postponement of the invasion for 24 hours, ruffled the Channel and caused "awful anxiety," said a spokesman at SHAEF [Supreme Headquarters Allied Expeditionary Force]. But the landings were made, although some of the troops undoubtedly were seasick.

For hours without interruption the vast armada of planes charged with softening up the defenses roared over the coast, while in the water more than 200 minesweepers cleared obstructions before the invasion fleet.

As a result comparatively light opposition was met from enemy naval forces and shore batteries. Coast defense guns were not nearly as effective as they might have been, and despite German claims of heavy damage inflicted by Nazi E-boats, the Allies' naval losses were "very, very small," a SHAEF spokesman said.

The Allied Command said nothing about the great battle being on at last until the Germans found it out for themselves. At 6:35 AM the German Overseas News Agency broadcast a bulletin: "The invasion has begun. German naval forces have engaged enemy landing craft. Paratroops have landed at the mouth of the Seine." Instantly the electrifying news was relayed around the world.

The Allied announcement came at 9:01 AM, when correspondents summoned to the elaborate invasion press room in London's Ministry of Information were given Communique No. 1:

"Under the command of Gen. Eisenhower, Allied naval forces, supported by strong air forces, began landing Allied armies this morning on the northern coast of France." . . .

1944

While the war raged in Europe, America entertained itself with a new broad of popular singer, the "crooner." And the crooner nonpareil was a slight, wan young man from New Jersey named Francis Albert Sinatra. A former singer with the bands of Harry James and Tommy Dorsey, Sinatra could transform legions of adulating women wearing fashionable, ankle-high bobby socks into screaming hysterics merely by stepping to the microphone. As this *New York Daily News* account of October 13, 1944, clearly | shows, Sinatra was one of America's first pop heroes, a teen idol.

'VOICE' WINS HIS LOUDEST SQUEAL

By Elaine Cunniffe and Gilbert Millstein

Thousands and thousands of shrill, flushed pilgrims surged into Times Square yesterday, their mecca the Paramount Theater, their prophet a languid baritone with big ears and a habit of writhing back of a microphone clutched in his hands.

They rose with the milkman. They brought their lunches, autograph books, bobby socks, short skirts and noisy ecstasy.

Shortly after 10 A.M., 3,600 of them were wedged into the theatre, while outside a passionate 25,000 contended with the cops. The chosen, who got inside, ripped ties from ushers and were lectured in classical music like "Old Man River," by that great classicist, Frank Sinatra.

The reason so many were able to show up was that yesterday was a holiday.

A Feint to the Larynx.

Several outside swooned on schedule. One 16-year-old, Loretta Dillon of 6 Calvin St., Lynbrook, L.I., rallied sufficiently to insist upon being allowed inside to look at The Voice. Her success prompted a succession of false faints thereafter, but none was successful.

The cops, mature and case-hardened, handled the idolators well—firmly but gently. On hand were two emergency trucks, 20 radio cars, four lieutenants, six sergeants, two captains, two assistant chief inspectors, two inspectors, 70 patrolmen, 50 traffic cops, 12 mounted men, 20 police women, 200 detectives and 41 temporary police, the later drawn from the ranks guarding the Columbus Day parade on Fifth Ave.

The crowd, four abreast, stretched from the Paramount's glided ticket office, right around 43d St. to Eight Ave., from there to 44th and then eastward to Broadway. All traffic had to be detoured between 43d and 44th Sts. for about an hour before noon.

The cause of it all, a vision in brown slacks, brown and yellow plaid jacket, flaming orange sweater and tie and a white shirt with points like two pieces of pie, came on the stage shortly after 10 A. M.

He opened his mouth. The auditorium trembled with juvenile acclaim and the audience rose. He closed his mouth.

Five minutes later he opened it again—and sang.

Music—and Words.

He sang "I'll Walk Alone," "Come Out" and "They'll be a Hot Time in the Town of Berlin," but no one could hear him for the applause. He smiled tentatively and the footlights shone on his healthy tan makeup.

"Now," he said, "I want to sing a very beautiful song, 'Old Man River.' "
He did and you were able to distinguish such phrases as "he don't say
nothin', he just keeps rollin'," etc. This classic sobered his audience down
to a roar.

"I hope you appreciated that song," he said, "because the music is very
beautiful. I don't want to preach to you about music, but I do want you to
realize there is more than one kind.

"And now, I'd like to sing a song which is often sung to babies, the
Brahms 'Lullaby.' " Many in the audience listened respectfully.

Anything Goes.

Frankie said he hopes they appreciated THAT. "As long as you sing it,
Frankie, we like it!" They intoned. Then he tried to go off-stage. He got
off once but was shouted back on. Finally, he refused encores, blew the
cultists a kiss with both hands and disappeared—until the next show.

The audience sat practically solid through two shows. After Frankie had
appeared the second time, however, about half departed, walking on air.

It was that way all day—and far into the night.

1945

The closer American soldiers and marines came to the home islands of Japan, the more bitter the fighting, and the greater the casualty tolls on both sides. The conquest of vital Iwo Jima, with its airfield just 750 miles south of Tokyo, would be remembered in Marine Corps legend as the bloodiest, the most costly of battles in the Pacific war.

Homer Bigart, covering Iwo Jima for *The New York Herald-Tribune*, wrote in the paper's March 14, 1945, edition of military doctors and medics' selfless efforts to save the wounded. Secure in the justness of an American victory, Bigart wrote his story in an unabashed style close to propaganda. It exemplifies the sort of coverage that would earn for Bigart a Pulitzer prize in 1946.

Iwo Hospital: War Rages Outside But Its Staff Performs Miracles

Surgeons, Aided by Blood Flown From U.S., Do 20 Major Operations a Day; Men Become Inured to Shootings on the Premises

By Homer Bigart
By Navy Wireless to the Herald Tribune.
Copyright, 1945, New York Tribune Inc.

IWO JIMA, March 12 (Delayed)—Tucked against the slope of a huge
brown ash heap overlooking the southern coast of Iwo is the hospital of a
marine division. Until a few days ago the hospital might just as well have

been sitting right on the front lines. It was within easy range of Japanese guns and mortars. Almost nightly enemy patrols sneaked past the darkened ward tents and operating huts.

One dark night five Japanese came marching down the road directly past the receiving tent. Private First Class Willard B. Young, a marine guard, saw their bayonets silhouetted against the sky and opened fire, killing one and scattering the others.

Another piece of excitement came the following night when a Japanese patient attempted to escape. He was frustrated by a wounded marine.

"Normally the Japanese patients are exceedingly co-operative," said Lieutenant Commander William W. Ayers, of New Orleans, the hospital commandant. "They always seem amazed that they aren't shot, and appear grateful for the treatment we give them."

Ayres and his staff have been too busy to pay much attention to the occasional shootings on the premises. On one particular sanguinary night several hundred casualties were cleared at the reception tent. The chief surgeon, Lieutenant Commander Thomas C. Butt, of Orlando, Fla., said the surgical teams averaged about twenty major operations daily, plus thirty to forty minors and numerous dressings.

"I've seen everything in the book and some things that weren't in the book," Butt said. "We are getting away with stuff that civilian surgeons would consider impossible—for example, bilateral amputations of the thigh."

Whole blood packed in ice and flown from San Francisco is being employed for the first time by the marines, and has saved at least twenty-five Leathernecks, according to Butt. Some were totally moribund when blood from West Coast civilians began surging into their bodies.

"There was one day—we had to amputate both legs," said Butt. "I wouldn't have given a nickle for his chances. There was just him.

"Well, we starte [sic] dgiving [sic] him transfusions. I tell you this blood is marvelous. Next morning as they were evacuating him he called from the stretcher: 'So long, Doc, I'll be seeing you.' "

Butt took us to the reception tent where Pharmacists Mate Edward Reinhart of Sheppardstown, W. Va., was uncrating blood bottles. All bore San Francisco tags giving the name of the donor.

Reinhart told us that the marine patients always noted the donor's name, and often asked the Red Cross to provide the address.

"I'll look up that babe when I hit Frisco," said one Leatherneck receiving blood donated by a woman. A card showed the donation had been made on Feb. 27.

Normally the hospital's twenty-five medical officers and six dentists work a twelve-hour stretch. But during the first week's bitter fighting here when the operating rooms were in constant use there was little sleep. Lieutenant Commander Henry Jernigan of Atlanta, Ga., orthopedist, worked thirty-six hours without a break.

"It was hard getting them to go to bed," said Ayres. "Long after they'd been relieved they stood by their cases and saw them through."

The short distance from the front to the hospital undoubtedly saved many lives, Ayres said. He told of corpsmen under fire driving jeep ambulances across the barren plateau to pick up the wounded.

Especially heroic was the work of Pharmacists Mate Filiberto Salaz, of Pueblo, Col., an Indian who on D Day went back and forth on the beach braving fierce mortar fire to rescue the wounded. Casualties among the corpsmen have been nearly as heavy as among the combat troops.

The hospital came ashore on D plus 1, and the tents were partly dug in as a protection both from dust. The surrounding area was shell fragments and the blinding a bleak and treeless dust bowl. The nights were sharp, with the temperatures sometimes falling to the lower 40s.

The tents were not heated, but Ayres got sufficient blankets from the quartermaster stores. Surprisingly few marines came down with colds. Lieutenant Commander Henry J. Fregori, of Proctor, Vt., the malarialogist, said the temperature and the climate made Iwo the healthiest spot yet captured in the Pacific.

Fregori was warned to expect scrub typhus bacillary and dysentery as well as an epidemic of colds. So far, no typhus nor dysentery has been found among the Japanese prisoners, although some were lousy and one had scabies.

Scrub typhus is carried by mites. Fregori said he has found some mites but that they have not been classified.

The island is remarkably free from mosquitoes, and Fregori's squads had to hunt all day before bagging some. They were dengue carriers, but too scarce to cause alarm. Sand crabs, flying ants and flies are the only other nuisances.

Hospital planes ease the burden of the medics by evacuating scores of wounded to the Marianas. Before the airport was opened "weasels" and "amtracs" [amphibious tractors small, and large variety] carried most of the seriously wounded to warships anchored off the coast.

1945

Newspapers are often and justifiably criticized for being shrill. But in one instance, a newspaper achieved distinction by understatement. On Friday, April 13, 1945, amid the tumult of editing news of the death of President Franklin Delano Roosevelt, an anonymous rewrite man on the tabloid *New York Post* quietly inserted two lines into the official casualty list released by the Pentagon each day. Forty-five years later, it still brings tears to the eyes of those who remember F.D.R. as the man historian James MacGregor Burns called "The Soldier of Freedom."

TODAY'S ARMY-NAVY CASUALTY LIST

Washington, Apr. 13.—Following are the latest casualties in the military services, including next-of-kin.

Army-Navy Dead

ROOSEVELT, Franklin D., Commander-in-Chief, wife, Mrs. Anne Eleanor Roosevelt, the White House.

Navy Dead

DECKER, Carlos Anthony, Fireman lc., Sister, Mrs. Elizabeth Decker Metz, 16 Concord Pl., Concord. S. I. . . .

1945

"I have become death . . . shatterer of worlds," physicist J. Robert Oppenheimer quietly quoted from the Hindu Bhagavad-Gita, as he watched the first nuclear blast fill the skies in New Mexico. Less than a month later, on August 6, 1945, an atomic bomb obliterated Hiroshima, and several days after that, another flattened Nagasaki. Now even Oppenheimer's words seemed inadequate.

A single bomb had destroyed 60 percent of Hiroshima. Japanese authorities put the climbing death toll at more than 50,000 several weeks after rescue workers arrived. Visiting the city weeks after the blast, *New York Times* correspondent W.H. Lawrence expressed the horror of such awesome devastation. His story ran in the *Times* of September 5, 1945.

VISTIT TO HIROSHIMA PROVES IT WORLD'S MOST-DAMAGED CITY

Four Square Miles Leveled by the Atomic Bomb—People Reported Dying at Rate of 100 a day—Hate for Us Shown

By W.H. Lawrence
By Wireless to The New York Times.

HIROSHIMA, Japan, Sept. 3 (Delayed)—The atomic bomb still is killing Japanese at a rate of 100 daily in flattened, rubble-strewn Hiroshima, where the secret weapon harnessing the power of the universe itself as a destructive agent was used for the first time on Aug 6.

Following a four-day battle, U.S. Marines plant "Old Glory" atop Iwo Jima's Mount Surabachi in Joe Rosenthal's famous photograph, February 23, 1945. The Library of Congress, Washington, D.C.

I was among the first few foreigners to reach the site of this historic bombing and walked for nearly two hours today through the streets where the stench of death still pervades and survivors or relatives of the dead, wearing gauze patches over their mouths, still probe among the ruins for bodies or possessions.

This is the world's most damaged city, worse than Warsaw or Stalingrad, which held the record in Europe. Fully four square miles, constituting 60 percent of the city, are absolutely levelled and the houses and buildings in the rest of the city are irreparably damaged.

Japanese announced that the death toll had passed 53,000, an increase of 20,000 in the figure reported Aug. 20 and last Saturday, and it was predicted the final count would exceed 80,000 dead.

On Aug. 20, the latest date for which Japanese official detailed statistics are available, the casualties were 33,000 dead, 30,000 missing, 13,960 seriously wounded and 43,000 listed as wounded "not so seriously."

This accounted for approximately one-third of Hiroshima's pre-war population of 343,000, but in addition it was stated that most of the other persons in the city suffered minor wounds that were not considered serious enough for medical treatment in view of the great shortage of doctors to deal with this disaster.

Japanese doctors told us they were helpless to deal with burns caused by the bomb's great flash or with other physical ailments caused by the bomb. Some said they thought that all who had been in Hiroshima that day would die as a result of the bomb's lingering effects.

They told us that persons who had been only slightly injured on the day of the blast lost 86 percent of their white blood corpuscles, developed temperature of 104 degrees Fahrenheit, their hair began to drop out, they lost their appetite, vomited blood and finally died.

The bomb fell about 8:15 A.M. on a clear day just after the "all clear" signal ending an air raid alert had been sounded, and many of Hiroshima's residents were in the streets when the sky above them was lighted by a brilliant flash that seared everything below it.

Most of the deaths and destruction that occurred in a fraction of a second, although fires smoldered for more than a day in the ruins of wooden and stone houses crumpled inward. Bodies of men women and children were thrown about the streets and the cries of the terrified wounded filled the air.

A witness of the bombing said "everything had been scorched to the ground, everything that still lived was waiting to die."

So terrible was the blast, that every wounded person thought he had been hit by an individual bomb, and it was not until hours later that it was recognized that a new weapon of undreamed of power had been utilized against them. . . .

As a war correspondent in Europe and the Pacific I have never looked upon such scenes of death and destruction. It was enough to take your breath away when standing in the center of the area where the bomb fell. You could see nothing but rubble and the seared walls of a few earthquake-proof buildings that remained upright.

Steel was twisted and the tile was burned into dust. The wood was charred and torn into small fragments. Air-raid shelters were crushed in.

The damage in Hiroshima is greater than that in Nagasaki, which I saw from a low level in an airplane, but there were indications that the Nagasaki bomb was in some ways more powerful. It appeared that most of the buildings of Nagasaki disintegrated, leaving no rubble to mark the damaged area. Only in a few places were piles of stone, steel, galvanized iron and wood, typical of bomb damage in any city. . . .

We walked past large granite buildings from which stone fragments still were dropping and peered inside a floorless stone structure that serves as the emergency headquarters for three banks, to which an imperial messenger had just delivered relief funds, for which residents were standing in line.

Surprisingly, the street cars which were not burned out, still operate and Japanese riding on them looked out with more curiosity than hostility at the tall white men in Army uniforms, studying the devastation their country had caused.

Some Bodies Still in Ruins

It was a chilly, drizzly day, but hundreds were moving amid the rubble from which most of the bodies had been removed and cremated, but a few still remain, giving off the awful, sickening odor of death.

Even the trees were killed by the bomb. Birds that looked like buzzards perched on the torn, leafless limbs.

Nobody was smiling. The patient, long-suffering Japanese, who believed they were winning the war up to the very day the Emperor announced he had surrendered, moved slowly and quietly through the streets to carry out their personal business. There is no work for them here, except in cleaning up, and, as in all Japanese cities, there is little to eat.

In the rubble of destroyed stone and wooden houses we saw, occasionally, an unbroken bottle of sake that, somehow, had survived the blast, but nobody seemed to be drinking.

A visit to Hiroshima is an experience to leave one shaken by the terrible, incredible sights. Here is the final proof of what the mechanical and scientific genius of America has been able to accomplish in war through the invention of the airplane, especially the B-29 Superfortress and the atomic bomb. It should be the last evidence needed to convince any doubter of the need to retain and perfect our air offense and defense lest the fate of Hiroshima be repeated in Indianapolis or Washington or Detroit or New York.

Three Japanese newspaper men who interviewed us wanted to know the role of the atomic bomb in future warfare. We told them it was our purpose as one of the United Nations to make certain that peace is maintained throughout the world. . . .

After walking through the city for about two hours we were taken to a modern undamaged building on the outskirts, where in the paneled former board room of the Eastern Oriental Manufacturing Company, motorcycle manufacturers, we were received by Hirokuni Dazai, who controlled the "Thought Police" in the Hiroshima prefecture. The "Thought Police" are similar to the Gestapo in Nazi Germany or the NKVD in the Soviet Union.

Dazai, who had returned to Hiroshima from Tokyo forty minutes before the bomb exploded, provided the official casualty statistics and gave us an account of what happened to him.

He was wearing a white gauze bandage around his head. He said he had suffered a slight wound when his house collapsed upon him and his family. His wife was knocked unconscious but his two children were only scratched.

He said he had not noticed the airplanes overhead and that the great flash that arced through the sky was his first knowledge that a bomb had fallen. He said he had believed hundreds of bombs had fallen when he felt the blast.

It was Dazai who sent the first report of the new bomb to Tokyo. His report undoubtedly played a major role in the emperor's decision four days later to advise the United Nations that Japan was willing to accept the Potsdam declaration [demanding Japan's surrender] if he could keep his job.

Dazai said great fires kept relief parties out of the central part of the city for hours and interfered with land transport, including railways, so that it was almost impossible to move doctors in or take patients out.

We asked him his opinion of the use of this type of bomb. He replied that he believed we had in our possession the ability to destroy every living thing of the civilization established by the gods.

1947

After playing for the International League's Montreal Royals, Jackie Robinson was brought up to the Brooklyn Dodgers in 1947. Two years earlier, Branch Rickey, the Dodgers' owner, had signed Robinson, an accomplished athlete who had played football, basketball, and baseball and run track at UCLA.

Robinson's mere presence on Brooklyn's Ebbets Field during a spring day in 1947 generated news coast to coast. The black ballplayer who was to make sports history by breaking the color line in major league baseball. Nowhere was Robinson more avidly written about than in the nation's black press, including Baltimore's *Afro-American,* which provided this small, affecting portrait of the major leaguer in its April 19, 1947, edition.

LOOKING 'EM OVER

With Sam Lacy

BROOKLYN—Jackie Robinson fell into the back seat of a friend's club coupe and gave vent to a heavy sigh.

The new Brooklyn Dodger rookie had finally reached the car after 20 minutes of pushing and mauling by a mob of approximately 250 well-wishers, most of them men and boys and a majority of them white.

They had waited more than an hour outside Ebbets Field for Jackie to appear. And as he stepped through the gate, he was set upon by his begging, cajoling, demanding admirers. Many wanted autographs, others simply wanted to touch him. It was just as though the former Negro American League ball player had suddenly been transformed into some kind of matinee idol—only his fans weren't bobby-soxers, nor did they capitalize on the swoon.

It was easy to see as he pitched himself into the car that Jackie was physically spent but mentally pleased. Like any other human being, Jackie showed clearly that, for the moment, all he wanted was to be left alone. Those of us who were with him sensed this and, as though the word had been passed around, each decided to keep quiet, to give him a moment to relax.

As he sat there looking out on the maelstrom of Brooklyn traffic, looking but not seeing, I caught a distinct gleam in the athlete's eyes. And in that fleeing moment I was made happy, for I realized that underneath Jackie's bored exterior was a genuine feeling of warm satisfaction over the attention he was getting. This was a normal reaction and augured well.

We had just run onto the ramp leading to Brooklyn Bridge, headed for Manhattan, when Jackie himself broke the silence. "You know," he began, "that went along swell. There's nothing wrong with those fellows that I can see."

The star was referring to his new Brooklyn Dodger teammates, with whom just a few hours before he had received his baptism in major league baseball.

Just Grinned

"There wasn't the slightest indication that I was anything but another ball player," Robbie went on, as if he were anticipating our questions.

"Several of them approached me when I went into the dressing room, and wished me luck. I can't say who all of them were but I distinctly remember Johnny Van Cyck, Gene Hermanski and Ralph Branca coming over and saying how glad they were to have me with the team.

"It sounded very good and I wanted very much to say something but I couldn't. I guess I just grinned.

"That's the way it was all through batting practice and in-field. They 'pepped it' with me the same as they did with the other fellows.

"Frankly, I wasn't conscious of being treated any different. I liked that. I don't want to be a 'special' guy. I just want to be another ball player.

"When we went into the meeting before the game, it was the same thing. Sukey [Clyde Sukeforth, acting manager] didn't say anything about my joining the team, or about how I should be welcomed the same as any other player. I thought that was wise and, under my breath, I thanked Sukey for it.

"After he'd finished giving instructions, Sukey turned to me and asked me how I felt. I told him fine, and he said, 'Good, you're starting at first base.'

"You could have knocked me over with a handkerchief. I didn't have any idea I'd be in there right away.

"But you know what?" Robbie went on, after a moment of thought. "What impresed [sic] me most was the way Eddie Stanky acted."

[Stanky, Dodger second baseman, is from Mobile, Ala., and the man for whose position Jackie was gunning when spring training began in February—Ed. note.]

"Why, that fellow's a real ballplayer," Jackie continued, with emphasis on the last two words. "I don't know how he may be in the locker room or on the road or after the game, but on the field he is a ballplayer—trying to win.

"He kept coaching me all through the game, pulling me in and telling me to move back or to one side or the other. Once he asked me if I wasn't too far off the bag, whether I could get to the bag in time.

"I told him I could get there, but he simply said, 'Move in closer anyway.' I did. Later, he explained that although my speed enabled me to get to the base in time for the putout, it wasn't soon enough.

"'You see,' Stanky said, 'it isn't simply to be there for the throw. What you want to do is to get to the base and be standing still so that you're a target for your infielders. It's better to have your third baseman and shortstop throwing at you than to have them throwing at the base.'

Big League

"Another time, he told me how to take relay throws on double plays. In those few minutes next to Stanky, I learned more than I could hope to learn in five years of playing the bag on my own. Suddenly I realized that this was big league.

"Two other things that happened today show me that the fellows are 'right guys.'

"When I missed a bunt signal in the sixth, it sounded like a hundred guys yelled at me from the bench. If I wasn't regarded as one of them, they'd have kept quiet. They'd have let me miss it and gotten a kick out of my humiliation.

"That was one. The other was the fellowship shown by Bruce Edwards, the catcher. He said nothing all through the game, but each time he passed me, Bruce either slapped me on the back or punched me on the arm, clicking his teeth as he did so.

"You know, I think they're okay—yeah, okay."

A joyous President Harry S Truman celebrates the November 2, 1948, defeat of both Republican Thomas E Dewey and the conservative Chicago Tribune, *which went to press early with a headline that could not have been more wrong.* St. Louis Globe-Democrat *photo, courtesy of the St. Louis Mercantile Library, St. Louis, Mo.*

1950

Joseph McCarthy, Republican senator from Wisconsin, was frankly looking for an issue with which to flay the Democrats and especially President Harry S. Truman. The question of Communist subversion in the Democratic Administration, and particularly in the State Department, would suit nicely for this Lincoln Day fund-raising speech the Republican Party had assigned him to give in Wheeling, West Virginia. The public was worried about the fall of China to the Reds, about Soviet possession of the atomic bomb, and its dominance of Eastern Europe, about American policy, once so mighty and now seemingly so impotent.

In a prepared text handed to the press, McCarthy claimed he had a list of the names of 205 Communists working in the Department of State—though apparently that figure did not particularly impress the reporter for *The Wheeling Intelligencer* who buried the number in his story. (McCarthy had no such list; in later talks he kept changing the figure.) Still, the claim riveted attention on McCarthy. Within months he would be the most strident of the many officeholders ferreting out suspected subversives, and so well publicized that his name became a synonym for the abuses of civil liberties that ensued in the hunt for domestic Communists. The publicity began in *The Wheeling* [West Virginia] *Intelligencer* on February 10, 1950.

M'CARTHY CHARGES REDS HOLD U.S. JOBS

Truman Blasted
For Reluctance
To Press Probe

Wisconsin Senator
Tells Lincoln Fete
Here 'Chips Down'

By Frank Desmond
Of the Intelligencer Staff

Joseph McCarthy, junior U.S. Senator from Wisconsin, was given a rousing ovation last night when, as guest of the Ohio County Republican Women's Club, he declared bluntly that the fate of the world rests with the clash between the atheism of Moscow and the Christian spirit throughout other parts of the world.

More than 275 representative Republican men and women were on hand to attend the colorful Lincoln Day dinner of the valley women which was held in the colonnade room of the McLure hotel.

Disdaining any oratorical fireworks, McCarthy's talk was of an intimate, homey nature, punctuated at times with humor.

But on the serious side, he launched many barbs at the present setup of the State Department, at President Truman's reluctance to press investigation of "traitors from within," and other pertinent matters.

He said that recent incidents which brought traitors to the limelight is [sic] the result of an "emotional hangover" and a temporary moral lapse which follows every war. However, he added:

"The morals of our people have not been destroyed. They still exist and this cloak of numbness and apathy needs only a spark to rekindle them."

Referring directly to the State Department, he declared:

"While I cannot take the time to name all of the men in the State Department who have been named as members of the Communist Party and members of a spy ring, I have here in my hand a list of 205 that were known to the Secretary of State as being members of the Communist Party and who, nevertheless, are still working and shaping the policy in the State Department. . . .

"Actually, ladies and gentlemen, the reason for the graft, the corruption, the disloyalty, the treason in high government positions—the reason this continues is because of the lack of moral uprising [sic] on the part of the 140 million American people. In the light of history, however, this is not hard to explain.

"It is the result of an emotional hangover and a temporary moral lapse which follows every war. It is the apathy to evil which people who have been subjected to the tremendous evils of war feel.

"As the people of the world see mass murder, the destruction of defenseless and innocent people and all of the crime and lack of morals which go with war, they become numb and apathetic. It has always been thus after war."

At another time, he declared:

"Today, we are engaged in a final all-out battle between Communistic atheism and Christianity. The modern champions of Communism have selected this as the time, and ladies and gentlemen, the chips are down—they are truly down." . . .

1953

It was the summer scourge, the terror of every parent. Each year, primarily during the hot weather, hundreds, thousands of children would complain of fever and sore throat, and of feeling tired. The next day they would be mysteriously paralyzed, most often permanently, some even condemned to live in great iron lungs which helped them to breathe.

Poliomyelitis or infantile paralysis knew no social boundaries. Franklin Delano Roosevelt, then a promising young politician from New York, had been stricken in 1921. With the help of his wife, he had partially recovered, though, crippled from the waist down, he would never walk again without leg braces, crutches, or a cane. As President of the United States, he became a moving force in the March of Dimes, an annual fund drive that raised money for polio research.

Those dimes funded the research that

led to the March 27, 1953, announcement that a University of Pittsburgh team headed by Jonas Salk had found a vaccine effective against the summer terror. *The Pittsburgh Press* assigned staff writer John Troan to the page one story.

Serum Effective in Tests

PITT VACCINE 'PROMISING' IN POLIO BATTLE

Immunity Reported for 4½ Months; None of 161 Subjects Harmed

By John Troan

One shot of the new Pitt polio vaccine apparently makes a child immune to the disease for at least 4½ months, Dr. Jonas E. Salk reported last night.

The vaccine not only seems to work but it also appears to be safe—for it hasn't harmed any of the 1651 persons in the Pittsburgh district whose parents had the courage to offer them up for the experiment.

Dr. Salk, the University of Pittsburgh scientist who heads up the research team which produced the vaccine, emphasized much work remains to be done before any such preventative agent can be released for general use, because a lot of questions still are unanswered.

Vaccine Not Ready

But, in an unprecedented medical broadcast, he told a nationwide radio audience that the results of the studies here "provide justification for optimism."

Dr. Salk said, "It does appear that the approach in these investigations may lead to the desired objective" of a safe, sure vaccine which will finally wipe out the scourge of infantile paralysis.

Dr. Salk made it clear "there will be no vaccine for widespread use" during the coming polio season. In other words, you won't be able to get any for your child this year.

However, both in his radio talk and in an accompanying report to be published tomorrow in The Journal of American Medical Assn., Dr. Salk left the door open for a possible large-scale field test in 1953.

Pleads for Patience

It is known that officials of the National Foundation for Infantile Paralysis are hopeful the Virus Research Laboratory at Pitt will be able to produce enough vaccine to stage such a test "under fire" in some polio epidemic area around August or September.

Dr. Salk, nevertheless, pleaded for public patience.

"I am certain," he said, "that you will understand that the actual accomplishment of our purpose cannot be achieved in a day."

Dr. Salk disclosed that the experimental human studies were undertaken first on patients at the D.T. Watson Home in Leetsdale and then on inmates of the Polk State School in Venango County.

"In none of the 161 persons involved," Dr. Salk stated, "have there been any signs of illness that could be attributed to the inoculaton."

Dr. Salk revealed he's actually working with two different vaccines.

One Confers Immunity

However, only the second seems to confer immunity to all three types of polio. This is the one which has had the entire scientific world agog since word leaked out in January that it had been tried on humans with encouraging results.

In the initial tests on children at the Watson Home, Dr. Salk used a watery vaccine. It had been shown to be safe in monkeys because animals which were inoculated with it escaped infection even when a polio virus was shot directly into their brains.

The vaccine contained the three different polio viruses, which had been cultivated in test tubes at the lab in Municipal Hospital.

To render the viruses harmless, they were given a special chemical bath. In this way it was hoped they would be too weak to cause paralysis, yet strong enough to "insult" the body and make it fight back—thus generating substances known as anti-bodies, which would provide the desired immunity.

Moving with extreme caution, Dr. Salk gave the first human injections to children who already had been crippled by one of the three types of the polio virus.

If the vaccine had gone haywire, these children could have been paralyzed a second time. But the only bad side effect the vaccine produced was a red swelling at the needle site which occurred in some cases. . . .

Dr. Salk reported that the information thus far available "suggests that it should be possible with a non-infectious preparation to approximate the immunology effect induced by the disease process itself."

That amounts to lifetime immunity. . . .

1954

The marriage of former Yankee centerfielder Joe DiMaggio and film siren Marilyn Monroe united a prince and princess of American popular culture. It also provided gossip columnists with material for weeks. Though "Joltin' Joe" and "blonde bombshell" Monroe had been dating for nearly two years, their afternoon wedding ceremony at San Francisco City Hall remained a secret. Even the battling queens of gossip, Louella Parsons and Hedda Hopper, failed to learn of it until afterwards. This did not stop Parsons from gushing about the wedding in the January 15, 1954, editions of the Hearst newspapers, such as in this story from *The Los Angeles Examiner*.

MARILYN MONROE, DIMAGGIO MARRIED;

Miss Monroe in
Satin, Ermine

By Louella O. Parsons
Motion Picture Editor International News Service

At long last, Marilyn Monroe and Joe DiMaggio are married.

The ceremony was performed yesterday in the San Francisco City Hall, by Superior Judge Charles S. Peery in his chambers at approximately 1:50 p.m.

Marilyn, who was hatless, wore a black satin coat with ermine collar over a street dress and carried white orchids. The witnesses were Reno Barsocchini, a longtime friend and business associate of the bridegroom, Frank (Lefty) O'Doul, who was Joe's first manager, and Mrs. O'Doul.

Keeps Word———

The first news that Marilyn planned to be married came when she put in a long distance call to Harry Brand, head of 20th Century-Fox publicity, and said:

"I promised you that if I ever got married, I'd let you know, so I'm keeping my word. Please tell all my friends."

Marilyn has been on suspension from her studio for not reporting for "Pink Tights," her next picture, but she'll be back at the end of next week to start work; good news not only to her studio, but to her friends as well.

She and Joe will honeymoon for a week.

I predicted this marriage would take place this month because our No. 1 boxoffice girl and her Joe went house-hunting in Burlingame, the fashionable suburb of San Francisco. This I had straight and not only printed it in my column, but told it on the radio.

Marilyn, who has been living with Joe's sister in San Francisco, had her telephone disconnected so that reporters could not reach her. Not that she minds publicity, but Joe, who had plenty of it when he was a baseball star with the Yankees, hates it. That was probably the reason for the secrecy on their marriage.

Meteoric Rise———

We were all alerted a week ago by reports that Marilyn and Joe were going to be married in Las Vegas. I have no doubt they did plan to be married there, but were frightened off when it was known they had reservations in the gambling city.

Marilyn's meteoric rise to fame is one of the stories that make Hollywood such a fabulous place. She started out as an aircraft worker on the assembly line, and it was [producer] Joseph Schenck who gave her her start at 20th Century-Fox.

Later she was let out at that studio and her first success came at M-G-M when she made "Asphalt Jungle." Curvaceous Marilyn first attracted attention with her swinging hips and her walk, which has been described as the most sexy one on the screen.

Later she was signed again by 20th, and [producer] Darryl Zanuck gave her such pictures as "Gentlemen Prefer Blondes" and "How to Marry a Millionaire," and so started her on the career that made her the most widely publicized actress of our day.

Blind Date———

Marilyn met Joe on a blind date about two years ago and, much to the surprise of everyone, they fell in love. Since Marilyn had never seen a baseball game in her life, and Joe was not interested in motion pictures, no one expected them to be interested in each other.

Joe took Marilyn right into the bosom of his family and to this girl brought up in an orphanage, it was the most perfect thing that could have happened. She had never had any family life and Joe, like all Italians, loves his family.

At the time of the death of her agent, Johnny Hyde, Marilyn came to see me and said she had been bitterly criticized for not marrying Johnny.

Grateful———

"I'd never marry a man I didn't love," she told me. "And though I admired and respected Johnny and am grateful for the way he steered my career and the great advice he gave me, I didn't love him."

There have always been jokes about Marilyn's highbrow inclinations, but I know she is sincerely interested in trying to improve herself. She has talked to me many times about books she is reading and wants to read.

I think that everyone who knows this girl, who has risen against such enormous odds, wishes her great happiness.

I believe they will make their home in San Francisco except for such times as she is working in Hollywood. San Francisco is Joe's home town, and his sister and brothers live there. Marilyn has already given up her apartment in Beverly Hills.

Second Marriages———

It is the second marriage for both. Marilyn was married to Jim Dougherty in 1942 and divorced him in Las Vegas in 1946. She was just another youngster when they were married, and they were divorced when he came out of the service.

Joe was formerly married to Dorothy Arnold, by whom he has a son, and I might add that the little boy adores Marilyn, as do all males, regardless of age.

1954

The ruling had stood in law for more than a half-century when on May 17, 1954, the Supreme Court of the United States held, 9–0, that "separate but equal" facilities for people of color were not constitutional. Reversing not only legal precedent but implicitly criticizing three centuries of practice, *Brown v. Board of Education of Topeka, Kansas,* was a beacon of decency.

Some threatened resistance. United States Senator James O. Eastland, a Mississippi Democrat, promised, "The South will not abide nor obey this legislative decision by a political court." Others, like the defendant school board insisted the problem had been corrected already. (Ironically, the grandchildren of plaintiff Oliver Brown were still attending segregated schools in Topeka, Kansas, thirty years after the *Brown* decision.)

Quite properly, *The Topeka Daily Capital* of May 18, 1954, reported *Brown v. Board,* the most important civil rights decision by the high court in this century, as a local story under the headline:

LITTLE EFFECT ON TOPEKA

The Supreme Court of the United States Monday declared unconstitutional an 1879 Kansas law allowing for segregation of Negroes and white elementary students in first class cities, but it appeared that the historic ruling will have no effect on Topeka schools where a movement to end segregation has been underway since September 1953. Similar movements are afoot in Salina and Atchison.

The Supreme Court ruling also overthrew a 1905 amendment to the 1879 law allowing Kansas City to segregate high school students.

Topeka Board of Education, along with the State of Kansas, was defendant in the original action. Other defendants before the Supreme Court were South Carolina, Virginia, Delaware and the District of Columbia.

A U.S. District Court had found that segregation in public education has a detrimental effect upon Negro children, but denied relief on the ground that the Negro and white schools were substantially equal with respect to buildings, transportation, curricula and educational qualifications for teachers.

Other first class Kansas cities practicing segregation are Coffeyville, Fort Scott, Leavenworth, Parsons and Lawrence. Baxter Springs, Bonner Springs, Chetopa, Manhattan, Oswego, Olathe, Paola and Ellinwood, while not first class cities, have in the past, also had segregation.

Some 10 Negro students in the Randolph and Southwest School districts were integrated for the 1953–54 school year. The Topeka Board of Education has 113 more students in 12 other districts for the 1954–55 year.

Five other elementary schools remain to be integrated. They are Lafayette, Lincoln, Parkdale, Van Buren and Lowman Hill.

The four all-Negro schools, McKinley, Buchanan, Monroe and Washington, will have an estimated enrollment of 711 for the 1954–55 school year. Before integration there were 824 students.

The Supreme Court's decision will have no effect on rural schools in Shawnee County.

Clifford Watson, county superintendent, said segregation is not practiced in the rural elementary and high schools.

The ruling by the Supreme Court was hailed by Topeka school officials.

Jacob Dickinson, president of the Board of Education, said the decision "is the finest spirit of the law and true democracy."

"In my opinion the court has been very wise in deciding the basic question and then calling for further discussion by all parties as to orderly and reasonable application of the ruling," Dickinson, an attorney, said.

"The Topeka Board of Education will of course continue the implementation of its policy to terminate the maintenance of segregation in the elementary grades as rapidly as practicable," he added.

Wendell Goodwin, superintendent of Topeka schools, said that altho he hasn't studied the high court's opinion, "I imagine segregation will be terminated in Topeka before the Supreme Court decides when and how it should be done."

Prominent Topeka Negroes also hailed the opinion.

M. L. Burnett, president of the Topeka branch of the National Association for Advancement of Colored People, which assisted in carrying the Topeka case to the Supreme Court, said, "I must say I'm completely overwhelmed."

"However, I will say thank God for the Supreme Court," he added. He said that altho the high court did not see a time and means, it has "broken the back of segregation" with its ruling.

"Since they have gone so far as to revise the former decision, we can leave it to them to abolish segregation as soon as practicable and by the best means," Burnett declared.

Burnett said the Topeka NAACP has planned a celebration for 8:15 p.m. today at Monroe School.

Another of the appellants, the Rev. Oliver L. Brown, pastor of St. Mark's AME Church, said, "I personally feel that this case has a deep bearing upon the hearts of our teachers. Certainly we must make an effort for them also, for there are many I know are capable of teaching anywhere.

"Secondly, I feel that this decision holds a better future, not only for one family, but for every child indicated. This will, no doubt, bring about a better understanding of our racial situation and will eliminate the inferiority complexes of children of school age.

"Every citizen of the United States needs equal education in order that the society in which we live may be met with intelligence. Such things as segregation have a tendency to shatter the morale of the people and leave a gap for communism to try to creep in. We must eliminate that by unity," the Rev. Mr. Brown concluded.

"I'm wonderfully happy by the decision, I think it is a great step forward to better relations between the races," said Mrs. Alvin Todd, another party to the case.

"We may have a long time to go before segregation is actually abolished, but we're just thankful we have come this far. The very fact that segregation was ruled illegal means a great deal, regardless of the machinery that must now be set up," she added. . . .

1955

Walt Disney's consuming fantasy became a physical reality the morning of July 18, 1955. Disneyland, a multimillion-dollar amusement park located on 160 acres of former orange groves 22 miles from downtown Los Angeles, opened to the public. A special Sunday dedication of Disneyland, a day before, featured bands and speeches, and was seen by more than 60 million viewers watching portions of the preceedings on television. Reporter Jerry Hulse was among the 30,000 guests invited to the dedication festivities at Disneyland; his story ran on page 1 of the July 18, 1955, *Los Angeles Times*.

DREAM REALIZED—DISNEYLAND OPENS

$17,500,000 World of Fantasy
Dedicated to Children and Hope

By Jerry Hulse

Once-upon-a-time land—that magical land of fantasy and faraway places in the minds of little children—became a dream come true yesterday.

It came true at the world premier opening the $17,500,000 Disneyland—land of childish dreams and adult hopes—in Anaheim.

Snow White lives. Donald Duck quacks. Captain Hook stalks the paths of Never Never Land.

These and other characters from the ages of ageless fairy tales came to life yesterday in the miracle of Disneyland's Fantasyland.

Time in Reverse

Time spun backward in this once-upon-a-time setting, back to the difficult days of America's pioneer past and daring exploits of the King of the Wild Frontier—Davy Crockett.

Davy Crockett lives again in a place called Frontierland, a land dedicated to the ideals, dreams and exploits that created America.

Stagecoaches jogged over the Painted Desert. Indians attacked. A river boat—the Mark Twain—moved lazily down the Mississippi.

In Frontierland, America's brave past was re-created.

Dreams of Youth

But its pioneer history was contrasted by a startling visit to Tomorrow-land—a land that may well be a prediction of things come true near the year 2000. A rocket shot forth to the moon, filled with squealing little boys and girls. And those adults young enough in mind to recapture the happy dreams of youth.

Youngsters caught in this dreamland discovered these adventures as they strolled happily down a path that led from this world of reality into Disney-land's wonderful world of dreams.

Adventureland

There was a place called Adventureland, where they rode an explorer boat down tropical rivers. Plastic crocodiles snapped. Lions roared. Tigers growled. The shore was lined with tropical flowers. Wild birds cried from the tree-tops.

This happy world of wonder within a troubled world came to life with magic wand-like suddenness when Walt Disney stepped off the Santa Fe and Disneyland train accompanied by Gov. Knight.

From there Disney strolled to the Town Square at the head of Main St., U.S.A. His dedication address was simple.

"All who come to this happy place—welcome," he said.

"Here age relives fond memories of the past . . . and here youth may savor the challenge and promise of the future.

"Disneyland is dedicated to the ideals, the dreams and the hard facts that have created America . . . with the hope that it will be a source of joy and inspiration to all the world."

Disney then joined the premiere opening parade.

There were bands, a color guard, horseless carriages carrying special guests, and the cartoon characters created by Disney.

Leading the Fantasyland division of the parade were mounted knights. They were followed by the Mouseketeers, the Disneyland band and then those wonderful cartoon characters . . . Dumbo, Pluto, Donald Duck, Mickey and Minnie Mouse. There was Pinocchio, the March Hare, the Mad Hatter and Sleeping Beauty.

Cinderella Rides

Cinderella rode in a golden pumpkin-type coach pulled by two ponies. Prince Charming rode nearby on a striking white horse.

Children lining the sidewalks of Main St. waved and shouted as a float passed carrying Snow White surrounded by the seven dancing dwarfs.

Frontierland's parade division included Fess (Davy Crockett) Parker and his sidekick Buddy Ebsen. Adding to the frontier atmosphere was Chief Flying Hoof riding Firewater.

Youngsters and adults alike laughed loudly as four cannibals marched up Main St. representing Adventureland.

Spaceman Preview

The future—Tomorrowland—was previewed by a spaceman. Following him were miniature gasoline-driven automobiles. Among the drivers was funnyman Jerry Colonna.

Finally, the parade ended with the Main St., U.S.A. division and the Dixieland music of the Firehouse Five Plus Two.

Disney then visited each of the four lands, giving short dedication addresses.

At Fantasyland, he said, "This is a timeless land of enchantment where fairy tales come true—dedicated to the young in heart."

Parade Telecast

The parade was telecast across the nation on a 90-minute ABC show.

Nearly 30,000 special guests visited Disneyland yesterday. Today it will open to the general public.

Among the special guests yesterday were 500 boys and girls from Orange County schools. They were escorted across the drawbridge and into Fantasyland by costumed Walt Disney characters.

Emceeing the parade was Art Linkletter, joined by scores of Hollywood film and television personalities.

Boat Christened

A highlight was the christening of the riverboat Mark Twain by actress Irene Dunne. She cracked a bottle filled with river waters gathered throughout the nation on the hull.

And as the sun set and dusk fell, shadowing towering Sleeping Beauty Castle, a lamplighter set aglow 100-year-old gas lamps lining Main St., U.S.A.

It was the end of the first day's chapter in the new magic world of Disneyland.

1957

Defying a federal court order to integrate Little Rock's Central High School, Arkansas Governor Orval E. Faubus mustered his National Guard and ordered the soldiers to turn away any black students who sought to enroll. Meanwhile restless crowds milled about outside the high school, waiting for the blacks to appear. Associated Press reporter Relman Morin, who was to win a Pulitzer Prize for his coverage at Little Rock, recorded what happened when the students showed up. This is Morin's story as it appeared in *The Los Angeles Times* of September 24, 1957.

EYEWITNESS TELLS STORY OF RIOTING

By Relman Morin

Little Rock, September 23—It was exactly like an explosion, a human explosion.

At 8:35 a.m., the people standing in front of the high school looked like the ones you see every day in a shopping center.

A pretty, sweet-faced woman with auburn hair and a jewel-green jacket . . . another, holding a white portable radio in her ear. "I'm getting the news of what's going on at the high school," she said . . . People laughed . . . A grey-haired man, tall and spare, leaned over the wooden barricade, "If they're coming," he said, quietly, "they'll be here soon" . . . "They better," said another. "I got to get to work."

Soon Became Mob

Ordinary people—mostly curious, you would have said—watching a high school on a bright, blue-and-gold morning.

Five minutes later, at 8:40, they were a mob.

The terrifying spectacle of 200-odd individuals, suddenly welded together into a single body, took place in the barest fraction of a second. It was an explosion, savagery chain-reacting from person to person, fusing them into a white-hot mass.

There are three glass-windowed telephone booths across the street from the south end of the high school.

At 8:35, I was inside one of them, dictating.

I saw four Negroes coming down the center of the street, in twos. One was tall and big-shouldered. One was tall and thin. The other two were short. The big man had a card in his hat and was carrying a Speed Graflex, a camera for taking news pictures.

A strange, animal growl rose from the crowd.

"Here come the Negroes."

Instantly, people turned their backs on the high school and ran toward the four men. They hesitated. Then they turned to run.

Ridden to Ground

I saw the white men catch them on the sidewalk and the lawn of a home a quarter block away. There were a furious, struggling knot. You could see a man kicking at the big Negro. Then another jumped on his back and rode him to the ground, forearms deep in the Negro's throat.

They kicked him and beat him on the ground and they smashed his camera to splinters. The other three ran down the street with one white man chasing them. When the white man saw he was alone, he turned and fled back toward the crowd.

Meanwhile, five policemen had rescued the big man.

I had just finished saying, "Police escorted the big man away—"

At that instant a man shouted, "Look the Negroes are going in."

Directly across from me three Negro boys and five girls were walking toward the side door at the south end of the school.

It was an unforgettable tableau.

They were carrying books. White bobby-sox, part of the high school uniform, glinted on the girls' ankles. They were all nicely dressed. The boys wore open-throat shirts and the girls' ordinary frocks.

Didn't Hurry

They weren't hurrying. They simply strolled across perhaps 15 yards from the sidewalk to the school steps. They glanced at the people and the police as though none of this concerned them.

You can never forget a scene like that.

Nor the one that followed.

Like a wave, the people who had run toward the four Negro men, now swept back toward the police and the barricades.

"Oh, god, they're in the school." a man yelled.

A woman—the one with the auburn hair and green jacket—rushed up to him. Her face was working with fury now.

Snarls and Screams

Her lips drew back in a snarl and she was screaming, "Did they go in?"

"They are in the school," the man said.

"Oh God," she said. She covered her face with her hands. Then she tore her hair, still screaming.

She looked exactly like the women who cluster around a mine head, when there has been an explosion and men are trapped below.

The tall, lean man jumped up on one of the barricades. He was holding on the shoulders of others nearby.

"Who's going through?" he roared.

"We all are," the people shrieked.

They surged over and around the barricades, breaking for the police.

About a dozen policemen, swinging billy clubs, were in front of them.

Men and women raced toward them and the policemen raised their clubs, moving this way and that as people tried to dodge around them.

A man went down, pole-axed, when a policeman clubbed him.

Meanwhile the women—the auburn-haired one, the woman with the radio, and others—were swirling around the police commanding officers.

Pure Hysteria

Tears were streaming down their faces. They acted completely distraught. It was pure hysteria.

And they kept crying, "They are in our school. Oh God, are you going to stand here and let them stay in school?"

Then, swiftly, a line of cars filled with State troopers rolled toward the school from two directions. The flasher-signals on the tops of the cars were spurting red warnings.

The troopers, big, thin-waisted men in broad-brimmed hats, moved inside the barricades with the policemen.

In an instant, they had the crowd—not wholly under control—but well away from the school.

Word of the violence that day forced President Dwight Eisenhower to take action, however reluctantly. He nationalized the Arkansas Guard, thereby removing the troops from Governor Faubus's control, and ordered 1,000 paratroopers to restore order in front of Central High. For the first time since Reconstruction, the federal government was using military force to assure the rights of blacks, and thereby affirming the supremacy of law. The following day, the nine students were enrolled at Central.

1960

The 1960s were to be the decade of the young. Nowhere was that clearer than in the segregated South, where students would take commanding positions in the civil rights movement. Brushing aside their elders' pleas of moderation or forbearance, the students pressed a new, vigorous activism and militancy.

The first outbreak of student protest took place on February 1 in the F.W. Woolworth five and dime in Greensboro, North Carolina. Though the sit-in movement was to spread to a half dozen other cities within days, its importance was not immediately recognized. *The Charlotte Observer* initially reported the Greensboro sit-ins, just fifty miles down the highway, with a wire-service story on its regional news page of Wednesday, February 3, 1960.

NEGROES SEEK DINER SERVICE

GREENSBORO—A group of Negro students—at one time numbering up to 27 men and four women—sat down at F.W. Woolworth's lunch counter here Tuesday in an attempt to obtain service.

They failed.

But one of the Agricultural & Technical students said the group is "prepared to keep coming for two years if we have to."

The student declined to give his name.

J. W. Largen of Atlanta, Woolworth's district superintendent, said, "We haven't refused anybody service. Our girls have been busy, and they couldn't get around to everybody."

The student who declined to give his name said, "They sell us merchandise from other counters. If they sell us other merchandise, we say they should serve us at the lunch counter."

Two city people detectives checked the store several times during the day. They said their only interest was to prevent any disorders.

The students sat quietly at the counter. Many of them studied as they waited.

The students said the demonstration was not organized by any particular group.

Dr. George C. Simkins Jr., head of the local NAACP chapter, said the NAACP had no previous knowledge of the demonstration.

But he said the group is 100 per cent behind the idea and "if any legal action arises as a result, the NAACP is prepared to back the group."

The demonstration apparently began Monday afternoon when four freshmen students sat down in the dime store about 4:30 p.m. and stayed until the store closed at 5:30 p.m.

They did not show up again, however.

Police said they were not notified of Monday's demonstration.

The Negroes formed a circle in front of Woolworth's before entering and said the Lord's Prayer.

C. L. Harris, manager of the store, declined to comment.

"They just sit there," he said. "It's nothing to me."

Woolworth's district superintendent, who was here also, declined to elaborate on his statement that the waitresses were too busy to serve the Negroes.

Several of the men students were dressed in their Reserve Officer's Training Corps uniforms.

Some of the students said they did not like the way they were treated at other eating places. But they declined to comment on this point further.

College officials at A&T said they had no knowledge of the demonstration until they were questioned by reporters.

Student spokesmen Franklin McLain and Ezell Blair Jr. stated that the group is seeking luncheon counter service and will continue its push "several days, several weeks . . . until something is done."

Both declared the movement is a student one, with no backing from National Association for the Advancement of Colored People.

They said they expect they could count on NAACP backing if needed.

The move is not school connected, they added, but they hope to encourage more students to participate and hope that Bennett College students will join.

1960

Flying almost silently through near space at an altitude 13 miles above the Soviet Union, U-2 reconnaissance aircraft Number 360 soared the early morning sky. Safely above the range of frustrated Russian surface-to-air missiles, the pilot, a Central Intelligence Agency employee, routinely ran through his flight plan, clicking ground-surveillance photographs as he flew from Peshawar, Pakistan, to Bodo, Norway. Exactly what happened as the plane approached the city of Sverdlovsk, 1300 miles inside the Russian border, remains classified. Most likely, the U-2 lost power, then glided earthward, into the range of Soviet anti-aircraft rockets.

By noon in Washington on that May 1, 1960, the CIA knew its plane and pilot Francis Gary Powers were overdue. The agency presumed the plane was down, and the pilot dead. The Soviets held their silence.

On May 3, the National Aeronautics and Space Agency released a cover story to the press stating a U-2 weather plane had gone down in "the area" of Lake Van, Turkey, after its pilot radioed he was experiencing oxygen difficulties. Two days later, Premier Nikita Khrushchev announced to the Supreme Soviet that the U-2 had been shot down, but said nothing about Powers, by then held in Lubyanka Prison. Khrushchev charged the flight an act of military aggression and snorted, "Just imagine what would have happened had a *Soviet* aircraft ap-

peared over New York, Chicago or Detroit."

On orders from the White House and the CIA, NASA reaffirmed one of its U-2 planes "in a continuing program to study gust-meterological conditions found at high altitude" was missing. Yes, the plane had cameras aboard, but they were to take cloud pictures, a NASA spokesman said.

American newspapermen were about to learn the enduring lesson of journalist I. F. Stone: All governments lie. On Saturday, May 7, Khrushchev sprang his trap, proudly telling the Supreme Soviet that the pilot, in Russian custody, had confessed to spying. In two related articles, *The Washington Post* of Sunday, May 8, 1960, reported President Dwight Eisenhower's tacit admission that the U-2 was on a spy mission, and recounted parallel events in Moscow. (Putting the word "proof" in quotation marks leaves little doubt where that paper's editors stood, despite the evidence.)

K. SAYS PILOT CONFESSES SPYING; U. S. TO DEMAND TALK WITH HIM

Premier Indicates Trial, Shows Deputies 'Proof' Jet Sought Red Targets

Bulletin
Associated Press

The United States admitted last night that "an unarmed civilian" aircraft probably made an information-gathering flight over the Soviet Union.

A statement cleared by President Eisenhower and released by the State Department in effect conceded the accuracy of much of Soviet Premier Nikita S. Khrushchev's charge that a plane shot down in Russia last Sunday was on a spy mission.

Russian Downers Of Plane Receive Medal Rewards

By Preston Grover

MOSCOW, May 7 (AP)—Premier Nikita S. Khrushchev said today that Francis G. Powers, pilot of a United States high-altitude jet plane shot down by rocket in the Urals Sunday, is safe in Soviet hands and has confessed he was spying. The Premier submitted film, money, weapons and an unused suicide kit as proof and indicated the flier will be tried.

Khrushchev waved pictures before a shouting, applauding Supreme Soviet—the Soviet version of a parliament—in support of his charge that the 30-year-old pilot was photographing Soviet military bases and industrial installations for the United States Central Intelligence Agency.

"This time the thief was caught red-handed," he said. ". . . We are going to decorate those soldiers who shot down this plane. We are proud of the fact that they fulfilled their duty."

Plane Trappers Honored

Decorations were reported awarded promptly by the Supreme Soviet to 18 officers and men for destruction of the plane. . . .

This is the way Khrushchev hinted that the American airman, who he said escaped by parachute when his speedy Lockheed U2 was hit, may be tried for espionage:

"I think that it will be correct to pose a question about the bringing of this pilot before a court in order that the public itself may become convinced of the actions undertaken by the United States, provoking the Soviet Union with a view to inflaming the atmosphere, brushing aside even the successes which had been achieved in the easing of international tension."

Rejects U.S. Claim

Khrushchev dismissed as a fabrication the United States State Department report that Powers, Lockheed test pilot from Pound, Va., was on a weather reserch [sic] mission from Adana, Turkey, when his plane vanished. . . .

[T]he Soviet Premier gave this account:

Powers flew from Turkey April 27 to Peshawar, then took off Sunday for a flight across Soviet territory toward a United States base at Bodo, Norway. He was flying at an altitude of 20,000 meters—more than 12 miles—when he was downed near Sverdlovsk in the Urals, deep in Soviet territory.

Both the pilot, "alive and well," and the wreckage of the plane were reported brought to Moscow. Khrushchev announced earlier this week that the plane had been brought down by a remarkable rocket.

Premier Quotes Pilot

Khrushchev quoted Powers as saying:

"I had to take off from the airdrome at Peshawar in Pakistan to cross the state frontier of the U.S.S.R. and to fly across Soviet territory to Norway to the airdrome at Bobo. I had to fly over definite points in the U.S.S.R. Of them, I remember Murmansk and Archangel. During the flight over Soviet territory I had to switch some apparatus on and off over definite landmarks which were shown on a map. I think my flight over Soviet territory was for the collection of information on Soviet guided missiles and radar stations."

Khrushchev told the deputies the plane was rigged with a demolition charge that should have been triggered by a catapult ejection device when the pilot bailed out, but that Powers avoided the ejector and jumped in taking to his parachute.

Powers also was equipped with a poison needle, Khrushchev said, and had been "told that he should not fall alive into the hands of Soviet authorities."

Tells of Spy Equipment

The plane was not fitted for weather study at all, he declared, "it was just an ordinary military reconnaissance aircraft equipped with various instruments for gathering espionage information." Its camera, he said, was good.

Of the poison needle, the Premier said Powers did not use it because "living things want to go on living."

The pilot also carried a silenced pistol, a dagger and a penknife, Khrushchev said.

He said Powers was also carrying 7500 Soviet rubles, some French gold francs and other foreign money, two gold watches in addition to Powers's own and seven gold bracelets for women.

The Premier said "we have not only the instruments found on the aircraft, but also a developed film consisting of several places on our territory."

"Here, look at this. Here are the airfields, here. Fighters in position on the ground. Two little white strips. Here you see another airfield. Here also a single line you see a long belt. They are our fighters in position on the ground. Again an airfield photographed. And again an airfield photographed. This is their film and we have developed it. Again an airfield photographed. Well, this will suffice. . . ."

He passed out the pictures for inspection by the deputies.

Khrushchev said he had delayed announcing capture of the pilot in order to expose "fabrications in the official American version."

Warns Other Nations

He suggested that Turkey, Pakistan and Norway take a second look at American use of bases on their sol [sic].

By Khrushchev's account, Powers said he went to work for an "American spy organization" in 1956 for $2500 a month. That was the year Powers signed up as a Lockheed test pilot.

Khrushchev also said, "I think it would be expedient to hold a press conference and to show during it all the (plane's) means for the exploration of the atmosphere. "He did not specify when this might be held.

The Premier said he got a very favorable impression from his talks with Americans last September, "but apparently militarists in the Pentagon . . . continue work for war purposes."

Warningly he said:

"A nuclear bomb can be dropped (by plane) in such a way, but such an aggressor can get back a more powerful nuclear bomb . . .

"What kind of morality are these people following if they consider themselves Christian?". . .

On Friday, August 19, 1960, a three-judge court in Moscow found a contrite and badly frightened Francis Gary Powers guilty of espionage. Although this was a "grave crime" against the Soviet Union, the presiding judge stated, the court was moved by Powers's "sincere repentence." "Socialist humaneness" therefore dictated that Powers suffer deprivation of liberty, the first three years to be spent in prison.

Powers actually spent less than eighteen months of his sentence in Vladimir Prison, 150 miles east of Moscow. On February 10, 1962, he was exchanged by the Soviet government for Rudolph Ivanovich Abel, a colonel in the KGB who had been convicted of spying for the Soviet Union in the United States and sentenced to 30 years in federal prison.

Abel returned to the U.S.S.R. a hero, awarded the Order of Lenin, and pensioned off to comfortable retirement. Powers worked for a time as a test pilot for Lockheed Aircraft, wrote his memoirs, then drifted about looking for work. He finally took a job as an airborne traffic reporter, flying over Los Angeles' crowded freeways. From that he went on to become a helicopter pilot, working for television station KNBC in Los Angeles. On August 1, 1977, while flying over the San Fernando Valley with a cameraman, Powers' helicopter lost power and spun into a softball diamond. Powers and the cameraman were instantly killed.

1960

Rarely has a social revolution of such vast consequence been announced with such a faint trumpet. The government's approval of the first birth control pill, reported in a routine dispatch by Associated Press, apparently got little news play. *The New York Times,* then in its encyclopedic mode as *the* journal of record, was one of the very few papers to run it—on page 75 of its May 10, 1960, issue. The social, sexual, and feminist upheavals that the drug fostered would keep platoons of reporters busy for years to come.

U. S. APPROVES PILL FOR BIRTH CONTROL

Washington, May 9 (AP)—For the first time the Food and Drug Administration has approved a pill as safe for contraceptive or birth control use.

"Approval was based on the question of safety," Associate Commissioner John L. Harvey said today. "We had no choice as to the morality that might be involved.

"When the data convinced our experts that the drug meets the requirements of the new drug provisions our own ideas of morality had nothing to do with the case."

The pill that has been approved is called Enovid. It is made by G. D. Searle and Co., Chicago.

Under the clearance granted by the agency it may be used only on doctor's prescription.

The drug has been on the market for several years but the previous clearance specified it was to be recommended only for treatment of female disorders.

1962

On October 22, 1962, President John F. Kennedy addressed the nation on television and radio, announcing that the Soviet Union had violated a promise not to build offensive missile bases in Cuba. Consequently, Kennedy was authorizing an arms blockade of the island to halt any further shipments of weapons. The broadcast, with its implicit threat of nuclear war, put America on alert. And around the globe, world leaders anxiously waited for the next move of what would be known as the Cuban missile crisis.

The international test of nerves was finally resolved on October 28, 1962, when Soviet Premier Nikita Khrushchev agreed to stop work on the bases and send the missiles already there back to Russia. In return, Kennedy promised an end to the blockade and a pledge not to invade Cuba.

Anthony Lewis's coverage of Kennedy's speech, which ran in *The New York Times* on October 23, 1962, succinctly caught the president's grim mood and the edgy state of international affairs.

U.S. IMPOSES ARMS BLOCKADE ON CUBA ON FINDING OFFENSIVE - MISSILE SITES; KENNEDY READY FOR SOVIET SHOWDOWN

PRESIDENT GRAVE

Asserts Russians Lied and Put Hemisphere in Great Danger

by ANTHONY LEWIS
Special to The New York Times

WASHINGTON, Oct 22—President Kennedy imposed a naval and air "quarantine" tonight on the shipment of offensive military equipment to Cuba.

In a speech of extraordinary gravity, he told the American people that the Soviet Union, contrary to promises, was building offensive missile and bomber bases in Cuba. He said the bases could handle missiles carrying nuclear warheads up to 2,000 miles.

Thus a critical moment in the cold war was at hand tonight. The President had decided on a direct confrontation with—and challenge to—the power of the Soviet Union.

Direct Thrust at the Soviet

Two aspects of the speech were notable. One was that its direct thrust at the Soviet Union as the party responsible for the crisis. Mr. Kennedy treated Cuba and the Government of Premier Fidel Castro as a mere pawn in Moscow's hands and drew the issue as one with the Soviet Government.

The President in language of unusual bluntness, accused the Soviet leaders of deliberately "false statements about their intentions in Cuba."

The other aspect of the speech particularly noted by observers here was its flat commitment by the United States to act alone against the missile threat in Cuba.

Nation Ready to Act

The President made it clear that this country would not stop short of military action to end what he called a "clandestine, reckless and provocative threat to world peace."

Mr. Kennedy said the United States was asking for an emergency meeting of the United Nations Security Council to consider a resolution for "dismantling and withdrawal of all offensive weapons in Cuba."

He said the launching of a nuclear missile from Cuba against any nation in the Western Hemisphere would be regarded as an attack by the Soviet Union against the United States. It would be met, he said, by retaliation against the Soviet Union.

He called on Premier Khrushchev to withdraw the missiles from Cuba and so "move the world back from the abyss of destruction."

All this the President recited in an 18-minute radio and television address of a grimness unparalleled in recent times. He read the words rapidly, with little emotion, until he came to the peroration—a warning to Americans of the dangers ahead.

"Let no one doubt that this is a difficult and dangerous effort on which we have set out," the President said. "No one can foresee precisely what course it will take or what costs or casualties will be incurred.

"The path we have chosen for the present is full of hazards, as all paths are—but it is the one most consistent with our character and courage as a nation and our commitments around the world," he added.

"The cost of freedom is always high—but Americans have always paid it. And one path we shall never choose is the path of surrender or submission.

"Our goal is not the victory of might but the vindication of right—not peace at the expense of freedom, but both peace and freedom, here in this hemisphere and we hope, around the world. God willing, that goal will be achieved."

The President's speech did not actually start the naval blockade tonight. To meet the requirements of international law, the State Department will issue a formal proclamation late tomorrow, and that may delay the effectiveness of the action as long as another 24 hours.

Crisis Before Public

The speech laid before the American people a crisis that had gripped the highest officials here since last Tuesday, but had only begun to leak out to the public over the weekend. The President said it was 9 A.M. Tuesday that he got the first firm intelligence report about the missile sites on Cuba.

Last month, he said, the Soviet Government publicly stated that its military equipment for Cuba was "exclusively for defensive purposes" and that the Soviets did not need retaliatory missile bases outside its own territory.

"That statement was false," Mr. Kennedy said.

Just last Thursday, he continued, the Soviet foreign minister, Andrei A. Gromyko, told him in a call at the White House that the Soviet Union "would never become involved" in building any offensive military capacity in Cuba.

"That statement was also false," the President said.

Appeal to Khrushchev

He made a direct appeal to Premier Khurshchev to abandon the Communist "course of world domination." An hour before the President spoke a personal letter from him to Mr. Khrushchev was delivered to the Soviet Government in Moscow.

Mr. Kennedy disclosed that he was calling for an immediate meeting of the Organ of Consultation of the Organization of American States to consider the crisis.

The O.A.S. promptly scheduled an emergency session for 9 A.M. tomorrow. State Department officials said they were confident of receiving the necessary 14 votes out of the 20 nations represented.

The President said the United States was prepared also to discuss the situation "in any other meeting that could be useful." This was taken as an allusion to a possible summit conference with Mr. Khrushchev.

But the President emphasized that discussion in any of these forums would be undertaken "without limiting our freedom of action." This meant that the United States was determined on this course no matter what any international organization—or even the United States allies—might say. . . .

1963

They came by chartered plane, by special train, by bus, 200,000 strong, gathered on August 28, 1963, on the Mall between the Washington Monument and Lincoln Memorial to petition their government for a redress of grievances.

The Washington Post assigned a dozen reporters to cover the largest mass demonstration in the nation's history. Robert D. Baker wrote a routine lead story for the August 29, 1963, edition; though large, the demonstration had been peaceful. Susanna McBee covered the speeches themselves, little realizing that with his speech would come the apotheosis of Martin Luther King, Jr.

Paradoxically, the March on Washington for Jobs and Freedom failed to produce any legislation. The Congress would not pass a civil rights bill for another year, and then only because of the heavy pressure brought by the new president, Lyndon Johnson.

200,000 JAM MALL IN MAMMOTH RALLY IN SOLEMN, ORDERLY PLEAS FOR EQUALITY

Largest Demonstration on Rights in U.S. History Urges Passage of Bill

By Robert E. Baker
Staff Reporter

More than 200,000 persons jammed the Mall here yesterday in the biggest civil rights demonstration in the Nation's history.

This was the "March on Washington for Jobs and Freedom," a one-day rally demanding a breakthrough in civil rights for Negroes.

The demonstrators came by special buses and trains in perfect order. They sang and gathered at the Lincoln Memorial to hear their leaders call on Congress to pass civil rights legislation.

In a mammoth display of fervor, they ended the day by pledging to return to their homes and keep up the battle for full equality by more demonstrations, if necessary.

A. Philip Randolph, director of the March and head of the Brotherhood of Sleeping Car Porters, drew great applause in his remarks at the Memorial when he said this was only the beginning of demonstrations here to gain equality for all.

The ten leaders, representing top Negro civil rights organizations, organized labor and religious denominations, visited Capitol Hill in the morning.

Top House and Senate leaders congratulated the marchers on their courteous behavior but were chary about saying that the demonstration would help the passage of pending civil rights legislation. House Speaker John W. [Mc]Cormack (D.Mass.) did go so far as to say that the impact of the orderly demonstration would help the bill.

After the demonstration, the leaders called on President Kennedy and Vice President Lyndon B. Johnson at the White House.

President's Statement

After the White House meeting, President Kennedy issued a statement in which he said that such demonstrations for equality are not new nor difficult to understand.

"What is different today is the intensified and widespread public awareness of the need to move forward in achieving these objectives—objectives which are older than the nation," the statement said. It concluded:

"The cause of 20 million Negroes has been advanced by the program conducted so appropriately before the Nation's shrine to the Great Emancipator, but even more significant is the contribution to all mankind."

The estimate of the size of the crowd was made by Police Chief Robert V. Murray. But no definitive estimate could be made of the number of white participants which numbered several thousands.

A hand count of 1038 persons in [a] panoramic photograph of the Washington Monument area, where the participants gathered before marching to the Lincoln Memorial, showed 718 Negroes and 320 whites—a Negro percentage of 69.1. A similar check of the order around the Lincoln Memorial yielded an almost identical percentage.

Because the people were rallying around an issue that raises emotions, the city had made unprecedented security arrangements, greater than for presidential inaugurations and for visits of heads of State.

But the crowd, which police said was the biggest within memory, was one of the most orderly. They were spirited but serious. . . .

1720 Persons Stricken

It was a perfect day for the rally, sunny with a high of 83 degrees. Even so, the emotion and packed conditions took their toll. By late afternoon, some 1720 persons had been treated at the first aid stations and 56 had been taken to hospitals, most of them heat victims.

The day started early. At dawn, while many of the marchers were en route to the demonstration, a 100-block area of Washington had been sealed off for the day.

George Lincoln Rockwell, head of the American Nazi Party, and 74 followers showed up at the Washington Monument grounds despite repeated police requests that he refrain from any counter-demonstration. . . .

Filled by 10:30

By 10:30 a.m., the Washington Monument grounds was filled with tens of thousands of demonstrators. There was a forest of placards.

Some had long messages: "We march together, Catholics, Jews, Protestants, for dignity and brotherhood of all men under God now."

Others were short: "Free in '63."

Near the base of the Monument, a group of 200 young NAACP members from Wilmington, N.C., were clapping and singing Negro protest songs. A legless Negro veteran pushed himself along the Monument walkway and told people he was 74 years old.

On the other side of the Monument, a group from Cambridge, Md., scene of civil rights demonstrations, sang "We Shall Overcome." Nearby, a peppery group of Negro children from Prince Edward County, Va., which closed its public schools rather than desegregate them, were also chanting and clapping.

Far down at the platform bordering Constitution Ave., singer Lena Horne was introduced and shouted only one word into the microphone: "Freedom!" . . .

The March from the Washington Monument to the Lincoln Memorial started at 11:30, with a sizable portion of the crowd upsetting program plans by getting in front of the ten March leaders. Some observers saw this as symbolic of the Negro movement for civil rights today: That some of the Negroes are in front of their leaders. . . .

In her story covering the speeches, Susanna McBee hinted this rally was more than an event, more than a one-day news story.

RESTRAINED MILITANCY MARKS RALLY SPEECHES

By Susanna McBee
Staff Reporter

America's top civil rights leaders, in tones of high emotionalism and fervent prayer, stood in the shadow of the Great Emancipator yesterday and told the Nation that until the Negro is free, no one will be free.

The theme of the giant rally emerged as one of restrained militancy—win "Freedom Now" but with love and non-violence and without bitterness. However, the theme emerged intact only after the speakers kept young John Lewis of the Student Non-violent Coordinating Committee from sounding a bitter, discordant note and compelled him to alter his previously prepared speech.

Only the Beginning

The temper was one of determination—this mass March on Washington for Jobs and Freedom was only the beginning, they were told again and again.

The call was one asking for passage of a strengthened civil rights package—"Pass the bill! Pass the bill!" cried the crowd as 150 members of Congress appeared on the steps of the Memorial to hear their pleas.

The hope was one for brotherhood—"I have a dream," the Rev. Dr. Martin Luther King Jr. cried again and again as he forecast a nation living up to its creed that all men are created equal.

Lewis's prepared speech, however, said, "We cannot support the Administration's civil rights bill, for it is too little, and too late."

Cites "Conspiracy"

After noting that the Justice Department brought charges of interfering with justice against nine leaders and members of the Albany, Ga., civil rights movement, Lewis in his prepared speech called the action a "conspiracy" between the Federal Government and local politicians.

In the speech he actually delivered he omitted the conspiracy charge.

In his prepared speech he accused an unnamed Administration spokesman of trying to kill a proposal to guarantee a "fair" Federal judge in voting cases. He also said President Kennedy "consistently" appointed "racist judges."

But in the revised speech he omitted these charges.

Backed Rights Bill

In the prepared text he threatened to march through the South "the way Sherman did" and proposed a "scorched earth policy" to "burn Jim Crow to the ground." He also left out these sentences in his actual talk.

Significantly, in his delivery, Lewis, a 25-year old Fisk University graduate student, did support the Kennedy civil rights bill.

He stressed, though, that it should be amended to protect Negroes against police brutality, to further insure Negro voting rights and to increase economic opportunities for Negroes.

His toned-down speech still was more militant than the rest. It was changed as a result of objections raised Tuesday night by the Most Rev. Patrick A. O'Boyle, Archbishop of Washington, who saw an advance copy of the speech.

The Catholic Archbishop, it was learned, relayed his objections to A. Philip Randolph, founder of the March, and said he would not give the invocation as scheduled unless the Lewis speech was changed.

Mrs. Murphy Rapped

In the other speeches, Mrs. Murphy, the symbolic rooming house owner who cites her property rights in order to bar Negroes, was soundly denounced.

Randolph said, "We must destroy the notion that Mrs. Murphy's property rights include the right to humiliate me because of the color of my skin."

And Roy Wilkins of the NAACP added that with a far-reaching public accommodations law, Mrs. Murphy "might get a Negro traveler in her tourist home, but then she might get a white procurer or a white embezzler."

The speech of CORE [Congress of Racial Equality] Director James Farmer, which was read by CORE Chairman Floyd McKissick because Farmer is in a Louisiana jail for a civil rights demonstration, was cheered loudly for the passage, "We will not slow down. We will not stop our militant, peaceful demonstrations."

Biggest Applause

But the loudest and most consistent applause came for Dr. King, whom Randolph introduced as the "moral leader of the Nation."

"I have a dream," Dr. King said, that in Georgia the sons of former slaves and the sons of former slave owners "will sit down at the table of brotherhood."

Then, with the crowd cheering wildly, the march deputy director, Bayard Rustin, read the marchers' civil rights demands, which they ratified with shouts of "Yes." Randolph read a pledge to continue the civil rights fight back home, which the crowd acknowledged with a loud "I do pledge."

Then, the throng, which Singer Marian Anderson had called a "salt and pepper crowd," began singing "We Shall Overcome." Many of the people, lining the Reflecting Pool in a magnificent picture postcard setting, held hands and swayed back and forth as they sang. Then they dispersed and it was all over.

1963

The visit by the charismatic, young President of the United States and his beautiful wife was intended to smooth a rift in the Texas Democratic Party. United Press International's White House correspondent Merriman Smith had already filed a routine story that morning about a routine trip.

But routine events sometimes became something else. This is the evolving story, paragraph by paragraph, as Smith reported it to UPI's Dallas bureau first from the mobile telephone in the press pool car, then from a pay phone at Parkland Memorial Hospital. Smith continued to grab people he knew as they walked past his telephone booth, pumping them for information. Improvising until help arrived, Smith filed details as the Dallas bureau wrote and rewrote the story through the early afternoon. Smith's reportage of the death of a President would win the Pulitzer Prize that year.

The wire service codes are easy to understand. "UPI" is, of course, the source. "A" refers to UPI's main news wire. The number of each story or partial story follows. "N" indicates this is for night or afternoon use by clients. "DA" is the originating bureau, Dallas. The last line of each file begins with the initials of the teletype operator. That is followed immediately by the time of transmission, beginning with UPI's A7N DA moving at 12:34 P.M. Central Standard Time.

UPI A7N DA

PRECEDE KENNEDY

DALLAS, NOV. 22 (UPI)—THREE SHOTS WERE FIRED AT PRESIDENT KENNEDY'S MOTORCADE TODAY IN DOWNTOWN DALLAS.

JT1234PCS. .

UPI A8N DA

URGENT

1ST ADD SHOTS, DALLAS (A7N) XXX DOWNTOWN DALLAS.
NO CASUALTIES WERE REPORTED.

THE INCIDENT OCCURRED NEAR THE COUNTY SHERIFF'S OFFICE ON MAIN STREET, JUST EAST OF AN UNDERPASS LEADING TOWARD THE TRADE MART WHERE THE PRESIDENT WAS TO MA

FLASH

FLASH

KENNEDY SERIOUSLY WOUNDED
PERHAPS SERIOUSLY
PERHAPS FATALLY BY ASSASSINS BULLET.

JT1239PCS

UPI A9N

BULLETIN
1ST LEAD SHOOTING
DALLAS, NOV. 22 (UPI)—PRESIDENT KENNEDY AND GOV. JOHN
B. CONNALLY OF TEXAS WERE CUT DOWN BY AN ASSASSIN'S
BULLETS AS THEY TOURED DOWNTOWN DALLAS IN AN OPEN
AUTOMOBILE TODAY.

MOREJT1241PCS

UPI A10N DA

1ST ADD 1ST LEAD SHOOTING DALLAS (9N DALLAS) XX TODAY.

THE PRESIDENT, HIS LIMP BODY CRADLED IN THE ARMS OF
HIS WIFE, WAS RUSHED TO PARKLAND HOSPITAL. THE GOVER-
NOR ALSO WAS TAKEN TO PARKLAND.

CLINT HILL, A SECRET SERVICE AGENT ASSIGNED TO MRS.
KENNEDY, SAID "HE'S DEAD," AS THE PRESIDENT WAS LIFTED
FROM THE REAR OF A WHITE HOUSE TOURING CAR, THE FA-
MOUS "BUBBLETOP" FROM WASHINGTON. HE WAS RUSHED TO
AN EMERGENCY ROOM IN THE HOSPITAL.

OTHER WHITE HOUSE OFFICIALS WERE IN DOUBT AS THE
CORRIDORS OF THE HOSPITAL ERUPTED IN PANDEMONIUM.

THE INCIDENT OCCURRED JUST EAST OF THE TRIPLE UNDER-
PASS FACING A PARK IN DOWNTOWN DALLAS.

REPORTERS ABOUT FIVE CAR LENGTHS BEHIND THE CHIEF
EXECUTIVE HEAREO
MORE 144PES

UPI A11N DA

2ND ADD 1ST LEAD SHOOTING (9N DALLAS) XXX DALLAS.

REPORTERS ABOUT FIVE CAR LENGTHS BEHIND THE CHIEF
EXECUTIVE HEARD WHAT SOUNDED LIKE THREE BURSTS OF
GUNFIRE.

SECRET SERVICE AGENTS IN A FOLLOW-UP CAR QUICKLY UN-
LIMBERED THEIR AUTOMATIC RIFLES.

THE BUBBLE TOP OF THE PRESIDENT'S CAR WAS DOWN.

THEY DREW THEIR PISTOLS, BUT THE DAMAGE WAS DONE.

THE PRESIDENT WAS SLUMPED OVER IN THE BACKSEAT OF

THE CAR FACE DOWN. CONNALLY LAY ON THE FLOOR OF THE REAR SEAT.

IT WAS IMPOSSIBLE TO TELL AT M
MORE 145PES

UPI A12N DA

IT WAS IMPOSSIBLE TO TELL AT ONCE WHERE KENNEDY WAS HIT, BUT BULLET WOUNDS IN CONNALLY'S CHEST WERE PLAINLY VISIBLE, INDICATING THE GUNFIRE MIGHT POSSIBLY HAVE COME FROM AN AUTOMATIC WEAPON.

THERE WERE THREE LOUD BURSTS.

DALLAS MOTORCYCLE OFFICERS ESCORTING THE PRESIDENT QUICKLY LEAPED FROM THEIR BIKES AND RACED UP A GRASSY HILL.

UV MORE 146PES

UPI A13N

AT THE TOP OF THE HILL, A MAN AND WOMAN APPEARED HUDDLED ON THE GROUND.

IN THE TURMOIL, IT WAS IMPOSSIBLE TO DETERMINE AT ONCE WHETHER THE SECRET SERVICE AND DALLAS POLICE RE-TURNED THE GUNFIRE THAT STRUCK DOWN KENNEDY AND CONNALLY.

IT WAS ALSO DIFFICULT TO DETERMINE IMMEDIATELY WHETHER THE FIRST LADY AND MRS. CONNALLY WERE IN-JURED.

BMMORE 148PES

UPI A14N DA

BOTH WOMEN WERE IN THE CAR.

BOTH WOMEN WERE CROUCHED DOWN OVER THE INERT FORMS OF THEIR HUSBANDS AS THE BIG CAR RACED TOWARD THE HOSPITAL.

MRS. KENNEDY WAS ON HER KNEES ON THE FLOOR OF THE REAR SEAT WITH HER HEAD TOWARD THE PRESIDENT.

JT 1249PCS

UPI A15N DA

VICE PRESIDENT LYNDON B. JOHNSON WAS IN A CAR BEHIND THE PRESIDENT'S.

THERE WAS NO IMMEDIATE SIGN THAT HE WAS HURT. IN FACT, THERE WAS NO EVIDENCE AT ALL AT WHAT MIGHT HAVE HAP-PENED TO JOHNSON SINCE ONLY THE PRESIDENT'S CAR AND ITS SECRET SERVICE FOLLOW-UP CAR WENT TO THE HOSPITAL.

JT1250PCS

UPI A16N DA

A SCREAMING MOTORCYCLE ESCORT LED THE CARS THERE.

THE PRESIDENT HAD LANDED ONLY A SHORT TIME BEFORE AT DALLAS LOVE FIELD AND WAS DRIVING TO THE TRADE MART TO DELIVER A LUNCHEON SPEECH SPONSORED BY THREE DALLAS, ORGANIZATIONS. THE LARGEST TURNOUT OF THE CURRENT TEXAS TOUR WAS ON THE STREETS TO GREET KENNEDY.

JT1251PCS

UPI A17N DA

AN ESTIMATED 250,000 PEOPLE LINED THE STREETS.

AT 12:50 P.M. CENTRAL STANDARD TIME, ACTING WHITE [HOUSE] SECRETARY MALCOLM KILDUFF WAS ASKED WHETHER THE PRESIDENT WAS DEAD.

"I HAVE NO WORD NOW," KILDUFF REPLIED.

JT1252PCS

UPI A18N DA

A FEW MINUTES LATER, REAR ADM. GEORGE BURKLEY, USN, THE WHITE HOUSE PHYSICIAN, RUSHED INTO THE HOSPITAL. HE HEADED FOR THE EMERGENCY ROOM WHERE THE PRESIDENT AND CONNALLY WERE TAKEN.

JT1253PCS

UPI A19N DA

THE MOTORCADE WAS SO STRUNG OUT AS THE RESULT OF THE SPEEDY SECRET SERVICE DEPARTURE FROM THE SCENE OF THE SHOOTING THAT MEMBERS OF THE KENNEDY STAFF WERE FROM 15 MINUTES TO A HALF HOUR BEHIND IN REACHING THE HOSPITAL.

IT WAS IMPOSSIBLE UNDER THE TENSION AT THE HOSPITAL TO ASSEMBLE A CLEARCUT STORY OF THE INCIDENT BECAUSE THE BURST OF GUNFIRE TOOK ONLY SECONDS.

JT1255PCS

UPI A2ON DA

SOME OF THE SECRET SERVICE AGENTS THOUGHT THE GUNFIRE WAS FROM AN AUTOMATIC WEAPON FIRED TO THE RIGHT REAR OF THE CHIEF EXECUTIVE'S CAR, PROBABLY FROM THE GRASSY KNOLL TO WHICH MOTORCYCLE POLICEMEN DIRECTED THEIR ATTENTION AS THEY RACED UP THE SLOPE.

JT1256PCS

UPI A21N DA
UPI WHITE HOUSE REPORTER MERRIMAN SMITH WAS IN À RA-
DIO-TELEPHONE "POOL" CAR ABOUT EIGHT CAR LENGTHS BE-
HIND THE PRESIDENT.
JT1257PCS

UPI A22N DA
HE AND THREE OTHER COLLEAGUES ALONG WITH KILDUFF
RACED TO THE HOSPITAL BEHIND THE PRESIDENT'S CAR AND
ARRIVED AT THE EMERGENCY ENTRANCE BEFORE LITTERS WERE
BROUGHT UP TO REMOVE THE PRESIDENT AND THE GOVERNOR
FROM THEIR CAR.
JT1258PCS

UPI A23N DA
EDITORS:
THE KENNEDY STORY, DALLAS, MAY BE SIGNED BY
MERRIMAN SMITH
UPI WHITE HOUSE REPORTER
JT12258PCS

UPI A24N DA
WHEN THE PRESIDENT WAS TAKEN INTO THE EMERGENCY
ROOM, A CALL WAS SENT OUT IMMEDIATELY FOR SOME OF THE
TOP SURGICAL SPECIALISTS IN DALLAS.
A CALL ALSO WAS SENT FOR A ROMAN CATHOLIC PRIEST.
JT1259PCS

UPI A25N DA
CONGRESSMAN JIM WRIGHT OF FORT WORTH SAID BOTH
KENNEDY AND CONNALLY WERE SERIOUSLY WOUNDED BUT
ALIVE.
JT1259PCS

UPI A26ND DA
BLOOD WAS SPATTERED OVER THE LIMOUSINE, WHICH HAD
BEEN FLOWN IN SPECIALLY TO CARRY THE PRESIDENT IN A
WELCOMING PARADE. THE DRIVER WAS SECRET SERVICE MAN
BILL GREER.
JT102PCS

UPI A27N DA
A SECOND PRIEST WAS ESCORTED IN A FEW MOMENTS LATER.
AT THE HEIGHT OF THE EMERGENCY ROOM DRAMA, A WEEP-
ING NEGRO WOMAN BEARING A SMALL BLOODY CHILD RUSHED

INTO THE HOSPITAL, WHERE A NURSE AND AN INTERN WENT
QUICKLY TO HER SIDE.
JT103PCS

UPI A28N DA
MRS. KENNEDY APPARENTLY WAS SAFE. MRS. CONNALLY
ALSO WAS SAFE, IT APPEARED. BOTH WOMEN WERE STUNNED.
KENNEDY, ACCORDING TO A MEMBER OF HIS STAFF, WAS
STILL ALIVE AT 12:55 P.M. CST.
JT105PCS

UPI A29N DA
BOTH WOMEN DISAPPEARED INTO THE EMERGENCY SECTION
OF PARKLAND HOSPITAL, TO WAIT NEWS OF THEIR HUSBANDS.
OUTSIDE THE EMERGENCY ROOM IN A BUFF-WALLED HALL-
WAY, ANXIOUS MEMBERS OF THE WHITE HOUSE STAFF GATH-
ERED, INCLUDING MAJ. GEN. CHESTER V. CLIFTON, MILITARY
AIDE TO THE PRESIDENT, AND BRIG. GEN. GODFREY MCHUGH,
AIR FORCE AIDE.
JT108PCS

UPI A30N DA
MRS. EVELYN LINCOLN, KENNEDY'S SECRETARY, PAMELA
TANURE, PRESS SECRETARY TO MRS. KENNEDY, AND OTHER
MEMBERS OF THE STAFF WERE SHOWN TO A SPECIAL WAITING
ROOM NOT FAR FROM THE EMERGENCY ROOM AREA.
JT109PCS

UPI A31N DA
MRS. LINCOLN BROKE INTO TEARS AT ONE POINT, BUT MAN-
AGED TO PULL HERSELF TOGETHER AND RESUME WHAT AP-
PEARED TO BE OFFICIAL CHORES.
MRS. JOHNSON, FLANKED BY TWO SECRET SERVICE AGENTS,
ARRIVED AT THE HOSPITAL SHORTLY AFTER.
JT111PCS

UPI A32N DA
SHE WALKED IN AT 1:10 P.M. AND WENT IMMEDIATELY TO
THE EMERGENCY WARD.
JT111PCS

UPI A33N DA
ALSO STANDING BY THE DOOR OF THE EMERGENCY SECTION
WAS MRS. MARY GALLAGHER, PERSONAL SECRETARY TO THE
FIRST LADY.
JT112PCS

UPI A34N DA

ALTHOUGH DALLAS IS REGARDED AS A CENTER OF STRONG
POLITICAL OPPOSITION TO KENNEDY, THE HEAVY STREET
CROWDS BETWEEN THE LOVE FIELD AIRPORT AND THE SCENE
OF THE SHOOTING WAS OVERWHELMINGLY FRIENDLY. THERE
WERE NUMEROUS "WELCOME KENNEDY" SIGNS, BUT A FEW
WERE ANTI-KENNEDY.
JT113PCS

UPI A35N DA

ONE MAN PERCHED ON THE FOOT OF HIS CAR HAD HELD OUT
TOWARD THE PRESIDENT A SIGN SAYING THAT BECAUSE OF
KENNEDY'S "SOCIALISTIC BELIEFS, I HOLD YOU IN COMPLETE
CONTEMPT."
JT114PCS

UPI A36N DA

A WOMAN A FEW BLOCKS LATER HELD UP A SIGN SAYING
"CAN THE KLAN."
JT115PCS

UPI A37N DA

ON OCT. 24, ADLAI STEVENSON, U.S. AMBASSADOR TO THE
UNITED NATIONS, WAS SPAT UPON AND WHACKED BY A PICKET
SIGN AFTER A SPEECH IN DALLAS.
JT116PCS

UPI A38N DA

AT 1:12 P.M. A SPECIAL CARTON OF BLOOD, APPARENTLY FOR
TRANSFUSION PURPOSES, WAS RUSHED INTO THE EMERGENCY
WARD BY TWO DALLAS POLICE OFFICERS.
JT116PCS

UPI A39N DA

THE PRESIDENT AND HIS WIFE HAD BEEN IN SPARKLING SPIR-
ITS THIS MORNING WHEN THEY LEFT FORT WORTH FOR THEIR
TWO-HOUR VISIT TO DALLAS.
JT117PCS

UPI A40N DA

THE PRESIDENT SPOKE AT A BREAKFAST GIVEN BY THE FORT
WORTH CHAMBER OF COMMERCE AND HIS WIFE, CLAD IN A PINK
WOOL SUIT WITH BLUE SATIN COLLAR AND A MATCHING PILL-
BOX HAT, MADE A STUNNING ENTRANCE.
JT117PCS

UPI A42N DA

THE LAST SHOOTING INCIDENT INVOLVING A PRESIDENT OC-
CURRED IN 1950 WHEN PRESIDENT HARRY S. TRUMAN WAS IN
OFFICE AND WAS LIVING IN BLAIR HOUSE IN WASHINGTON. THE
WHITE HOUSE WAS BEING RENOVATED AT THE TIME.
    JT119PCS

UPI A43N DA

TWO PUERTO RICAN NATIONALISTS TRIED TO GUN THEIR WAY
INTO BLAIR HOUSE AND ASSASSINATE TRUMAN, WHO WAS
TAKING A NAP AT THE TIME ON THE SECOND FLOOR. ONE WHITE
HOUSE POLICE OFFICER WAS KILLED AND ANOTHER SERIOUSLY
WOUNDED.

ONE OF THE ASSASSINS WAS KILLED IN A BLAZE OF GUNFIRE
ON PENNSYLVANIA AVENUE.
    JT120PCS

UPI A44N DA

BILL STINSON, AN ASSISTANT TO GOV. CONNALLY, SAID HE
TALKED TO THE GOVERNOR IN THE HOSPITAL OPERATING ROOM.
HE SAID THE GOVERNOR WAS SHOT JUST BELOW THE SHOUL-
DER BLADE IN THE BACK.
    JT121PCS

UPI A45N DA

STINSON SAID HE ASKED CONNALLY HOW IT HAPPENED AND
HE SAID: "I DON'T KNOW. I GUESS FROM THE BACK. THEY GOT
THE PRESIDENT, TOO."
    JT121PCS

UPI A46N DA

STINSON SAID HE ASKED CONNALLY IF THERE WAS ANY-
THING HE COULD DO AND CONNALLY REPLIED, "JUST TAKE
CARE OF NELLIE (HIS WIFE) FOR ME."
    JT122PCS

UPI A47N DA

A FATHER HUBER, OF HOLY TRINITY CHURCH IN DALLAS, AD-
MINISTERED THE LAST SACRAMENT OF THE CHURCH TO THE
PRESIDENT.
    JT123PCS

UPI A48N DA

SHERIFF'S OFFICERS TOOK A YOUNG MAN INTO CUSTODY AT
THE SCENE AND QUESTIONED HIM BEHIND CLOSED DOORS.
    JT124PCS

UPI A49N DA

THE SACRAMENT WAS ADMINISTERED SHORTLY BEFORE 1 P.M.

ANOTHER PRIEST, WHO DECLINED TO GIVE HIS NAME, SAID THE CHIEF EXECUTIVE STILL WAS ALIVE AT THE TIME.

JT124PCS

UPI A50N DA

THE VICE PRESIDENT'S WIFE, AFTER A QUICK CHECK OF CONDITIONS IN THE EMERGENCY SECTION, SAID HER HUSBAND WAS UNHARMED.

JT125PCS

UPI A51N DA

THE VICE PRESIDENT WAS SOMEWHERE IN THE HOSPITAL, BUT IT WAS IMPOSSIBLE TO DETERMINE HIS PRECISE WHEREABOUTS AT ONCE.

HE WAS REPORTED BADLY SHAKEN BY THE SHOOTING. DOCTORS WERE TRYING TO KEEP HIM AS QUIET AS POSSIBLE.

JT126PCS

UPI A52N DA

HE WAS UNDER HEAVY SECRET SERVICE AND POLICE PROTECTION.

THROUGHOUT THE TEXAS TRIP, WHEN KENNEDY AND JOHNSON HAD BEEN IN THE SAME MOTORCADE, AS AN OBVIOUS SECURITY MEASURE, THEY HAVE RIDDEN IN SEPARATE CARS. THE JOHNSON CAR HAS ALWAYS BEEN SOME DISTANCE FROM THE KENNEDY CAR, SOMETIMES BY AS MUCH AS 60 YARDS.

JT126PCS

UPI A53N DA

SEN. RALPH YARBOROUGH, D-TEX., IN A NEARBY CAR, SAID HE SAW THE PRESIDENT'S LIPS MOVING "AT A NORMAL RATE OF SPEED" WHILE HE WAS BEING RUSHED TO THE HOSPITAL.

JT128PCS

UPI A54N DA

MALCOLM KILDUFF, AN ASSISTANT PRESS SECRETARY, SAID HE "CANNOT SAY" WHETHER THE PRESIDENT IS ALIVE AND "CANNOT SAY WHERE HE WAS HIT. THERE ARE TOO MANY STORIES."

JT129PCS

UPI A55N DA

PERHAPS IT WAS THIS GAP IN THE MOTORCADE THAT SAVED JOHNSON FROM BEING A TARGET TODAY.

THE PRIEST WHO ACCOMPANIED FATHER HUBER DID NOT GO INTO THE EMERGENCY ROOM HIMSELF. HE SAID HE UNDERSTOOD THE PRESIDENT'S CONDITION WAS "CRITICAL." BUT HE SAID HE WAS STILL ALIVE AT 12:55 P.M.
JT130PCS

UPI A56N DA
AS THE PRESIDENT FOUGHT FOR LIFE, SPECIALISTS ARRIVED AT THE HOSPITAL, ONE, A DR. WILSON, IDENTIFIED HIMSELF AS A NEUROSURGEON.
JT131PCS

UPO A57N DA
TELEVISION NEWSMAN MAL COUCH SAID HE LOOKED UP JUST AFTER THE SHOT WAS FIRED AND SAW A RIFLE BEING WITHDRAWN FROM A 5TH OR 6TH FLOOR WINDOW OF A NEARBY BUILDING (THE TEXAS BOOK DEPOSITORY).
JT132PCS

UPI A58N DA
"A POLICEMAN FELL TO THE GROUND AND PULLED HIS PISTOL AND YELLED, 'GET DOWN.' "
JT132PCS

UPI A59N DA
"A NEGRO MAN ACROSS THE STREET PICKED UP HIS LITTLE GIRL AND RAN. THIS WAS THE MAN THE POLICE FIRST CHASED. A WOMAN NEARBY FAINTED AS POLICE AT FIRST THOUGHT SHE, TOO, HAD BEEN SHOT."
JT133PCS

UPI A60N DA
FATHER OSCAR HUBER OF HOLY TRINITY CHURCH SAID HE ADMINISTERED THE LAST RITES TO THE PRESIDENT.
JT134PCS

UPI A61N DA
DR. WILSON SAID HE WAS FROM RICE UNIVERSITY. HE ARRIVED AT THE HOSPITAL ABOUT 1:30 P.M.
"THEY HAVE SENT OUT A CALL FOR ALL NEUROSURGEONS," HE SAID.
JT134PCS

UPI A62N DA
CHARLES BREHM, 38, WAS 15 FEET AWAY WHEN THE PRESIDENT WAS SHOT.

"HE WAS WAVING AND THE FIRST SHOT HIT HIM AND THAT AWFUL LOOK CROSSED HIS FACE," B

FLASH
   PRESIDENT KENNEDY DEAD
   JT135PCS

UPI A63N DA
   BULLETIN
   2ND LEAD ASSASSINATION (PREVIOUS SHOOTING A9N)
   BY MERRIMAN SMITH
                    UPI WHITE HOUSE REPORTER
DALLAS, NOV. 22 (UPI)—PRESIDENT KENNEDY WAS ASSASSI-
NATED TODAY IN A BURST OF GUNFIRE IN DOWNTOWN DAL-
LAS. TEXAS GOV. JOHN CONNALLY WAS SHOT DOWN WITH HIM.
   MORE JT138PCS

1964

It was either a great send-up or nothing less than the perfect promotion scheme. Four mop-haired musicians, their behavior as tongue-in-cheek, as outlandish as their trigged out Edwardian clothes, landed in New York to appear on television's "The Ed Sullivan Show," and kick off their first American tour.

The press responded—with literary snickers and smirks, or, at least, good humor. After all, how could you take any of this seriously, especially when these "Beatles" themselves did not? Who could know the musical and social revolutions that these long-haired Liverpudlians heralded?

John Hughes, himself a British citizen, had a bit of fun on the front page of the august *Christian Science Monitor* of Tuesday, February 11, 1964, at the expense of British-American relations. (The British attempt to capture the Suez Canal, the stationing of the American Skybolt missile, and the maneuvering between Barry Goldwater, Richard Nixon, and Nelson Rockefeller for the Republican presidential nomination all figured in Hughes's story.)

BEATLES TEST TIES—YEAH!

by John Hughes
Assistant Overseas Editor of The Christian Science Monitor

The Beatles have crossed the Atlantic. And frankly, one wonders whether Anglo-American relations can survive the strain.

Britons and Americans may have had their differences over Suez and Skybolt. There was even quite a to-do over the Boston Tea Party. But for

After being sacked by an onrushing Steeler, New York Giants' quarterback Y. A. Tittle kneels dazed on the turf at Pittsburgh's Forbes Field, September 20, 1964. Copyright by AP/Wide World Photos

sheer British ruthlessness, nothing can compare with the dispatch to the United States of four screaming, strumming, young Liverpudlians with golliwog haircuts known as the Beatles.

For years, patriotic Americans have sought to solve the problem of rock 'n' roll singers by exporting them. They've been sent to Britain and Germany and some even as far away as Australia. The campaign was not entirely successful. Some eventually came back. But while they were away there was relief.

Barber Allies Appalled

Now Britain has flung back the Beatles—a group which this British writer can assert has a capacity for musical bedlam that far outstrips any American invention. It is difficult to see how the State Department can regard this as anything but "An Unfriendly Act." This may be the end of a beautiful Anglo-American friendship.

Of course, it is only fair to report that American reaction is not unanimous. Several million young Americans apparently think the Beatles are great. They made one Beatle record the current best-seller even before the Beatles set foot here.

Three thousand screaming teen-agers met the Beatles at New York's Kennedy Airport Friday, and one airport official said: "I see it, but I don't believe it."

Parts of the country are swept by Beatlemania. On sale are Beatle sweatshirts, T-shirts, boots, and pillows. And Beatle wigs. So many of these are being sold that some people want to start a "Society for the Prevention of Cruelty to the American Barber."

Spotlight Stolen

Sunday night the nation got its first television exposure to the Beatles when they appeared on the "Ed Sullivan Show." The CBS network reported it received more than 50,000 applications for the 1,500 seats available in the studio, where American teen-agers squealed in ecstasy throughout the performance. And as this writer said to his wife: "I see it, but I don't believe it."

All this has had a melancholy effect on the American political scene. The Beatles have been hogging all the publicity.

Almost nobody heard Senator Goldwater this weekend calling Fidel Castro names. Nobody noticed whether Richard Nixon was standing in a draft. And if they'd lowered the voting age overnight, the Beatles, and not Rocky, would have been elected.

As for President Johnson, as soon as he heard the Beatles were coming, he took off for Texas and a weekend on his ranch.

Another consequence of the Beatles' American visit is that it has transformed the popular American image of Britain. It's no good the British Travel Office putting out that stuff about Olde Worlde Charm and 400 years of Shakespeare any more. We know now that every beefeater's foot is tapping to "Yeah, yeah, yeah," and that behind every pair of English chintz curtains the Beatles are on the telly.

1964

The story is self-explanatory. Responding to a reported attack on American naval vessels cruising off the coast of North Vietnam, President Lyndon Baines Johnson ordered aircraft from two carriers to retaliate. Even as he addressed the American people on television on August 4, 1964, 64 carrier planes were attacking oil storage facilities just north of the partition line between North and South Vietnam. Without a declaration of war, the United States had directly entered the war in Vietnam.

Further, the President had in his hands a long-ready resolution he intended to ask of Congress authorizing him to take "all necessary measures [to] repel any armed attack" on United States forces in Southeast Asia. The resolution, adopted in the Senate by a vote of 88–2, also approved in advance "all necessary steps, including the use of armed force" to meet request for assistance from South Vietnam. It was a blank authorization for further escalation of American commitment to the Government of South Vietnam.

There was only one trouble, and it illumes one of the great difficulties of the press. The Government was, if not lying, then bending the truth to its own purposes. There had been an attack two days before on an American destroyer; carrier planes had sunk two of the three attacking torpedo boats. But the second attack—the attack about which the President was speaking—never took place. A confused sonarman, bad weather, nerves, all combined to lead the U.S.S. *Maddox* to report falsely it was under attack. Even though the commander retracted his report of being under fire, President Johnson pressed ahead with his retaliation, and escalation.

Though the nation would not realize it

for some time, the United States was effectively at war. Dependent upon the government for information, first the press—including one of the finest report-ers on the staff of the *New York Times* of August 5, 1964. most authoritative newspaper—then the public were deceived.

U.S. PLANES ATTACK NORTH VIETNAM BASES; PRESIDENT ORDERS 'LIMITED' RETALIATION AFTER COMMUNISTS' PT BOATS RENEW RAIDS

Forces Enlarged

Stevenson to Appeal for Action by U.N. on 'Open Aggression'

By Tom Wicker

WASHINGTON, Aug. 4—President Johnson has ordered retaliatory action against gunboats and "certain supporting facilities in North Vietnam" after renewed attacks against American destroyers in the Gulf of Tonkin.

In a television address tonight, Mr. Johnson said air attacks on the North Vietnamese ships and facilities were taking place as he spoke, shortly after 11:30 p.m.

State Department sources said the attacks were being carried out with conventional weapons on a number of shore bases in North Vietnam, with the objective of destroying them and the 30 to 40 gunboats they served.

The aim, they explained, was to destroy North Vietnam's gunboat capability. They said more air strikes might come later if needed. Carrier-based aircraft were used in tonight's strike.

2 Boats Believed Sunk

Administration officials also announced that substantial additional units, primarily air and sea forces, were being sent to Southeast Asia.

This "positive reply," as the President called it, followed a naval battle in which a number of North Vietnamese PT boats attacked two United States destroyers with torpedoes. Two of the boats were believed to have been sunk. The United States forces suffered no damage and no loss of lives.

Mr. Johnson termed the North Vietnamese attacks "open aggression on the high seas."

Washington's response is "limited and fitting," the President said, and his Administration seeks no general extension of the guerrilla war in South Vietnam.

Goldwater Approves

"We Americans know" he said, "although others appear to forget, the risks of spreading conflict."

Mr. Johnson said Secretary of State Dean Rusk had been instructed to make this American attitude clear to all nations. He added that Adlai E. Stevenson, chief United States delegate, would raise the matter immediately in the United Nations Security Council. [The Council was expected to meet at 10:30 A.M. Wednesday.]

The President said he had informed his Republican Presidential rival, Senator Barry Goldwater, of his action and had received his endorsement.

Congressional leaders of both parties, the President went on, have assured him of speedy and overwhelming passage of a resolution "making clear that our Government is united in its determination to take all necessary measures in support of freedom and defense of peace in Southeast Asia." . . .

Mr. Johnson said the retaliatory action he had ordered had been taken against "vessels and facilities used in these hostile operations."

Thus, despite Mr. Johnson's assurances that the United States sought no "wider war," it was plain that the sitation [sic] in South Vietnam and surrounding area had reached new gravity.

In South Vietnam, American forces have been advising and training the South Vietnamese Army in its resistance against Communist guerrillas.

American naval vessels have been patrolling the Gulf of Tonkin, both as a show of force and to offer naval support for situations that might develop in Southeast Asia.

The first North Vietnamese attack came Sunday when torpedo boats attacked the destroyer Maddox. They were driven off.

The new attacks came in spite of orders Mr. Johnson had given that United States naval forces destroy any attackers. . . .

1965

The civil rights movement was a series of grinding, bitter struggles in a number of southern counties. No place resisted any harder than Selma, Alabama, where a sheriff enforced his rule with electric cattle prods and billy clubs. When the Reverend Martin Luther King, Jr. led a protest march around the county courthouse on February 1, 1965, law enforcement officers responded by arresting 770 people. Then a thousand students were arrested in nearby Marion. To focus national attention on segregation in Selma, Reverend King proposed a peaceful 50-mile march from that city to the state capital, Montgomery. But peaceful the march was not to be. Sheriff James Clark blocked the marchers with clubs and tear gas; a white civil rights activist, the Reverend James Reeb, was beaten to death by unidentified men.

King secured a federal court order authorizing the march on March 17, and three days later President Lyndon Johnson ordered 4,000 troops to enforce the court order and to guard the marchers. On March 20, 3,200 stalwarts began the hike, their numbers, and press attention, growing each day. Yet another civil rights worker, Detroit housewife Viola Liuzzo, would die, murdered by members of the Ku Klux Klan, but on March 25, 1965, the federal court and the laws of the United States affirmed, they reached the birthplace of the Confederacy. The local paper, *The Montgomery Advertiser*, cov- ered the arrival of the march gingerly on March 26, 1965.

25,000 CONVERGE ON STATE CAPITOL, END 5-DAY PROTEST TREK FROM SELMA

By TOM MACKIN

A five-day civil rights march from Selma ended at the State Capitol Thursday when an estimated 25,000 Negro and white demonstrators converged to protest discrimination in Alabama.

A 20-member committee designated by Dr. Martin Luther King, leader of the march, was unsuccessful in attempts to present a list of grievances to Gov. George Wallace late Thursday afternoon but indicated it will ask the governor for the appointment at an undisclosed future date.

A message from Wallace issued while the marchers were listening to numerous addresses from figures high in the "movement," said Wallace would receive a petition from any group of citizens of the State of Alabama, not to exceed 20, at any time after this demonstration and march had dispersed.

The committee, headed by Joseph Lowery of Birmingham, vice president of King's Southern Christian Leadership Conference (SCLC), was turned away from the Capitol at 5:20 p.m. by Highway Patrol Maj. Walter L. Allen Jr.

They regrouped and returned and were admitted to the Capitol building. The governor's executive secretary, Cecil Jackson, met the committee and informed them the Capitol was closed for the night.

Jackson told them it would be "appropriate" if they could seek an appointment for a future date.

The speeches delivered in front of the Capitol were the climax of the march which, in its final phase, drew participants from all over the United States, from Canada and from Europe. Dr. King was the final speaker.

"Our feet are tired, but our souls are rested," King told the throng. "We are on the move now and we are not about to turn around. We are on the move now, and no wave of racism can stop us."

"Segregation is on its deathbed," King said. "The only thing that is not certain is how costly will the segregationalists and Wallace make the funeral."

He said the segregationist doctrine of "Jim Crow" was a creature of the Southern aristocracy, devised to head off the Populist Movement of the late 19th Century which was uniting poor whites and Negroes against the "Bourbon interests."

"Alabama has tried to nurture and defend evil," King said, "but evil is choking to death in Alabama's dusty streets. We are moving toward the land of freedom.

"Editorial writers and others across Alabama have asked how long it will be before civil rights workers, outsiders, invading clergymen and others leave and let Alabama return to normalcy," King said.

"I have a message to leave with Alabama—we do not intend to let the state return to 'normalcy.' We will have a new Alabama. The only normalcy that is worthwhile is the normalcy that recognizes the decency of every man, the normalcy of brotherhood, true peace and justice," he said.

King had predicted 30,000 marchers would be on hand for the march. Spokesmen of the federalized Alabama National Guard and the regular Army, assigned by President Johnson to protect the march, and city police had figured on 10,000. That figure was upped to 15,000 about an hour before the march left the City of St. Jude, and additional demonstrators joined in as the parade wound through the Negro section of West Montgomery.

The Rev. Ralph Abernathy, treasurer of SCLC, said his "official" counters numbered the crowd at 50,000 when it reached the Capitol.

The official estimate by Asst. Police Chief D.H. Lackey however, was 25,000.

Dr. Ralph Bunche, U.S. undersecretary of state for the United Nations, challenged the "outsider" designation applied to him and other marchers from outside Alabama.

"I am here because I belong here," Bunche said. "My conscience and my mind tell me this is where I must be. No American can ever be an 'outsider' anywhere in this nation." . . .

The petition unanimously ratified by the marchers for presentation to Gov. Wallace protested alleged police brutality, voter registration discrimination, denial of adequate education and opportunities to earn sufficient income, and "the psychotic climate of this state (which) produced the men who savagely attacked and killed the Rev. James Reeb in Selma."

It called for an end to the poll tax on state elections, opening of voter registration offices "at times which are convenient to working people—such as nights and Saturdays," the encouragement of county officials "in the democratic process," the appointment of Negroes to boards and agencies of the state in policy making positions, an end to police brutality and an end of the "climate of violence and hatred" in Alabama.

1967

Little about the first gridiron contest between the champions of the American and the National Football conferences suggested it would become the single most popular sporting event in the United States. The promoters might call it the "Super Bowl," but the public was hardly overwhelmed; indeed, about one-third of the seats in the Los Angeles Memorial Coliseum were unsold at kickoff. Not until a decade after *Los Angeles Times* sports editor Paul Zimmerman wrote his story for the Monday, January 16, 1967, edition did the Super

Bowl actually become "super." It would go on to become a deliberately stage-managed affair, propelled by wink- of-the-eye hype that turned a sporting event into a huge contest for television ratings.

PACKERS PROVE NFL'S BRAND BEST, 35-10

By Paul Zimmerman
Times Sports Editor

Like a stern parent chastizing a mischievous child, the Green Bay Packers soundly thrashed the upstart Kansas City Chiefs, 35–10, Sunday in Memorial Coliseum in the first Super Bowl game.

The outstanding master of the whip-lash on a gorgeous summer-like afternoon was Bryan Bartlett Starr, who had been playing in the NFL four years before the junior circuit was born.

The great Packer quarterback completed key third-down passes with abandon, to the amazement of 63,036 shirt-sleeved spectators, connecting on 16 of 23 throws for 250 yards and two touchdowns as he riddled the Kansas City defense. He was named player of the game.

Kansas City, the recalcitrant child, bitterly opposed the lessons its elders sought to teach in the first half, and left the field before the spectacular half-time show trailing only 14–10.

That was the end of the line for coach Hank Stram's Chiefs, who never got deep into Green Bay territory during the second half as the always rugged Packer defense turned back to the AFL champions at the 40-yard line twice—the deepest penetrations.

"We mangled 'em a little bit," was the understatement of Packer fullback Jim Taylor after the game.

Victorious coach Vince Lombardi kindly called the vanquished a good team but honesty got the better of him when he added:

"The Chiefs are not as good as the Cowboys (who lost to Green Bay in the NFL playoff game). They are not as good as the good NFL teams."

The first championship game provided the answer to the question the football world had been asking ever since the AFL was formed.

Naturally, Stram didn't quite agree.

"After the first half I thought we could win. But once the Packers got their third touchdown we had to play to catch up," he pointed out.

That was when the Packer defense really asserted itself, early in the third quarter, blitzing quarterback Len Dawson and turning back the Kansas City ground game.

Stram felt Willie Wood's interception and 50-yard return with a Dawson pass turned the tide in Green Bay's favor. It set the stage for Elijah Pitts' 5-yard touchdown run.

"The interception changed the personality of the game," Stram said.

There was no question about that, but the Packers were going to accomplish the change sooner or later, anyway.

By a quirk of fate, 34-year old Mac McGee emerged from the contest as

Starr's key receiver. The 11-year veteran end, who had caught only four passes for 90 yards all season, plus another in the playoff game, replaced the injured Boyd Dowler and snagged seven for 138 yards and a pair of touchdowns.

He made some fantastic catches as Starr riddled the Kansas City deep defense behind a wall of superb protection.

It was McGee who started the scoring with as spectacular a catch as anyone would want to see.

He made a one-handed reception over his right shoulder at the 25-yard line, spun away from defender Willie Mitchell, and rambled into the end zone—a 37-yard touchdown play.

That came midway through the first quarter on the end of an 80-yard drive in six plays with Starr completing tosses to Marv Fleming, Pitts and Carroll Dale along the way.

Mike Mercer's attempted 40-yard field goal that sailed wide closed out the initial quarter. But the Chiefs bounced right back in the second to score when they put together a 66-yard push in half a dozen plays. . . .

That was the closes the Chiefs came all afternoon.

The Packers got it right back. . . .

Starr was quickly back at his old tricks. Passes to Dale for 25 and McGee for 37 took the ball to the 18, midway through the final quarter. A short one to Dale went to the 12 and from there Taylor and Pitts punched it over, with Elijah going the final yard.

Beathard Gets In

Their wasn't much after that. The pro-Chief crowd got a chance to roar a little when Pete Beathard, former USC star, took over for the much harassed Dawson, but the Trojan could do nothing.

With reserves in from both benches and time running out, that was the ball game.

Where Kansas City had left the field at halftime leading in most statistical departments, the Chiefs took the long walk to the dressing room at the end badly mauled.

In addition to the score, they trailed Green Bay 17–21 in first downs, 239–358 in total yards, and 167–228 in passes. Only in the punting game did they hold the edge. . . .

If Sunday's game is any indication, the AFL has a long journey ahead before it catches up with the old establishment, the NFL.

1968

The attacks during the Vietnamese New Year's holiday of Tet came as a stunning blow. In virtually every province of war-ravaged South Vietnam, Viet Cong guerrillas struck, seemingly at will. To millions of Americans, the coordinated assaults and the raid on the United States Embassy in Saigon, the symbol of the American presence in that country, were a shock. If the Embassy was not safe, after more than five years of fighting and tens of thousands dead, after repeated promises of a "light at the end of the tunnel," what was the United States accomplishing in Vietnam?

United States soldiers and marines, with Republic of South Vietnam troops would recover from the surprise attack, handing the enemy a stinging battlefield defeat in coming weeks. But that costly tactical victory would come too late. The North Vietnamese and their Viet Cong allies had scored a major propaganda victory;

from Tet on, American public opinion in support of the war began to ebb.

The Des Moines Register is published in the largest city of a conservative state, Iowa, in the heartland of the United States. Its coverage of the opening day of the Tet offensive on Wednesday morning, January 31, 1968, is representative of the news stories that would eventually move a large number of Americans to protest continued American involvement in the Vietnam war.

Critics later scored this coverage as inaccurate (first reports said the suicide squad broke into the embassy building proper) and implicitly negative. Stories such as these, they asserted, cost the United States victory in Vietnam by alienating the American people.

SUICIDE SQUAD CAPTURES U. S. EMBASSY IN SAIGON

Yank Troops Retake It In 6-Hour Fight

Several Americans, 19 Reds Killed

Leased Wire to the Register

SAIGON, SOUTH VIETNAM (WEDNESDAY)—A Viet Cong suicide squad seized and held parts of the U.S. embassy for six hours today before being wiped out by American troops counterattacking on the ground and from helicopters landing on the roof of the building.

The guerrillas reportedly captured five floors of the six-story building in fierce fighting before dawn.

All the Viet Cong commandos were killed in the embassy battle, climaxing a series of guerrilla assaults and shellings in Saigon that brought warfare deep into the South Vietnamese capital.

First reports told of 19 Communist bodies counted on the embassy grounds. At least five U.S. military policemen and Marines were reported killed and eight were wounded.

After the battle, Gen. William Westmoreland, commander of U.S. forces in Vietnam, arrived at the scene and said none of the enemy had penetrated the building proper.

Reports Conflict

This report conflicted with the versions of U.S. military police and South Vietnamese who said the Viet Cong had taken control of several floors of the building.

Dozens of persons on the scene said that Vietnamese had entered the building.

Westmoreland told newsmen, "Obviously the enemy had been planning the assault on the American embassy for some time. They chose the Tet [lunar new year] period for this assault. The enemy obviously assumed the security would be lessened during this period.

"There was superficial damage to the embassy.

"In summary," Westmoreland said, "the enemy's well-laid plans went afoul. There was some superficial damage. All of the enemy who entered the compound were killed: Nineteen bodies have been found on the premises."

The Viet Cong wore gray uniforms with cartridge belts. Some had red arm bands.

The embassy building was badly shot up and the Great Seal of the United States was dislodged from the wall above the entrance by bullets.

The building is enclosed in a shell of reinforced concrete and the architect said it is designed to withstand riot, siege, and mortar attacks. The compound was surrounded by an eight-foot high concrete wall.

At last report, fighting was still going on near Tan Son Nhut airport in the suburbs of the city, military officials said.

Simultaneously with the strikes against Saigon, the Reds for the second straight day exploded guerrilla assaults on cities up and down the country in an unprecedented offensive against urban centers.

Battle Imminent

The Red attacks appeared aimed at diverting allied strength from the northern provinces where a major battle seemed imminent.

Among key buildings attacked in Saigon were Independence Palace, where [South Vietnamese] President Nguyen Van Thieu has offices.

Also shelled or attacked with small-arms fire were the building of the Vietnamese joint chiefs of staff, Vietnamese navy headquarters, three U.S. officers' billets, the Philippine Embassy and the vicinity of Tan Son Nhut Air base.

The embassy and its grounds were declare secured at 9:05 a.m.

Three U.S. Marines raised the Stars and Stripes in front of the scarred embassy at 11:45 a.m., nearly five hours later than normal.

Fighting that had ripped through the area near the heart of the city for hours died out, but other pockets of Viet Cong still were holding out in other areas.

Blast Hole in Wall

The Red commandos blew a hole in a wall to enter the embassy grounds about 3 a.m.

The gleaming white $2.6-million building was opened only last November to replace one wrecked by a previous guerrilla attack.

The bullet-proof building was designed for maximum security against a Viet Cong attack.

In Washington, a State department spokesman said the embassy staff was "regarded as safe." . . .

Although the situation in Saigon was confused, the capital appeared in no danger of a full scale invasion.

There was no immediate information on the number of rounds that had hit the capital, or on casualties.

Military ambulances, red lights blazing and sirens blaring, sped through the streets. They apparently were en route to military hospitals with persons who had been wounded in the attacks.

Other Viet Cong wrecked the gates of Independence Palace with grenades. Another unit tried to infiltrate near the government radio station and the prime minister's office.

Some of the guerrillas carried bazookas. Street fighting raged at several points.

Among other cities shelled was Can Tho, the biggest city in the Mekong Delta, about 80 miles south of Saigon. It was the first attack this week in the sprawling, canal-laced delta below Saigon.

Air Base Shelled

Also attacked either by shell or ground assault were the air base at Bien Hoa, 20 miles northwest of Saigon; U.S. Army installations at Long Binh, 15 miles north of the capital; the airstrip at Ban Me Thuot, a province capital in the central highlands; Kontum, another provincial capital in the highlands and Da Nang, second largest city in South Vietnam.

Unlike the Tuesday attacks on key cities that caught allied defenders by surprise, the attack on Saigon was not entirely unexpected.

The U.S. Command had circulated a notice several days ago warning: "There may be Viet Cong activities aimed at various U.S. and Vietnamese headquarters and government billets during the Tet holidays. Viet Cong artillery units and Viet Cong suicide cadres are infiltrating into the capital area." . . .

The attacks Tuesday and Wednesday broke open the Communists' announcement of a truce to cover the lunar new year.

The Communists' widespread assaults led the U.S. Command to express belief they were probably intended "to draw attention from the major area of threat," just below the demilitarized zone, where an offensive by three or four Hanoi divisions, perhaps 35,000 to 40,000 men, is feared.

The attacks on eight cities and five airfields farther south, the biggest such coordinated Red drive of the war, raised a possibility the allies may abandon their practice of proclaiming cease-fires for future holidays.

Sees "Violation"

President Thieu, in calling off the allied stand-down ahead of time, accused the Communist of "a premeditated and callous violation" of their own truce.

General Westmoreland said the Viet Cong's truce proclamation "is clearly revealed as a hoax and a fraud." . . .

Still incomplete reports showed 18 U.S. servicemen had been killed and 41 wounded in incidents across the country. About 70 South Vietnamese government troops were reported killed. It appeared about 300 of the enemy died in the attacks. . . .

1968

Three assassinations shaped America during the turbulent 1960s and beyond. The deaths of John Fitzgerald Kennedy and his brother Robert deprived the nation of men of promise. Worse still, the slaying of Martin Luther King, stole the nation's very conscience; the civil rights movement has yet to recover.

The death of Dr. King was a national tragedy. But for John Means of *The Memphis Commercial Appeal*, this was a big local story to be put together from the information gathered by reporters all over town for the edition of Friday morning, April 5, 1968.

DR. KING IS SLAIN BY SNIPER

Intensive Manhunt
Is Quickly Mounted

President Johnson's Plane Is Reported
En Route To Memphis;
State Guard Alerted

By JOHN MEANS

A sniper shot and killed Dr. Martin Luther King last night as he stood on the balcony of a downtown hotel.

The most intensive manhunt in the city's history was touched off minutes after the shooting.

Violence broke out in Memphis, Nashville, Birmingham, Miami, Raleigh, Washington, New York and other cities as news of the assassination swept the nation.

National leaders, including President Lyndon Johnson, and aides close to the slain 39-year-old Nobel Peace Prize winner, urged the nation to stand calm and avoid violence.

The entire nation was tense.

It was learned early this morning that Air Force One—the President's plane—had left Washington. It may be en route to Memphis.

There was no confirmation that the President was aboard.

The slaying of Dr. King brought Tennessee National Guardsmen back into Memphis. The entire 11,000 men in the state guard were on alert early today.

Memphis was placed under a tight, 24-hour curfew by Mayor Henry Loeb.

All schools will be closed today. Parents were urged to keep their children at home.

A rifle bullet slammed into Dr. King's jaw and neck at 6:01 p.m.

He died in the emergency room at St. Joseph Hospital at 7:05 p.m.

King, the foremost American civil rights leader, was alone on the second-floor walk of the Lorraine Hotel at 406 Mulberry when the bullet struck.

A young white man is believed to have fired the fatal shot from a nearby building.

Looters and vandals roamed the streets despite the imposition of a tight curfew. Shooting was widespread. National Guardsmen were rushed to the North Memphis area of Springdale and Howell after bullets blasted the windshield out of a police car near there.

Police—estimated at more than 150—descended on the south Memphis hotel, sealed off the area, and almost immediately broadcast a description of the sniper: a white male, 30 to 32 years old, 5 feet, 10 inches tall, about 165 pounds, dark to sandy hair, medium build, ruddy complexion as if he worked outside, wearing a black suit and white shirt.

Frank R. Ahlgren, editor of the Commercial Appeal, announced that the newspaper will pay a $25,000 reward for information leading to the arrest and conviction of Dr. King's assassin.

Dr. King returned to Memphis Wednesday morning to map plans for another downtown march—scheduled for next Monday—in support of the city's striking sanitation workers. He had spent part of the day yesterday awaiting reports from his attorneys, who were in Federal Judge Bailey Brown's courtroom asking that a temporary restraining order against the proposed march be lifted.

The injunction was obtained by the city after Dr. King's first march broke out in violence downtown, brought the National Guard to the city in strength and seriously damaged the Negro leader's reputation for nonviolence, and it was this picture he was planning to dispel with the march next Monday.

Mayor Loeb declared today, tomorrow and Sunday as days of mourning, and said all flags in the city would be lowered "with appropriate observances."

All ministers, priests and rabbis in the Memphis area have been asked to meet at 10 a.m. today at St. Mary's Cathedral (Episcopal).

Frank Holloman, fire and police director, who took personal command of the murder investigation minutes after the shooting, said "every resource" of city, county, state and federal law enforcement agencies "is committed and dedicated to identifying and apprehending the person or persons responsible."

Mayor Loeb ordered a tight curfew, much stricter than the one imposed after last week's rioting. "All movement is restricted except for health or emergency reasons," the order said.

A few minutes after the shooting, police reported a high-speed chase in which a blue Pontiac was being pursued by a white Mustang out the Austin Peay Highway. Shots were reported fired between the two cars. A white Mustang, seen near the scene of the slaying, was still being sought by police early today.

Officials of Dr. King's Southern Christian Leadership Conference, some of whom were standing near him on the narrow balcony of the hotel when he was shot, continued to urge his nonviolent teachings. His chief lieutenant, Dr. Ralph Abernathy, went to the Mason Temple last night to address a gathering of Dr. King's followers.

"Let us live for what he died for," Dr. Abernathy told the mourning group. "If we respect his leadership, if we appreciate the service that he rendered, then we must do all in our power to carry forth the work that is incomplete.

"If a riot or violence would erupt in Memphis tonight, Dr. King in Heaven would not be pleased."

A few had other ideas. "He died for us and we're going to die for him," a young man shouted.

Early Friday morning, Mr. Holloman said police believe the murder weapon was a 30-caliber pump action Remington rifle equipped with a telescopic sight. Such a weapon was among those stolen Tuesday night from Dowdle Sporting Goods Co. at 2896 Walnut Grove Road.

"The distance over which the bullet traveled before it struck Dr. King was 205 feet, 3 inches, at a down angle," Mr. Holloman said.

He also detailed "other evidence . . . that may help us identify the assassin. The shot was fired from the window of a common bathroom at the end of the hall on the east side of the building at 420 South Main. The suspect checked into the boarding house between 3 and 3:30 p.m. His room was close to the bathroom. The suspect was a white man, 6 feet tall, about 165–175 pounds, between 26 and 32 years of age.

"We do know he bought a pair of binoculars this (Thursday) afternoon in Memphis . . . The man was seen to run from the 420 South Main building and discard the gun and a suitcase at 424 South Main. He simply faded. Nobody saw him get in the car, but a white Mustang was seen to flee the area." . . .

"The bullet knocked him off his feet," said the Rev. Jesse Jackson, executive staff member of SCLC. "It sounded like a stick of dynamite, or a big firecracker." . . .

Moments before, Dr. King was talking to Ben Branch, singer and bandleader who was to appear with him at the Mason Temple rally.

"I want you to sing for me tonight," the world's youngest Nobel Peace Prize winner said. "I want you to do that song for me, 'Precious Lord.' Sing it real pretty." . . .

Two weeks after King's death, the Federal Bureau of Investigation announced it was seeking a sometime drifter and escaped convict, James Earl Ray, for questioning. Ray was arrested on June 8, 1968, at London Airport and extradited to the United States where he pled guilty on March 11, 1969. Sentenced to a prison term of 99 years, the 40-year-old Ray twice tried to escape. He remained at large for three days on his second attempt, but was recaptured on June 13, 1977.

1969

It remains an awesome feat, unmatched still, a brave first step into the cosmos. Less than ten years after President Kennedy committed this nation to the quest, three men not only hurtled into orbit about the moon, but two walked on its pristine surface, and returned once more safely to earth. If the achievement had a somewhat ignoble motive—to beat the Soviet Union to the moon for purposes of international prestige—it was nonetheless majestic, and thought-provoking.

For Skip Johnson of *The Orlando Sentinel,* however epochal it might be, this was a local story. Many of the men and women who helped to send the astronauts thundering aloft from Cape Kennedy days before were residents of Orlando. Johnson's story of July 21, 1969, celebrated their triumph also.

AMERICAN ON THE MOON

Earth's Finest Hour

By Skip Johnson
Sentinel Staff

SPACE CENTER, Houston—Man walked on the moon's face for two hours Sunday, completing his exploration shortly after 1 a.m. today.

Neil Armstrong walked on its cracky, desolate surface for two hours and 10 minutes, shattering forever the bonds which have held man to his own soil since time began.

Edwin Aldrin spent an hour and 51 minutes walking on the moon with Armstrong. He first touched lunar soil 20 minutes behind Armstrong.

Armstrong, the commander of Apollo 11, crept out of the grotesque lunar module—nicknamed Eagle—about 10:40 p.m. and slowly began descending the nine steps along its spindly front leg.

And, as people throughout the world watched on television, he became history's footprint on the moon.

"That's one small step for man, one giant leap for mankind," he said as he placed his left foot on the powdery lunar soil.

The time was 10:56 p.m. The place, the Sea of Tranquility, 62 miles east of the Sabine Crater.

Both astronauts described the moon as strangely beautiful.

"It has a stark beauty all its own. It's different, like a high desert, but it is very pretty out here," Armstrong said.

When Aldrin joined him, his first words were simply, "It's a beautiful view."

Armstrong described the moon surface as "fine and powdery."

"I can pick it up loosely with my toe. It adheres in fine layers like powdered charcoal to the soles and sides of my boots.

"I sink in about an eighth of an inch, and I can see my footprints."

Armstrong said he had no difficulty in moving around.

"It's easier than the simulators in one-sixth G [gravity] we performed on the ground."

Millions, perhaps a billion, people throughout the world watched Armstrong, and later Aldrin, as they moved like gorillas on the lunar surface.

Before Aldrin joined Armstrong on the surface, Armstrong began collecting samples, putting some in his suit and some in rock boxes to hoist them into the Eagle.

"It's a very hard surface with a powder top," Armstrong said. . . .

Aldrin joined Armstrong on the moon's surface 20 minutes later.

"Isn't it something," Armstrong said. "Isn't this fun?"

Aldrin described the rocks as "rather slippery, very powdery."

"Neil, didn't I say we'd find a purple rock here?" Aldrin said.

"Did you find the purple rock?" Armstrong asked.

"Yep. Small and sparkly."

Aldrin packed the purple rock into the box and said he would leave it up to earth's scientists to decide what it was.

A few seconds after Aldrin climbed down to the lunar surface, the two of them installed a plaque on the bottom of the descent stage of the LEM [Lunar Excursion Module], which will remain on the lunar surface.

The nine-by-seven inch stainless steel plaque is signed by President Richard M. Nixon and the three Apollo 11 crewmen—Armstrong, Aldrin, and Michael Collins.

The plaque bears images of the earth's two hemispheres and this inscription which was read aloud by Armstrong.

"Here, men from the planet earth first set foot on the moon July, 1969 A.D. We came in peace for all mankind."

The astronauts also unfurled an American flag which they planted in the moon's soil.

And they also left a one and one-half inch silicon disc bearing messages of goodwill from heads of state of many nations.

And then while they undertook experiments and picked up more rocks, the astronauts had a ball bouncing around in the one-sixth gravity.

Before leaving the moon's surface, they left the patches of three American astronauts killed in a space capsule fire on earth and medals belonging to the wives of two Russian cosmonauts who were killed when their parachutes malfunctioned as they returned to earth from a space mission.

The touchdown came at 4:17 Sunday afternoon 62 miles east of Sabine Crater, and about four miles downrange from the scheduled landing site.

A few minutes after landing, Armstrong and Aldrin removed their helmets and gloves and, for the first time, had a chance to look at the moon's surface from only a few feet away.

Aldrin described the view:

"It looks like a collection of just about every variety of shape, angularity, granularity, and every variety of rock you could find.

"The color is going to vary pretty much on how you look at it relative to the sun. There doesn't appear to be much of a general color at all.

"However, the rocks and boulders of which there are quite a few in the near area look as though they are going to have some interesting color to them."

Fifteen minutes later, after the astronauts exchanged technical data with mission control in Houston, Aldrin continued:

"We landed on a relatively level plain cratered with a large number of craters of the five to 50-foot variety, and some reached 20 to 30-feet high. There are thousands of little one and two-foot craters in the area.

"We see some rocks out several hundred feet in front of us that are probably two feet in size and have angular edges. There is a hill in view south of us, about a half-mile to a mile away."

He also said the rocket's engine cracked open several lunar rocks as they descended. He described these rocks as being chalky gray on the outside and a darker, ashen gray on the inside.

Aldrin removed an overhead hatch and said he could see the earth.

"It's big and bright and beautiful," he said.

Aldrin also paused to make a simple request on behalf of the astronauts.

"We ask every person listening in, whoever and wherever they may be, to pause for a moment and contemplate the events of the past few hours and to give thanks in his or her own way."

As the Eagle neared the lunar surface a few minutes earlier, Armstrong had to take manual control of the flight to avoid crashing into a rocky crater located at the site scheduled for the landing.

He said the selected site turned out to be a football field sized crater with a large number of boulders and rocks. "I had to fly manually over the rock field to find a reasonably good landing area."

The landing site selected was within the margin of safety.

The rocket's engines began kicking up lunar dust at an altitude of about 40 feet. It smashed the rocks as the Eagle touched down.

"You've got a bunch of guys about to turn blue," mission control radioed. Then mission control radioed to Michael Collins, orbiting about in the command module:

"He has landed at Tranquility base. He is at Tranquility base."

"Yea, I heard the whole thing," Collins said. "It was fantastic."

"Be advised there are a lot of smiling faces in this room and all over the world," mission control told the moon astronauts.

"And don't forget one in the command module," Collins said from his vantage point 60 miles above. . . .

1969

The greatest gathering in the name of peace, love, and rock 'n' roll occurred in mid-August, 1969. More than 400,000 people, most of them young, some of them free-spirited, all of them beside themselves in the excitement of the moment, convened in a meadow in Max Yasgur's dairy farm outside the town of Woodstock, New York, beginning on Friday, August 15, 1969. Though the press was there in force, most reporters covered the three days of the Woodstock Music and Art Fair as a freak show, a hippie convention, or a criminal convocation spiced with drugs and nudity. Only a few reporters, chief among them Alfred G. Aronowitz in the August 18, 1969, *New York Post,* strove to explain Woodstock and the Aquarian generation.

BENIGN MONSTER DEVOURED MUSIC

By Alfred G. Aronowitz
New York Post Correspondent

Bethel, N.Y.—You sat on the big stage watered by the blue spotlights while the Big Pink Band plays Bob Dylan's "I Shall be Released" and you look out into the eyes of the monster.

It has been there for three days now, this monster, benign, magnificent, sometimes larger, sometimes smaller, roosting on a hillside where alfalfa once grew, drowning in mud, thirsting for water, chilled by rain, unsheltered, unfed, yet kept alive by something on stage that can't be explained except in terms of magic. Is music alone miracle enough to sate the appetites of 450,000 people?

You sit on the big stage listening to the sweet plea of innocence of a singer who tells you that every distance is not near, and on the ground 20 feet below a state trooper is chasing a bunch of kids off their perch on a heavy construction crane while a bearded acid head stands next to him stark naked.

The rain has left an early-morning chill that is warping the piano strings out of tune and there is no excuse to be walking around without any clothes on, but the state trooper ignores the acid head and instead turns his attention to getting permission for a 15-year old boy to sit on the stage. When you learn that the 15-year old boy is the state trooper's son you realize where the monster comes from. It is America's child.

Your feet are puffed with the blisters of no-other-way-to-get-there and your head tilts to one side with the weight of your eyelids and you wonder why the monster doesn't just go home. But out there on the rain-sogged hillside it lives, reminding you of its existence every now and then with a full-throated roar that also tells you how terrifying a monster can be. There are bonfires on the hillside and you can smell the marijuana smoke on the monster's breath and you wonder what dreams it sees when it looks down at the stage you're standing on. Is it music that dreams are made of?

There were two births reported at the Woodstock Music and Art Fair, called Aquarian Exposition because we are at the end of the Age of Pisces and the 2000 years of the Christian era and the promoters thought they could earn a few dollars by capitalizing on an underground which fancies itself the secret early Christians of a new religion.

Woodstock? It's an hour and a half away in light traffic, but then listen to the testimony of Artie Kornfeld, who is one of the promoters of the fair and who now feels absolved of all guilt because he stands to lose a fortune.

"From now on," he says, "when people hear the name Woodstock they won't think of the town, they'll think of our festival." Has Kornfeld found a new religion? "This weekend turned me around so much," he says, his eyes burning with the passion of some unknown fuel, "that I could never go back to what I was doing." Artie Kornfeld was a commercial record producer whose greatest credit was the Cowsills, but now he's going to spend more time with his wife and daughter.

Meet Mike Lang, host to his generation. At 24, Mike dreamed up the Woodstock Music and Art Fair, and his plans were so thorough that when you sat down for bologna and cheese snacks in the performers' pavilion, there were boxes of Wash 'n' Dry on the tables. But yesterday morning, the 800 portable toilets on the festival site were filling up.

Is it an indictable offense to underestimate your power? If the promoters didn't realize how easy it was to get so many kids in one place, then perhaps they shouldn't have tried to get any.

When you first came over the hill in a helicopter three days ago, the site was breathtaking. Only the Pope could draw a crowd like that. The monster came dressed for a picnic, but it would have worn a shirt and tie if it had to.

Wilted collars? First it rained, then the sun shone too brightly. The crowds walking on the temporary plastic water pipes caused leaks, and then the wells didn't deliver as promised. The showers and drinking fountains which had been placed so thoughtfully throughout the festival site turned out to be as useful as the tickets that had been sold to get into the place: Not at all.

The 150,000 who bought advance admissions ended up subsidizing the whole show. By the time the festival management was ready to open its gates, the monster was already inside. With close to 200,000 on the alfalfa

William K. Schroeder, 19, lies dead after being shot by Ohio National Guardsmen during an anti–Vietnam War protest at Kent State University, Ohio, May 4, 1970. Copyright by AP/ Wide World Photos

field, another 100,000 milling throughout the nearby campsites, and as many as a million waiting in long lines of traffic trying to get there. Max Yasgur's 600-acre dairy farm had become one of the most populous cities in the state. All told, an estimated 450,000 made it there. By yesterday morning Max was on the great stage greeting the monster with a peace sign.

Is the freakout scene over? More than 40 kids had to be carried away, flipping out from bad trips. One of them reportedly died in Middletown Hospital. Still another was run over by a tractor.

Most of the LSD cases were treated by members of the Hog Farm, long experienced with acid. "The cops like that," said Hugh Romney, who patrolled the festival site, as Police Chief, with his front teeth missing, carrying a staff struck through a tiny drum, wearing a 10-gallon hat, consciously doing the work of the Lord and giving lessons in gentleness.

By this morning, the monster was almost gone. Jimi Hendrix, the biggest star of the festival, had to play to the smallest crowd of the weekend. When you left by helicopter you looked down at the mud and the exhaustion and wondered which would you remember more, the monster or his footprint.

1971

The war in Vietnam had ground on, ever more costly, year after year, with no sign of either a victory or an end to American involvement. When President Richard Nixon approved a further widening of the war in January 1971, into neighboring Laos, the decision provoked a former Defense Department analyst, Daniel Ellsberg, to leak to *The New York Times* a copy of a four-year-old 7,100-page secret history of the Vietnam war. First Ellsberg and then the *Times* editors who subsequently read the 47-volume history, carefully purged it of documents that might reveal military secrets. On June 13, 1971, the *Times* began printing its series on what would be called "The Pentagon Papers."

Fearing that revelation of the convoluted history of United States involvement in Vietnam would undercut his bargaining position as he sought to negotiate an end to the fighting, President Nixon instructed the Department of Justice to seek an unprecedented court order to bar the paper from continuing to publish the series.

A federal court judge in New York granted the injunction on June 15, with the third installment on the newsstands that morning. The *Times* appealed this first-ever prior restraint, even as *The Washington Post* began *its* series based on yet another purloined copy of the Pentagon papers. The government sought to block the *Post* series as well, and the two legal cases went before the Supreme Court of the United States with a rare haste. *The New York Times* reported the high court's decision on July 1, 1971.

SUPREME COURT, 6-3, UPHOLDS NEWSPAPERS ON PUBLICATION OF THE PENTAGON REPORT; TIMES RESUMES ITS SERIES, HALTED 15 DAYS

Burger Dissents

First Amendment Rule Held to Block Most Prior Restraints

By Fred P. Graham
Special to the New York Times

Washington, June 30—The Supreme Court freed The New York Times and The Washington Post today to resume immediate publication of articles based on the secret Pentagon papers on the origins of the Vietnam war.

By a vote of 6 to 3 the Court held that any attempt by the Government to block news articles prior to publication bears "a heavy burden of presumption against its constitutionality."

In a historic test of that principle—the first effort by the Government to enjoin publication on the ground of national security—the Court declared that "the Government has not met that burden."

The brief judgment was read to a hushed courtroom by Chief Justice Warren E. Burger at 2:30 P.M. at a special session called three hours before. . . .

The case had been expected to produce a landmark ruling on the circumstances under which prior restraint could be imposed upon the press, but because no opinion by a single Justice commanded the support of a majority, only the unsigned decision will serve as precedent.

Uncertainty Over Outcome

Because it came on the 15th day after The Times had been restrained from publishing further articles in its series mined from the 7,000 pages of material—the first such restraint in the name of "national security" in the history of the United States—there was some uncertainty whether the press had scored a strong victory or whether a precedent for some degree of restraint had been set.

Alexander M. Bickel, the Yale law professor who had argued for The Times in the case, said in a telephone interview that the ruling placed the press in a "stronger position." He maintained that no Federal District Judge would henceforth temporarily restrain a newspaper on the Justice Department's complaint that "this is what they have printed and we don't like it" and that a direct threat of irreparable harm would have to be alleged.

However, the United States Solicitor General, Erwin N. Griswold, turned to another lawyer shortly after the Justices filed from the courtroom and remarked: "Maybe the newspapers will show a little restraint in the future." All nine Justices wrote opinions, in a judicial outpouring that was described by Supreme Court scholars as without precedent. They divided roughly into groups of three each.

The first group, composed of Hugo L. Black, William O. Douglas and Thurgood Marshall, took what is known as the absolutist view that the courts lack the power to suppress any press publication, no matter how grave a threat to security it might pose.

Justices Black and Douglas restated their long-held belief that the First Amendment's guarantee of a free press forbids any judicial restraint. Justice Marshall insisted that because Congress had twice considered and rejected such power for the courts, the Supreme Court would be "enacting" law if it imposed restraint.

The second group, which included William J. Brennan Jr., Potter Stewart and Byron R. White, said that the press could not be muzzled except to prevent direct, immediate and irreparable damage to the nation. They agreed that this material did not pose such a threat.

The Dissenters' Views

The third bloc, composed of the three dissenters, declared that the courts should not refuse to enforce the executive branch's conclusion that material should be kept confidential—so long as a Cabinet-level officer had decided that it should—on a matter affecting foreign relations.

They felt that the "frenzied train of events" in the cases before them had not given the courts enough time to determine those questions, so they concluded that the restraints upon publication should have been retained while both cases were sent back to the trial judges for more hearings.

The New York Times's series drawn from the secret Pentagon study was accompanied by supporting documents. Articles were published on June 13, 14 and 15 before they were halted by court order. A similar restraining order was imposed on June 19 against The Washington Post after it began to print articles based on the study.

Justice Black's opinion stated that just such publications as those were intended to be protected by the First Amendment's declaration that "Congress shall make no law . . . abridging the freedom of the press."

Paramount among the responsibilities of a free press, he said, "is the duty to prevent any part of the Government from deceiving the people and sending them off to distant lands to die of foreign fevers and foreign shot and shell.

"In my view, far from deserving condemnation for their courageous reporting, The New York Times, The Washington Post and other newspapers should be commended for serving the purpose that the Founding Fathers saw so clearly," he said. "In revealing the workings of government that led to the Vietnam war, the newspapers nobly did precisely that which the founders hoped and trusted they would do."

Justice Douglas joined the opinion by Justice Black and was joined by him in another opinion. The First Amendment's purpose, Justice Douglas argued, is to prohibit "governmental suppression of embarrassing information." He asserted that the temporary restraints in these cases "constitute a flouting of the principles of the First Amendment."

Justice Marshall's position was based primarily upon the separation-of-powers principle, assumed that under extreme circumstances the courts would act without such powers.

Justice Brennan focused on the temporary restraints, which had been issued to freeze the situation so that the material would not be made public before the courts could decide if it should be enjoined. He continued that no restraints should have been imposed because the Government alleged only in general terms that security breaches might occur.

Justices Stewart and White, who also joined each other's opinions, said that though they had read the documents they felt that publication would not be in the national interest.

But Justice Stewart, a former chairman of The Yale Daily News, insisted that "it is the duty of the executive" to protect state secrets through its own security measures and not the duty of the courts to do it by banning news articles.

He implied that if publication of the material would cause "direct, immediate, and irreparable damage to our nation or its people," he would uphold prior restraint, but because that situation was not present here, he said that the papers must be free to publish.

Justice White added that Congress had enacted criminal laws, including the espionage laws, that might apply to these papers. "The newspapers are presumably now on full notice," he said, that the Justice Department may bring prosecutions if the publications violate those laws. He added that he "would have no difficulty in sustaining convictions" under the laws, even if the breaches of security were not sufficient to justify prior restraint.

The Chief Justice and Justices Stewart and Blackman echoed this caveat in their opinions—meaning that one less than a majority had lent their weight to the warning.

Chief Justice Burger blamed The Times "in large part" for the "frenetic haste" with which the case was handled. He said The Times had studied the Pentagon archives for three or four months before beginning its series, yet it had breached "the duty of an honorable press" by not asking the Government if any security violations were involved before it began publication.

He said it found it "hardly believable" that The Times would do this, and he concluded that it would not be harmed if the case were sent back for more testimony.

Justice [Harry] Blackman, also focusing his criticism on The Times, said there had been inadequate time to determine if the publications could result in "the death of soldiers, the destruction of alliances, the greatly increased difficulty of negotiation with our enemies, the inability of our diplomats to negotiate." He concluded that if the war were prolonged and a delay in the return of United States prisoners result from publication, "then the nation's people will know where the responsibility for these sad consequences rests."

In his own dissenting opinion, Justice [John] Harlan said: "The judiciary must review the initial executive determination to the point of satisfying itself that the subject matter of the dispute does lie within the proper compass of the President's foreign policy relations power.

"The judiciary," he went on, "may properly insist that the determination that disclosure of that subject matter would irreparably impair the national security be made by the head of the executive department of State or the Secretary of Defense—after actual personal consideration.

"But in my judgment, the judiciary may not properly go beyond these two inquiries and redetermine for itself the probable impact of disclosure on the national security."

The Justice Department initially sought an injunction against The Times on June 15 from Federal District Judge Murray I. Gurfein in New York.

Judge Gurfein, who had issued the original temporary restraining order that was stayed until today, ruled that the material was basically historical matter that might be embarrassing to the Government but did not pose a threat to national security. Federal District Judge Gerhard A. Gesell of the District of Columbia came to the same conclusion in the Government's suit against The Washington Post.

The United States Court of Appeals for the Second Circuit, voting 5 to 3, ordered more secret hearings before Judge Gurfein and The Times appealed. The United States Court of Appeals for the District of Columbia upheld Judge Gesell, 7 to 2, holding that no injunction should be imposed. Today the Supreme Court affirmed the Appeals Court here and reversed the Second Circuit. . . .

1972

It would be hard to imagine a bigger political story that began in such an inauspicious manner. But a veteran police reporter's story about "a third-rate burglary," as a White House press secretary described the break-in, would become Watergate, and bring down a president of the United States.

Alfred E. Lewis wrote the initial Watergate story for *The Washington Post* of June 18, 1972. In a credit line at the end of Lewis' copy, a desk editor added, "Contributing to this story were Washington Post Staff Writers Bob Woodward, Carl Bernstein. . . ." The two young reporters would pursue the story when others dropped it, making it their own.

5 HELD IN PLOT TO BUG DEMOCRATS' OFFICE HERE

by Alfred E. Lewis
Washington Post staff writer

Five men, one of whom said he is a former employee of the Central Intelligence Agency, were arrested at 2:30 a.m. yesterday in what authorities described as an elaborate plot to bug the offices of the Democratic National Committee here.

Three of the men were native-born Cubans and another was said to have trained Cuban exiles for guerrilla activity after the 1961 Bay of Pigs invasion.

They were surprised at gunpoint by three plainclothes officers of the metropolitan police department in a sixth-floor office at the plush Watergate, 2600 Virginia Ave., NW, where the Democratic National Committee occupies the entire floor.

There was no immediate explanation as to why the five suspects would want to bug the Democratic National Committee offices or whether or not they were working for any other individuals or organizations.

A spokesman for the Democratic National Committee said records kept in those offices are "not of a sensitive variety" although there are "financial records" and other such information.

Police said two ceiling panels in the office of Dorothy V. Bush, secretary of the Democratic Party, had been removed.

Her office is adjacent to the office of Democratic National Chairman Lawrence F. O'Brien. Presumably, it would have been possible to slide a bugging device through the panels in that office to a place above the ceiling panels in O'Brien's office.

All wearing rubber surgical gloves, the five suspects were captured inside a small office within the committee's headquarters suite.

Police said the men had with them at least two sophisticated devices capable of picking up and transmitting all talk, including telephone conversations. In addition, police found lockpicks and door jimmies, almost $2,300 in cash, most of it in $100 bills with the serial numbers in sequence.

The men also had with them one walkie-talkie, a short wave receiver that could pick up police calls, 40 rolls of unexposed film, two 35 millimeter cameras and three pen-sized tear gas guns.

Near where they were captured were two open file drawers, and one national committee source conjectured that the men were preparing to photograph the contents.

In Court yesterday, one suspect said the men were "anti-Communists" and the others nodded agreement. The operation was described in court by prosecutor Earl J. Silbert as "professional" and "clandestine." One of the Cuban natives, The Washington Post learned, is now a Miami locksmith.

Many of the burglary tools found at the Democratic National Committee offices appeared to be packaged in what police said were burglary kits.

The five men were identified as:

● Edward Martin, alias James W. McCord, of New York City and perhaps the Washington metropolitan area. Martin said in court yesterday that he retired from the CIA two years ago. He said he presently is employed as a "security consultant."

● Frank Sturgis of 2515 NW 122d St., Miami. Prosecutors said that an FBI check on Sturgis showed that he had served in the Cuban Military army intelligence in 1958, recently travelled to Honduras in Central America, and presently is the agent for a Havana salvage agency. He has a home and family in Miami. Sturgis also was once charged with a gun violation in Miami, according to FBI records.

● Eugenio R. Martinez of 4044 North Meridian Ave., Miami. Prosecutors said that Martinez violated the immigration laws in 1958 by flying in a private plane to Cuba. He is a licensed real estate agent and a notary public in Florida.

● Virgilio R. Gonzales of 930 NW 23d Ave., Miami. In Miami yesterday, his wife told a Washington Post reporter that her husband works as a locksmith at the Missing Link Key Shop.

● Bernard L. Barker of 5229 NW 4th St., Miami. Douglas Caddy, one of the attorneys for the five men, told a reporter that shortly after 3 a.m. yesterday, he received a call from Barker's wife. "She said that her husband told her to call me if he hadn't called her by 3 a.m.; that it might mean he was in trouble."

All were charged with felonious burglary and with possession of implements of crime. All but Martin were ordered held in $50,000 bail. Martin, who has ties in the area, was held in $30,000 bail. . . .

The early morning arrests occurred about 40 minutes after a security guard at the Watergate noticed that a door connecting a stairwell with the hotel's basement garage had been taped so it would not lock.

The guard, 24-year-old Frank Wills, removed the tape, but when he passed by about 10 minutes later a new piece had been put on. Wills then called police. . . .

1974

What had begun with the Watergate break-in, the "third-rate burglary" discovered by security guard Frank Wills on the night of June 16, 1972, ended almost twenty-seven months later, with the resignation from office of a discredited President of the United States. By then the Nixon administration was a shambles. Vice-President Spiro Agnew, in a separate scandal, had resigned, pleading guilty to income tax evasion. Seventeen others, including three former cabinet members and three of Nixon's closest advisors in the White House, had been sentenced to prison for Watergate-related crimes.

Nixon himself had been named by a federal Grand Jury as an unindicted co-conspirator in the attempt to obstruct the investigation of the Watergate break-in. Compounding his credibility problems, he also faced three counts of impeachment by the House of Representatives and a trial in the Senate. The usually combative Nixon chose instead to resign his office.

The Washington Post, which had pursued the story largely through the dogged efforts of reporters Robert Woodward and Carl Bernstein, reported the climax on August 9, 1974.

NIXON RESIGNS

By Carroll Kilpatrick
Washington Post Staff Writer

Richard Milhous Nixon announced last night that he will resign as the 37th President of the United States at noon today.

Vice President Gerald R. Ford of Michigan will take the oath as the new President at noon to complete the remaining 2-1/2 years of Mr. Nixon's term.

After two years of bitter public debate over the Watergate scandals, President Nixon bowed to pressures from the public and leaders of his party to become the first President in American history to resign.

"By taking this action," he said in a subdued yet dramatic television address from the Oval Office. "I hope that I will have hastened the start of the process of healing which is so desperately needed in America."

Vice President Ford, who spoke a short time later in front of his Alexandria home, announced that Secretary of State Henry A. Kissinger will remain in his Cabinet.

The President-to-be praised Mr. Nixon's sacrifice for the country and called it "one of the very saddest incidents that I've ever witnessed."

Mr. Nixon said he decided he must resign when he concluded that he no longer had "a strong enough political base in the Congress" to make it possible for him to complete his term of office.

Declaring that he has never been a quitter, Mr. Nixon said that to leave office before the end of his term "is abhorrent to every instinct in my body."

But "as President, I must put the interests of America first," he said.

While the President acknowledged that some of his judgments "were wrong,'' he made no confession of the ''high crimes and misdemeanors'' with which the House Judiciary Committee charged him in its bill of impeachment.

Specifically, he did not refer to Judiciary Committee charges that in the cover-up of Watergate crimes he misused government agencies such as the FBI, the Central Intelligence Agency and the Internal Revenue Service.

After the President's address, Special Prosecutor Leon Jaworski issued a statement declaring that ''there has been no agreement or understanding of any sort between the President or his representatives and the special prosecutor relating in any way to the President's resignation.''

Jaworski said that his office ''was not asked for any such agreement or understanding and offered none.''

His office was informed yesterday afternoon of the President's decision, Jaworski said, but ''my office did not participate in any way in the President's decision to resign.''

Mr. Nixon's brief speech was delivered in firm tones and he appeared to be in complete control of his emotions. The absence of rancor contrasted sharply with the ''farewell'' he delivered in 1962 after being defeated for the governorship of California.

An hour before the speech, however, the President broke down during a meeting with old congressional friends and had to leave the room.

He had invited 20 senators and 26 representatives for a farewell meeting in the Cabinet room. Later, Sen Barry M. Goldwater (R-Ariz.), one of those present, said Mr. Nixon said to them very much what he said in his speech.

''He just told us that the country couldn't operate with a half-time President,'' Goldwater reported. ''Then he broke down and cried and he had to leave the room. Then the rest of us broke down and cried.''

In his televised resignation, after thanking his friends for their support, the President concluded by saying he was leaving office ''with this prayer: may God's grace be with you in all the days ahead.''

As for his sharpened critics, the President said, ''I leave with no bitterness toward those who have opposed me.'' He called on all Americans to ''join together . . . in helping our new President succeed.''

The President said he had thought it was his duty to preservere in office in face of the Watergate charges and to complete his term.

''In the past days, however, it has become evident to me that I no longer have a strong enough political base in the Congress to justify continuing that effort,'' Mr. Nixon said.

His family ''unanimously urged'' him to stay in office, and fight the charges against him, he said. But he came to realize that he would not have the support needed to carry out the duties of his office in difficult times.

''America needs a full-time President and a full-time Congress.'' Mr. Nixon said. The resignation came with ''a great sadness that I will not be here in this office'' to complete work on the programs started, he said.

But praising Vice President Ford, Mr. Nixon said that ''the leadership of America will be in good hands.''

President Gerald R. Ford refuses to come to the aid of a bankrupt New York City, as translated by that city's leading tabloid, the Daily News, *October 30, 1975.* Copyright by the *New York Daily News*

In his admission of error, the outgoing President said, "I deeply regret any injuries that may have been done in the course of the events that led to this decision."

He emphasized that world peace had been the overriding concern of his years in the White House.

When he first took the oath, he said, he made a "sacred commitment" to "consecrate my office and wisdom to the cause of peace among nations."

"I have done my very best in all the days since to be true to that pledge," he said, adding that he is now confident that the world is a safer place for all people. . . ."

Mr. Nixon has served 2,026 days as the 37th President of the United States. He leaves office with 2-1/2 years of his second term remaining to be carried out by the man he nominated to be Vice President last year. . . .

1978

Horror heaped upon horror. Nothing could prepare reporters for the bodies found sprawled across the rough-hewn floor of the pavilion and in the surrounding community. In that jungle clearing in Guyana, inland from the Caribbean Sea, a charismatic cult leader from San Francisco had led his flock first to murder, then to mass suicide.

Congressman Leo Ryan, accompanied by a group of newsmen, had flown from California to a small airstrip near the agricultural settlement in the jungle to investigate charges that Reverend Jim Jones was holding people against their will. Apparently at Jones' orders, members of the community opened fire on the Ryan party, killing the congressman and four others, including three newsmen. When the government of Guyana sent troops to investigate, Jones assembled members of the People's Temple and led them in a mass suicide.

San Francisco Chronicle correspondent Keith Power caught the horror on November 21, 1978, of finding the first of 909 victims of the Reverend Jim Jones' paranoia.

400 STOOD IN LINE TO DIE

Hundreds Fled
Into the Jungle

By Keith Power
Chronicle Correspondent

Georgetown,
Guyana

The death toll at Jonestown grew to 405 last night from the mass suicides and killings that began Saturday when the babies at the People's Temple settlement were lined up and given cups of purple Kool-Aid laced with cyanide.

Then the older children and adults took their turn, marching past the big soup kettle to receive their fatal doses.

It took the victims five minutes to die, one of the three survivors at the scene reported.

Most went to an altar at the end of the open-air pavilion where the Rev. Jim Jones had summoned his flock to tell them that the plan to kill not only Congressman Leo J. Ryan but also the visiting newsmen and relatives had failed.

The bodies of the dead were clustered so tightly it wasn't possible to see the ground near the altar.

Jones was one of the only three who died by gunshot. He was shot in the right temple, apparently a suicide.

Jones' wife, Marceline, and their three children were also dead.

Apparently about 400 managed to flee into the jungle, escaping a fusillade of shots fired by guards stationed outside the central area of the colony.

Earlier estimates that Jonestown had a population of 1200 were scaled down when it was discovered that there were only 800 passports in Jones' office.

The first reporters to reach the scene found the dazed survivors.

One was Grover Davis, 79, who had been able to run away and hide in the brush. Another was Hyacinth Prash, a white-haired woman who stayed in her dormitory bed because she was too ill to get up and attend the ghastly ceremonies.

The third survivor was Odell Rhodes, 36, a former teacher, who said he had been asked by the camp's doctor, Lawrence Schact, to bring him a stethoscope after Schact and the colony's nurses had completed making their cyanide brew.

Rhodes left on the errand as requested—and he didn't return.

Instead, he found a nearby refuge in the jungle, where he could view and hear the terrible scene.

It took five minutes for the convulsions that came from drinking the poison to result in death, Rhodes said—time enough for families to reunite with arms closed about one another before falling.

There was supposed to be a radioed signal as well, Rhodes said, with the words "White Knight," ordering People's Temple members in San Francisco, Los Angeles and Georgetown to kill themselves in Jones' name.

But the signal never went out.

Rhodes told reporters what the original attack plan against the Ryan mission had been:

Larry Layton, a fanatically loyal cult member, was to pose as a refugee seeking Ryan's help. And then when Ryan's charter plane was airborne, Layton was to shoot the pilot so the 18-passenger plane would crash—killing everyone in the congressman's party.

The scheme collapsed when Ryan told Layton he had to leave on a second, smaller plane brought in to take out those members who sought to leave Guyana.

Layton, now under arrest in Georgetown, got into the smaller craft and fired his pistol at two fugitives until he was subdued and his gun taken away.

Richard Dwyer, deputy chief of the United States mission in Guyana, was given the gun, and Guyanese police seized Layton.

The shots Layton fired were the signal for other gunmen on the field to fire their weapons, Rhodes told reporters in Guyana. The gunman killed Ryan and four others, but they had to return to Jonestown to report that "the mission had failed," Rhodes said.

Only one woman protested, Rhodes continued, when Jones assembled the group and announced the suicide plan would go into effect.

She was shouted down.

"Most of the people did it more or less willingly," Rhodes said.

As for those who might have some doubts, Jones offered words of comfort and promises of heaven.

"We're going to meet," he said, "in another place."

About a dozen of the dead were in Jones' house. Maria Katsaris, 24, whose brother, Anthony, was injured in the airstrip attack after making a vain effort to persuade her to come home, was found dead in Jones' bed— a bullet in her head.

Jones' wife, Marceline, and their children died of poisoning.

There were two other witnesses within earshot of the scene—attorneys Mark Lane, known for his [Kennedy] assassination conspiracy theories, and Charles Garry of San Francisco, longtime defender of Jones and his temple.

As Lane and Garry escaped into dense rain forest, they could héar Jones telling his followers over the settlement's loudspeaker that it was time for them to die.

Then came the final six words of the former San Francisco evangelist's address: "Mother, mother, mother, mother, mother, mother."

Lane said he counted 85 shots. Then there was silence.

The first outsiders to reach the carnage were Guyanese soldiers.

They had expected to find many victims of gunfire, but apparently the shots Lane heard were fired at successful escapers.

The Guyanese forces found, to no one's surprise, a store of arms and ammunition in the deserted settlement.

And there was also an unexpected discovery: a large quantity of United States currency, checks and gold apparently worth more than a million U.S. dollars.

It will be at least a day or two before a list of the dead can be prepared, Shirley Field-Ridley, Guyana's minister of information, declared at a press conference.

Most of the dead are believed to be from Northern California.

"Please be patient," the information chief pleaded.

Field-Ridley said 30 members of the People's Temple residing at a house in Georgetown have agreed to go to Jonestown, 150 miles away, to try to identify the dead.

The police kept the house at Georgetown under close guard, protecting the residents from possible attack by the guards who had overseen the suicide ceremony at Jonestown.

It was not known how many of the guards themselves escaped after the other settlers died.

As the long and dreadful task of trying to learn the names of the dead goes on, first priority will be placed on finding temple members who fled into the jungle to avoid the slaughter.

Commissioner of Police Lloyd Baker held little hope that many of the escapers could survive for long without help.

"They will die of exposure, insects or snake bite if they stay in there too long," Barker said.

By dark, police and soldiers had found only 12 survivors from among those who had fled into the bush.

Anyone who loses his bearings more than few hundred yards away from a road or clearing may end up entrapped in the dark green jungle.

The area is almost uninhabited. The only established settlements are in Port Kaituma, six miles to the east. Tiny bands of Amerindians, Guyana's indigenous inhabitants, are camped at irregular intervals.

The landscape may be familiar to movie buffs: Jonestown is 60 miles away from the beautiful but wild setting where "Lost Horizons" was filmed.

While work continued in the vast interior, planeloads of American officials—diplomatic and medical—kept arriving in Georgetown during the day to bolster the small diplomatic mission here.

The U.S. Army team trained in handling corpses is due at Jonestown today.

The soldiers, many of them veterans of similar duty in Vietnam, will pick up the bodies in helicopters and fly them to Wheeler Ridge, where the corpses will be transferred to military airplanes. . . .

1979

On March 28, 1979, at Three Mile Island near Harrisburg, Pennsylvania, there occurred what the federal Nuclear Regulatory Commission opaquely terms an "anomalous incident." Due to a succession of operator errors, a nuclear reactor at TMI vented radiation into the atmosphere and sparked fears of a thermonuclear meltdown. Federal officials maintained that only a minimal amount of radiation had escaped. Yet the situa-tion in the reactors seemed increasingly grave, perhaps even beyond control. Pennsylvania Governor Richard Thornburgh, faced with a crisis of confidence in the reports, advised pregnant women and children within a five-mile radius of the nuclear power plant to evacuate.

While the full story, or some approximation of it, would be a long time coming, *The Philadelphia Inquirer* was to earn a Pulitzer Prize for its continuous coverage of the incident at Three Mile Island, which began with this story on March 29, 1979.

POWER PLANT LEAKS RADIATION

Mishap south of capital

By Thomas Ferrick Jr.
and Susan Q. Stranahan
Inquirer Staff Writers

Radiation was released yesterday within 16-miles radius of the Three Mile Island nuclear power plant southeast of Harrisburg, after a valve broke about 4 a.m. in the cooling system of the reactor. The interior of the plant also was contaminated.

Officials at the plant, operated by Metropolitan Edison Co. of Reading, declared a general emergency about 7:45 a.m. at the site. It was the first time that a general emergency, which is one based on radiation levels, had ever been declared at a commercial nuclear reactor, according to the federal Nuclear Regulatory Commission. The leak was in the form of steam carrying radioactive iodine.

"This situation is more complex than the company first led us to believe," said Lt. Gov. William W. Scranton 3d at a news briefing in Harrisburg. "Metropolitan Edison has given you (the news media) and us (the state) conflicting information."

"There has been a release of radioactivity into the environment," Scranton said. "The magnitude of that release is still being determined, but there is no evidence yet that it has resulted in the presence of dangerous levels (of radiation).

"At this point, we believe there is still no danger to public health," he said.

The plant, on the island in the Susquehanna River, was closed shortly after the incident.

Radiation beamed through the four-foot thick walls housing the reactor throughout most of the day, according to the Nuclear Regulatory Commission.

By last night, however, the reactor had been brought to a "safe condition" as a result of emergency cooling measures, federal officials said. Low levels of radiation still emanated from auxiliary buildings at the plant where radioactive waste water from [the] bottom of the reactor was being stored temporarily, they said.

Radioactive steam was vented during the morning and early afternoon to try to relieve pressure in the reactor building, officials of the Pennsylvania Department of Environmental Resources (DER) said.

Federal officials said that intense heat, caused by the loss of circulating water, had apparently damaged the reactor core. It was not known whether part of the radioactive fuel might have melted before emergency measures to halt nuclear reaction were instituted, a spokesman for the regulatory commission said.

It may be several days before anyone can enter the reactor building.

Radiation levels of 5 to 15 millirems per hour were measured outside the plant during the day, the regulatory commission spokesman said. In the United States, the average level is 100 to 120 millirems per year from background sources. A chest X-ray emits about 30 millirems.

The highest level of radiation measured at the plant was 70 millirems at the north gate of the sprawling facility, according to Dr. Charles Gallina of the regulatory commission.

Although a cloud of radioactive steam was released into the atmosphere about 4 a.m., according to Metropolitan officials, the Nuclear Regulatory Commission, which licenses all nuclear plants, said it was not notified until about 3 hours and 45 minutes later. State officials sharply criticized Metropolitan for the long delay in reporting the leak and providing information. Company spokesmen were not available for comment on the delay.

Light winds in the area did not scatter the contamination very far, according to William Dornsife, a DER nuclear engineer.

Company officials described the radioactivity as "minimal." "There will be no adverse effect on the people there," a spokesman in Reading said.

However, that assessment was challenged by at least one organization, the Union of Concerned Scientists, which maintained that the potential had existed for a much more serious incident.

"An interruption of the cooling system is an accident of the utmost seriousness," said Daniel Ford, executive director of the union, an independent group of scientists and engineers who have studied nuclear power and challenged its safety record.

"The name of the game in reactor safety is keeping the nuclear fuel, the core, adequately cooled." Ford said in Cambridge, Mass. "If you don't keep it cool, it can overheat and melt. This can set the stage for a devastating accident."

Details of the incident remained unclear. At the plant investigators from the Nuclear Regulatory Commission and the DER were attempting last night to piece together what happened.

The problem occurred in the plant's number two generator, which was first tested a year ago yesterday. The generator was operating at near 100 percent capacity, 880 megawatts. (The plant's other nuclear generator is shut down for refueling.)

According to Dornsife of the DER, company news releases and federal officials, the following occurred:

An air valve in a water pump in the secondary (non-radioactive) circulating system malfunctioned, but the exact time is not known. The increased workload on a second valve caused it to break down. Water feeding the generator that produces steam was shut off, and the turbine which is driven by the steam, automatically shut down.

The steam generator automatically dropped to about 15 percent of its capacity. However, the reactor continued to produce heat and because there was no water circulating in the steam generator, pipes in the steam generator cracked. Water used to cool the primary (radioactive) system and water from the secondary system combined in the generator.

In the meantime, the pressurizer, which stands between the reactor and the steam generator, reacted to the intensifying heat by overflowing, spilling water onto the bottom of the reactor-containment area. The superheated water produced large volumes of steam in the containment area.

The whole chain of events is believed to have happened in a short period of time. In an effort to relieve the pressure, radioactive steam was vented— either by the company or through safety valves, it was not known which— about 4 a.m. The venting process [was] resumed by the company at 11 a.m. and continued for 2½ hours, according to DER officials.

Only a few workers were in the plant at the time of the leak. They were being tested for radiation exposure. Workers reporting for the day shift were not permitted to enter the plant. About 500 people are employed at Three Mile Island.

Loss of power from the plant had no effect on the Pennsylvania-New Jersey-Maryland power grid because of reserve capacity available in the system to offset the closing.

The plant's second generating unit began full-scale operations Dec. 30. Reports filed with the Nuclear Regulatory Commission indicate a history of problems with the unit prior to start-up and afterward. The unit was shut for about five months last year during the testing phase for various modifications, according to federal officials.

On Jan. 15, according to a report published by the commission, problems within the unit occurred, forcing another shutdown. The report indicated that a condenser malfunctioned, resulting in the rupture of the bellows around the atmospheric release valve. The unit was shut down for 15 days.

It could not be immediately determined whether the Jan. 15 incident was related to yesterday's malfunction. . . .

1982

The spread of a mysterious, fatal disease sent a chill through the homosexual community. Randy Shilts of *The San Francisco Chronicle*, who is himself gay, realized early on that the disease's impact was a story with implications well beyond that city's homosexual community. When Shilts wrote the following article for the *Chronicle* of May 13, 1982, the term AIDS, for acquired immune defi-

ciency syndrome, had not entered the | illness as GRID—gay-related immuno-
language. Scientists then referred to the | deficiency diseases.

THE STRANGE, DEADLY DISEASES
THAT STRIKE GAY MEN

By Randy Shilts

A 43-year-old San Francisco man looked at the purple spots covering his arms, face and chest and contemplated the death sentence they might foreshadow.

"Every time I see a new spot I think I'm a step closer to death," said Jerry, a former waiter. "I don't even look in the mirror any more."

Jerry is a victim of one of a series of baffling diseases hitting primarily gay men with increasing frequency across the country.

Scientists have lumped the various illnesses together under the acronym of GRID—for gay-related immuno-deficiency diseases—and public health officials have come to view them as the most startling health problem to hit the United States since the first outbreak of Legionnaire's disease in 1976.

The numbers of gay men struck by the GRID diseases passed epidemic proportions long ago, and are now frightening public health officials for a number of reasons.

• In the 11 months since the first American case of a rare skin cancer known as Kaposi's sarcoma was reported to federal authorities, the cancer and the other GRID illnesses have reportedly struck 335 Americans and almost all of them gay men, killing 136—a higher death toll than both toxic shock syndrome and Legionnaire's disease combined.

• The diseases, most of which were previously unheard of among healthy young men, offer few hopes for survival. Only 15 percent of the men diagnosed in 1979 for Kaposi's sarcoma, now colloquially known as "gay cancer," are alive now, say federal officials. Two thirds of the reported 1980 victims have died.

• The overall death rate for patients with Pneumocystis pneumonia, the "gay pneumonia," which is the deadliest GRID, now stands at 50 percent.

• Public health officials are also discovering that a laundry list of other strange diseases are striking gay men, apparently associated with a dysfunction of the patient's immune system. These "opportunistic" diseases now account for one-sixth of the GRID victims.

• Even more mysterious than the fact that diseases are attacking a group with few if any common genetic physical or racial characteristics, is the isolated geographic regions where GRID victims have been found. About half come from New York, with another quarter split almost evenly between Los Angeles and San Francisco. The remaining quarter is scattered through smaller centers of gay populations around the country.

Public health officials also worry that so far they have seen only the "tip of the iceburg'' because of the increase in frequency with which the diseases are being reported. GRID victims have been reported since January and the federal Center for Disease Control now average one new case a day.

Scientists fear the GRID problems may spread into the mainstream population before they find the solution. New figures are showing a growing number of women and bisexual or heterosexual men who have come down with one of the mysterious diseases.

In the Bay Area, GRID diseases have stricken 65 gay men and killed 19, authorities have responded quickly to the threats, establishing one of the nation's first GRID clinics at the University of California-San Francisco.

"In San Francisco, it's an epidemic beyond anything that's acceptable," says Dr. Selma Dritz, assistant director of the bureau of communicable disease control for San Francisco's Department of Public Health. "It's like nothing we've ever had."

A major comfort for GRID victims has come with the weekly meetings of a support group, sponsored by the Shanti Project, a Berkeley-based organization specializing in grief counseling with terminally ill patients.

Every Wednesday, a half-dozen GRID victims discuss the turns of their unusual illness in conversations ranging from jokes about how they sneak marijuana into hospitals to counter their chemotherapy to more somber thoughts about the five group members who have died from the baffling malaises.

For Jerry, the 45-year-old waiter, having a cancer associated with a stigmatized minority meant waiting six months before telling his religious mother for fear that she might say that that [sic] he was only experiencing what God does to the immoral.

And when one gay victim of Pneumocystis lapsed into a semi-coma, his relatives tried to strike his lover's name from the guest list and forbid him from seeing the dying man, says Geary.

Bobbi Campbell, a gay cancer victim who writes a column on the disease for a local gay paper, says he has found that many in the gay community are eager to pin the diseases on the drug use and exotic sexual practices that some medical officials have found to be associated with victims.

"There's this need to focus on these aspects of the disease—so people can put the victims at arm's length from themselves, so it doesn't hit close to home," says Campbell.

The victims' search for a cure remains the most disheartening aspect of the strange diseases.

Jerry, a KS victim, already has gone through chemotherapy, a month of expensive and scientifically unproven interferon injections and is now being treated with another drug, all with no apparent effect on the disease.

"We keep revising our treatment protocols," worries Dritz of city public health. "But nothing seems to work, so we just have to keep experimenting."

Scientists have had as much trouble isolating a cause of the outbreaks as finding a cure. Put simply, researchers attribute the GRID diseases to a massive breakdown in the victim's immune system. This stops the body's ability to arrest the development of cancer cells, or pneumonia, or any other invading organism to which most people are exposed. . . .

GRID—AIDS—has raged on, unchecked, among intravenous drug users and heterosexuals, no longer a "gay disease." By late 1989, public health officials estimated that 60,000 men, women and children had died of AIDS, and another 250,000 were infected—with no cure in sight.

1982

From the moment South African Dr. Christiaan Barnard performed the first human heart transplant in 1967, medical researchers—like alchemists of old seeking to transmute base metals into gold—had sought to create a mechanical heart, an artificial implant with which to replace a diseased organ. Dozens of researchers and institutions craved the honor and publicity of being the first. When the University of Utah Medical Center's Dr. William C. DeVries won the laurel on Thursday, December 2, 1982, *The Salt Lake City Tribune* of Friday, December 3, 1982, covered the first artificial heart implant as the local story it was.

UTAH ARTIFICIAL HEART PUMPING LIFE THROUGH SEATTLE DENTIST

By JoAnn Jacobsen-Wells
Tribune Medical Editor

A courageous 61-year old Seattle man, deteriorating rapidly from a failing heart muscle, received a new lease on life Thursday morning when he became the first human recipient of the University of Utah's Jarvik-7 artificial heart.

The tedious, complicated seven-and-a half hour surgery, done at the university's Medical Center in Salt Lake City, made medical history. It is the first permanent artificial heart to be implanted in a human being. Without the implant, the man would have surely died soon.

The success of the long-awaited surgery was heralded throughout the halls of the Medical Center once the word got out that Dr. Barney B. Clark, a retired dentist, was being kept alive by a plastic, fist-size mechanical device.

But few people were more thrilled than Dr. William C. DeVries, who described the surgery as "almost a spiritual experience."

"The entire team worked so nicely together," he said in a press conference Thursday afternoon. "It was a very touching experience to see him

(Dr. Clark) this morning nod his head, move his hands, recognize his wife and indicate he wasn't in pain.

"It was a deep and touching experience for everyone on the team—something we have worked hard for a very long time. And we are all very proud."

Unable to Talk

Dr. DeVries, the only surgeon authorized by the Federal Food and Drug Administration to put an artificial heart in a human, said his first recipient is hooked up to a respirator. Because there is a large tube in Dr. Clark's mouth, he is unable to talk, but he is able to shake his head "yes" and "no," and he tries to mouth words.

"I definitely think the surgery was a success because last night (Monday) I had no doubt but that he would be dead. And he isn't," Dr. DeVries said, emphasizing that, "It's not over yet, it's just the beginning."

The surgeon, who gained instant stardom at the university (so much so that three of the physician jackets bearing his name were "borrowed" Thursday morning), said the prognosis for his patient is "very good!"

Late Thursday, hospital spokesmen said his condition was still critical, but improving. Dr. Clark was awake and alert and complaining of a sore throat and thirstiness—routine complaints for heart surgery patients.

The recipient, a retired dentist who was born in Provo, entered the Medical Center at 5:30 p.m. Monday. It was then he signed a highly "negative, discouraging," but extremely informative 11-page consent form. As FDA protocol demands, he signed it again 24 hours later.

Abnormal Heart Rhythms

Dr. Clark's surgery was originally scheduled for 8 a.m. Thursday but DeVries decided to move the operation up because the patient began developing abnormal heart rhythms.

Dr. Chase N. Peterson, vice president of health sciences at the university, said the change in plans was fine with Dr. Clark, his wife, Una Loy Clark, and their three grown children.

"He had a marvelous attitude," the Dr. Peterson said. "In fact he turned to his wife Wednesday afternoon and said, 'You know I am a little nervous.' She said, 'You know there is no reason to be nervous, is there?'

He said, 'No, come to think about it, none at all.' Then, they both laughed. Later in the afternoon, the patient told Mrs. Clark he'd like to have it done then and 'get it over with.' "

He got his wish. Dr. DeVries walked into his room only minutes later and informed the couple he had decided to proceed with the operation immediately.

Dr. Peterson said the decision to advance the pioneering surgery was made because the patient's failing heart began to beat abnormally, a condition called cardiac arrhythmia, which cannot be treated by drugs.

"The picture was rather ominous for further deterioration and possible death," he said. The hurried-up surgery was an attempt to "move in while the heart was still pumping reasonable volumes of blood to the body and not take the risk that we would have him [Clark's heart] pump inadequate amounts to the body. . . ."

Dr. Peterson said a number of different chemicals were given Tuesday and Wednesday to smooth out the heart to protect it from those extra beats. Physicians also attempted to dry him out to get the extra fluid out of his body, which was a consequence of his heart failure. He was also given medicine to improve the coagulation of his blood, which was abnormally low.

But he continued to deteriorate at a rapid rate so Dr. DeVries proceeded early with the operation he had waited for since September 1981, when the FDA had given him the initial go-ahead to implant the Jarvik-7.

Without the implant, Dr. DeVries said Dr. Clark would have died this weekend.

Operation Chronology

Once the decision was made by Dr. Clark and his family at about 9 p.m. Wednesday, here's what happened:

—10:20 p.m.: Members of the surgical team began preparing for the operation. Team members, who gathered in the large operating room on the third floor of the Medical Center, were Dr. DeVries (chief surgeon) and Drs. Lyle Joyce, Chuck Berry, Tom Ross, Jeff and Fred Anderson. Anesthesiologists were Drs. Nathan Pace, WenShin Liu and Morris Matthews.

—11:27 p.m.: The initial incision was made in Dr. Clark's chest.

—12:07 a.m.: His heart was removed. There was no turning back.

—1:55 a.m.: The artificial heart's right ventricle was attached.

—2:07 a.m.: The left ventricle was attached.

Throughout the early morning hours, Dr. Peterson and John Dwan, director of development and community relations, visited the cafeteria-turned-press center in the Medical Center to give members of the press updates on the progress of the implant. Their usual reply was "Things are going well."

For about two hours, however, they didn't appear in the cafeteria. Tension mounted. Rumors flew.

5 a.m. Briefing

Dr. Peterson, who finally met the anxious press at 5 a.m., said the physicians had considerable difficulties the last few hours associated with pulmonary edema (swelling of the lungs), caused by Dr. Clark's previous heart failure. . . .

Shortly after 6 a.m., Dr. Peterson happily announced that the pressures coming out of the artificial heart surgery were entirely normal and satisfactory to support Dr. Clark. Although he was unconscious—still under the anesthesia—he had a blood pressure equivalent to an 18-year old man.

Low Pressure

His heart had not been beating hard enough to generate much blood pressure. His pressure had been 85 over 90. It should have been 135 over 85.

Dr. Peterson said his heart wasn't really pumping; it was just quivering.

The team Thursday concurred the Jarvik-7 is a mechanical success. But its principal designer, Robert K. Jarvik, said: "It's going to be years before we see what really develops from the surgery. It's going to depend on the development of much improved equipment over what we have now."

Drs. Jarvik and DeVries agree that if a portable artificial heart becomes usable, it could potentially help tens of thousands of people suffering from degenerative heart diseases.

The young medical genius, who insists he didn't think the surgery could have gone better—but had fears that it could have gone worse—said he believes the implantation procedure will be a success when the patient says "it was worthwhile for him to do it."

While the surgery in Salt Lake City made front-page headlines throughout the world, it's not the first time an artificial heart has been implanted in a human being.

Attempt in 1969

Dr. Denton Cooley, Texas Heart Institution in Houston, conducted the first implant of an artificial heart into a human in 1969 without FDA approval. The patient, Haskell Karp, lived 68 hours with the artificial heart, but died of overwhelming infection within hours after the subsequent transplant of a donor heart.

In July, 1981, Dr. Cooley implanted another artificial heart in a man, again without the approval of the FDA. The patient died a week after receiving the donor heart.

Contacted Thursday in Houston, the flamboyant Dr. Cooley said he is "impressed" with the Utah team's success, but had no further comment.

But, however, Dr. Christiaan Barnard, who performed the first heart transplant in 1967, did. From his home in Capetown, South Africa, the transplant pioneer said he has doubts about the effectiveness of implanting an artificial heart.

"The Utah heart does not seem to be the solution," he said, adding the need for such a heart to be hooked to a machine outside the body was a problem. "The best solution remains the heart transplant."

Dr. Clark was not within the age restrictions to be eligible for a transplant. Dr. Jarvik, notified of Dr. Barnard's remark, said, "He has a right to his opinion."

The FDA has given the university heart team permission to implant seven Jarvik-7 hearts. But the physicians have none on the shelf, and they want to see how effective[ly] the heart works in Dr. Clark before they try again.

Still tethered to an external unit of the artificial heart, the courageous Barney Clark died of what doctors termed "secondary complications" on March 23, 1983. The Jarvik-7 was temporarily shelved for further study.

1984

The headline in the newspaper that considered her a hometown girl said it all: "A Ticket for History." Indeed, Geraldine Ferraro, a three-term congresswoman from Queens, New York, was capping 150 years of the struggle for women's rights. That triumph was reported by Long Island, New York, *Newsday* on July 13, 1984.

A TICKET
FOR HISTORY

Mondale Picks Ferraro
For 2nd Spot on Ticket

By Judith Bender
Newsday Washington Bureau

St. Paul, Minn.—Walter Mondale made political history yesterday, announcing that Rep. Geraldine Ferraro of Forest Hills was his choice to be the Democratic vice presidential candidate.

"History speaks to us today," Mondale said to a packed and cheering House chamber at the Minnesota State Capitol. "Our founders said in the Constitution, 'We the People,' not just the rich, or men, or white." It was a reference to the fact that in picking Ferraro, a feisty three-term congresswoman, the Democrats were breaking new ground as the first major party to put a woman on the ticket.

"I looked for the best vice president and I found her in Gerry Ferraro," he said.

In introducing Ferraro, Mondale outlined his campaign against Ronald Reagan as one that would "honor basic American values and those who embody them." In an apparent appeal to the middle-class Americans who deserted the Democratic Party in droves for Reagan in 1980, he said the Queens congresswoman—whose father was an Italian immigrant who died when she was eight and whose mother worked as a crochet beader to put her daughter through school—epitomized "a classic American dream."

"She's earned her way here today," Mondale said of the woman who had worked as a lawyer in a corner of her husband's real estate firm while raising three children. Ferraro's first governmental job was as an assistant prosecutor in the office of her cousin, then Queens District Attorney Nicholas Ferraro, a job she held until she challenged the choice of party leaders for congressman in 1978.

Ferraro, who will be 49 next month, ebullient and smiling, picked up

Mondale's theme, but not before she drew laughter by saying "Thank you, Vice President Mondale. Vice President. It has a nice ring to it."

Later, she said that in choosing her as his running mate, Mondale "sent a powerful signal about the direction he wants to lead our country."

As her husband John Zaccaro and her younger daughter, Laura, looked on, she said, "American history is about doors being opened, doors of opportunity being opened for everyone. No matter who you are, you can get anything you want if you're willing to earn it."

Asked how she felt after the speech, Ferraro smiled broadly and said: "Good."

Mondale's announcement ended a month-long selection process and a parade of mostly minority and female candidates to the North Oaks community where Mondale has his home. The process had raised questions about whether Mondale would be successful in channeling enthusiasms of the various constituency groups of the Democratic Party or whether he would be perceived as pandering to the same special interest groups and not seriously considering a breakthrough choice at all.

Even though Mondale chose not to dwell on the obvious, Mondale aides believed that his choice had produced an immediate, positive response, even among southern Democrats who have been aggressively pushing a Southerner for a running mate as the only way to make a dent in that region.

"It's a whole new phenomenon," said Robert Beckel, Mondale's campaign manager. . . .

One of Mondale's rivals, the Rev. Jesse Jackson, called the decision "courageous."

Sen. Gary Hart, maintaining he's still in the race for the presidential nomination, said that Ferraro was "an excellent vice presidential nominee for Mondale and that her selection is "a significant advance for women in American politics."

President Reagan said only that he is "looking forward to running against the Democratic ticket."

Although she started out as the popular favorite of feminist groups, of her congressional colleagues and of House Speaker Thomas P. O'Neill, some Mondale aides apparently did not believe she had done well during her interview with Mondale. Those reports angered Ferraro and were denied by Mondale.

On Tuesday, a visit by Mondale senior adviser John Reilly to Ferraro's San Francisco hotel seemed to put her in a different category from all the other candidates except for San Francisco Mayor Dianne Feinstein, who met with another adviser, campaign chairman James Johnson. Aides declined to say what was discussed, and so far, Ferraro has not granted any interviews herself.

As Mondale worked on his acceptance speech and considered his decisions on a running mate, there came a time, according to Johnson, where the two "converged in a single moment," and he saw the Ferraro choice as an opportunity to personify the issues he intends to raise during the campaign.

"It was clearly a choice to illustrate his intention to open up doors in American society," Johnson said at a press briefing, "and given her background, her district, it was clearly a choice to say something about the average American, who cares about taxes, about their children's education. . . .

"He felt the case he wanted to make to the American people was a case she had been making and making very effectively in her district."

Ferraro's district in central Queens is sometimes referred to as the "Archie Bunker" district, a district in which basically conservative voters have nonetheless elected a liberal Democrat three times. It is also a polyglot with an ethnic variety that includes Greeks and Asians as well as Italians and Jews. It includes families earning from moderate to middle-to-upper incomes.

Mondale's decision was made late Wednesday, according to Johnson, and the call was placed to Ferraro in San Francisco, where she had gone earlier in the week in her role as head of the platform committee.

"Here goes," said Mondale, as he picked up the phone and asked the fateful question. "Will you be my runnning mate?" said Mondale, according to his aides.

Ferraro accepted. "She told him she was 'very honored' and she told him she would work very hard," said a Mondale aide.

In all, seven candidates had been interviewed. Beside Ferraro and Feinstein, they were Mayor Tom Bradley of Los Angeles, W. Wilson Goode of Philadelphia and Henry Cisneros of San Antonio, Gov. Martha Layne Collins of Kentucky and Sen. Lloyd Bentsen of Texas. . . .

1986

By the time of her death, at age 98 in 1986, artist Georgia O'Keeffe had passed from mere celebrity status to a revered figure. Her life had spanned artistic generations; her work had mothered more than a few younger artists. Her studies of flowers were bright, bold icons, precursors to Pop Art, and her oil paintings of sun-bleached cow skulls and New Mexican desert landscapes played a part in triggering new directions in architecture and interior design. Indeed, O'Keeffe, whose early paintings tended toward abstraction, helped establish America's place in the modernist movement and cleared the way for artists as diverse as Frank Stella and Andy Warhol.

Sam Atwood of the *Santa Fe New Mexican,* O'Keeffe's hometown paper, wrote an appreciative sidebar to her obituary on March 7, 1986.

THE VISION OF GEORGIA O'KEEFFE

By SAM ATWOOD
The New Mexican Staff

From a small garage framing a dramatic view of flat-topped Cerro Pedernal, Santa Fe sculptor Una Hanbury chipped away at a portrait of Georgia O'Keeffe.

It was 1968. Hanbury spent a month at O'Keeffe's ranch in the red rock country east of Abiquiu Lake, working side by side with the aging artist.

"I hope you understand I don't want to see this portrait until it's finished," O'Keeffe told Hanbury.

Hanbury obliged her by concealing her work at the end of each day with a Safeway shopping bag. When the portrait was complete, she snatched the wrapper off and O'Keeffe circumnavigated her likeness.

"I didn't know you were going to do such a personal portrait of me," O'Keeffe told the sculptor, adding "I'm very, very flattered."

O'Keeffe died Thursday in Santa Fe. At 98, she came close to achieving her dream of living to be 100. To her friends and followers, she left behind memories of an iron-willed pioneer with an artistic vision as sharp as the Southwestern light she painted in.

"I think without question she is the most important American artist, and will be for years," Sante Fe art historian Sahryn Udall said.

"She put American abstraction on the map. She legitimized it . . . she said it so early and so clearly at a time when almost no one else was pushing abstraction," Udall said.

She also achieved a remarkable career at a time when women were supposed to be content making babies, not art. "Women can only create babies say the scientists, but I say they can produce art—and Georgia O'Keeffe is the proof of it," Alfred Stieglitz declared at her 1923 show.

Stieglitz, the pioneer of fine art photography, launched O'Keeffe's career and married her on a cold day in December, 1924. But the fiercely independent artist never gave up her name and Stieglitz balked when reporters referred to her as his "wife."

"I've had a hard time hanging on to my name, but I hang onto it with my teeth," she once said. "I like getting what I've got on my own."

O'Keeffe is probably best known for her oil paintings of animal skulls and flowers. Some say her white calla lilies and purple jack-in-the-pulpits are erotic, but O'Keeffe hated that suggestion and resisted any attempt to read symbolism into her paintings, Udall said.

The flowers and skulls have been popularized in posters and post cards, but those subjects represent only a small part of her visionary palette. She also painted New York City skyscrapers, lonely crosses and flowing abstractions.

"She had an extraordinary breadth to her career," said James Wood, director of the Art Institute of Chicago, where O'Keeffe studied as a young artist. "She created a style that Americans identify with. An O'Keeffe speaks across a very broad audience," Wood said.

O'Keeffe loved the dry desert landscape of northern New Mexico, where she first came to visit in 1929, and returned to some of her favorite places time and again to capture their shapes and colors. She camped out at those spots and gave them names like the Black Place, White Place and Gray Hills.

In her travels, she pursued something more elemental than lovely landscapes.

"It wasn't just what she saw, but something she filtered through her mind . . . She had these ideas that were so powerful, she would return to them time and time again," Udall said.

Stieglitz hung O'Keeffe's works—at first, without her permission—in his New York gallery and helped her win recognition early in her career. Before her death, at least one of her paintings sold for $1 million—an unusual accomplishment for a living artist.

Georgia O'Keeffe was born on Nov. 15, 1887 near Sun Prairie, Wisconsin. Her first memory, as told in a 1976 autobiography, was of bright light, white cotton pillows and a cotton patchwork quilt when she was just 9 months old.

She attended a local school and a convent classroom near Madison, then completed junior and senior high school in Chatham, VA. She studied art at the Art Institute of Chicago in 1905 and 1906, and by 1909, worked as a commercial artist in Chicago.

In the fall of 1912, she began a two-year tenure as supervisor of art in public schools in Amarillo, Texas. Her teaching career later took her to the University of Virginia, and Columbia College in Columbia, S.C.

In 1918, O'Keeffe settled in New York City, painting there and in Lake George, N.Y. In the 1920s, she exhibited regularly at Stieglitz's Intimate Gallery.

O'Keeffe made a summer trip to New Mexico in 1929 and visited Mabel Dodge Luhan in Taos. She returned to New Mexico every summer thereafter and first visited Ghost Ranch, near Abiquiu, in 1934.

Six years later, she bought the three-wing adobe hacienda at Ghost Ranch that would become her home base and inspiration for more than four decades. Sandstone cliffs towered above the house, and Cerro Pedernal stood like a sentinel to the south.

The ranch house was sparsely furnished, with only blankets covering bare bancos. Shells, skulls and rocks filled window sills and corners, said Jim Hall, who still manages Ghost Ranch, now a conference center for the Presbyterian Church.

"She had a very high tactile sense. She liked to feel things," Hall said.

Hall helped protect O'Keeffe from the hordes of curious tourists. To the public, she seemed an austere, self-centered artist. But in private, she was a warm person with a deep concern for the people of Abiquiu, Hall said.

If a young local student needed money to go to college, O'Keeffe made sure the means were available.

"She'd always do it quietly, always sort of under the table, but she always had a concern for youngsters with promise," Hall said. O'Keeffe also contributed to a community hall and school in Abiquiu, he said.

In 1945, O'Keeffe bought and renovated an abandoned hacienda in Abiquiu. In recent years, she considered donating the house to the National Park Service, but withdrew her offer because she felt it would draw unwanted hordes of tourists to the small town, Hall said.

In 1971, at age 84, O'Keeffe was shocked to realize that the world she saw through the blue-green eyes was turning into a blur. Doctors diagnosed an irreversible vision loss, and she stopped painting.

It took a young man's vision to recapture her desire to create.

One autumn day in 1972, a tall man with a pony tail and a mustache knocked at her door. The man was Juan Hamilton, a recently divorced potter and sculptor searching for a fresh start. He was in his 20s; she was 85.

O'Keeffe hired Hamilton to do odd jobs around the hacienda, but required him to take up his art work again. Hamilton built asymmetrical pots on her kitchen table, and O'Keeffe, who had previously shown little interest in ceramics, started experimenting with coiled clay pots.

Her success in clay gradually led her back to painting, and she and Hamilton became inseparably close friends.

Now, after her death, the value of her paintings will likely rise steeply, at least for a few years, according to art dealer Forrest Fenn, who knew O'Keeffe and has sold her works to such admirers as Calvin Klein. "She's probably done more to open doors for women than any other artist," Fenn said. . . .

1989

It came as a stunning blow; to many it seemed a betrayal of trust. For ten years the oil companies had assured the American public that they were not only very cautious, but prepared for any emergency should their operations foul the pristine Alaskan wilderness. And then, shortly after midnight on Friday, March 24, 1989, in the frigid waters of Prince William Sound 100 miles south of Anchorage came the inevitable accident. Two articles in *The Anchorage Daily News* of March 25 revealed the sham promises.

CRUDE OIL FOULS SOUND

Tanker Spill is largest ever in U.S.

By Patti Epler and David Hulen
Daily News Reporters

More than 11 million gallons of North Slope crude oil poured through the punctured steel hull of a tanker grounded on a well-charted reef in Prince William Sound on Friday, unleashing the largest crude oil spill ever to foul U.S. waters.

The Exxon Valdez, one of the newest tankers in Exxon Shipping Co.'s fleet, ran aground shortly after midnight on Bligh Reef, about 25 miles from the Alyeska Pipeline Service Co. shipping terminal. Navigation charts show the reef to be about three miles from the outbound shipping lane.

Frank Iarossi, president of Exxon Shipping, blamed the disaster on "human error," but declined to go into specifics.

"At this stage we don't understand the sequence of events," he said. "As far as we could tell, everything on the ship was operational. There was no rudder failure. I think we would need to address the actions (of crew members)."

The fully laden tanker was on its way to a refinery in Long Beach, Calif., when it struck the reef, which Valdez-area boaters call the best-known hazard in the sound. By sundown Friday, people who had flown over the ship estimated the oil slick to be roughly eight miles long and four miles wide, stretching southwest into the middle of the Sound.

The disaster threatened to wreak havoc in one of [the] continent's richest marine environments just as herring were returning to spawn and juvenile salmon were migrating from the rivers where they hatched.

State and federal officials have just begun to assess the danger that the oil poses to the Sound's rich abundance of migratory birds and marine mammals, including fin, orca, minke and humpback whales.

Scientists and officials were debating whether they should attempt to control the spill with chemical dispersants. While the chemicals could help save the lives of marine mammals and birds, they could kill whole schools of fish and contaminate herring roe laid in kelp.

At a press conference Friday evening, Exxon officials said their first priority would be to try to limit the damage, and then to investigate what caused the accident. . . .

Valdez Coast Guard Cmdr. Stephen McCall said Friday that his agency was puzzled by the accident. "We know that she left without a hitch from the terminal," he said. "All her equipment was operating properly." . . .

The pilot who steered the tanker out of the port area and through the narrows—a three-quarter-mile-wide stretch of treacherous waterway just outside the harbor—already had been dropped off, McCall said.

The tanker was under the command of Exxon Capt. Joe Hazelwood, who has been with the company 20 years and has skippered vessels in and out of Valdez for about 12 years, [Exxon spokesman Tom] Cirigliano said.

The Valdez was carrying about 53 million gallons—1.26 million barrels—of crude, according to Coast Guard and Exxon officials.

At least 150,000 barrels immediately ran from ruptures in three starboard cargo tanks, and the oil continued to leak throughout much of the early morning at the rate of 20,000 gallons an hour, the Coast Guard said.

The crude coated icebergs black. Sea lions sought the high ground of buoys.

State environmental officials estimated the spill at about 265,000 barrels—or 11.3 million gallons—late Friday afternoon.

The 987-foot Valdez, which needs 55 feet of water when fully loaded to stay afloat, notified the Coast Guard at 1:38 a.m. that it had run atop the 36-foot shoal, said Coast Guard Spokesman Petty Officer John Gonzales. Coast Guard and state Department of Environmental Conservation officials immediately went out to the ship, some of them staying on the vessel through the rest of the day.

The spill first was reported to be a half-mile long. By morning light, when at least 200,000 barrels had spilled, the slick had grown to an amoeba-like creature some five to six miles long and one to three miles wide. The tides that swirl through that area of the sound kept changing the slick's shape, but also worked to keep most of the oil from moving on out into the Gulf of Alaska. . . .

OIL OFFICIALS REACT SLOWLY TO DISASTER

by Larry Campbell
Daily News Reporter

VALDEZ—As the largest oil spill in the history of the United States entered its second day, only a feeble containment effort had been mounted and a crowd of state, federal and oil company officials remained undecided about how to clean up the mess.

A 32-square-mile, multi-hued sheen continued to float and spread atop the waters of Prince William Sound. The Sound is surrounded by land on three sides. Two large islands, Hinchinbrook and Montague, lie across its open, southern end. That means that unless the spilled oil can be dealt with, it is a near-certainty that it will wash ashore somewhere in the Sound.

Valdez residents grew increasingly critical Friday of what seemed to be sluggish movement by Alyeska Pipeline Service Co., which operates the oil terminal here, and Exxon Shipping Co. in dealing with the spill. Nearly 24 hours after the Exxon Valdez ran aground on Bligh Reef about 25 miles southwest of here, officials had done little to contain the spill or clean up what was beyond containment.

"We're disappointed that it seems to have taken so long," said Valdez city manager Doug Griffin. "I've left messages all day with (Alyeska and Exxon) people, but I haven't heard from any of them yet."

Frank Iarossi, president of Exxon Shipping Co., said his firm spent Friday doing exactly what it was supposed to, mobilizing experts and equipment from around the world for the Valdez cleanup. Alyeska spokesman Tom Brennan said his company did all it could as well, as soon as day broke.

Late Friday morning, more than eight hours after the accident, the Valdez sat motionless on the shallow bottom. A slick some 5 to 6 miles long reached from the vessel's bow to the southwest. U.S. Coast Guard and private aircraft flew overhead, but on the water only the tanker and the oil—no containment booms or other oil spill equipment—were visible. . . .

By Friday evening a few containment booms made an appearance, wrapped around the bows of three Alyeska skimmers that were barely making a dent in the 11 million gallons of spilled oil.

Most of the response by oil industry officials has, so far, been invisible. Alyeska apparently made all the right telephone calls, including one [to] Iarossi, at his Houston, Texas, home. Exxon then began mobilizing a spill response team and gathering machinery and manpower from San Francisco, Florida and London.

But while that elaborate equipment was being pulled together, containment booms at Alyeska's terminal lay idle. A barge that could have been used to carry them to the spill site was undergoing repairs and couldn't be used for some hours, according to Brennan.

Still, Brennan said, nothing could have been done on the site until daybreak, anyway, when flyovers could be made to better assess damage.

"I know these people are upset by what seems to be slow response, but they just don't understand that you can't move that fast in a situation like this," Brennan said.

Exxon and Alyeska officials still have lots of decisions to make. The vessel must be inspected to make sure it won't be further damaged once its remaining cargo is taken off and it begins to float again.

In addition, even though the oilmen have been given permission to use chemical dispersants, no final decision on their use has been made.

Dispersants are chemicals that bond with the oil to break it up and sink it. Critics of dispersion say the sinking oil threatens a wide range of fish and other marine life.

Meanwhile the people who make their living off the fish in Prince William Sound are getting more impatient.

"I couldn't believe when we flew over there this morning that nothing was being done," said Riki Ott, an official with the Cordova District Fisherman's United. "Something should have been done immediately. And now (oil officials) are talking about dispersants. I can't believe any of this."

As the Alaskan winter set in, Exxon suspended its clean-up operation. Oil still coated the rocky shoreline, and the slick had congealed into heavy globs that sank to the bottom of Prince William sound. Exxon was evasive when asked if it would resume the billion-dollar clean-up when warmer weather returned in the spring. Neither the waters nor Exxon's reputation as a protector of the environment remained unsullied.

1989

Unyielding, the symbol of a divided city and nation, east and west, and of a world torn asunder, the Berlin Wall stood for 28 years while discontent grew within the communist Democratic Republic of Germany.

The once-fearsome wall, erected by the Stalinist East German government in 1961 as the most visible and infamous part of the Iron Curtain, was finally doomed when Soviet President Mikhail Gorbachev, himself coping with an imploding nation, secretly informed the East German government that the U.S.S.R. would not support the East German ban on easy travel between the two Germanys.

The *New York Times* of November 10, 1989, reported the opening of the Berlin Wall and with it the first step toward the end of the cold war and the nuclear terror it posed.

CLAMOR IN THE EAST

East Germany Opens Frontier to the West for Migration or Travel

Thousands Cross

By Serge Schmemann
Special to the New York Times

EAST BERLIN, Friday, Nov. 10—East Germany on Thursday lifted restrictions on emigration or travel to the West, and within hours tens of thousands of East and West Berliners swarmed across the infamous Berlin Wall for a boisterous celebration.

Border guards at Bornholmer Strasse crossing, Checkpoint Charlie and several other crossings abandoned all efforts to check credentials, even though the new regulations said East Germans would still need passports and permission to get across. Some guards smiled and took snapshots, assuring passers-by that they were just recording a historic event.

Politburo Announcement

The mass crossing began about two hours after Gunter Schabowski, a member of the Politburo, had announced at a press conference that permission to travel or emigrate would be granted quickly and without preconditions, and that East Germans would be allowed to cross at any crossing into West Germany or West Berlin. . . .

Once Mr. Schabowski's announcement was read on radio and television, a tentative trickle of East Germans testing the new regulation quickly turned into a jubilant horde, which joined at the border crossings with crowds of flag-waving, cheering West Germans. Thousands of Berliners clambered across the wall at the Brandenburg Gate, passing through the historical arch that for so long had been inaccessible to Berliners of either side.

Similar scenes were reported in Lubeck, the only other East German city touching the border, and at other border crossings along the inter-German frontier.

All through the night and into the early morning, celebrating East Berliners filled the Kurfurstendamm, West Berlin's "great white way," blowing trumpets, dancing, laughing and absorbing a glittering scene that until now they could glimpse only on television. . . .

The extraordinary breach of what had been the most infamous stretch of the Iron Curtain marked the culmination of an extraordinary month that has seen the virtual transformation of East Germany under the dual pressures of unceasing flight and continuing demonstrations. It also marked a breach of a wall that had become the premier symbol of Stalinist oppression and of the divisions of Europe and Germany into hostile camps after World War II. . . .

The Berlin Wall—first raised on Aug. 13, 1961, to halt a vast hemorrhage of East Germans to the West—evolved into a double row of eight-foot-high concrete walls with watchtowers, electronic sensors and a no man's land in between. Frequent attempts to breach the barrier often ended in death, and the very sophistication of the wall became a standing indictment of the system that could hold its people only with such extraordinary means.

The decision to allow East Germans to travel freely came on a day when Egon Krenz, the new East German leader, was reported to have called for a law insuring free and democratic elections. In a speech to the Communist Party's Central Committee on Wednesday night that was published today, Mr. Krenz also called for new laws on freedom of assembly, association and the press. But he gave no details.

Mr. Schabowski's announcement about the unimpeded travel was greeted with an outburst of emotion in West Germany, whose Constitution sustains the hope of a reunited Germany and whose people have seen in the dramatic changes in East Germany the first glimmers of an end to division.

The West German Parliament abandoned a heated debated after learning of the new developments, and ended its session with a spontaneous singing of the national anthem.

"We demand of the responsible people in the German Democratic Republic that they start tomorrow to tear down the wall," declared Friedrich Bohl, the chief whip of the governing Christian Democrats.

In West Berlin, Eberhard Diepgen, the former Mayor, said: "This is a day

I have been awaiting since Aug. 13, 1961. With this the wall has lost its function. It can and must be torn down.'' . . .

Marked 40th Anniversary

The announcement of the travel measure was the latest in an extraordinary chain of events that has profoundly transformed East Germany since it marked its 40th anniversary on Oct. 7.

Shocked into action by the mass flights that have gathered pace all through the summer, hundreds of thousands of East Germans have taken to the street in the last months to press with increasing urgency for profound change in their society, which under Erich Honecker ranked among the most iron-clad Communist strongholds in Eastern Europe.

The double pressure of the mass exodus and mass demonstrations (have) sent the Communist Party into headlong retreat. Mr. Honecker was ousted Oct. 18, and at the start of the extraordinary Central Committee session now under way, the entire Politburo resigned to enable Mr. Krenz, the new leader, to select a smaller and younger panel, including only five of the former members. . . .

1990

On April 6, 1990, thousands of art lovers and the merely curious had attended the opening of *Robert Mapplethorpe: The Perfect Moment* at Cincinnati's Contemporary Arts Center. The exhibit, which consisted of 175 photographs by Mapplethorpe, several of which were seen as strongly homoerotic and sadomasochistic, ignited a firestorm of protest. The focus of this fury was the CAC's director, Dennis Barrie, who would become the target of a court battle pitting those who saw the work as pornographic against those championing freedom of expression.

When a grand jury indicted the Contemporary Arts Center and Barrie on obscenity charges, the case made headlines nationwide. Though Barrie would subsequently be acquitted of these charges, the initial finding signaled the start of a larger "culture war," championed by the National Endowment for the Arts, involving federal funding of controversial art.

The *Cincinnati Enquirer* of April 8, 1990, reported on the grand jury's indictment and its repercussions.

ARTS CENTER, DIRECTOR INDICTED

Grand Jury: Mapplethorpe Photos Obscene

By Jane Prendergast
The Cincinnati Enquirer

The Robert Mapplethorpe controversy spilled from the courtroom to gallery and back to courtroom Saturday after a Hamilton County grand jury issued obscenity indictments against the Contemporary Arts Center and its director, Dennis Barrie.

The photo exhibit, "Robert Mapplethorpe: The Perfect Moment," opened to the public for the first time Saturday, and nine of the early viewers—anonymous members of a Hamilton County grand jury—set in action the day's events:

The grand jury decided that seven of the 175 photos were obscene and charged the CAC and Barrie with two misdemeanor counts each of pandering obscenity and illegal use of a child in nudity-related material.

At midafternoon, police officers cleared the packed CAC gallery amid shouts of "Gestapo go home" and "Sieg Heil" from the hundreds who assembled to view the exhibit. Police reopened the gallery after videotaping the artwork.

Saturday night, CAC attorneys asked U.S. District Judge Carl B. Rubin for a temporary order to protect the show from police action.

The action might be the first time in U.S. history that a museum's display of sexually explicit photos will be challenged in court.

Hamilton County Prosecuting Attorney Arthur M. Ney Jr. announced the indictments flanked by Cincinnati Police Chief Lawrence Whalen and Hamilton County Sheriff Simon Leis.

No photos were confiscated, although Ney challenged the CAC to remove the photos in question—which depict homosexual acts and nude or partially clothed children—until a jury could decide if they are obscene.

But Ney said additional charges could be filed each day the exhibit remains open.

"As responsible citizens," Leis said, "the (CAC) board now has an obligation to remove those pictures."

Ney did not say whether he would seize the photos if the CAC refused to remove them: instead, he gave the center "a reasonable time," possibly until Thursday, before acting.

But Barrie, CAC attorney H. Louis Sirkin and CAC board President Roger Ach insisted that the exhibit would remain intact.

"There's simply nothing wrong with this exhibit," Barrie said. "It's important for this city that it be seen here."

In their request to federal court, CAC attorneys accused county and city authorities of using unconstitutional prior restraint and malicious harassment in an unsuccessful attempt to deter CAC from showing the entire Mapplethorpe exhibit.

Rubin set a hearing for 10 a.m. today in the University of Cincinnati Law School courtroom.

Barrie, who intends to plead not guilty, and a representative of the CAC are scheduled to be arraigned Friday before Common Pleas Judge Gilbert Bettman.

. . . The indictments touched off an emotional reaction at the Fifth Street gallery by visitors who were ordered out of the center while police videotaped the display.

... Barrie tried to calm the crowd.

"It's a very dark day," he said. "We all know that. But we don't want anyone to get hurt."

In all, more than 3,000 viewed the exhibit Saturday, easily breaking the center's attendance record for an opening day, officials said.

Enquirer reporter Ben L. Kaufman contributed to this report.

1991

A rakish cat cavorting in a towering stripped hat. An earnest elephant hatching an egg. An ornery beast filching Christmas.

For nearly half a century these and other fantastic creatures have been the very stuff of growing up, sparking the wonder of reading in millions of kids worldwide. But it was not always so. Once upon a time it was a Dick and Jane world of "see Spot run." However, in 1937, children's literature took a joyful leap when a soft-spoken man named Theodor Geisel, who called himself Dr.

Seuss, wrote and illustrated *And to Think That I Saw It on Mulberry Street.* The inventive author went on to create drawings and text for a batch of kicky fantasies filled with captivating nonsense and oddball characters who spoke in rhyme most of the time.

The following obituary for Dr. Seuss, published in the *San Diego Union-Tribune* on September 26, 1991, assesses the enduring influence of this puckish genius, offering insight into why his work transcends generations and lives on as more than child's word play.

GOODBYE TO DR. SEUSS

Prolific Master of Charm and Whimsy, Whose Tales Taught Generations of Children the Joy of Reading Is Dead at 87

John Wilkens and Robert P. Laurence
Staff Writers

The Cat takes off his Hat. The Green Eggs are blue. The Grinch has stolen something else, three months before Christmas.

Theodor "Dr. Seuss" Geisel, the writer whose wildly imaginative works of rhyme and reason spurred generations of children to read and love books, died late Tuesday at his La Jolla home.

The most popular author of children's books in American history was 87.

He had been ill off and on for several years, battling cancer and other diseases, and recently told doctors not to make any dramatic efforts to keep him alive, friends said. His wife of 23 years, Audrey, was with him when he died.

Services Are Pending

"I hope he's in one of his own happy worlds," said Peter Neumeyer, an English professor at San Diego State and a specialist in children's literature.

Seuss was only his middle name, and the only doctorates he had were honorary.

But it was as Dr. Seuss that Geisel won the adoration of millions and led a revolution in children's literature.

Working with a vocabulary of 348 words, he created "The Cat in the Hat" in 1957 and proved that with enough wit, charm and humor, the smallest child could be lured between the covers of a book.

In that same year, he published "How the Grinch Stole Christmas!" an instant classic that has become to 20th-century yuletide what Charles Dickens' "A Christmas Carol" was to the 19th century.

"I think the fact that I entertain the kids is the greatest satisfaction, rather than teach them anything," Geisel once said. "I think that when they get entertained they learn."

His most important achievement, he said on another occasion, was having had "something to do with kicking Dick and Jane out of the school system."

Perfecting what he liked to call "illogical insanity," Seuss wrote 47 books filled with quirky, dancing poetry and whimsical, endearing drawings. From 1937's "And to Think That I Saw It on Mulberry Street!" through 1990's "Oh, the Places You'll Go," his books sold more than 200 million copies and were translated into 20 languages.

For all their zaniness, sometimes they carried an important moral, too. "Grinch" was about commercialism, "The Lorax" about conservation and "The Butter Battle Book" about the nuclear arms race. . . .

Married twice, he never had children of his own. "You have 'em, I'll amuse 'em," was his motto.

He felt, though, as if each of the kids who read his books belonged in some way to him. "I love them all," he once joked, "as long as they don't all show up at once."

But show up they often did, finding their way along the winding road to his doorstep high on Mount Soledad, wanting to meet the man who gave them "Yertle the Turtle," "Horton Hears a Who," "Green Eggs and Ham," "Thidwick the Big-Hearted Moose" and so many other stories. . . .

Virtually every day's batch of mail included a packet of letters from youngsters. One of his favorites came from an 8-year-old who wrote: "Dear Dr. Seuss, You sure thunk up a lot of funny books. You sure thunk up a lot of funny animals. Who thunk you up, Dr. Seuss?"

The thunking was years in the making.

Turns to Drawing

He was born in Springfield, Mass., on March 4, 1904, the middle child between two sisters. His father helped run the family brewery, called Kuhlmback & Geisel but known fondly by the locals as Come Back and Guzzle. . . .

He graduated in 1925 [from Dartmouth College] and journeyed to Oxford University in England, to study the writings of Jonathan Swift, the 18th-century social critic. There, another American student, Helen Palmer, noticed him doodling winged horses in the margins of his notebook. "You're not very interested in the lectures," she said.

She encouraged him to make drawing his career, and he dropped out of Oxford. They were married in November 1927, and she became his editor and harshest critic. She wrote children's books, too, under her maiden name.

Helen died in 1967. A year later, Geisel married the former Audrey Stone Dimond. . . .

Returning to New York from Oxford, Geisel began earning his living as a cartoonist and humorist, drawing and writing for the humor magazine Judge. Existence was precarious and he was often paid not in cash but in the products of advertisers.

But it was at Judge that he bestowed on himself the title of "Dr."

He'd used the name Seuss before, at the Jack-o-Lantern. Then at Judge, "I was writing mock scientific stories. They were crazy science fictions. They needed a doctorate. So I wrote under the name of Dr. Theoprastus Seuss."

Geisel also liked to joke that by giving himself the title, instead of staying at Oxford to earn it, "I saved my father $10,000."

He kept using the pseudonym, but thought it would be only a temporary disguise. "I was saving my own name for the great American novel, which I was planning to do as a serious writer," he once explained.

The novel got written, but it was, in Geisel's words, "a pretentious, sophomoric thing" that was never published. "It didn't sell as a novel, so I boiled it down to a long, long short story. Then I boiled it down to a short story. Then I finally found a joke in it that I sold to Judge for $15."

Finds Fame

He took his first step toward fame in 1928. Standard Oil hired him to draw cartoons advertising its bug killer, a product called Flit. Geisel penned the "Quick, Henry! The Flit!" series until 1942, when he joined the Army. The slogan became a common household phrase.

In 1937, Dr. Seuss wrote his first children's book, "And to Think That I Saw It on Mulberry Street," because he figured that was the only kind of outside writing his Flit contract would allow. It is the story of a boy, Marco, and the outrageous things he dreams up while walking home from school. . . .

A couple of years later, he moved into editorial cartooning, drawing for the short-lived, progressive New York newspaper PM. He'd dabbled in cartooning before with a comic strip called "Heiji," published by the Hearst newspapers.

World War II saw him move to a different medium. He joined the Army and served four years with the documentary filmmaking unit directed by the late Frank Capra.

One of his films, "Your Job in Germany," later released by Warner Bros. as "Hitler Lives," received an Academy Award in 1946 for Best Documentary Short. A year later, a second Oscar for Best Documentary Feature went to "Design for Death," a history of the Japanese people written with his wife, Helen.

Geisel also won an Academy Award for animation in 1951 for the cartoon "Gerald McBoing-Boing." He also wrote the screenplay in 1952 for "The 5000 Fingers of Dr. T," a full-length fantasy about a wild music teacher and his piano. Seuss was unhappy with the final product but it became a cult classic.

Taps Baby Boom

. . .

In 1956, his alma mater, Dartmouth, gave him an honorary degree, a Doctor of Humane Letters. "I'm legitimate," he laughed afterward.

Then, amid a national outcry over the inability of many children to read, he was given a simple vocabulary of 348 words and asked to come up with a primer for youngsters.

He worried over the job for months until one day, rummaging through old discarded drawings, he came across a mischievous cat wearing a tall, bent stovepipe hat cocked at a jaunty angle. "Cat" and "hat" were both on his list of allowed words, so he was on his way. Or so he thought.

1995

It began with a "low-speed" car chase, viewed live by millions on television screens across the country, the white Ford Bronco at the head of a convoy of police vehicles, driving slowly along L.A.'s freeways. It ended, some 474 days later, with the reading of a jury's verdict in a nondescript courtroom in Downtown Los Angeles.

In between, through more than 15 months of sensationalistic headlines and pandering journalism, the nation eavesdropped, transfixed by the latest "trial of the century." As the *Los Angeles Times*'s lead story made clear on October 4, 1995, *People v. Simpson* was not just a murder trial laced with sex but a courtroom drama rivaling any paperback crime story, as well as a disquieting look at race in America at the end of the 20th Century.

SIMPSON NOT GUILTY

Drama Ends 474 Days After Arrest

Verdicts: The ex-football star expresses gratitude and returns to his Brentwood estate where friends and family celebrate. Relatives of the victims react with pain and grim silence to the jurors' decision.

By Jim Newton
Times Staff Writer

Bringing one of history's most riveting courtroom dramas to a stunning climax, O.J. Simpson was acquitted of two counts of murder Tuesday, verdicts that set the Hall of Famer free 474 days after he was arrested and charged with a brutal double murder.

At 11:16 a.m., Simpson returned home to his Brentwood estate, embracing longtime friend Al Cowlings in the same driveway where the two were arrested on June 17, 1994. As night fell, crowds of well-wishers and detractors gathered beyond police barricades while the Simpson entourage partied inside the famous home.

Within hours of the verdicts—broadcast live and bringing businesses around the country to a temporary standstill—family members of the victims retreated in grief, and the first of the anonymous jurors emerged to give The Times an interview in which he dismissed the prosecution's physical evidence as "garbage in, garbage out."

While jurors scattered to their homes, prosecutors, defense lawyers and family members of the victims and defendant gathered in an extraordinary series of news conferences.

In a statement read by his eldest son during one of the media sessions, Simpson expressed relief, gratitude and a commitment to finding whoever murdered his ex-wife Nicole Brown Simpson and her friend Ronald Lyle Goldman.

"I am relieved that this part of the incredible nightmare that occurred on June 12, 1994, is over with," Simpson said. "My first obligation is to my young children, who will be raised in the way that Nicole and I had always planned."

Simpson vowed to pursue "as my primary goal in life" the killer or killers responsible for the murders, concluding: "I only hope someday that—despite every prejudicial thing that has been said about me publicly, both in and out of the courtroom—people will come to understand and believe that I would not, could not and did not kill anyone."

After 266 days of sequestration at the Inter-Continental Hotel in Downtown Los Angeles, jurors deliberated a mere three hours before accepting Simpson's contention that the charges against him were unproven.

Their verdicts, which were delivered in a courtroom so tense that some spectators trembled visibly in anticipation, united jurors and Simpson in a strangely triumphant moment.

Simpson smiled thinly and mouthed the words ''thank you'' as the not guilty verdicts were read. Two jurors smiled back. Another, Lionel (Lon) Cryer, raised his left fist in a salute toward Simpson as the panel left the courtroom.

But the same finale was greeted with shock by the family of Nicole Simpson, and it wrenchingly broke the spirits of Goldman's relatives.

Nicole Simpson and Goldman were knifed to death outside her Brentwood condominium on June 12, 1994, a foggy summer evening in an otherwise quiet neighborhood. O.J. Simpson pleaded not guilty to the crimes, but he was the only suspect, and members of both victims' families came to believe that he was responsible for the murders.

In court, Fred Goldman, the victim's father, stared in pain at the ceiling, his wife in one arm and his daughter in the other, both sobbing openly as the verdicts were read. In the quiet courtroom, Kim Goldman's gulping sobs were the only sounds that accompanied the reading.

''Oh my God,'' Patti Goldman said, turning to her shaken husband.

''Murderer'' he said under his breath, repeating that later as he left the courtroom.

Kim Goldman, Ronald's sister, fought to keep herself from speaking out while court was in session—Superior Court Judge Lance A. Ito had warned that any other outbursts would be grounds for ejection. But after the verdicts were delivered, she could not contain herself. She quietly burst out a short string of expletives, then turned to the people near her on the courtroom bench and apologized.

''I'm sorry,'' she said, repeating that twice more as her long red hair cascaded over her tear-stained cheeks.

Later, Fred Goldman said the night of the murders ''was the worst nightmare of my life.''

''This,'' he added, ''is the second.''

1997

Dismissed by some sports pundits as just another prodigy who would wilt as soon as he felt the pressure from golf's most prestigious event, 21-year-old old Tiger Woods left all doubters—and competitors—in his wake on the way to a new Masters tournament record.

Woods, the first person of African American descent to win a major golf tournament, not only scored an unprecedented victory on the links but shattered the barriers that marked golf as the last major sport in the United States to bar men and women of color from the clubhouse and country club. That he did so with such grace and athletic ability transformed him into a national hero—on the links and off.

The *Atlanta Journal-Constitution* covered the story in neighboring Augusta, home of the Masters, and ran this piece on April 14, 1997.

RUNAWAY TIGER

Woods Wins Masters by Record 12 Shots
With 18-Under Total

Glenn Sheeley
Staff Writer

Well, one green jacket down, nine to go.

Culminating four days of fantasy golf, 21-year-old Tiger Woods officially starting living out Jack Nicklaus' prediction Sunday, capturing the 1997 Masters title with a record-wrecking performance of staggering proportions.

With a display only he might someday equal, Woods blew away the Masters field by a record 12 strokes, establishing a new 72-hole record of 18-under-par 270 with a final round of 69.

In his first Masters as a professional, Woods became the youngest champion in tournament history and the first man of African-American heritage to win one of golf's major championships.

After making a 4-foot putt at the 18th green to preserve the record, Woods raised his arms to the overcast sky. He hugged his caddie, "Fluff" Cowan, and his parents, Earl and Tida, coming to tears during a long exchange on the shoulder of his father. He later accepted the green jacket from defending champion Nick Faldo, who had missed the cut and finished 20 strokes behind him on Friday.

It was such an astounding 72 holes of golf for Woods that even his own childhood dreams were surpassed.

"I never thought I would have a lead like that," said Woods, who started the day with a 9-shot advantage. "You envision dueling it out with Faldo or Nicklaus or Watson, someone who's awfully tough to beat down the stretch."

It was last year when Nicklaus, a six-time Masters champion, predicted that Woods eventually would win more green jackets that he and Arnold Palmer (four wins) combined. It sounded at the time like a Nicklaus exaggeration. Now it might be an understatement. Who's going to beat Woods those other 15 or 20 times?

There was no Greg Norman-type collapse for this Masters and nothing resembling it. Although Earl Woods warned his son of the toughest round of his life, Tiger made it look easy, smiling broadly and never losing his focus.

From the point where Woods shot a back-nine 30 on Thursday, nothing emerged but forward progress. Woods shot rounds of 70–66–65–69. He went 37 holes without a bogey.

With more domination than in any of his tour wins or three U.S. Amateur titles, Woods went to 17-under with a birdie at the par-5 13th, stopping his eagle putt from 15 feet on the lip. After a 3-wood and a sand wedge to the 404-yard 14th, Woods nailed an 8-footer for a birdie to reach 18-under.

Almost as an afterthought, second place went to Tom Kite, 47, who shot a 70 to finish at 6-under 282. Former Georgia player Tommy Tolles (67) was third. Kite, the Ryder Cup captain, congratulated Woods who ran his points total to 800 and officially made the team.

With a smile as wide as his lead, Woods wore the green jacket, a 42-long, over his red sweater in the interview room.

"It fits pretty good," Woods said.

1998

The last decade of the 20th Century had not been kind to the "national pastime." By 1998, baseball had fallen behind in the intense competition for the leisure dollar. But two men, an agile Dominican named Sammy Sosa, a Chicago Cubs outfielder, and the Bunyanesque Mark McGwire, a first baseman for the St. Louis Cardinals, changed all that.

In a two-man attack on Roger Maris's 37-year-old single-season home run record of 61, McGwire and Sosa traded prodigious blows in the final months of the season, treating millions of enthralled baseball fans and non-fans alike to a gentlemanly contest of athletic power. In doing so, they helped to restore baseball as America's national sport.

Rick Hummel of the *St. Louis Post-Dispatch* reported the last day of the great home run derby. His story appeared on September 28, 1998.

SWING KING, AMAZING!

McGwire Hits Two to Finish With 70 Homers
Even the Slugger Can't Believe He Did It

By Rick Hummel
of *The Post-Dispatch*

In his final triumphant act, Mark McGwire rang the curtain down on his most magical season the same way he began it.

McGwire started by homering in the Cardinals' first four games and finished by hitting five homers in their last three games. His final number is a staggering 70 home runs. That's 27 homers more than Johnny Mize's previous Cardinals record, 10 homers more than Babe Ruth and nine more than Roger Maris. It's also nine homers more than the number of singles (61) McGwire had this year.

His two homers Sunday, giving him five homers in his final 11 at-bats, sparked the Cardinals to a closing 6-3 win over the Montreal Expos at Busch Stadium.

For his first homer, in the third inning, McGwire whipped a 1-1 breaking pitch from Mike Thurman into the left-field seats. His second homer, off rookie Carl Pavano, his 66th victim, was a line shot off a fastball over the left-field wall. That broke a 3-3 tie in the seventh inning.

After this homer, McGwire was congratulated by the entire Montreal infield and catcher Mike Barrett before pointing to a close friend in the stands, saluting the owners, who tipped their caps in return, and making his usual curtain calls.

Technically, we still don't know if McGwire will wind up with the single-season record. Sammy Sosa of the Chicago Cubs has "just" 66 with one playoff game—which counts in the statistics—remaining as the Cubs try to win the wild-card bid by beating the San Francisco Giants tonight in Chicago. Just two days before, McGwire actually was behind Sosa, 66 homers to 65, for 45 minutes.

"But it's not like I'm calling Sammy up on the phone and saying, 'You hit one? I'm coming right back,' " McGwire said.

"What's been happening the last few months, there's no explanation for it."

. . .

While McGwire broke the home run record for the seventh and eighth times this season, he fell just short of his goal of hitting .300. He wound up at .299 after his third straight two-hit game.

"That (.300) is something nobody's really talked about—I've hit a lot of home runs, but I've maintained an average," McGwire said. "And I'm proud of it." . . .

McGwire agreed to being both amazed and exhausted by what he had done.

"To say the least, I'm amazed," McGwire said. "Hitting 70, I've never thought about it or dreamt about it. When I got to 62 early in September, everybody said 'Shoot for 70.'

"I'm speechless really. I can't believe I did it. Can you? It blows me away."

1999

Almost from the moment of Bill Clinton's inauguration as president, his administration came under partisan fire and judicial scrutiny. As charge after charge—of crooked land deals, insider trading, even complicity in the international drug trade and murder—fell short of proof, frustrated Republicans pressed ahead in their investigation of his alleged extramarital affairs. Chiefly, this included an affair with a White House intern—and whether or not he had obstructed justice and then committed perjury before a grand jury. This effort would end with only the second impeachment of a U.S. president in the nation's history and a solemn trial in the Senate.

The acquittal of President Clinton was reported by the *Washington Post* on February 13, 1999.

CLINTON ACQUITTED

2 Impeachment Articles Fail to Win Senate Majority;

Five Republicans Join Democrats in Voting Down Both Charges

By Peter Baker, Helen Dewar
Washington Post Staff Writers

The United States Senate acquitted William Jefferson Clinton yesterday on charges that he committed perjury and obstruction of justice to hide sexual indiscretions with a onetime White House intern, permitting the 42nd president to complete the remaining 708 days of his term.

After a tumultuous year of scandal that tested the Constitution and tried the nation's patience, neither of the two articles of impeachment brought by the House garnered a simple majority, much less the two-thirds necessary to convict Clinton of high crimes and misdemeanors. Article I alleging perjury was defeated on a 45 to 55 vote at 12:21 p.m. Just 18 minutes later, Article II charging obstruction failed on a 50 to 50 tie. Five Republicans joined all 45 Democrats in supporting full acquittal.

"It is, therefore, ordered and adjudged that the said William Jefferson Clinton be, and he hereby is, acquitted of the charges in the said articles," declared Chief Justice William H. Rehnquist, the presiding officer, marking the conclusion of the first impeachment trial of a president in 131 years. . . .

The Senate's decision to spare Clinton gives him the opportunity to try to repair his battered presidency and find a way to mitigate the legacy of the Monica S. Lewinsky saga that will mark him in the history books as only the second president impeached by the House of Representatives. . . .

The constitutional crisis ended 13 months to the day after Linda R. Tripp started it by telling independent counsel Kenneth W. Starr's office that she had secret tapes of her friend, Lewinsky, suggesting that Clinton wanted her to lie under oath in the Paula Jones case about their affair.

That phone call led to an unprecedented investigation and a virtual carnival of unseemliness in which tawdry sexual escapades and the deceptions they inspired ultimately set in motion the impeachment formalities. In the end, the 13 House Republican "managers" who relentlessly pressed the case not only failed to force Clinton from power but could not even persuade all of their party brethren to endorse their cause. . . .

For such a momentous occasion, though, the verdict was anticlimactic. The trial began five weeks ago with no suggestion that conviction was a realistic possibility. And what little suspense there was faded with disclosures about individual senators' intentions earlier this week. . . .

Unlike Clinton, who did not watch the proceedings and instead received the news by telephone from Chief of Staff John D. Podesta, some of the other principle players were glued to their television sets. Lewinsky watched live coverage in New York. Paula Jones expressed discouragement.

"I'm not happy, you know, for sure," she told Fox News. "I just expected it because he gets away with everything."

Beyond the Beltway, much of the country wanted him to, with opinion polls showing that the public overwhelmingly believed Clinton lied under oath and obstructed justice yet did not want him removed from office for it. Just a handful of protesters held a lonely vigil outside the Capitol yesterday with signs such as "Jail to the Chief."

In the year since the story about the president and the intern first broke, the nation has been exposed to a sex scandal that dwarfed any before it, as the most excruciating intimate details poured forth through news accounts and the explicit report that Starr sent Congress in September alleging 11 impeachable offenses by the president. Clinton became the first president ever to testify in his own defense before a grand jury. The Supreme Court wiped away attempts to shield White House aides and Secret Service officers from testifying. And the House of Representatives, on a largely party-line vote, impeached a president for the first time since Andrew Johnson in 1868. . . .

2000

It was the closest presidential election since 1876, when the Republican candidate, Rutherford B. Hayes, defeated his Democratic opponent, Samuel Tilden, by one vote in the decisive electoral college balloting. And perhaps it was the most confusing, settled only by a murky 5-4 decision by the justices of the Supreme Court of the United States, voting along conservative-liberal lines.

Months later, newspapers were still counting improperly marked ballots, attempting to sort out just who did garner the most votes in Florida and take the state's 25 electoral votes. If all disputed ballots had been counted, George W. Bush would have won by at least 225 or as many as 493 votes. If so-called dimpled ballots had been counted, Bush's victory margin would have fallen to just 60 votes. At the same time, if every "overvote" on a confusing "butterfly ballot" in heavily Democratic Palm Beach County had been counted, Al Gore would have eked out a 350-vote victory.

Gore and his supporters could take some consolation in the fact that nationally he had tallied 540,000 votes more than did the president-elect. But that was cold comfort, since Bush's victory in Florida gave him 271 electoral votes to Gore's 266. In the end, those were the only ones that counted.

The *Palm Beach Post* reported the U.S. Supreme Court's decision on December 13, 2000.

DIVIDED SUPREME COURT HANDS BUSH PROBABLE VICTORY; GORE TO REACT TODAY

No More Counting

Larry Lipman and Brian E. Crowley
Palm Beach Post Staff Writers

WASHINGTON—A fractured U.S. Supreme Court late Tuesday reversed the Florida Supreme Court's ruling authorizing manual recounts of the state's disputed ballots, effectively ending Al Gore's quest for the presidency.

Coming just two hours before the deadline for Florida to select its Electoral College electors, the ruling apparently squelched the judicial battle over whether Gore or George W. Bush should win the state's 25 electoral votes.

In practical terms, the court ruling handed the state's electors to Bush and cemented his claim to become the 43rd president.

"Obviously without a recount, it's impossible for Gore to get ahead in the vote," said state House Minority Leader Lois Frankel after the court's ruling just before 10 p.m. . . .

In the 13-page unsigned order, seven of the nine federal justices agreed that "there are constitutional problems with the recount ordered by the Florida Supreme Court," because the order violated constitutional equal protection requirements. But they noted there was "disagreement . . . as to the remedy."

The justices concluded that the Florida Supreme Court's recount order could not meet Tuesday's deadline because it did not adhere to "minimal constitutional standards."

"Because it is evident that any recount seeking to meet the December 12 date will be unconstitutional for the reasons we have discussed, we reverse the judgment of the Supreme Court of Florida ordering a recount to proceed," the order said. . . .

With the ruling, Bush will go on record as having won Florida with 2,912,790 votes to Gore's 2,912,252 votes. What is not in the total are scores of lawyers and court hearings, thousands of protesters, and countless numbers of chads all contributing to one of the closest and most contested elections in the nation's history.

It wasn't expected to be this hard for George W. Bush. Younger brother Jeb [governor of Florida] and a powerful state Republican Party were supposed to be enough to carry the state.

But a determined Gore—and a "butterfly ballot" in Palm Beach County—brought the race to a standstill for the past 35 days. . . .

Although the order was issued in the name of the court, the opinion contained deeply fractured views among the nine justices.

Chief Justice William Rehnquist and Justices Antonin Scalia and Clarence

Thomas issued a separate concurring opinion spelling out in greater detail why they voted to reverse the Florida Supreme Court's ruling.

Meanwhile, the four dissenting justices—John Paul Stevens, David Souter, Ruth Bader Ginsburg and [Stephen] Breyer—each wrote dissenting opinions and joined various portions of each others dissents. . . .

In its order, the court ruled that Florida's recount procedures appeared to violate the 14th Amendment's "equal protection" clause because it did not "satisfy the minimum requirement for non-arbitrary treatment of voters necessary to secure the fundamental right."

While acknowledging that Florida's standard which requires canvassers and courts to determine the "intent of the voter" is "unobjectionable as an abstract proposition and a starting principle," the justices said the problem was a lack of specific standards to ensure that the principle would be applied equally.

"The want of those rules here has led to unequal evaluation of ballots," the court wrote, noting that the standards for accepting dimpled or partially punched chads "might vary not only from county to county but indeed within a single county from one recount team to another."

The court concluded that "it is obvious that the recount cannot be conducted" in a manner that would fulfill the constitutional requirements of equal protection and due process "without substantial additional work.". . .

September 11, 2001. A bright, clear morning. Then, within minutes of each other, two hijacked American Airlines jets plowed into the twin towers of the World Trade Center in New York City. It was Pearl Harbor for the new millennium, a sudden act of international terrorism that signaled an insidious new kind of war. Steve McCurry, a photographer for the esteemed photo agency Magnum, had a chilling view of the subsequent collapse of the towers from the roof of his office on the north side of Washington Square Park in Lower Manhattan. Copyright Steve McCurry / Magnum Photos

NEWSPAPERS AND SYNDICATES

Represented in This Volume

Alexander's Weekly Messenger	April 1, 1840
Alta California	May 10, 1869
	May 11, 1869
Anchorage Daily News	March 25, 1869
Atlanta Constitution	December 16, 1939
Atlanta Journal	August 17, 1915
Atlanta Journal-Constitution	April 14, 1997
Appeal to Reason	February 25, 1905
Associated Press	January 3, 1920
	August 18, 1920
	October 31, 1938
	June 7, 1942
	September 24, 1957
	May 8, 1960
	May 10, 1960
Baltimore Afro-American	April 19, 1947
Baltimore Patriot (and Commercial Gazette)	May 25, 1844
	October 17, 1859
	October 18, 1859
Baltimore Sun	August 30, 1926
Boston Daily Globe	May 6, 1904
	January 12, 1912
	August 23, 1927
Boston Gazette	August 31, 1812
Boston Gazette and Country Journal	October 7, 1771
Boston News-Letter	April 24, 1704
Boston Transcript	March 17, 1885
Bozeman Avant Courier	July 6, 1876
Californian	March 15, 1848
	May 2, 1848
	July 15, 1848
Charleston Daily Courier	April 12, 1861
Charlotte Observer	February 3, 1960
Chattanooga Daily Times	July 22, 1925
Chicago Daily News	July 27, 1919
	September 28, 1920
Chicago Herald Examiner	February 15, 1929
Chicago Inter-Ocean	May 5, 1886
	December 30, 1903

Christian Science Monitor	August 15, 1935
	February 11, 1964
Cincinnati Argus	June 14, 1849
Cincinnati Enquirer	April 8, 1990
Cleveland Plain Dealer	July 18, 1941
Daily National Intelligencer	February 6, 1815
	July 7, 1863
Des Moines Register	January 31, 1968
Detroit Free Press	March 6, 1898
Detroit News	January 6, 1914
Dunlap's Pennsylvania Packer or	
the General Advertiser	December 27, 1776
Honolulu Star-Bulletin International	
tional	December 7, 1941
International News Service	January 15, 1954
Jackson Daily Clarion-Ledger	April 30, 1900
Kansas City Star	April 21, 1918
Knoxville Journal and Tribune	August 19, 1920
Liberator	September 28, 1855
Los Angeles Evening Herald	November 11, 1918
Los Angeles Examiner	January 15, 1954
Los Angeles Illustrated News	April 15, 1935
Los Angeles Times	May 17, 1929
	July 18, 1955
	September 24, 1957
	January 16, 1967
	October 4, 1995
Massachusetts Gazette and Boston	
News-Letter	December 23, 1773
Massachusetts Spy	May 3, 1775
Memphis Commercial Appeal	April 5, 1968
Montgomery Advertiser	March 26, 1965
National Intelligencer	July 7, 1863
New Orleans Picayune	January 25, 1887
New York American	April 19, 1927
New York Daily Mirror	August 26, 1939
New York Daily News	May 1, 1939
	October 13, 1944

New York Evening Journal	February 16, 1898
	July 4, 1898
New York Evening Post	July 13, 1804
New York Herald	July 5, 1910
New York Herald-Tribune	October 19, 1924
	November 8, 1931
	January 8, 1932
	May 13, 1932
	April 1, 1943
	March 14, 1945
New York Independent Journal	October 27, 1787
New York Journal and American	June 23, 1938
New York Mercury	August 9, 1755
New York Morning Chronicle	December 24, 1803
	July 18, 1804
New York Morning Herald	April 24, 1838
New York Post	June 3, 1941
	April 13, 1945
	August 18, 1969
New York Sun	September 3, 1833
	January 17, 1938
New York Time Piece	July 20, 1798
New York Times	July 8, 1871
	September 7, 1909
	February 23, 1913
	April 8, 1927
	May 21, 1927
	October 1, 1927
	May 2, 1931
	October 11, 1935
	September 5, 1945
	May 10, 1960
	October 23, 1962
	August 5, 1964
	July 1, 1971
	November 10, 1989
New York Tribune	July 14, 1863
	May 16, 1911
	May 8, 1915
	June 6, 1918
New York Weekly Journal	November 24, 1734
	August 18, 1735
New York World	January 26, 1890
	November 1, 1925
Newsday	July 13, 1984
Norfolk Virginian Pilot	December 17, 1903

Orlando Sentinel	July 21, 1969
Pacific Citizen	March 1, 1942
Palm Beach Post	December 13, 2000
Pennsylvania Mercury	September 21, 1787
Philadelphia Inquirer	March 29, 1979
Pittsburgh Dispatch	June 1, 1889
Pittsburgh Press	March 27, 1953
Richmond Dispatch	July 20, 1861
Salt Lake City Tribune	December 3, 1982
San Diego Tribune-Sun	June 7, 1942
San Diego Union-Tribune	September 26, 1991
San Felipe de Austin Telegraph and Texas Register	March 24, 1836
San Francisco Call-Chronicle-Examiner	April 19, 1906
San Francisco Chronicle	October 31, 1938
	November 21, 1978
	May 13, 1982
San Francisco Daily Dramatic Chronicle	April 15, 1865
San Francisco Examiner	June 3, 1888
	July 4, 1898
	January 15, 1954
San Francisco News	October 5, 1936
Santa Fe New Mexican	March 7, 1986
Scripps Howard Syndicate	January 10, 1944
Stars and Stripes	June 7, 1944
St. Louis Post-Dispatch	April 4, 1882
	September 28, 1998
St. Louis Republican	July 7, 1876
Topeka Capital Daily	May 18, 1954
United Press International	November 22, 1963
Ventura Free Press	May 20, 1876
Vicksburgh Daily Citizen	July 2, 1863
	July 4, 1863
Wall Street Journal	October 30, 1929
Washington Evening Star	March 7, 1857
Washington Globe	September 2, 1831

Washington Post	November 4, 1903
	January 9, 1918
	January 30, 1920
	May 8, 1960
	August 29, 1963
	June 18, 1972
	August 9, 1974
	February 13, 1999
Wheeling Intelligencer	February 10, 1950

ACKNOWLEDGMENTS

The editors and publisher gratefully acknowledge the following for permission to reproduce the stated copyrighted material: The Afro-American Newspaper Company for "Looking 'em Over," by Sam Lacy, April 19, 1947. Anchorage Daily News for "Crude Oil Fouls Sound," by Patti Epler and David Hulen, March 25, 1989. Copyright © 1989 Anchorage Daily News. Associated Press for "U.S. Agents Capture 2,500 'Reds,' " as it appeared in the *Washington Post*, January 3, 1920; "Tennessee's Legislature Ratifies Amendment Giving Suffrage to Women," as it appeared in the *Knoxville Journal and Tribune*, August 19, 1920; "The Great Radio Scare," as it appeared in the *San Francisco Chronicle* of October 31, 1938; "Jap Fleet Reeling Under U.S. Blows," as it appeared in the *San Diego Tribune-Sun* of June 6, 1942; "Eyewitness Tells Story of Rioting," by Relman Morin, as it appeared in the *Los Angeles Times* of September 24, 1957; "K. Says Pilot Confesses Spying," by Preston Grover, as it appeared in the *Washington Post* of May 8, 1960; and "U.S. Approves Pill for Birth Control," as it appeared in the *New York Times* of May 10, 1960. Atlanta Journal and the Atlanta Constitution for "Leo Frank Forcibly Taken from Prison," *Atlanta Journal*, August 17, 1915; " 'Gone With the Wind' Enthralls Audience with Magnificence," *Atlanta Constitution*, December 16, 1939; and "Runaway Tiger," *Atlanta Journal-Constitution*, April 14, 1997. The material is reprinted by permission of the Atlanta Journal-Constitution. The Boston Globe for "Greatest Game Ever," *Boston Daily Globe*, May 6, 1904; "Girls Beaten Down by a Lawrence Mob," *Boston Daily Globe*, January 12, 1912; "Madeiros, Sacco, Venzetti Died in Chair This Morning," *Boston Daily Globe*, August 23, 1927. Reprinted courtesy of The Boston Globe. The Charlotte Observer for "Negroes Seek Diner Service," February 3, 1960. Reprinted with permission from the *Charlotte Observer*. The Chattanooga Times for "Jury Finds Evolution Teacher 'Guilty,' " July 22, 1925. Reprinted from the *Chattanooga Daily Times*. The Christian Science Monitor for "Beatles Test Ties—Yeah!" by John Hughes, February 11, 1964. Reprinted by permission from the *Christian Science Monitor*. Copyright © 1964 The Christian Science Publishing Society. All rights reserved. The Cincinnati Enquirer for "Mapplethorpe Photos Obscene," April 8, 1990. Reprinted by permission of The Cincinnati Enquirer. The Commercial Appeal for "Dr. King Is Slain by Sniper," *Commercial Appeal*, April 5, 1968. Reprinted by permission of The Commercial Appeal. Daily Capital, Topeka, Kans., for "Little Effect on Topeka," *Topeka Daily Capital*, May 18, 1954. The Des Moines Register and Tribune Company for "Suicide Squad Captures U.S. Embassy in Saigon," *Des Moines Register*, January 31, 1968. Copyright © 1990 Des Moines Register and Tribune Company. Reprinted with permission. Dow Jones & Company, Inc., for "Stocks Steady After Decline," *Wall Steet Journal*, October 30, 1929. Enoch Pratt Free Library for "Valentino," by H. L. Mencken, *Baltimore Sun*, August 30, 1926. Reprinted by permission of the Enoch Pratt Free Library in accordance with the terms of the will of H. L. Mencken. Harvard College for "Today and Tomorrow," by Walter Lippmann, *New York World*, January 8, 1932. Used with the permission of the President and Fellows of Harvard College. Hearst Newspapers for permission to reprint "Terms of Armistice," *Los Angeles Evening Herald*, November 11, 1918; "Can't Agree on Snyder Jury," by Damon Runyon, *New York American*, April 19, 1927; "Seven Lined Up and Slain by Gangland Firing Squad," *Chicago Herald Examiner*, February 15, 1929; "Louis Tells Cannon He Made Schmeling Quit," by James Cannon, *New York Journal and American*, June 23, 1938; "The Inside Story: How Lepke Gave Up to Winchell," by Walter Winchell, *New York Daily Mirror*,

August 26, 1939. The Honolulu Star Bulletin for "War!" as printed in an extra edition
of the *Honolulu Star,* December 7, 1941. I.H.T. Corporation for "American Fire
Spread Havoc in Foe's Lines," by Wilbur Forrest, *New York Tribune,* June 6, 1981;
"Notre Dame's Cyclone Beats Army, 13-7," by Grantland Rice, *New York Herald
Tribune,* October 19, 1924; "O'Neill's Own Story of 'Electra' in the Making," by
Eugene O'Neill, *New York Herald-Tribune,* November 8, 1931; "Lindbergh Baby Is
Found Slain Near Hopewell," *New York Herald-Tribune,* May 13, 1932; "The The-
aters: Lilacs to Oklahoma," by Howard Barnes, *New York Herald-Tribune,* April 1,
1943; "Iwo Hospital: War Rages Outside But Its Staff Performs Miracles," by Homer
Bigart, *New York Herald-Tribune,* March 14, 1945. I.H.T. Corporation. Reprinted by
permission. The Intelligencer for "M'Carthy Charges Reds Hold U.S. Jobs," by
Frank Desmond, *Wheeling Intelligencer,* February 10, 1950. The Kansas City Star
for "Mix, War, Art and Dancing," *Kansas City Star,* April 21, 1918. Knoxville
Journal for "Tennessee's Legislature Ratifies Amendment Giving Suffrage to
Women," *Knoxville Journal and Tribune,* August 19, 1920. Los Angeles Times for
"Film—Merit Trophies Awarded," *Los Angeles Times,* May 17, 1929; "Dream Re-
alized—Disneyland Opens," by Jerry Hulse, *Los Angeles Times,* July 18, 1955;
"Packers Prove NFL's Brand Best, 35-10," by Paul Zimmerman, *Los Angeles Times,*
January 16, 1967; "Simpson Not Guilty," by Jim Newton, *Los Angeles Times,* Oc-
tober 4, 1995. Copyright © Los Angeles Times. Reprinted by permission. The Mont-
gomery Advertiser for "25,000 Converge on State Capitol, End 5-Day Protest Trek
from Selma," by Tom Mackin, *Montgomery Advertiser,* March 26, 1965. The New
Mexican, Santa Fe, N.Mex., for "The Vision of Georgia O'Keeffe," by Sam Atwood,
New Mexican, March 7, 1986. New York Daily News for "History's Most Costly
Exhibits Shown at Fair," by Leo Casey, May 1, 1939; Copyright © 1939 New York
News Inc. Reprinted with permission; " 'Voice' Wins His Loudest Squeal," by
Elaine Cunniffe and Gilbert Millstein, October 13, 1944. Copyright © 1944, New
York News Inc. Reprinted by permission. New York Post for "Stanley Frank Reports:
Gehrig Was Game, Grand Character," by Stanley Frank, *New York Post,* June 3,
1941; "Today's Army-Navy Casualty List," *New York Post,* April 13, 1945; "Benign
Mobster Devoured Music," by Alfred G. Arnowitz, *New York Post,* August 18, 1969.
Reprinted with permission from the New York Post. The New York Times for "More
Ring Villainy," July 8, 1871. Copyright © 1871 by The New York Times Company.
Reprinted by permission. "Peary Discovers the North Pole After Eight Trials in 23
Years," September 7, 1909. Copyright © 1909 by The New York Times Company.
Reprinted by permission. "Art at Home Abroad," February 23, 1913. Copyright ©
1913 by The New York Times Company. Reprinted by permission. "Far Off Speakers
Seen as Well as Heard Here in a Test of Television," April 8, 1927. Copyright ©
1927 by The New York Times Company. Reprinted by permission. "Lindbergh Does
It!" by Edwin L. James, May 21, 1927. Copyright © 1927 by The New York Times
Company. Reprinted by permission. "Home Run Record Falls as Ruth Hits 60th,"
October 1, 1927. Copyright © 1927 by The New York Times Company. Reprinted
by permission. "Porgy and Bess, Native Opera Opens at Alvin," by Brooks Atkinson,
October 11, 1935. Copyright © 1935 by The New York Times Company. Reprinted
by permission. "Visit to Hiroshima Proves It World's Most Damaged City," by
W. H. Lawrence, September 5, 1945. Copyright © 1945 by The New York Times
Company. Reprinted by permission. "U.S. Approves Pill for Birth Control," May
10, 1960. Copyright © 1960 by The New York Times Company. Reprinted by per-
mission. "U.S. Imposes Arms Blockade on Cuba on Finding Offensive-Missile
Sites," by Anthony Lewis, October 23, 1962. Copyright © 1962 by The New York
Times Company. Reprinted by permission. "U.S. Planes Attack North Vietnam Bas-
es," by Tom Wicker, August 5, 1964. Copyright © 1964 by The New York Times
Company. Reprinted by permission. "Supreme Court, 6-3 Upholds Newspapers on
Publication of the Pentagon Report," by Fred P. Graham, July 1, 1971. Copyright ©
1971 by The New York Times Company. Reprinted by permission. "Clamor in the

East," by Serge Schmemann, November 10, 1989. Copyright © 1989 by The New York Times Company. Reprinted by permission. Newsday for "A Ticket for History," by Judith Bender, *Newsday,* July 13, 1984. The Orlando Sentinel for "American On the Moon," by Skip Johnson, *Orlando Sentinel,* July 21, 1969. Pacific Citizen for "West Half of Washington, Oregon, California, Southern Arizona Designated as Military Areas," *Pacific Citizen,* March 1, 1942. The Palm Beach Post for "Divided Supreme Court Hands Bush Probable Victory," by Larry Lipman and Brian E. Crowley, *Palm Beach Post,* December 13, 2000. Used by permission. The Philadelphia Inquirer for "Power Plant Leaks Radiation" by Thomas Ferrick Jr. and Susan Q. Stranahan, *Philadelphia Inquirer,* March 29, 1979. Used by permission. The Pittsburgh Press for "Serum Effective in Tests," by John Troan, *Pittsburgh Press,* March 27, 1953. The Plain Dealer for "DiMaggio Stopped, But Yankees Win," by Gordon Cobbledick, *Plain Dealer,* July 18, 1941. "Swing King," *St. Louis Post-Dispatch,* September 28, 1998. Reprinted with permission of the St. Louis Post-Dispatch. Copyright © September 28, 1998. The Salt Lake Tribune for "Utah Artificial Heart Pumping Life through Seattle Dentist," by JoAnn Jacobsen-Wells, *Salt Lake Tribune,* December 3, 1982. Courtesy of The Salt Lake Tribune. San Diego Tribune for "Jap Fleet Reeling Under U.S. Blows," *San Diego Tribune,* June 7, 1942. The San Diego Union-Tribune for "Goodbye Dr. Seuss," September 26, 1991. Reprinted with permission of The San Diego Union-Tribune, copyright © The San Diego Union-Tribune. San Francisco Chronicle for "The Great Radio Scare," October 31, 1938; "400 Stood in Line to Die," by Keith Power, *San Francisco Chronicle,* November 21, 1978; "The Strange, Deadly Diseases That Strike Gay Men," by Randy Shilts, *San Francisco Chronicle,* May 13, 1982. Copyright © San Francisco Chronicle. Reprinted by permission. San Francisco Examiner for "Tokio, 3 Other Great Cities Blasted by U.S., Japs Assert," *San Francisco Examiner,* April 19, 1942; "Marilyn Monroe, DiMaggio Married: Miss Monroe in Satin, Ermine," by Louella O. Parsons, *San Francisco Examiner,* January 15, 1954. Reprinted with permission of The San Francisco Examiner. Copyright © 1990 The San Francisco Examiner. Carl Sandburg Family Trust for "Says Lax Conditions Cause Race Riots," by Carl Sandburg, July 27, 1919. Carl Sandburg Family Trust, Maurice C. Greenbaum and Frank M. Parker, Trustees. Scripps Howard for "The Story of Captain Waskow," by Ernie Pyle, January 10, 1944. Reprinted by permission of the Scripps Howard Foundation. The Washington Post for "200,000 Jam Mall in Mammoth Rally in Solemn, Orderly Pleas for Equality," by Robert E. Baker, *Washington Post,* August 29, 1963. © 1963 The Washington Post. Reprinted by permission. "Restrained Militancy Marks Rally Speeches," by Susanna McBee, *Washington Post,* August 29, 1963. © 1963 The Washington Post. Reprinted with Permission. "5 Held in Plot to Bug Democrats' Office Here," by Alfred E. Lewis, *Washington Post,* June 18, 1972. © 1972 The Washington Post. Reprinted with permission. "Nixon Resigns," by Carroll Kilpatrick, *Washington Post,* August 9, 1974. © 1974 The Washington Post. Reprinted with permission. "Clinton Acquitted," by Peter Baker and Helen Dewar, *Washington Post,* February 13, 1999. © 1999 The Washington Post. Reprinted with permission.

INDEX

Abel, Rudolph I., 303
Abernathy, Ralph, 327, 335
Abolitionism, 28, 41-44, 46-49
Academy Awards, 214-15, 380
Ach, Roger, 376
Adams, John, 17
Adams, Samuel, 5
Adventures of Huckleberry Finn, 80-81
Afro-American, 282-84
Agnew, Spiro, 348
Ahlgren, Frank R., 334
AIDS (1982), 357-60
Alamo (1836), 32-34
Alcott, Louisa May, 80
Aldrin, Edwin, 336-38
Alexander's Weekly Messenger, 36-37
Allen, Walter L., Jr., 326
Allen, William, 223-24
Alsace-Lorraine, 161-62
Alta California, 65-68, 72
American Civil Liberties Union, 183
"American Crisis," 11-13
American Nazi Party, 307
American Woolen Mills strike (1912), 134-38
Anchorage Daily News, 370-73
Anderson, Bill, 79
Anderson, Fred, 362
Anderson, Jeff, 362
Anderson, Louis B., 168
Anderson, Marian, 311
Anderson, Robert, 49-51
And to Think That I Saw It on Mulberry Street, 377, 378, 379
Anthony, Susan B., 173
Anti-Semitism, 153-58
Appeal to Reason, 116-20
Apprenticeship of Ernest Hemingway, 162
Armory Exhibition (1913), 138-44
Armstrong, Louis, 242
Armstrong, Neil, 336-38
Arnold, Dorothy, 290
Aronowitz, Alfred O., 339
Around the World in Eighty Days, 93
Artificial heart implant (1982), 360-63
Assassinations: JFK (1963), 311-21; King (1968), 333-36; Lincoln (1865), 64-65

Associated Press, 169, 303
Atkinson, Brooks, 234
Atlanta Constitution, 252-55
Atlanta Journal, 153-58
Atlanta-Journal Constitution, 382-84
Atlantic Charter, 272
Atrocities, 153-58, 351-54
AT&T, 190-93
Attell, Abe, 178
Atwood, Sam, 366
Augusta, Ga., 382
Automobile industry, 99, 145-47
Aviation, 106-9
Ayers, Lemuel, 268
Ayers, William W., 276-77

Bache, Benjamin F., 19
Bagby, Jim, 258-59
Baker, Lloyd, 354
Baker, Peter, 386-87
Baker, Robert D., 306
Baltimore Patriot, 46-49, 67
Baltimore Patriot and Commercial Gazette, 38-39
B&O Railroad, 46
Barker, Bernard L., 347
Barnard, Christiaan, 360, 363
Barnes, Howard, 267
Barrett, Mike, 385
Barrie, Dennis, 376-77
Barsocchini, Reno, 289
Baseball, 114-16, 175-79, 207-8, 210, 256-59, 282-84, 384-85
Basie, Count, 241
Beathard, Pete, 329
Beatles, The, 321-23
Beauregard, Pierre P. T., 49-50, 52-54
Beckel, Robert, 365
Beiderbecke, Bix, 241
Bel Geddes, Norman, 247
Bell, Alexander Graham, 192
Bender, Judith, 364
Bennett, James Gordon, 34
Bentsen, Lloyd, 366
Bergen, Edgar, 244
Berlin. *See* East Berlin; West Berlin

The University of Illinois Press
is a founding member of the
Association of American University Presses.

University of Illinois Press
1325 South Oak Street
Champaign, IL 61820-6903
www.press.uillinois.edu